THE PROCESS
OF LEGAL RESEARCH

D0025892

ASPEN COURSEBOOK SERIES

THE PROCESS OF LEGAL RESEARCH AUTHORITIES AND OPTIONS

Eighth Edition

Christina L. Kunz
Professor of Law
William Mitchell College of Law

Deborah A. Schmedemann
Professor of Law
William Mitchell College of Law

Ann L. Bateson
Director of the Schoenecker Law Library
Associate Dean and Professor of Law
University of St. Thomas School of Law

Mehmet Konar-Steenberg
Associate Professor of Law
William Mitchell College of Law

Anthony S. Winer
Professor of Law
William Mitchell College of Law

Sarah Deer
Assistant Professor of Law
William Mitchell College of Law

Wolters Kluwer
Law & Business

Published by Wolters Kluwer Law & Business in New York.

Wolters Kluwer Law & Business serves customers worldwide with CCH, Aspen Publishers, and Kluwer Law International products. (www.wolterskluwerlb.com)

To contact Customer Service, e-mail customer.service@wolterskluwer.com, call 1-800-234-1660, fax 1-800-901-9075, or mail correspondence to:

Wolters Kluwer Law & Business
Attn: Order Department
PO Box 990
Frederick, MD 21705

Printed in the United States of America.

1 2 3 4 5 6 7 8 9 0

ISBN 978-1-4548-0552-6

Library of Congress Cataloging-in-Publication Data

The process of legal research : authorities and options / Christina L. Kunz . . . [et al.]. — 8th ed.
    p. cm. — (Aspen coursebook series)
  Includes index.
  ISBN 978-1-4548-0552-6
  1. Legal research — United States.   I. Kunz, Christina L.
  KF240.P76 2012
  340.072'073 — dc23
                            2012018042

About Wolters Kluwer Law & Business

Wolters Kluwer Law & Business is a leading global provider of intelligent information and digital solutions for legal and business professionals in key specialty areas, and respected educational resources for professors and law students. Wolters Kluwer Law & Business connects legal and business professionals as well as those in the education market with timely, specialized authoritative content and information-enabled solutions to support success through productivity, accuracy and mobility.

Serving customers worldwide, Wolters Kluwer Law & Business products include those under the Aspen Publishers, CCH, Kluwer Law International, Loislaw, Best Case, ftwilliam.com and MediRegs family of products.

CCH products have been a trusted resource since 1913, and are highly regarded resources for legal, securities, antitrust and trade regulation, government contracting, banking, pension, payroll, employment and labor, and healthcare reimbursement and compliance professionals.

Aspen Publishers products provide essential information to attorneys, business professionals and law students. Written by preeminent authorities, the product line offers analytical and practical information in a range of specialty practice areas from securities law and intellectual property to mergers and acquisitions and pension/benefits. Aspen's trusted legal education resources provide professors and students with high-quality, up-to-date and effective resources for successful instruction and study in all areas of the law.

Kluwer Law International products provide the global business community with reliable international legal information in English. Legal practitioners, corporate counsel and business executives around the world rely on Kluwer Law journals, looseleafs, books, and electronic products for comprehensive information in many areas of international legal practice.

Loislaw is a comprehensive online legal research product providing legal content to law firm practitioners of various specializations. Loislaw provides attorneys with the ability to quickly and efficiently find the necessary legal information they need, when and where they need it, by facilitating access to primary law as well as state-specific law, records, forms and treatises.

Best Case Solutions is the leading bankruptcy software product to the bankruptcy industry. It provides software and workflow tools to flawlessly streamline petition preparation and the electronic filing process, while timely incorporating ever-changing court requirements.

ftwilliam.com offers employee benefits professionals the highest quality plan documents (retirement, welfare and non-qualified) and government forms (5500/PBGC, 1099 and IRS) software at highly competitive prices.

MediRegs products provide integrated health care compliance content and software solutions for professionals in healthcare, higher education and life sciences, including professionals in accounting, law and consulting.

Wolters Kluwer Law & Business, a division of Wolters Kluwer, is headquartered in New York. Wolters Kluwer is a market-leading global information services company focused on professionals.

This book is dedicated to our families,
our colleagues who have taught legal research with us,
and our students of the past three decades.

Summary of Contents

CONTENTS

EXHIBITS

CHAPTER 8 RESEARCH IN RULES OF PROCEDURE

CHARTS AND EXAMPLES

PREFACE

Whatever career you choose in the law, to help your clients — the people and organizations that are relying on you — you must know the pertinent law. To know the pertinent law, you must know how to conduct legal research. This book's aim is to help you develop that skill, which, like other legal skills, will continue to improve with experience.

Since the first edition of this book was published (1986), we have become its primary authors. We have worked with excellent reference librarians and hundreds of practitioners who teach in our law schools' legal writing courses. Most important, we have taught literally thousands of law students.

In writing this edition, we came to the following two-part thesis about learning research: First, in an environment with a dizzying array of legal research resources, your first and fundamental task is to understand legal authorities — hence the emphasis throughout the book on what the types of law are, how they are made, how they fit together, and how to derive the pertinent rules from them. Second, once you have that core knowledge, you must wisely select from the options that provide what you need and use them proficiently — hence the emphasis on the various research options, their major attributes, advantages, and disadvantages.

To be frank, some people think of "research" as dry and tedious. In fact, legal research conducted on behalf of a client whose well-being is at stake is challenging and creative. There is some resemblance to a hunt for treasure, the law you find may be downright interesting, and your ability to use your findings to help your client is often rewarding.

We have yet to figure out a way to have a real client "live" in this book so that you can experience these feelings. We have, instead, included a series of realistic client situations and shown you how legal research would help to solve the clients' problems. Here are the basic issues, so you can think about them before you begin reading:

- Is it permissible for an employer to decline to hire a qualified applicant because the applicant would work with her spouse and coworkers would be uncomfortable with this arrangement?
- Can a former employee of a grocery store recover money for the harm to his reputation when his manager tells coworkers he was fired for pilfering food, which was not in fact true but rather a story made up by a disgruntled coworker?
- Could an employer be liable to a driver injured in a crash caused by one of its employees who was backing out of a parking lot after picking up donuts for a work meeting — and also talking on his cellphone?

- Is an employee of a company with fifty-one employees spread over two worksites eligible for reinstatement after adoption leave under the federal family leave statute?
- May an employer discipline workers for writing disparaging messages on Facebook about their working conditions?
- What happens when a lawyer fails to properly sign an answer to a complaint within the specified time period? Does the other side win?
- Once a lawsuit is filed over an employee's termination, can the fired employee still talk with friends at the former employer?

(As you can see, one benefit of reading this book will be learning a bit about your rights as an employee.) We have included the bumps we experienced along the way, to show you that legal research is not always smooth sailing.

Each chapter here contains a fair amount of information. To help you read the chapters actively, they begin not only with a table of contents but also with a list of key concepts and tools. As you read the chapter or as you review it, you may want to define these terms. Also, we have included some reflection questions at the end of the chapters to help you think more broadly and critically about what you have read. Finally, "the proof of the pudding is in the eating": the chapters conclude with a realistic client situation for *you* to research, which unfolds as the chapters unfold.

We wish you the best as you take on the challenge of learning legal research.

Deborah Schmedemann
Ann Bateson
Mehmet Konar-Steenberg

May 2012

ACKNOWLEDGMENTS

Listing the authors of this edition of this book is not an easy matter. Christina Kunz, who appears as the lead author, does not in fact continue to work on it, but it was her idea to begin with, and she was its most dedicated shepherd for a number of editions. Thus it will always be "the Kunz book." Others who were involved at various stages and whose contributions continue to linger here are Matthew Downs, Cliff Greene, Peter Erlinder, and Susan Catterall.

The long-time authors are delighted to welcome two new contributors: Anthony Winer and Sara Deer, both professors at William Mitchell, who have contributed a new chapter on international law and tribal law. We are grateful for their expertise.

We have had many colleagues assisting us not in the direct writing of this book but in teaching from it. We sincerely thank in particular the following reference librarians: Valerie Aggerbeck, Deborah Hackerson, and May Wells at the University of St. Thomas; Neal Axton, Janelle Beitz, Jean Boos, Sonya Huesman, and Karen Westwood at William Mitchell. At William Mitchell, practicing lawyers teach students to research and write; they are too numerous to mention by name, but we heartily thank them for their insights.

More broadly we thank those who teach legal research around the country who have shared their insights into how students learn and how this book can assist that process. And we thank our students who have been just as insightful over the years!

The administrations and staff at our law schools have provided considerable resources, financial and otherwise, in support of this project for many years. Two students at St. Thomas — Samuel Johnson and Gerald McCabe — provided able assistance. Cal Bonde and Lynette Fraction at William Mitchell ably oversaw the process of creating the manuscript and managing the copyright permissions.

We send off our manuscript and then depend on the skills of many other professionals to make it an actual book. We thank in particular Christine Hannan and her team at Aspen, Gretchen Otto of Motto Publishing Services, and Michele Deangelis.

It takes time and considerable energy to write this book. Not surprisingly, our families and friends pay a bit of a price when we are engaged in this project. Thanks for your tolerance — for the eighth time!

A book on legal research depends, of course, on the willingness of legal publishers to permit copying of their materials. Thus we thank the following publishers for permission to use the following exhibits:

American Bar Association

ABA Formal Ethics Opinion: Formal Opinion © 2011 by the American Bar Association. Reprinted with permission. Copies of ABA Formal Ethics Opinions are available from Service Center, American Bar Association, 321 North Clark Street, Chicago, IL 60654, 1-800-285-2221. All rights reserved. This information or any portion thereof may not be copied or disseminated in any form or by any means or stored in an electronic database or retrieval system without the express written consent of the American Bar Association.

American Law Institute

Restatement (Third) of Agency § 7.07 (American Law Institute 2006); and Case Citation for Restatement (Third) of Agency § 7.07 (American Law Institute 2007) (found through LexisNexis).

Restatement, Third, Agency, copyright 2006 by The American Law Institute. Reprinted with permission. All Rights Reserved.

LexisNexis

Judicial Council of California, California Civil Jury Instruction § 3724 (Matthew Bender/LexisNexis 2011) (found through California Courts Website);

Search in LexisNexis' KS State Cases, Combined for "supervisor or coworker or job w/p defam! or libel or slander w/ privilege" (run July 13, 2011);

Dobbyn v. Nelson, 1978 Kan. App. LEXIS 192 (Kansas Court of Appeals 1978);

Shepard's Report for Dobbyn v. Nelson (Kansas Court of Appeals 1978) (LexisNexis) (2011);

Deering's California Code Annotated (LexisNexis 2011);

Shepard's Report for California Vehicle Code § 23123 (LexisNexis 2011);

Deering's California Advance Legislative Service (Matthew Bender/Lexis Nexis 2011);

93 CIS PL 1033, 103 CIS Legis. Hist. P.L. 3 (CIS/Index LexisNexis); and

2011 Bill Tracking H.R. 1440 (LexisNexis 2011).

Reprinted with the permission of LexisNexis.

McGraw-Hill

Burton's Legal Thesaurus 210 (McGraw-Hill 2007). Reprinted with permission of The McGraw-Hill Companies, Inc.

ProQuest Congressional

Legislative History Report from ProQuest Congressional: 93 CIS PL 1033,
    103 CIS Legis. Hist. P.L. 3 (CIS/Index LexisNexis).
Reprinted with permission of ProQuest Congressional.

Thomson Reuters

Stephen F. Befort, Employment Law and Practice § 10.11 (West 2003 &
    Supp. 2010-2011);
First Page of Taylor v. LSI Corp. (Minnesota Court of Appeals 2010)
    (Westlaw);
Westlaw KeyCite Report for Taylor v. LSI Corp. (Minnesota Court of
    Appeals 2010);
Taylor v. LSI Corp. (Minnesota Supreme Court (2011) (Westlaw);
Black's Law Dictionary 534 (West 2009);
American Jurisprudence 2d Index;
45A American Jurisprudence 2d, Job Discrimination, table of contents
    § 445 (West 2002 & 2011);
Jane M. Draper, Defamation: publication by intracorporate communication
    of employee's evaluation, 47 A.L.R.4th 674, opening page and text
    (West 1986) (Westlaw);
17A American Jurisprudence Pleading & Practice Forms, Master and
    Servant § 70 (West 2011) (Westlaw);
Luttrell v. United Telephone System, Inc., 683 Pacific Reporter 2d 1292
    (Kansas Court of Appeals 1984);
20B Kansas Digest 2d 30, 51 (West 2003);
37B Minnesota Digest 2d 13 (2002);
Results List from Westlaw: "libel slander /s publish publication" in KS-CS-
    all database run on June 15, 2011;
Results List from WestlawNext: "defamation publication employment" run
    in Kansas sources run on June 15, 2011;
Luttrell v. United Telephone System, Inc., 695 P.2d 1279 (Kansas Supreme
    Court 1985) (WestlawNext);
KeyCite Report for Case for Luttrell v. United Telephone System, Inc.
    (Kansas Court of Appeals 1984) (Westlaw);
West's Annotated California Codes: General Index A-C (2010); Table of
    Titles, Chapters, Articles and Section for Title 9 Agency (1985); § 2338
    text (1985); notes of decisions (2011);
1993 United States Code Congressional and Administrative News 3 (West);
Legislative History Information in 29 United States Code Annotated § 2611
    (West 2009);
Regulation Information in 29 United States Code Annotated § 2611
    (Westlaw);
KeyCite Report for 29 Code of Federal Regulations § 825.111;
Rule 11, Federal Civil Judicial Procedure and Rules (West 2011); and

5A Charles Alan Wright & Arthur R. Miller, Federal Practice and Procedure
     § 1333 (2004).
Used with permission of Thomson Reuters.

University of Dayton

Frank J. Cavico, Defamation in the Private Sector: The Libelous and
     Slanderous Employer, University of Dayton Law Review 431-32
     (1998-1999). Reprinted with permission of University of Dayton Law
     Review.

THE PROCESS
OF LEGAL RESEARCH

INTRODUCTION: LITERACY IN THE LAW

Contents

This chapter explores the issue of marital status discrimination.

Key Concepts and Tools in This Chapter

- four elements of FEAT and their meaning
- sources and resources
- legal citation
- legal authority
- jurisdiction
- mandatory and persuasive authority
- commentary
- quasi-authority
- attributes of research resources
- planning research
- four searching steps
- recall and precision

(continued)

- author-driven and researcher-driven access tools
- monitoring research
- stopping research

THE FEAT OF LEGAL RESEARCH

This is both the best of times and the worst of times[1] for those who perform legal research. In this day of pervasive legal regulation of American life and sophisticated communications technology, the amount of law is enormous, and means of finding it abound—seemingly a researcher's dream. However, in this environment of plenty, a researcher runs very real risks of spending a lot of time without finding the needed information, despite significant effort. The goal of this book is to provide you with the knowledge, skills, and attitudes to research successfully in this challenging environment.

Researching *un*successfully is not an option for a legal researcher. Unlike academic research, legal research is aimed at solving a real and pressing problem for someone else—the lawyer's client. If the research misfires, the lawyer may not know the rule to apply to the client's situation, and the advice given may be skewed. The client's transaction may be configured improperly, a legal claim may be misframed, or a key defense may be overlooked. The client's situation may worsen, not improve. Furthermore, the lawyer may face adverse consequences, such as a professional discipline[2] or a legal malpractice claim.[3]

As you work through this book, you will read repeatedly about four cornerstones of successful legal research, which form the acronym FEAT. We have framed them as questions, so that at every phase of a research process you may ask and answer them as a means of guiding your activity:

1. Focus: What is the research situation before me: my client's facts and goals, the timing and location of the situation, and the legal topics involved?
2. Efficiency: Which resources will accomplish the task at hand most productively, given the value each resource provides, the time it will take me to use it, and its cost?

---

1. To paraphrase the classic opening line of Charles Dickens' *A Tale of Two Cities*, book 1, ch. 1 (1859).
2. Rule 1.1 of the Model Rules of Professional Conduct, a widely adopted ethics code developed by the American Bar Association, states: "A lawyer shall provide competent representation to the client. Competent representation requires the legal knowledge . . . reasonably necessary for the representation."
3. *E.g., Smith v. Lewis*, 530 P.2d 589 (Cal. 1975), *overruled on other grounds, In re Marriage of Brown*, 544 P.2d 561 (Cal. 1976) (court approved an award of $100,000).

3. Analysis: What legal rules have I learned thus far that will help me solve my client's problem?
4. Thoroughness: Have I covered the range of authorities I need to discern the complete and current legal rule(s) applicable to my client's problem?

This book is titled "The Process of Legal Research: Authorities and Options." The first phrase emphasizes that legal research is not so much something you know as something you do.

At the same time, as indicated by the second phrase, you cannot do legal research without knowing about legal sources. The universe of legal research encompasses a wide range of sources. You must know about the various sources that constitute the law, such as cases and statutes; the sources that comment on the law, such as treatises and periodical articles; and the relative weight each source carries. Because authority is such an important dimension of legal research, the chapters are organized by type of authority.

The second phrase also emphasizes the concept of options. Within each chapter, the text discusses options for researching the authority. Options revolve around the resources in which the authority is found and the skills you need to use those resources effectively. For example, a statute is a source; statutes appear in such resources as books published by commercial companies and databases on legislatures' websites. Some options are more efficient than others. That is, they generally yield strong results compared to the investment of time and other costs, such as fees to purchase or use resources. The chapters focus on optimal options and include boxes summarizing them.[4]

Because legal analysis is based to such a great extent on legal authority, citation to authorities on which an analysis relies is a significant element of most legal documents. Legal citation is complicated, a reflection of the range of legal authorities and the resources in which they are published. Because developing a citation for an authority occurs during the research process, this book provides some preliminary instruction in legal citation throughout the chapters. It draws on the two major legal citation manuals, *The Bluebook: A Uniform System of Citation* (19th ed. 2010) and *ALWD Citation Manual: A Professional System of Citation* (4th ed. 2010) by the Association of Legal Writing Directors. The short citation notes, found in boxes, focus on citing the various authorities in a document submitted in the course of law practice, such as a memorandum to a court, rather than on citation forms used in legal scholarship.

Attitudes are an important determinant of the success of one's research. First, curiosity drives legal research. Legal research is a quest for answers to important questions: Can my client do that? How much trouble is my client

---

4. Our recommendations come not only from our own experience in teaching law students and working with the practicing lawyers who teach in William Mitchell's skills courses but also from various formal studies of legal research practices, including Laura K. Justiss, *A Survey of Electronic Research Alternatives to LexisNexis and Westlaw in Law Firms*, 103 Law Lib. J. 71 (2011), and Patrick Meyer, *Law Firm Legal Research Requirements for New Attorneys*, 101 Law Lib. J. 297 (2009).

in? How can I maximize the advantages and minimize the disadvantages for my client in this deal? Second, because legal research can take time, may entail some misfires, and must be accomplished to a high standard, persistence is also a key attitude shared by strong legal researchers.

To give you a feel for the interaction of knowledge of legal authorities, the skills in using various options, and the attitudes of curiosity and persistence, this book takes you inside a fictional but generally realistic law firm as it handles various matters for its clients. There is one variance from real life in that most firms operate in one state and we have, for variety, set the matters in various states. All matters involve one of the more accessible and varied legal specialties: employment law.

Each chapter begins with a list of key concepts and tools covered in the chapter that you should be able to define to function competently in the field of legal research. Each chapter concludes with a section titled "Test Your Understanding." Those sections include questions to prompt you to think about some of the current functional or philosophical questions involved in legal research. They conclude with a scenario in which you, as the researcher, are asked to think through a situation; this situation spans the entire book.

The remaining parts of this chapter provide a big-picture overview of three fundamental topics—American legal sources, research resources, and work-flow in legal research—along with an illustration of their use in answering a client's question about hiring a new employee.

AMERICAN LEGAL SOURCES

Legal sources are not all created equal; rather, they occupy various places in an elaborate hierarchy. Thus, to research competently, you must know who generates a particular source, how it is generated, and where it fits in the hierarchy.

Some sources are legal authority: they constitute the law. These sources emanate from a government body acting in its law-making capacity. Thus, when a court issues a decision, a legislature enacts a statute, or an administrative agency promulgates a rule, law is created. In many areas, the law consists of a combination of legal authorities, as when a court issues a decision that applies a statute to a specific situation.

Each of these types of law operates within a jurisdiction. The word "jurisdiction" has many meanings in the law. As used here, it signifies a law-making body's power to govern the activities within a geographic location. For example, a decision by the Minnesota Supreme Court governs within Minnesota, whereas a decision of the U.S. Supreme Court has national applicability. The law of a different jurisdiction than the client's may provide insight into a problem when the law within the client's jurisdiction is not fully developed, but it is not binding. The law of the jurisdiction of the client's situation is called "mandatory authority"; the law of other jurisdictions is called "persuasive authority."

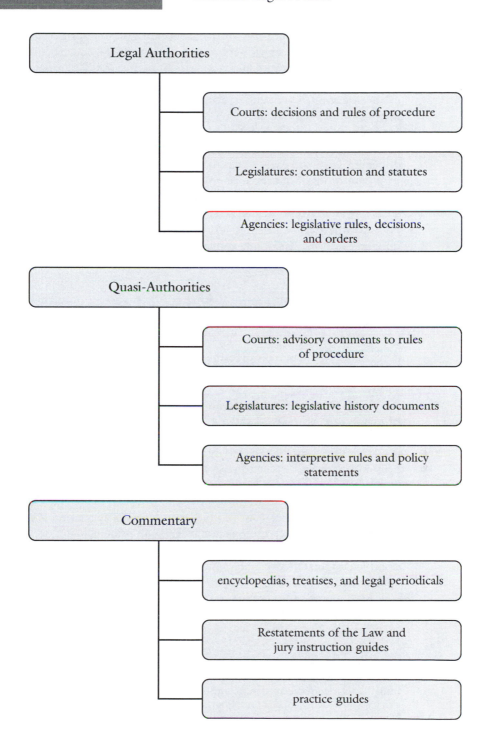

CHART 1.1   American Legal Sources

Legal Authorities

Courts: decisions and rules of procedure

Legislatures: constitution and statutes

Agencies: legislative rules, decisions, and orders

Quasi-Authorities

Courts: advisory comments to rules of procedure

Legislatures: legislative history documents

Agencies: interpretive rules and policy statements

Commentary

encyclopedias, treatises, and legal periodicals

Restatements of the Law and jury instruction guides

practice guides

Some sources are not the law itself but rather comment on the law; this book uses the term "commentary" for these sources.[5] These sources typically are created through a nongovernmental process, which may be a professor writing a treatise, a group of experts developing a synopsis of the law, or a publishing company's staff writing descriptions of the courts' decisions. Not surprisingly, some commentary sources are considered more credible than others.

Some sources are neither legal authority nor commentary but rather fall into an in-between category, which this book labels "quasi-authority." As one example, during the process of considering a statute, legislative committees hold hearings and write reports. The statute itself is the law; these other documents are considered helpful to consult—but not truly authoritative—when questions about the meaning of the statute arise.

Finally, in conducting legal research, you will encounter tools that are not authority at all. Nonetheless, these tools form an integral part of the research process, whether by assisting you to find pertinent sources or by providing updating information about a source you have found.

LEGAL RESEARCH RESOURCES

Any source you may want to read is likely to be available in multiple resources or publications. As you decide which resource to use, you should consider various factors.

First, unless you are researching an obscure issue requiring consideration of materials from many decades ago, you likely will be operating in print or online.[6] Each medium has distinct advantages. A book has a more obvious structure and may be easier to browse than an online database. A page of printed text is still easier to read for some people than a computer screen. Thus many lawyers routinely use print resources for some tasks and read important legal sources in print, even those obtained online. On the other hand, an online source may be more readily available, can be updated more quickly, and has search options not available in print. Some older sources are available only in print;[7] some newer sources are available only online. Thus good legal researchers are able to operate equally well in print and online as appropriate.

Second, the publisher of a resource is also a key variable. Some sources are published by the government, others by private companies. Traditionally,

5. Others use the term "secondary authority" to refer to commentary and "primary authority" to refer to the law itself.
6. As this book is being written, the traditional distinction between these two is blurring as electronic readers provide an electronic means of reading what would otherwise be considered a print source. These readers likely will represent the next step in a long evolution in the publication formats of legal sources, which has, over the years, included microfilm, microfiche, and CD-ROMs.
7. Indeed, some are available only in microforms.

government resources containing the law have taken longer to be published, provided only the law itself, and offered fewer editorial enhancements than commercial resources. However, these disadvantages, especially timeliness, have been eroding in recent years. Furthermore, government resources generally are the official—and hence the most credible—resources. Finally, most government resources are free or low-cost—a major advantage over commercial resources, which can be expensive.

Even so, many of the resources that are used most extensively in American legal research are commercial products. As you might expect, legal publishing has been dominated by a handful of major companies.[8] Currently, much of the development of commercial products is in online services. For decades and to a certain extent still today, two services have dominated legal research: Westlaw and LexisNexis (commonly shortened to "Lexis"). This book discusses also some services that are less ambitious in scope but also significant, such as HeinOnline. As you research in the coming years, you should stay up-to-date on new resources in the areas of your practice so that you are fully aware of your available options.

A third variable is the power of the resource, in particular its scope and sophistication. The best commercial products, in particular, provide a wide range of sources, considerable editorial material beyond the law itself, rapid updating, and tools to help the researcher find pertinent material and move easily among the materials within the resource. However, not all research tasks call for the most powerful resources, so matching tasks to resources is important to researching efficiently.

A closely related variable is the quality of the resource. For example, if you have a choice of several treatises (an expert's book-length discussion of a single legal subject), as you select one or two to use, you should consider the extensiveness of each treatise's discussion of the law and references to legal authorities, the quality of its organization and analysis, its currency, and the author's and treatise's reputations among lawyers in that practice area.

Last but certainly not least, a key variable is cost. Commercial publications, both print and online, can be more or less costly to purchase outright, subscribe to, or use on a per-transaction basis. Generally, the more extensive and elaborate the resource, the higher its cost. Some resources have costs that vary according to the specific use, such as which database is searched. Fortunately, some resources may be available to you at low or no cost through a public or academic library or as a benefit of membership in a bar association. While cost should not be the only consideration in your choice of resource, asking yourself whether there is a less costly option of accomplishing the specific task at hand is always wise.[9]

---

8. The current list includes Bloomberg/BNA, Reed Elsevier (which includes LexisNexis and Matthew Bender), Thomson Reuters (which includes West), and Wolters Kluwer (which includes Aspen and Commerce Clearing House).

9. During law school, you are likely to have ready access to Westlaw and LexisNexis. This is a good time to learn how to use them efficiently; it is not a good time to become dependent on them. Overdependence on these services by law students and new lawyers is a very common concern of their supervisors.

WORK-FLOW IN LEGAL RESEARCH

Because legal research is an activity, whether you are intentional about it or not, there will be a flow to your work. Strong researchers are highly meta-cognitive; that is, they are mindful of how they are going about the research process. This section describes the activities involved in legal research in a sequence that works across research projects.

Planning. As you will soon see, the options for any research project are many; you will not be able to, or want to, pursue every one. Rather, you will want to pursue enough fruitful options to do the job well. Thus you must plan your research: deciding how much time you have to get the job of research done, noting what you already know that could be pertinent, anticipating what you hope to find, considering the range of available resources, choosing a fruitful starting point, plotting the next steps, and having fallback plans if something does not pan out as planned. Planning entails careful consideration of the various resources to use for each task. Indeed, as to some sources, such as cases, you generally will use more than one resource. As detailed throughout this book, careful choice of a resource contributes greatly to the efficiency of your research.

Searching. Much of your research time will be spent working on a series of research projects, each involving a particular source and resource. In this era of online research, the standard means many people use to find pertinent information is to type several words into a search engine (such as Google) covering a broad range of sources and consider the results obtained sufficient. The most common complaint by supervising lawyers about research performed by new lawyers is that they conduct only this type of research and thereby miss what they need to find—a serious complaint indeed. Legal research requires much more sophisticated searching methods.

At the risk of oversimplification, searching methods in legal research fit within four somewhat sequential steps: (1) finding pertinent portions of the resource (such as a chapter in a treatise or a case within a database), (2) reading that portion for points to use in analyzing your client's situation, (3) mining the references to older sources, and (4) updating to find newer information and sources. The following picture is painted in very broad strokes. The four steps are detailed in subsequent chapters as they play out in commentary sources and the various forms of legal authority.

First, rarely will you read the entire text of a resource; rather, your goal is to identify and read the pertinent portions and little else. That is, you will want to conduct a search that has both high recall—it identifies all or nearly all pertinent portions—and high precision—it screens out all or nearly all non-pertinent portions. As developed in Chapter 2, your success on this score is a direct function of the vocabulary you identify to use in your research.

Another determinant of your success in finding pertinent portions is your skill in using the various access tools available in legal resources, some of which are very sophisticated. In general terms, the access tools can be categorized as either author-driven or researcher-driven.

Author-driven tools are (obviously) created by the author of a source and thus reflect the author's thinking about the subject. For example, many legal treatises include both a general and a detailed table of contents; an excellent strategy is to scan both to find pertinent topics. Treatises also contain indexes, alphabetical lists of major and minor topics along with pertinent page numbers. Although perusing an index may seem tedious, it is an excellent way to locate pertinent material within a resource.

Researcher-driven tools are primarily an option with online research. Here the researcher enters words in some configuration and asks the program to locate documents meeting the requirements of the search. Searches can vary from a single word to a set of words set out in a specific order. The program may provide a thesaurus to assist the researcher in searching for additional words. Some programs permit the researcher to tailor the search, for example, by instructing the program to locate the words in a specific portion of a document or to locate only documents from a certain time period. Some programs do more than follow the exact requirements entered by the researcher; they apply algorithms designed to produce more powerful results. For example, a natural-language search permits a researcher to key in words in a fairly unstructured manner; the program identifies and weights the most distinctive concepts in the search and displays a predetermined number of documents that should be the most pertinent based on the presence of those concepts in each document. Because these search options vary widely from online resource to online resource and evolve over time, a key skill is to master the search options of each online resource you use.

Second, you will carefully read the pertinent portion with two related goals: to discern what it says about the law in general and to ascertain its implications for your client's specific situation. As explained throughout this book, each legal source is distinctive in structure and content and must be read accordingly. Although reading the law is the topic of other books and many law school courses, this book touches on it because it is so integral to legal research.

Third, once you have identified and read the pertinent portion, you will mine its references to identify additional sources that precede the source you are reading. Rare is the legal source that does not refer to some other legal source. Commentary, of course, must refer to the law under discussion. In addition, many legal authorities refer to other ones. For example, most decisions written by the courts refer to pertinent statutes or to decisions in previous cases on the same topic. In addition, some of the more sophisticated resources containing legal authority also provide editorial notes pointing to additional sources. For example, some resources providing the language of a statute also provide synopses of decisions interpreting the statute.

Fourth, you will update important sources for two related purposes: to verify that what you have read is still valid and to identify new sources that may be helpful to read. This step is especially critical as to legal authority, which changes over time as courts issue new decisions, legislatures amend statutes, and agencies revise regulations. Every type of legal authority has one or more updating devices permitting you to ascertain that the source is still "good law." Not infrequently, you will identify additional sources to read through use of these updating devices.

Monitoring. As you research in various resources, it is critical to monitor your research, noting as to each resource what search methods you tried; what pertinent portions you identified and read (if any); what points you learned; what references you found; and how you updated the source. Note the timing of your research as well. Methods for processing your research abound, from the traditional index cards to research trails provided through the major online services.

Stopping. Finally, and often most difficult for new researchers, you must stop researching. This decision is often difficult because what you have found does not provide an unequivocal answer to your client's question and there are additional options you could pursue. This is the nature of legal research. Nonetheless, stop you must. Experienced researchers offer the following tests for knowing it is time to stop: you have a firm grasp on the legal framework and have explored the pertinent aspects; you have found authority that provides substantial guidance; you have confirmed that your authorities are good law; you have used a reasonable number of credible options, given the nature of the project; and you are seeing the same points over and over again (the law of diminishing returns).

CHART 1.2	Work-Flow of Legal Research

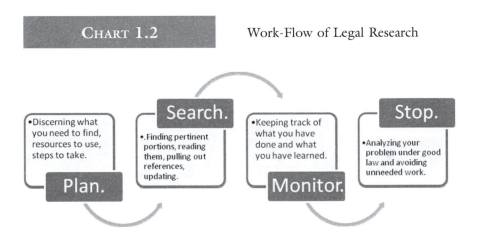

With this general overview in mind, consider now the first of the problems researched by our fictional firm.

AN ILLUSTRATION

Consider this situation: Our client, a retailer of high-end home furnishings, was hiring a new marketing manager for its Upper Midwest region, with offices in Minneapolis, Minnesota. One applicant was the wife of the current sales manager. The two managers would work closely together, and some employees expressed concern that having a married couple in these positions could be complicated. This concern aside, the wife was a strong candidate for the open position. Thus our client wanted to know whether it could lawfully decline to consider the wife under these circumstances. We conducted the research in Minnesota[10] state law in May 2011.

While the goal of research is to find and read legal authority on the topic, starting with commentary is often advisable as a means of getting an overview of the legal principles along with some references to actual legal authority. To learn the major rules in Minnesota, a treatise on Minnesota employment law was a good choice. We used *Employment Law and Practice,* a well-regarded source that we read in print; its third edition was published a few months before our research. We located the pertinent sections through the tables of contents and the index.

One section, excerpted in Exhibit 1.1, discussed the topic in several paragraphs. From this brief discussion we learned that Minnesota had a pertinent statute, the Minnesota Human Rights Act, and that its courts had applied that statute in various cases. With these general principles and references in mind, we turned to researching the legal authorities themselves.

Various resources could provide the Minnesota statute to which we found a reference. One option was to go to the legislature's own website, a free resource that was easy to use especially because we had a reference to the specific statute. Exhibit 1.2 presents two key provisions from the statute, as found on the Minnesota Legislature's website: section 363A.08 subdivision 2, which generally prohibits discrimination on the basis of marital status, and section 363A.03 subdivision 24, which defines "marital status." Combining the two sections, we determined that the statute prohibited discrimination on the basis of a spouse's identity or situation absent a bona fide occupational qualification.

The treatise referred as well to several cases decided by the Minnesota courts—the Minnesota Supreme Court, which is the highest court in the state, and the Minnesota Court of Appeals, which is one level down. We zeroed in on two fairly recent court of appeals cases: *Taylor* decided in 2010 and *Belton-Kocher* decided in 2000. As with the statute, we could find the cases in various resources. As discussed in Chapter 4, researching cases is done primarily in commercial services, whether print or online. We pulled up the cases on one such service, Westlaw.

We looked first at the more recent case, *Taylor.* We noticed two things adjacent to the title on Exhibit 1.3, the first page of the case from Westlaw: the letter H and a reference to "review granted." These flagged that the court of appeals decision was reviewed by the Minnesota Supreme Court. As you would expect, you should rely on the highest court decision in a case as a general rule. By clicking on the H, we obtained Exhibit 1.4, an updating

10. Employment discrimination is also governed by federal and local law, which we would also research in real life. For purposes of this illustration, we are focusing on state law, which provided the most straightforward rule.

| EXHIBIT 1.1 | Treatise Excerpt (*Employment Law and Practice*) |

Beyond the existence of a written policy, it is important that all employees in the workforce be familiar with the contents of the policy and how it is applied as a practical matter. To this end, it is useful to engage in training sessions for all employees. Because supervisors and managers often play unique roles in harassment situations, additional training should be provided for these individiuals.

iii. Investigation of Complaints

Finally, the individual or individuals charged with responsibility of investigating allegations of harassment must be thoroughly schooled in the process of conducting investigations, so that they are conducted promptly and are fair to all parties involved.

§§ 11:10 to 11:11 *[Reserved]*

D. MARITAL STATUS

§ 11:12   Marital status—In general

Research References

West's Key Number Digest, Civil Rights ⬥1195
C.J.S., Civil Rights §§ 56 to 58

The Minnesota Human Rights Act prohibits discrimination on the basis of marital status.[1] This protection refers to a person's status as single, married, remarried, divorced, separated, or a surviving spouse. The statute prohibits discrimination on the basis of the spouse or former spouse's identity, situation, actions, or beliefs.[2] The Minnesota Court of Appeals has held that marital status discrimination encompasses an employee's claim that she was terminated because her spouse was going to be terminated.[3] The protection of this provision extends to individuals living with, but not married to, a person of the opposite sex.[4]

Issues which arise under this provision often concern anti-nepotism employment rules. In 1979, the Minnesota Supreme Court held that an anti-nepotism rule denying full time employment to individuals married to persons already employed full time by the employer was illegal under the Act absent a compelling and overriding bona fide occupational qualification.[5] The requirement that a job candidate not be married to the person who would supervise the employment is a permissible bona fide

---

[Section 11:12]

[1]M.S.A. § 363A.08.

[2]M.S.A. § 363A.03, subd. 24.

[3]Taylor v. LSI Corp. of America, 781 N.W.2d 912 (Minn. Ct. App. 2010).

[4]State by Johnson v. Porter Farms, Inc., 382 N.W.2d 543, 547 (Minn. Ct. App. 1986).

[5]Kraft, Inc. v. State, 284 N.W.2d 386 (Minn. 1979).

459

Exhibit 1.1   (continued)

§ 11:12   Employment Law and Practice

occupational qualification if this anti-nepotism rule is essential for job performance.[6]

§§ 11:13 to 11:14 *[Reserved]*

E. SEXUAL ORIENTATION

§ 11:15   Sexual orientation—In general

Research References
West's Key Number Digest, Civil Rights ⚷1191
C.J.S., Civil Rights §§ 56 to 58

In 1993, the Minnesota Legislature added "sexual orientation" as a protected category under the Minnesota Human Rights Act.[1] Sexual orientation is defined as "having or being perceived as having an emotional, physical or sexual attachment to another person without regard to the sex of that person or having or being perceived as having an orientation for such attachment, or having or being perceived as having a self-image or identity not traditionally associated with one's biological maleness or femaleness." Sexual orientation does not include a physical or sexual attachment to children by an adult.[2]

Certain exceptions apply to the prohibition against discrimination on the basis of sexual orientation. In the employment context, the prohibition does not apply to a religious or fraternal cooperation, association, or society, with respect to qualifications based on sexual orientation, when sexual orientation is a bona fide occupational qualification for employment.[3] Also exempted are non-public service organizations whose primary function is providing occasional services to minors, youth theater, dance, music or artistic organizations, agricultural organizations for minors, and other youth organizations.[4]

Finally, nonprofit religious associations, religious corporations, and religious societies, and institutions organized for educational purposes that are operated, supervised, or controlled by a nonprofit religious association, religious corporation, or religious society, may take action with respect to employment on the basis of sexual orientation. The prohibition against discrimination in employment based on sexual orientation applies to the secular business activities engaged in by the religious organization. Such

---

[6]Belton-Kocher v. St. Paul School Dist., 610 N.W.2d 374 (Minn. Ct. App. 2000).

[Section 11:15]

[1]M.S.A. § 363A.08. Title VII does not ban discrimination on the basis of sexual orientation.

[2]M.S.A. § 363A.03, subd. 44.
[3]M.S.A. § 363A.20, subd. 2.
[4]M.S.A. § 363A.20, subd. 3.

460

EXHIBIT 1.2   Statutory Sections

1 | MINNESOTA STATUTES 2010 | 363A.03

363A.03 DEFINITIONS.

Subdivision 1. **Terms.** For the purposes of this chapter, the words defined in this section have the meanings ascribed to them.

Subd. 24. **Marital status.** "Marital status" means whether a person is single, married, remarried, divorced, separated, or a surviving spouse and, in employment cases, includes

protection against discrimination on the basis of the identity, situation, actions, or beliefs of a spouse or former spouse.

1   MINNESOTA STATUTES 2010   363A.08

363A.08 UNFAIR DISCRIMINATORY PRACTICES RELATING TO EMPLOYMENT OR UNFAIR EMPLOYMENT PRACTICE.

Subdivision 1. **Labor organization.** Except when based on a bona fide occupational qualification, it is an unfair employment practice for a labor organization, because of race, color, creed, religion, national origin, sex, marital status, status with regard to public assistance, disability, sexual orientation, or age:

(1) to deny full and equal membership rights to a person seeking membership or to a member;

(2) to expel a member from membership;

(3) to discriminate against a person seeking membership or a member with respect to hiring, apprenticeship, tenure, compensation, terms, upgrading, conditions, facilities, or privileges of employment; or

(4) to fail to classify properly, or refer for employment or otherwise to discriminate against a person or member.

Subd. 2. **Employer.** Except when based on a bona fide occupational qualification, it is an unfair employment practice for an employer, because of race, color, creed, religion, national origin, sex, marital status, status with regard to public assistance, membership or activity in a local commission, disability, sexual orientation, or age to:

(1) refuse to hire or to maintain a system of employment which unreasonably excludes a person seeking employment; or

(2) discharge an employee; or

(3) discriminate against a person with respect to hiring, tenure, compensation, terms, upgrading, conditions, facilities, or privileges of employment.

EXHIBIT 1.3	First Page of Case

Westlaw.

Page 1

781 N.W.2d 912, 109 Fair Empl.Prac.Cas. (BNA) 159
(Cite as: 781 N.W.2d 912)

H

Court of Appeals of Minnesota.
LeAnn TAYLOR, Appellant,
v.
LSI CORPORATION OF AMERICA, Respondent.

No. A09-1410.
April 27, 2010.
→ Review Granted July 20, 2010.

Background: Employee brought action against employer alleging marital-status discrimination. The District Court, Hennepin County, 2009 WL 2912707,Stephen C. Aldrich, J., granted summary judgment in favor of employer, and employee appealed.

Holdings: The Court of Appeals, Bjorkman, J., held that:
(1) in a matter of first impression, employee's claim that her termination was based on identity and situation of her spouse, a co-employee, fell squarely within statutory definition of marital status; and
(2) Court of Appeals would not consider whether or not employee met her initial burden of establishing a prima facie case under Minnesota Human Rights Act (MHRA).

Reversed and remanded.

West Headnotes

[1] Statutes 361 ☞188

361 Statutes
    361VI Construction and Operation
        361VI(A) General Rules of Construction
            361k187 Meaning of Language
                361k188 k. In general. Most Cited

Statutes 361 ☞190

361 Statutes

361VI Construction and Operation
    361VI(A) General Rules of Construction
        361k187 Meaning of Language
            361k190 k. Existence of ambiguity.
Most Cited Cases
    To ascertain and effectuate the intention of the legislature, the Court of Appeals first determines whether the statutory language is clear; if a statute, construed according to the ordinary rules of grammar, is unambiguous, the Court of Appeals may not engage in further statutory construction and must apply its plain meaning.

[2] Civil Rights 78 ☞1197

78 Civil Rights
    78II Employment Practices
        78k1195 Discrimination by Reason of Marital, Parental, or Familial Status
            78k1197 k. Particular cases. Most Cited Cases
    Employee's claim that employer terminated her based on the identity and situation of her spouse, a co-employee whose forced resignation was occurring at the same time as employee's, in violation of the Minnesota Human Rights Act, fell squarely within the statutory definition of "marital status," and did not require a showing that her termination was directed at her marital status itself. M.S.A. §§ 363A.03(24), 363A.08(2); Minn.St.1988, § 363.01 (40).

[3] Appeal and Error 30 ☞242(4)

30 Appeal and Error
    30V Presentation and Reservation in Lower Court of Grounds of Review
        30V(B) Objections and Motions, and Rulings Thereon
            30k242 Necessity of Ruling on Objection or Motion
                30k242(4) k. Rulings on evidence in general. Most Cited Cases
    On appeal of District Court's grant of summary

| EXHIBIT 1.4 | Updating Report for Case |

Westlaw

AUTHORIZED FOR EDUCATIONAL USE ONLY

Date of Printing: May 04, 2011

| KEYCITE |

H Taylor v. LSI Corp. of America, 781 N.W.2d 912, 109 Fair Empl.Prac.Cas. (BNA) 159 (Minn.App.,Apr 27, 2010) (NO. A09-1410)

History

Direct History

▶   1 Taylor v. LSI Corp. of America, 2009 WL 2912707 (Trial Order) (Minn.Dist.Ct. Apr 21, 2009) (NO. 27-CV-08-10689)

Reversed by

=>   2 **Taylor v. LSI Corp. of America**, 781 N.W.2d 912, 109 Fair Empl.Prac.Cas. (BNA) 159 (Minn.App. Apr 27, 2010) (NO. A09-1410), review granted (Jul 20, 2010)

Affirmed by

H   3 Taylor v. LSI Corp. of America, --- N.W.2d ----, 2011 WL 1376737, 112 Fair Empl.Prac.Cas. (BNA) 30 (Minn. Apr 13, 2011) (NO. A09-1410)

Court Documents

Appellate Court Documents (U.S.A.)

Minn.App. Appellate Briefs

4 LeAnn TAYLOR, Appellant, v. LSI CORPORATION OF AMERICA, a Minnesota Corporation, Respondent., 2009 WL 6477123 (Appellate Brief) (Minn.App. Aug. 31, 2009) **Appellant's Brief and Appendix** (NO. A09-1410)

5 Leann TAYLOR, Appellant, v. LSI CORPORATION OF AMERICA, A MINNESOTA COR-PORATION, Respondent., 2009 WL 6477124 (Appellate Brief) (Minn.App. Sep. 30, 2009) **Re-spondent's Brief** (NO. A09-1410)

Trial Court Documents (U.S.A.)

Minn.Dist.Ct. Trial Pleadings

6 LeAnn TAYLOR, Plaintiff, v. LSI CORPORATION OF AMERICA, A MINNESOTA COR-PORATION, Defendant., 2006 WL 6352257 (Trial Pleading) (Minn.Dist.Ct. Nov. 20, 2006) **Complaint** (NO. 27CV0810689)

7 LeAnn TAYLOR, Plaintiff, v. LSI CORPORATION OF AMERICA, a Minnesota corporation, Defendant., 2008 WL 6855289 (Trial Pleading) (Minn.Dist.Ct. Apr. 28, 2008) **Defendant's An-swer** (NO. 27CV0810689)

(KeyCite) report for *Taylor*. Item 3 on that report was a link to the Minnesota Supreme Court opinion in *Taylor*. Reading the supreme court decision, including the two pages in Exhibit 1.5, we learned that the employee there, LeAnn Taylor, could proceed with her lawsuit against an employer that terminated her after her husband, the employer's president, resigned.[11]

We also read *Belton-Kocher*. There the court of appeals upheld a school district policy that prohibited one employee from being supervised by his or her spouse. The court found that the policy was permissible as a bona fide, essential management standard.

In assessing whether we had a sufficiently thorough package of materials, we returned to the treatise. It listed two additional cases, but we learned from *Taylor* that the key statutory language dated to 1988 and those cases predated 1988.[12] Furthermore, we had two recent cases, including a very recent one from the state's highest court. Thus we decided to work with the two cases, in addition to the statute.

The employer won in *Belton-Kocher*; that case involved a hiring decision, but the concern was one spouse's supervision of the other, not their interaction as peers. The employee won in *Taylor*; that case involved termination and the presumption that a wife would not want to stay with an employer that terminated her husband.

Combining the authorities we found, we gleaned the following points: Generally an employer should not consider the identity of a candidate's spouse. It may legally do so only when there is a bona fide, essential management reason. Assumptions about how people will feel do not suffice; careful consideration of actual management difficulties may. Thus, to resolve our client's problem, we would need to have a serious discussion about the nature and realism of the concerns the coworkers had expressed. In short, the preliminary answer was (as is often the case): "It depends. Let's talk about this some more."

This is a good point to observe that a legal researcher must deal with less-than-complete pictures. This pattern—a generally phrased statute, various stories, and various outcomes in the cases—is common in the law. Often no case is identical to the client's situation. The lawyer's task is to make a cohesive whole out of the pieces that each authority contributes, with due regard for the weightiness of each authority. Often this will involve educated guessing.

11. The decision of the Minnesota Supreme Court was not discussed in the treatise because it post-dated the treatise's publication.

12. The points in this sentence were stated on pages not excerpted here.

Exhibit 1.5	Court's Opinion (*Taylor v. LSI Corp.*)

--- N.W.2d ----, 2011 WL 1376737 (Minn.), 112 Fair Empl.Prac.Cas. (BNA) 30
(Cite as: 2011 WL 1376737 (Minn.))

tion of marriage; MHRA broadly stated that an employer could not discharge an employee because of marital status, and, reading each term with its plain and ordinary meaning, this language extended protection against marital status discrimination to include the identity of the employee's spouse and the spouse's situation, as well as the spouse's actions and beliefs. M.S.A. § 363A.08.

Syllabus by the Court

*1 A claim of marital status discrimination under Minn.Stat. § 363A.08 (2010) does not require the plaintiff to allege that the employer's conduct was "directed at the institution of marriage."

Michael L. Puklich, Neaton & Puklich, PLLP, Chanhassen, MN, for respondent.

Thomas E. Marshall, V. John Ella, Jackson Lewis LLP, Minneapolis, MN, for appellant.

OPINION

PAGE, Justice.

Respondent LeAnn Taylor's employment with appellant LSI Corporation of America (LSI) was terminated after her husband was forced to resign his employment as president of LSI. Taylor filed a lawsuit against LSI claiming marital status discrimination in violation of the Minnesota Human Rights Act, Minn.Stat. ch. 363A (2010) (MHRA). The district court granted summary judgment to LSI, dismissing Taylor's claims on the grounds that existing case law requires a plaintiff claiming "marital status" discrimination to allege that the termination was a "direct attack on the institution of marriage," which Taylor admits she did not assert. The court of appeals reversed, concluding that the plain language of the MHRA does not require a "direct attack on the institution of marriage" and that remand was necessary because a genuine issue of material fact existed as to whether Taylor had made a prima facie showing of "marital status" discrimination. *Taylor v. LSI Corp. of Am.,* 781 N.W.2d 912, 917 (Minn.App.2010). We granted review and now, for the reasons discussed below, we affirm.

Taylor began her employment with LSI in 1988 as a receptionist/secretary. [FN1] In February 2001, Taylor was promoted to Sales and Marketing Coordinator; in June 2001, she married Gary Taylor, the president of LSI. [FN2] In August 2006, Gary Taylor resigned from LSI, effective August 31. Between Gary Taylor's offer to resign and its effective date, Taylor's employment was terminated. LSI did not hire anyone to replace Taylor and her duties were reassigned to other employees.

In her complaint, Taylor alleged that she was terminated due to her "marital status," in violation of Minn.Stat. § 363A.08, subd. 2 (2010). Section 363A.08, subdivision 2, provides that "it is an unfair employment practice for an employer, because of ... sex [or] marital status ... [to] discharge an employee." According to Taylor, the chief executive officer of LSI's parent company told Gary Taylor that he would like to terminate Taylor because "she would be uncomfortable or awkward remaining employed with [LSI] after Mr. Taylor left Defendant's employ." She also claims that the CEO told her directly that "due to her husband's situation ... and the fact that it was likely [the Taylors] were going to have to relocate, [LSI] was eliminating [her] position." LSI denies that such statements were made regarding Taylor's termination, and instead claims that Taylor was fired for legitimate business-related reasons.

In January 2009, LSI moved for summary judgment seeking dismissal of Taylor's lawsuit, arguing that the complaint failed to establish a prima facie case of marital status discrimination because it did not allege that Taylor's termination was an act "directed at the institution of marriage," as required by our decision in *Cybyske v. Independent School District No. 196,* 347 N.W.2d 256, 261 (Minn.1984). Taylor conceded that her termination did not involve a direct attack on the institution of marriage; however, Taylor argued that our decision in *Cybyske* was overruled by the Legislature's subsequent amendment of the MHRA to define "marital status" as "protection against discrimina-

EXHIBIT 1.5   (continued)

--- N.W.2d ----, 2011 WL 1376737 (Minn.), 112 Fair Empl.Prac.Cas. (BNA) 30
(Cite as: 2011 WL 1376737 (Minn.))

tion on the basis of the identity, situation, actions, or beliefs of a spouse or former spouse." Minn.Stat. § 363A.03, subd. 24 (Minn.2010). The district court granted LSI summary judgment after concluding that it was bound by the court of appeals' decision in *Kepler v. Kordel, Inc.,* 542 N.W.2d 645 (Minn.App.1996), *rev. denied* (Minn. Mar. 19, 1996). The district court read this case to require a plaintiff to allege a direct attack on the institution of marriage in order to make out a prima facie case of marital status discrimination. *Id.*

*2 The court of appeals found the language of the statute to be unambiguous and concluded that the "legislature defined 'marital status' to expressly include the 'identity, situation, [and] actions' of an employee's spouse." *Taylor,* 781 N.W.2d at 916 (alteration in original). Consequently, the court of appeals concluded that the district court erred by requiring "a direct attack on the institution of marriage" and reversed the grant of summary judgment and remanded to the district court for further proceedings. *Id.*

[1][2][3][4] The issue presented by the parties in this case is whether "marital status" discrimination as defined in Minn.Stat. § 363A.03, subd. 24, requires a plaintiff to prove that the employer's action constitutes a direct attack on the institution of marriage. When reviewing a grant of summary judgment, we consider two questions, "whether there are any genuine issues of material fact and whether the lower courts erred in their application of the law." *Cummings v. Koehnen,* 568 N.W.2d 418, 420 (Minn.1997). We review questions of statutory interpretation de novo. *Eagan Econ. Dev. Auth. v. U–Haul Co. of Minn.,* 787 N.W.2d 523, 529 (Minn.2010). To interpret a statute, we first assess "whether the statute's language, on its face, is clear or ambiguous." *Am. Family Ins. Grp. v. Schroedl,* 616 N.W.2d 273, 277 (Minn.2000). If the law is clear and free from ambiguity, then the plain meaning of the statute's words controls our interpretation of the statute. *Krummenacher v. City of Minnetonka,* 783 N.W.2d 721, 726 (Minn.2010) (citing

Minn.Stat. § 645.16 (2010)); *see also Schroedl,* 616 N.W.2d at 277 (stating that we construe "words and phrases according to their plain and ordinary meaning"). We "only look outside the statutory text to ascertain legislative intent if the statute's language is ambiguous." *Erdman v. Life Time Fitness, Inc.,* 788 N.W.2d 50, 56 (Minn.2010); *see also* Minn.Stat. § 645.16.

[5] We conclude that the language of the MHRA, on its face, is unambiguous because it does not lend itself to multiple interpretations or logical inconsistencies in its application. The language of the statute is clear: under Minn.Stat. § 363A.08, subd. 2, an employer cannot discharge an employee "because of ... marital status." Under Minn.Stat. § 363A.03, subd. 24, "marital status" includes "protection against discrimination on the basis of the identity, situation, actions, or beliefs of a spouse or former spouse." Reading each term with its "plain and ordinary meaning," this statute's language extends protection against marital status discrimination to include the identity of the employee's spouse and the spouse's situation, as well as the spouse's actions and beliefs. Therefore, we conclude, as did the court of appeals, that Minn.Stat. § 363A.08, subd. 2, in conjunction with Minn.Stat. § 363A.03, subd. 24, does not require a plaintiff to show that termination was "directed at the institution of marriage" in order to establish a "marital status" discrimination claim.

*3 While we do not rely on it for our conclusion that section 363A.03, subdivision 24, does not require a plaintiff to show that the employer's actions were "directed at the institution of marriage" to establish a marital status discrimination claim, we note that the statute's history supports that conclusion. The MHRA was originally enacted as the Minnesota State Act for Fair Employment Practices to "foster the employment of all individuals ... regardless of their race, color, creed, religion, or national origin." Act of April 19, 1955, ch. 516, §§ 1–2, 1955 Minn. Laws 802, 802–03. The Legislature subsequently amended the act to make it an

A COUNTERPOINT: GOOGLE RESEARCH

You may be wondering at this point why legal research needs to be so complicated. Put another way: why would it not suffice to simply enter some key words into an Internet search engine, such as Google? We did exactly that with the issue of marital status discrimination to document the differences between lay research and legal research.

Our search was *marital status discrimination Minnesota*.[13] We obtained 2,350,000 results in 0.15 seconds; the first seven are listed in Exhibit 1.6. Almost all of the documents are short summaries of the law posted on law firm websites. Some were too old to reflect current law. As for the current ones, we found discussion of the Minnesota Supreme Court decision in *Taylor* in all of them and in some a reference to the statute or pre-2000 cases. None referred to *Belton-Kocher* or the concept of a bona fide, essential management standard. Because anyone can create a blog or website, there was no way of knowing how credible the various writers were, and some articles seemed slanted (some firms represented employers, some employees). The most promising document, located at minnlawyer.com, a newspaper for Minnesota lawyers, was available only by subscription. The website unmarried.org (the paid ad) did provide a table of statutes around the country on the topic of marital status discrimination.

This experience was typical for Google research: we obtained some useful information; however, much of it was dated and not obviously so, some of it was slanted, none was itself a legal authority, and key information was missing. For some legal researchers, a Google search is a place to start. Chapters 2 and 3 cover more finely tuned and reliable ways to get started.

---

13. Using Google in a more sophisticated way, to research cases, is covered in Chapter 4.

| EXHIBIT 1.6 | Google Search Results |

Web   Images   Videos   Maps   News   Shopping   Gmail   more ▾   Sign in

Google | marital status discrimination minnes ✕   Search |

About 2,350,000 results (0.15 seconds)   Advanced search

Everything
Images
Videos
News
Shopping
More

Saint Paul, MN
Change location

All results
Wonder wheel
Related searches
Timeline

More search tools

▸ **Minnesota Marital Status Discrimination** Law
Clarified : **Minnesota ...**
Aug 5, 2010 ... It seems like I have been blogging a lot
recently about **discrimination** cases, but new and
interesting cases keep coming across my desk.
www.minnesotalaboremploymentlawblog.com/.../discrimination/minnesota
-marital-status-discrimination-law-clarified/ - Cached

**Marital Status Discrimination | Bench and Bar of
Minnesota**
Dec 13, 2010 ... The right of spouses to pursue
discrimination claims under the **Minnesota** Human Rights
Act was clarified last spring by a ruling of the ...
mnbenchbar.com/2010/12/marital-status-discrimination/ -
Cached

Marital Status Discrimination Clarified |
Mansfield Tanick & Cohen ...
Apr 13, 2011 ... The **Minnesota** Supreme Court today
issued a ruling clarifying what types of actions may
constitute **marital status discrimination** under ...
mtc-lawwatch.com/http:/mtc.../marital-status-
discrimination-clarified/ - Cached

Marital Status Discrimination
Minnesota Supreme Court Decides Case of First
Impression Construing the 1988 Amendments to "**Marital
Status**" Discrimination Under the **Minnesota** Human
Rights ...
www.w-
p.com/.../Marital_Status_Discrimination_Under_MHRA.asp
- Cached

MINNESOTA: No Discrimination Based On The
Employee's **Marital ...**
MINNESOTA: No **Discrimination** Based On The
Employee's **Marital Status** May 2009 ...
www.w-p.com/CM/Articles/No-Discrimination-Based-
On.asp - Cached

    Show more results from w-p.com

Minnesota Supreme Court broadens definition of
marital ...
Apr 13, 2011 ... Thus, the statute extends protection against
marital status discrimination to include the identity of the
employee's spouse and the spouse's ...
www.minnesota-litigator.com/.../minnesota-supreme-court-
broadens-definition-marital-discrimination.html - Cached

Employment **Discrimination** - **Marital Status** -
Minnesota Lawyer
Apr 18, 2011 ... Respondent filed a lawsuit alleging marital
status discrimination. The District Court granted summary
judgment to appellant on the grounds ...
minnlawyer.com › Opinions - Cached

TEST YOUR UNDERSTANDING

Reflection Questions

1. Consider how you would research a nonlegal question of some interest to you, perhaps through Google or a similar tool. From what you can tell so far, how does legal research differ from that process?

2. American law exists of laws made by three branches at three levels of government. Is this complexity justified? For example, what might be the advantage of shifting to a single level of government? Or of eliminating agencies and limiting the courts to application of laws made by the legislature, without the effect of creating law?

Your Scenario

When you were sworn in as a member of the bar, the chief justice of the state's supreme court encouraged all new lawyers to serve the public interest by taking cases for people who could not afford to pay a lawyer's fees. You picked up a flyer for a volunteer lawyer network and registered on the website. A few weeks later, you received a call to represent a client in a rental housing dispute. At this stage, you know nothing about housing law. How do you make sure that you learn what you need to know to handle this client's matter effectively and efficiently?

FOCUSING ON YOUR CLIENT'S SITUATION

Contents

- Study Your Client's Situation
- Develop Your Research Vocabulary
- An Illustration
  - Example 2.1. Summary of Client Situation
  - Exhibit 2.1. Legal Thesaurus Entries
  - Exhibit 2.2. Legal Dictionary Entries
- Test Your Understanding

This chapter explores the issue of marital status discrimination (also covered in Chapter 1).

Key Concepts and Tools in This Chapter

- tools for synthesizing information
- five journalist questions
- research terms and issues
- legal rule
- types of alternative terms
- substantive and procedural rules
- uses of legal dictionaries and thesauri

A novice's typical response to a research project might be to read the problem once or perhaps twice and then search for pertinent authority through some online service. This is not the best way to start legal research—it is too simplistic and likely to lead to shallow, if not off-target, results. Rather, to accomplish the complex task of legal research, one must work through several steps that together serve the first of the FEAT four touchstones—focus. Those steps are:

1. Study the client's situation.
2. Develop research terms and issues.

3.   Acquire an overview of the law through research in commentary.
4.   Plan your research in legal authorities.

This chapter covers the first and second steps, and Chapter 3 covers the third and fourth steps.

Every reference librarian can recount stories of research that misfired because the researcher either did not study the client's situation carefully enough or did not develop enough research vocabulary. For example, a researcher who has not studied the dates on which key events occurred may research law that was not in effect at the time. A researcher who has only one or two terms in mind may spend a lot of time looking for those terms when the law uses different terms. The steps described here will provide the focus necessary to get your research off to a good start.

The chapter first describes these steps (and sub-steps), then illustrates them by reference to the marital status discrimination problem featured in Chapter 1.

STUDY YOUR CLIENT'S SITUATION

Legal research is aimed at solving a real and pressing problem for a client; it is not an exercise in idle curiosity. Because the client is paying for the research[1] and wants practical answers, it is your professional responsibility to provide those answers. Thus, focusing on the client's problem is imperative.

Gather information.   The complicated process of learning about the client's situation is well beyond the scope of this book. Nonetheless a few general observations merit stating. First, the situation includes not only specific events but also the client's context and, most important in many cases, the client's goals.

Second, information comes from various sources. The client is the source of much of your information, in particular as to goals; this information may come through interviews and materials the client provides. Lawyers often investigate beyond what the client provides; they interview other people, read additional materials regarding the specific events, research the industry in which the client operates, and sometimes explore nonlegal research on the topic.

Third, facts are far less fixed than most people expect before they become lawyers. People often disagree about an event or its significance due to differences in perspective, perception, recall, and motive. Furthermore, client goals often evolve over time as the situation changes and the client learns what is and is not possible, both legally and practically. This is especially so when you are

---

1. Many lawyers do some work pro bono, that is, with little or no compensation and for the public good. Even if the client is not paying for the research, the lawyer's professional responsibility to provide focused research remains the same.

providing advice about a future transaction rather than resolving a dispute arising out of past events.

Finally, you may well know less than you would like to know when you undertake a research project. If a problem involves a future transaction, only some actual facts are known; the rest is prediction. If a problem involves past events, there may be a missing or contested piece of information—a document no one kept, an event people perceived differently. The solution in such situations is to research with built-in contingencies, i.e., to note what is not known, research the most probable situations, note the various possible legal conclusions, and refine the research when new information is available.

Synthesize information. If, as is often the case, you obtain information about your client's situation from various sources, you will need to synthesize the information somehow. A classic means of sequencing information is through a timeline. As for divergent views, one tempting option is to simply go with whatever the client says and disregard inconsistent information obtained from other sources. Because your professional duty—and your best service to your client—is to provide candid advice,[2] this is not a good strategy. It is wiser to employ some type of synthesizing tool, such as a grid in which you list the views of various sources on the same topic and indicate the credibility of the various sources.

Summarize information. To provide a means of focusing your research, as you transition from gathering information about the client's situation to conducting legal research, generate a summary of the key client facts to refer to throughout the research process. One useful tool is a template based on the standard questions journalists ask as they gather information and write stories:

1. Who are the important actors (including people and organizations) in the situation?
2. What is going on with them? What happened between them, or how might they interact in the future?
3. When did key events occur, or when will they occur?
4. Where did or will the events occur?
5. Why is my client seeking advice? For example, is it considering bringing a claim, has it been sued and you are defending it at a particular stage of litigation, or is it seeking advice about a future transaction?

As you answer these questions, aim for over- rather than under-inclusiveness. Until you have begun to learn the law, it is difficult to know whether a particular fact is pertinent or not.

---

2. According to Rule 1.2 of the American Bar Association's Model Rules of Professional Conduct, the client decides the objectives of the representation, and the lawyer and client consult as to the means by which the objectives are pursued. Model Rule 2.1 requires that the advice be candid and that the lawyer exercise independent professional judgment.

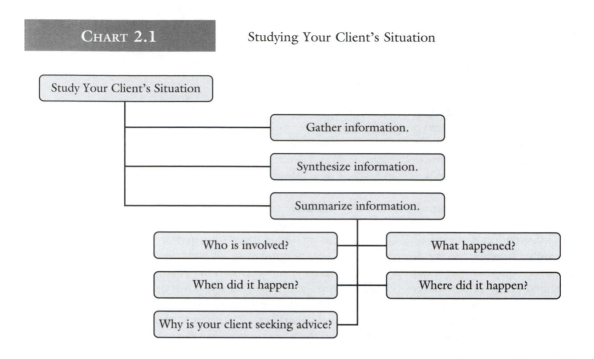

CHART 2.1   Studying Your Client's Situation

DEVELOP YOUR RESEARCH VOCABULARY

Once you have developed your summary of the key facts, you may be tempted to move directly into seeking pertinent sources. But there is an important intermediate step that can make or break your research, at least in the first few hours. This two-part step is to generate research terms and then draft research issues. Terms are words or phrases; issues are questions combining terms. Legal research is the process of matching your words of interest to the words chosen by the writers of pertinent commentary and authorities. Thus, if your vocabulary is deficient, you will not find what you need to find, or you will find too much non-pertinent information.

As you work on this step, keep in mind how legal sources use words. The core of a legal source is a legal rule: a statement connecting certain factual conditions to legal consequences. The factual conditions are expressed in more or less general terms depending on the scope of the rule, and the language tends to be more or less formal. For example, a rule on hiring new employees is likely to use "applicant," not "marketing manager" (too specific), and "employer," not "boss" (too colloquial).

The second half of a legal rule is the legal consequence of situations falling within the specified factual conditions. In common parlance, people say that conduct is "illegal" or "against the law." The American legal system is far more varied and refined than this. In basic terms, conduct may constitute a crime, leading to imprisonment and fines; be the basis of civil liability to the harmed party, leading to the payment of damages; or be regulated by an administrative agency, leading to fines and orders to alter the conduct. A legal rule thus uses a label for the type of legal wrong (e.g., wrongful termination) and either states or implies the nature of the legal consequence (e.g., recovery by the employee of lost wages).

Generate research terms. To develop a sound research vocabulary, you must draw on all of the dimensions in your summary of the client's key facts. As to each, think expansively, e.g., identify not just one or two but all actors; list not just their actions but their methods and reasons.

Furthermore, it is important to develop alternative words for the various factual concepts you identify. This is a matter of acquired skill. If you are researching in an area you have had some experience with, you may have a good feel for the words likely to be used in pertinent sources. In general, a good strategy is to generate reasonably precise words. A pertinent source is very unlikely to use your client's actual name—that is too narrow; nor is the source likely to use a very broad word, such as "person"—that is too broad. Rather, a source is likely to use a word reflecting the client's role in the situation, such as "applicant" or "employer."

In many areas of law, the chances are high that more than one word will be used across various sources for any factual facet. Thus you should consider alternatives to your original choice: synonyms, antonyms, and somewhat narrower or broader terms.

To develop a strong research vocabulary, you must also encompass a range of legal concepts that may pertain to your client's situation. The pertinent law may have two dimensions:

1. What is the substantive legal rule governing the situation? By "substantive legal rule," lawyers mean the rule that specifies whether conduct is legally required, permissible, or prohibited.
2. What is the procedural rule governing my client's case? If your client's situation involves litigation, a key component of your research may well be the rules governing litigation. If your client's situation does not involve a dispute in litigation, this will not factor into your research vocabulary.

Furthermore, as you generate your legal terms, think expansively, aim for reasonable precision, and develop a list of related words. For example, "liability" is an exceedingly broad word, so it is generally not a good choice. A better strategy is to use a word that captures the kind of liability that may be involved in your client's situation, such as "discrimination."

Obviously, your terms relating to legal concepts will be tentative, especially when you are researching a very new topic with little guidance from someone with more experience. Happily, more often than not, you will have some guidance—what you have learned in a class, what the lawyer who assigned you the project suggested, what you can learn from contacting someone who generally practices in the area, or what a reference librarian can suggest.[3]

Dictionaries and thesauri have an important role to play at this stage of the research process. For a factual concept, a nonlegal dictionary may be useful. For legal concepts, consulting a legal dictionary or thesaurus is often wise. The law is comprised largely of words most literate people would recognize, but many have specialized legal meanings that may or may not align with their meanings outside the law. Thus, especially when you are new to legal research, looking up a term is a wise precaution. Chart 2.2 lists some major legal dictionaries and thesauri. As useful as they are in building research vocabulary, they are not authoritative. Only rarely should you actually refer to a dictionary (and never a thesaurus) to establish the definition of a legal word; rather, you should use the law itself or a commentary source covered in Chapter 3.

CHART 2.2	Major Legal Dictionaries and Thesauri

Black's Law Dictionary (Bryan A. Garner ed., 9th ed. 2009, available on Westlaw).

Ballentine's Law Dictionary (3d ed. 2010, available on LexisNexis).

Bryan A. Garner, *Garner's Dictionary of Legal Usage* (3d ed. 2011).

William C. Burton, *Burton's Legal Thesaurus* (4th ed. 2007).

Daniel Oran, *Oran's Dictionary of the Law* (4th ed. 2008).

Draft research issues. By following these steps, you should have a solid list of terms capturing important factual facets and potential legal concepts in your client's situation. To focus even more, draft potential research issues, or questions, by combining factual facets and legal concepts to the extent your current knowledge permits you to do so. This final step serves two purposes. First, writing tentative issues prompts you to begin your analysis of the client's situation; research and analysis go hand-in-hand. Second, questions pique curiosity (more than lists do), and curiosity can drive a researcher to persist through a lengthy or challenging project.

---

3. Model Rule 1.6 generally requires a lawyer to keep information confidential unless the client gives consent or the disclosure is impliedly authorized to carry out the representation. Thus lawyers generally couch their discussions about client work in hypothetical or abstract terms.

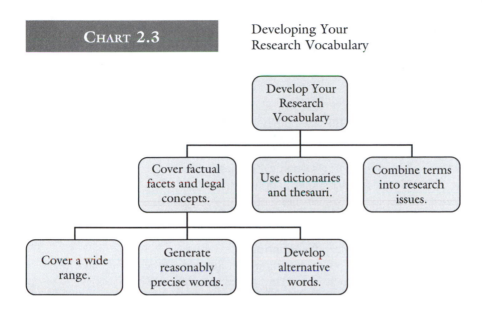

CHART 2.3   Developing Your
                   Research Vocabulary

The following illustration explains how the steps described here played out in the problem featured in Chapter 1.

AN ILLUSTRATION

Consider the problem presented in Chapter 1, in which a company sought advice as it considered a particular candidate for a marketing manager position. Our summary of the client's situation appears in Example 2.1.

Given the posture of the problem—the client was seeking advice at a preliminary stage, during its decision making—the only source of information was the client's representative, the client's human resources manager.

There was some uncertainty around a key matter: Would there really be difficulties if the two spouses were to work closely together? This became a built-in contingency in the research.

A key factual facet to capture in the research vocabulary was the client's identity. It was a retailer of high-end furnishings, but its specific business seemed unlikely to be important. It could matter that it was a private business and that it was fairly large.[4] The key point was that it was acting as an employer in this situation. See Exhibit 2.1, a thesaurus entry, which presents a variety of alternatives to the word "employer."

Another key player in the situation was the applicant. She was an applicant for a marketing position, a strong candidate, a female, and the wife of the

---

4. In the area of employment law, some statutes do differentiate between employment sectors (public and private) and by employer size. In this situation, the state statute covered private employers of one or more employees.

EXAMPLE 2.1	Summary of Client Situation

1. Who:
    a. Employer = retail operation
    b. Current employee = sales manager
    c. Applicant for marketing manager = spouse of current employee
        and future close colleague; highly qualified
    d. Also coworkers on sales/marketing staffs
2. What: consider spouse/applicant or not; qualifications are strong;
    concern is awkwardness of interaction with already employed
    spouse—as anticipated by coworkers
3. When: May 2011
4. Where: Minneapolis, Minnesota
5. Why: advice as to handling candidate's application, make legal
    decision, respect coworker concerns, avoid litigation

client's sales manager, with whom she would work closely if hired. In discerning which of these attributes mattered, we considered the reasons the client would give for its reaction to her application: that she was a strong candidate, on the one hand; that she was married to the sales manager, on the other hand. As to the latter, the concern was not that she was female, but that they were married—an important distinction. The research should focus not on her gender but rather on her role as a wife. A broader term for "wife" is "spouse," and an even broader term is "marital status." Furthermore, it was her status as the spouse of a current employee, not her marital status in general, that was the concern.

Thus a key legal concept to capture in the research vocabulary was the motivation for the potential decision not to pursue the candidate. In our culture, decisions that harm someone based on who they happen to be are thought of as "discrimination." See Exhibit 2.2, a dictionary entry for the word "discrimination." This exhibit confirmed that "discrimination" was a good word choice; indicated that federal and state statutes, as well as court decisions, prohibited various types of discrimination; and stated that an important consideration, in addition to the differential treatment, would be the lack of a reasonable distinction between those favored and those not favored.

Linking the terms we developed this issue: *Would it be discriminatory to decline to hire an otherwise strong applicant on the grounds of her marriage to a current employee with whom she would interact closely?*

EXHIBIT 2.1	Legal Thesaurus Entries (*Burton's Legal Thesaurus*)

ENCLOSURE

EMPLOYER, noun   administrator, boss, chief, controller, director, executive, head, leader, management, manager, master, overseer, owner, patron, proprietor, superintendent, superior, supervisor, taskmaster
ASSOCIATED CONCEPTS: employers' liability acts

EMPLOYMENT, noun   activity, appointment, assignment, avocation, berth, billet, business, calling, capacity, career, commission, craft, duty, employ, engagement, enterprise, field, function, incumbency, industry, job, labor, lifework, line, livelihood, living, means of livelihood, means of support, *negotium*, occupation, office, position, post, practice, profession, pursuit, retainment, service, situation, specialty, task, trade, vocation, work
ASSOCIATED CONCEPTS: abandonment of employment, arising out of and in course of employment, available for employment, casual employment, conditions of employment, contract of employment, course of employment, covered employment, dangerous employment, duration of employment, during term of employment, engaged in employment, exempt employment, extrahazardous employment, extraordinary employment, general employment, grade of employment, injury arising in course of employment, permanent employment, place of employment, private employment, professional employment, public employment, scope of employment, seasonal employment, temporary employment, tenure of employment

EMPLOYMENT DISCRIMINATION, noun   bias in the workplace, prejudice in an employment environment *Generally:* differentiation, disequalization, inequality, injustice, unfairness

EMPOWER, verb   accredit, activate, aggrandize, allow, appoint, arm, assign, authorize, capacitate, commission, confer power on, delegate, depute, deputize, enable, endow, energize, entrust, franchise, give ability, give authority, give permission, give power, give right, grant, grant authority, grant power, *homini rei*, impart power to, implement, invest, license, make able, make capable, make potent, permit, potentiate, *potestatem facere*, privilege, qualify, render competent, sanction, strengthen, train, vest, warrant

EMPTY (Nothing left), adjective   all gone, bare, blank, depleted, devoid, drained, exhausted, hollow, nothing left inside, unfilled, vacuous, void, without contents
ASSOCIATED CONCEPTS: empty judgment, empty law

EMPTY (Vacant), adjective   abandoned, available, barren, deserted, fruitless, idle, no one home, not inhabited, unclaimed, uninhabited, unoccupied, untenanted, up for grabs
ASSOCIATED CONCEPTS: empty premises

EMPTY (Without substance), adjective   devoid of merit, inconsequential, ineffective, ineffectual, insignificant, insubstantial, meaningless, meritless, unavailing, unimportant, unreal, unsatisfying, useless, vain, valueless, without substance, worthless
ASSOCIATED CONCEPTS: an empty threat, veiled threat of law suit

EMULOUS, adjective   admiring, competing, competitive, contending, copying, envious, follow the example of, following, imitative, jealous, rival

EN BANC, adverb   all together, as a unit, as a whole, collectively, *en bloc, en masse,* entirely, in a body, in a mass, in sum, *in toto,* one and all

EN MASSE, adverb   all together, as a body, as a group, as a whole, as one, at the same time, collectively, *en bloc,* ensemble, in assembly, in mass, in the aggregate, together

EN ROUTE, adverb   along the way, bound, during the journey, during travel, in passage, in progress, in transit, midway, on the journey, on the road, on the way

ENABLE, verb   abet, aid, allow, approve, arm, assist, authorize, capacitate, confer, consent, emancipate, empower, endow, facilitate, *facultatem facere,* give ability, give authority, give means, give permission, give power, grant, help, *homini rei,* implement, indulge, invest, let, liberate, license, make able, make capable, make possible, make practicable, permit, privilege, provide, provide means, qualify, release, remove a disability, render assistance, render competent, sanction, strengthen, supply with means, support
ASSOCIATED CONCEPTS: enabling act, enabling legislation, enabling statute

ENABLING LEGISLATION, noun   establishing legislation, first initiative, law giving authority, law giving power, law granting authority, law granting license, law investing power, original ordinance, seminal measure, underlying act, underlying legislative pronouncement
ASSOCIATED CONCEPTS: enacting clause

ENACT, verb   adopt a measure, appoint by act, codify, command, declare, decree, dictate, enjoin, establish, establish by law, give legislative sanction, institute by law, issue a command, legislate, make into a statute, make laws, ordain by law, order, pass, *perferre,* prescribe, put in force, put into effect
ASSOCIATED CONCEPTS: enacting clause
FOREIGN PHRASES: *Non obligat lex nisi promulgata.* A law is not obligatory unless it is promulgated. *Ejus est interpretari cujus est condere.* It is for him who enacts anything to give it interpretation.

ENACTMENT, noun   act, bill, charter, codification, decree, dictate, edict, establishment, fiat, law, legislation, *lex,* measure, ordinance, *plebiscitum,* regulation, rule, ruling, *sanctio,* statute, statutory law
FOREIGN PHRASES: *Leges suum ligent latorem.* Laws should bind their own proposer. *Jus constitui oportet in his quae ut plurimum accidunt non quae ex inopi nato.* Laws ought to be made with a view to those cases which occur most frequently, and not to those which are of rare or accidental occurrence. *Leges figendi et refigendi consuetudo est periculosissima.* The practice of making and remaking the laws is a most dangerous one. *Quod populus postremum jussit, id jus ratum esto.* What the people have last enacted, let that be the settled law.

ENCLOSE, verb   blockade, bound, bracket, capture, *cingere,* circumscribe, circumvallate, close in, compass, confine, contain, embrace, encase, encincture, encircle, encompass, enfold, envelop, environ, fence in, gird, girdle, hem in, immure, impound, imprison, incarcerate, *includere,* insert in a wrapper, insert in an envelope, keep behind bars, keep in, keep in custody, limit, pen, put a barrier around, put into a receptacle, restrain, restrict, retain, ring, *saepire,* shut in, surround, take into custody, trammel, wall in

ENCLOSURE, noun   arena, barrier, blockade, border, boundary, bracket, cincture, circle, circumjacence, circumscription, circumvallation, confine, confinement, container, containment, custody, edge, embrace, encasement, encirclement,

Exhibit 2.2	Legal Dictionary Entries (*Black's Law Dictionary*)

discovery vein. See VEIN.

discredit, *vb.* To destroy or impair the credibility of (a witness, a piece of evidence, or a theory); to lessen the degree of trust to be accorded to (a witness or document). [Cases: Witnesses ⊘330.] — **discredit,** *n.*

discreet (di-**skreet**), *adj.* Exercising discretion; prudent; judicious; discerning.

discrete (di-**skreet**), *adj.* Individual; separate; distinct.

discretion (di-**skresh**-ən). (14c) **1.** Wise conduct and management; cautious discernment; prudence. **2.** Individual judgment; the power of free decision-making.

　　sole discretion. An individual's power to make decisions without anyone else's advice or consent.

3. *Criminal & tort law.* The capacity to distinguish between right and wrong, sufficient to make a person responsible for his or her own actions. [Cases: Criminal Law ⊘46.] **4.** A public official's power or right to act in certain circumstances according to personal judgment and conscience, often in an official or representative capacity. — Also termed *discretionary power.*

　　administrative discretion. A public official's or agency's power to exercise judgment in the discharge of its duties. [Cases: Administrative Law and Procedure ⊘324, 754.]

　　judicial discretion. (17c) The exercise of judgment by a judge or court based on what is fair under the circumstances and guided by the rules and principles of law; a court's power to act or not act when a litigant is not entitled to demand the act as a matter of right. — Also termed *legal discretion.* [Cases: Courts ⊘26.]

　　prosecutorial discretion. (1966) A prosecutor's power to choose from the options available in a criminal case, such as filing charges, prosecuting, not prosecuting, plea-bargaining, and recommending a sentence to the court. [Cases: Criminal Law ⊘29(3); District and Prosecuting Attorneys ⊘8.]

discretion, abuse of. See ABUSE OF DISCRETION.

discretionary (di-**skresh**-ə-ner-ee), *adj.* (18c) (Of an act or duty) involving an exercise of judgment and choice, not an implementation of a hard-and-fast rule. ● Such an act by a court may be overturned only after a showing of abuse of discretion.

discretionary account. An account that allows a broker access to a customer's funds to purchase and sell securities or commodities for the customer based on the broker's judgment and without first having to obtain the customer's consent to the purchase or sale. [Cases: Brokers ⊘19.]

discretionary act. A deed involving an exercise of personal judgment and conscience. — Also termed *discretionary function.* See DISCRETION; ABUSE OF DISCRETION.

discretionary bail. See BAIL (3).

discretionary commitment. See COMMITMENT.

discretionary damages. See DAMAGES.

discretionary duty. See DUTY (2).

discretionary function. See DISCRETIONARY ACT.

discretionary immunity. See IMMUNITY (1).

discretionary order. See ORDER (8).

discretionary power. 1. See POWER (3). **2.** See DISCRETION (4).

discretionary review. See REVIEW.

discretionary sentencing. See *indeterminate sentencing* under SENTENCING.

discretionary-transfer statute. See TRANSFER STATUTE.

discretionary trust. See TRUST.

discretion statement. *Hist. English law.* In an action for divorce or judicial separation, a written request for the court to consider granting a judgment favorable to a spouse who has admittedly committed a matrimonial offense, esp. adultery.

　　"In a suit for divorce or judicial separation, the defendant's own adultery is a discretionary bar. The petitioner asking the court to exercise its discretion to grant a decree notwithstanding his own adultery must lodge in the Divorce Registry a statement, known as a `discretion statement,' dated and signed by him or his solicitor, stating that the court will be asked to exercise its discretion on his behalf notwithstanding his own adultery, and setting forth particulars of his acts of adultery and of the facts which is it material for the court to know for the purpose of exercising its discretion." N. Simon Tessy, *Is a Discretion Statement Really Necessary?*, 21 Mod. L. Rev. 48, 48 (1958).

discriminant function (di-**skrim**-ə-nənt). An IRS method of selecting tax returns to be audited. ● The method consists of (1) using a computer program to identify returns with a high probability of error (such as those showing a disproportionate amount of deductible expenses), and (2) having examiners manually review the selected returns to determine which ones should be audited. — Also termed *DIF system.* [Cases: Internal Revenue ⊘4443.]

discriminatee (di-**skrim**-ə-nə-tee). A person unlawfully discriminated against. [Cases: Civil Rights ⊘1007.]

discrimination, *n.* (1866) **1.** The effect of a law or established practice that confers privileges on a certain class or that denies privileges to a certain class because of race, age, sex, nationality, religion, or disability. ● Federal law, including Title VII of the Civil Rights Act, prohibits employment discrimination based on any one of those characteristics. Other federal statutes, supplemented by court decisions, prohibit discrimination in voting rights, housing, credit extension, public education, and access to public facilities. State laws provide further protections against discrimination. [Cases: Civil Rights ⊘1001–1263.] **2.** Differential treatment; esp., a failure to treat all persons equally when no reasonable distinction can be found between those favored and those not favored. [Cases: Civil Rights ⊘1033, 1138.]

　　"The dictionary sense of 'discrimination' is neutral while the current political use of the term is frequently non-neutral, pejorative. With both a neutral and a non-neutral use of the word having currency, the opportunity for confusion in arguments about racial discrimination is enormously

Exhibit 2.2   *(continued)*

multiplied. For some, it may be enough that a practice is called discriminatory for them to judge it wrong. Others may be mystified that the first group condemns the practice without further argument or inquiry. Many may be led to the false sense that they have actually made a moral argument by showing that the practice discriminates (distinguishes in favor of or against). The temptation is to move from 'X distinguishes in favor of or against' to 'X discriminates' to 'X is wrong' without being aware of the equivocation involved." Robert K. Fullinwider, *The Reverse Discrimination Controversy* 11–12 (1980).

age discrimination. Discrimination based on age. ● Federal law prohibits discrimination in employment against people who are age 40 or older. [Cases: Civil Rights ⌒1014, 1199.]

content-based discrimination. A state-imposed restriction on the content of speech, esp. when the speech concerns something of slight social value and is vastly outweighed by the public interest in morality and order. ● Types of speech subject to content-based discrimination include obscenity, fighting words, and defamation. *R.A.V. v. City of St. Paul*, 505 U.S. 377, 383–84, 112 S.Ct. 2538, 2543 (1992).

gender discrimination. See *sex discrimination.*

invidious discrimination (in-**vid**-ee-əs). (1856) Discrimination that is offensive or objectionable, esp. because it involves prejudice or stereotyping.

racial discrimination. Discrimination based on race. [Cases: Civil Rights ⌒1009, 1107.]

reverse discrimination. (1964) Preferential treatment of minorities, usu. through affirmative-action programs, in a way that adversely affects members of a majority group. See AFFIRMATIVE ACTION. [Cases: Civil Rights ⌒1033(3), 1232.]

sex discrimination. Discrimination based on gender, esp. against women. ● The Supreme Court has established an intermediate-scrutiny standard of review for gender-based classifications, which must serve an important governmental interest and be substantially related to the achievement of that objective. *Craig v. Boren*, 429 U.S. 190, 97 S.Ct. 451 (1976). — Also termed *gender discrimination*. [Cases: Civil Rights ⌒1011, 1164, 1236.]

viewpoint discrimination. Content-based discrimination in which the government targets not a particular subject, but instead certain views that speakers might express on the subject; discrimination based on the content of a communication. ● If restrictions on the content of speech are reasonable and not calculated to suppress a particular set of views or ideas, a governmental body may limit speech in a nonpublic forum to expressions that serve a specific purpose. For example, an agency holding a workshop to inform state employees of laws related to the agency's functions may reasonably prohibit the expression of opinions regarding the motives of the legislators. But if speech favorable to the legislators' intent is allowed and opponents are denied the opportunity to respond, the restriction would constitute viewpoint discrimination. —

Also termed *viewpoint-based discrimination*. [Cases: Constitutional Law ⌒1507, 1516.]

3. The effect of state laws that favor local interests over out-of-state interests. ● Such a discriminatory state law may still be upheld if it is narrowly tailored to achieve an important state interest. Cf. FAVORITISM. [Cases: Commerce ⌒54.1.] — **discriminate,** *vb.* — **discriminatory,** *adj.*

discriminatory tariff. See TARIFF (2).

discussion. 1. The act of exchanging views on something; a debate. 2. *Civil law.* A creditor's act of exhausting all remedies against the principal debtor before proceeding with a lawsuit against the guarantor. See BENEFIT OF DISCUSSION. [Cases: Guaranty ⌒42, 77; Principal and Surety ⌒138, 168.]

disease. 1. A deviation from the healthy and normal functioning of the body <the drug could not be linked to his disease>. 2. (*pl.*) Special classes of pathological conditions with similar traits, such as having similar causes and affecting similar organs <respiratory diseases> <occupational diseases>. 3. Any disorder; any depraved condition.

functional disease. A disease that prevents, obstructs, or interferes with an organ's special function, without anatomical defect or abnormality in the organ itself.

industrial disease. See OCCUPATIONAL DISEASE.

occupational disease. See OCCUPATIONAL DISEASE.

organic disease. A disease that is caused by an injury to, or lesion or malfunction in, an organ.

disembarrass, *vb.* To free from embarrassment; to extricate or disentangle one thing from another.

disembodied technology. *Intellectual property.* Know-how or knowledge that is in the form of information only. ● Disembodied technology includes proprietary technology and information in the public domain. Cf. EMBODIED TECHNOLOGY.

disenfranchise (dis-ən-**fran**-chIz), *vb.* (17c) To deprive (a person) of the right to exercise a franchise or privilege, esp. to vote. — Also termed *disfranchise.*

disenfranchisement (dis-ən-**fran**-chiz-mənt or -**fran**-chIz-mənt). 1. The act of depriving a member of a corporation or other organization of a right, as by expulsion. 2. The act of taking away the right to vote in public elections from a citizen or class of citizens. — Also termed *disfranchisement.* [Cases: Elections ⌒87.]

disentailing assurance. See DISENTAILMENT.

disentailing deed. See DEED.

disentailing statute (dis-ən-**tayl**-ing). A statute regulating or prohibiting disentailing deeds. See *disentailing deed* under DEED. [Cases: Deeds ⌒127.]

disentailment (dis-ən-**tayl**-mənt), *n.* (1886) The act or process by which a tenant in tail bars the entail on an estate and converts it into a fee simple, thereby nullifying the rights of any later claimant to the fee tail. — Also termed *disentailing assurance.* See BARRING OF

> **Citation to Legal Dictionaries**
>
> The most often cited legal dictionary, *Black's*, used in this chapter, is cited as follows:
>
> BLUEBOOK: *Black's Law Dictionary* 534 (9th ed. 2009). [See rule B8.1.]
> ALWD: *Black's Law Dictionary* 534 (Bryan A. Garner ed., 9th ed., West 2009). [See rule 25.]

TEST YOUR UNDERSTANDING

Reflection Questions

1. The early stages of research entail thinking both expansively and meticulously about how words are used. In what ways have you been a wordsmith? What lessons can you transfer from that setting to generating legal research terms?

2. It is often said that language is a lawyer's stock-in-trade. Not only do we use words in legal research, we also sell words in the various forms of communication for which clients pay, whether advice letters, negotiation, arguments to the jury, or briefs to a court. The law—and thus lawyers too—are very particular about which words to use when. Why? Why not, for example, simply prohibit "unfair hiring," in lieu of "discrimination based on marital status"?

Your Scenario

You have met with your client and learned about her situation. Her name is Elaine Wilson, and she lives in Buckley, West Virginia. Now twenty-five, she is a cook in a local restaurant and returned six months ago from a year-long tour of duty in Afghanistan as an Army reservist. She manages to get by, in part because she has a decent apartment at a decent price in one of the few such buildings in town. She clearly could not afford to pay for a lawyer to handle the following situation.

Her concern began several months ago when she developed symptoms of post-traumatic stress disorder, diagnosed by her Army physicians as stemming from her experiences in Afghanistan. She finds it difficult to sleep, is edgy when awake, has disturbing flashbacks when not otherwise occupied, and can be confrontational. Her physicians are working with her on counseling and medication. Recently she was given a puppy through a group that provides pets to veterans with ongoing psychological issues. The puppy has indeed served its purpose, providing a calming influence when she is most vulnerable to the effects of the PTSD, including when she is at home and alone.

While her employer (himself a veteran of the war in Vietnam) has been understanding, her landlord has raised a concern about the puppy. Ms. Wilson believes that the landlord is generally not pleased to have her in the apartment building since she developed PTSD. His stated complaint to her is that the building is a no-pet building. Her lease indeed stipulates that no pets are allowed. Her landlord says she is breaching that clause, and he is concerned that other tenants will also want to have pets for their psychological reasons. Thus he has told her that she must either give up the puppy or move in a month.

Think through this situation using the process described in this chapter. What are your research terms and issues?

FRAMING YOUR LEGAL RESEARCH

Contents

The issues explored in this chapter are marital status discrimination (also covered in Chapters 1 and 2), defamation within the workplace (also covered in Chapter 4), and an employer's liability for an employee's car accident (also covered in Chapter 5).

Key Concepts and Tools in This Chapter

- three advantages of early use of commentary sources
- citable commentary
- encyclopedias

(continued)

- treatises
- access tools for organized print resources
- updating publications for print resources
- legal periodicals
- indexes to legal periodicals
- *American Law Reports Annotations*
- searching an online catalog or index
- conducting key-word searches in full-text databases
- Restatements of the Law and American Law Institute
- jury instructions
- practice guides and sample forms and pleadings

Once you have carefully studied your client's situation and developed your initial research terms and issue(s), your next step is to frame your legal research. Although your ultimate goal is to find and rely on legal authority and commentary is not the law, framing your research is best done through commentary for several reasons. First, commentary provides an overview of an area of law; without this overview, you may not see the proverbial forest for the trees. Second, commentary provides references to legal authorities; to continue the analogy, it identifies some of the major trees. Third, commentary sources are generally easier to research in and understand during the early stages of research than the law itself. A treatise, for example, is much easier to read than a statute.

Experienced lawyers supervising new lawyers often complain that the complete legal framework for the client's problem is missing. This is of major significance in the law, where all pieces must be present for the problem to be solved properly. For example, assume that the statute governing a situation encompasses large but not small companies or provides exemptions in certain situations; failure to take these provisions into account could render the entire analysis, simply put, wrong. Using commentary as suggested in this chapter solves that problem. It thus serves the fourth of the FEAT cornerstones—thoroughness.

This chapter first provides an overview of the many forms of legal commentary. The chapter then discusses each of the major forms of commentary in more detail, with illustrations of their use in providing overviews of issues explored elsewhere in this book. Throughout the chapter are skill-set discussions, each covering a skill set that is used not only with the resources discussed in this chapter but also with other resources. For example, the discussion of using print-finding tools applies as well to print statutes, and the discussion of key-word searching applies to case law research. The chapter concludes with a chart presenting optimal options for commentary research.

OVERVIEW OF COMMENTARY SOURCES

As with legal authorities, legal commentary is created through various processes, by various people, and in various formats. Each form of commentary has its place in a fairly fixed hierarchy of credibility, its particular strengths and weaknesses as a research tool, and its best uses. While you need not be able to use all forms of commentary equally well, you should be able to use all proficiently.

Some commentary sources have as their primary purpose presenting a discussion of the law, with or without critical analysis. In this category are legal encyclopedias, treatises, and periodicals, which resemble sources found in most other disciplines. These sources fall on a spectrum: some consist of over a hundred volumes and cover nearly every legal topic; others are much more limited in size and scope. These sources are written by one person or a team of authors, in either an academic or commercial publishing setting. Based on the credibility of the authors and publishers, some are considered credible enough to be used in presenting a legal analysis to a court—what lawyers call "citable."

Some of these sources—encyclopedias and treatises—are published as coherent, organized wholes. Others—periodicals—are published in issues over time with no overarching organization. Thus encyclopedias and treatises are researched somewhat differently from periodicals, so this chapter takes up this category in two sections.

Another category of commentary is generated through a very different process involving cycles of debate and drafting by a group of experts over an extended period of time. The two main examples of this category are the Restatements of the Law and jury instructions. These sources are intended to provide a statement of what the law is in a form that closely replicates a legal rule. These sources are generally highly citable.

A third category of commentary is considered less credible than the first two. Sources in this category, which this book calls "practice guides," may provide some exposition of the law but exist primarily for a different reason: to provide practical guidance on how to handle a typical legal matter. For example, a source in this category may provide sample pleadings (documents used in litigation), sample contract language, or a checklist for handling the various phases of a legal process. These sources are published by commercial publishers and by organizations that provide continuing legal education to lawyers.[1] These sources are generally not cited and are less useful during the early stages of a typical research project. At the same time, they are integral to many lawyers' practices.

ENCYCLOPEDIAS AND TREATISES

Encyclopedias sweep the most broadly of the various commentary sources, as you would expect. The quintessential encyclopedias are *American Jurisprudence*

---

1. Almost every state requires lawyers to take seminars to update their knowledge and skills in order to retain their licenses to practice.

(second edition) and *Corpus Juris Secundum*. Both provide an overview of about 400 topics of federal and state law and run about 150 volumes in print form. Even at this size, the coverage is fairly general. The chief advantages of these two encyclopedias are that your research issue is very likely to be covered, they are very well organized with detailed tables of contents and indexes, you can easily browse them (particularly if you read them in print form), and they are updated annually. On the other hand, because they are so general and are not written by widely recognized experts, they are not particularly citable. Encyclopedias are best used to obtain a broad overview of your topic and perhaps a useful reference or two.

Some states have a state encyclopedia. State encyclopedias are more valuable than the national encyclopedias on a state law topic because they are more specific in both the discussion of the law and references, are less bulky and thus generally easier to use, and may be viewed as citable at least as to general propositions.

Treatises sweep less broadly than encyclopedias. A good treatise provides a detailed discussion of a single area of law, with many references. Indeed, while most treatises are only one volume long, others run many volumes. Most are well organized, and you can find pertinent material through tables of contents and indexes. Browsing treatises can be very helpful and works especially well in print. Many, but not all, treatises are updated every year or so, if not more often. A major advantage of some treatises is that they are written by respected experts and are thus highly citable. Thus, if you already know the subject of your research issue, a treatise can be a very good source to use early in your research.

At times, identifying a treatise to use can be vexing. Few use the word "treatise" in their titles. What may seem to be a treatise at first glance may in fact be something else. For example, as useful as they are for classes, casebooks and law school study aids (such as outlines) are not treatises for research purposes. On the other hand, some treatises are published in abridged versions specifically for law students.[2] Thus, as you begin to research a new area, you may want to ask a more senior colleague for the name of an influential treatise on your subject or ask for a treatise on reserve in a library.

The classic publication format for encyclopedias and treatises is print. At present, a good number of encyclopedias (including *American Jurisprudence Second* and *Corpus Juris Secundum*) are available online through commercial services (namely Westlaw and LexisNexis). Treatises continue to be predominately print sources, but this is changing fairly rapidly. While it obviously makes sense to use an encyclopedia or treatise online when that is the only way you have access to it, using them in print takes advantage of their particular utility in the research process. When working with a book in print, you can easily see the organization the author has brought to the topic, browse for pertinent sections, move readily from one section to another, identify references to pertinent material, and read extended passages. Some of these tasks are still somewhat more difficult to accomplish online. Furthermore, using an available treatise in print avoids online fees.

---

2. Student-oriented treatises are called "hornbooks," which is derived from the name for children's books of years ago, which were covered with horn to protect them from soiling.

Skill Set 1: Using Print Finding Tools. Recall that one of the searches in the work-flow of legal research described in Chapter 1 is to find pertinent portions of a resource. As shown in Chart 3.1, highly organized print sources provide several options.

First, take a careful look at its organization. Authors of legal commentary are much taken with subdividing their texts. In encyclopedias, subjects, called "topics," appear in alphabetical order; the discussion of a topic is presented in logically ordered, numbered sections. Treatises, in covering one subject in depth, typically consist of a series of logically ordered chapters divided into sections. In either source, the text of a section may run a few paragraphs up to a few pages.

One way to identify the sections you should read is to look at the various outlines within the source, such as the overall and detailed tables of contents, located at the beginning of an encyclopedia topic or treatise. In doing so, you will not only identify sections to read but also see how the author has framed the discussion, which should provide a good start for your own analysis. See Exhibit 3.1, a table of contents from *American Jurisprudence Second.*

Another way to find pertinent sections is through the index, which typically appears at the back of a single volume or in a set of separate volumes shelved at the end of a multivolume set. A multivolume treatise may have volume-specific indexes in each volume. Legal indexes are very detailed, alphabetical lists of major topics, with subtopics and even sub-subtopics listed alphabetically under each topic heading. Many indexes also include cross-references, which direct the user to other topics for additional guidance. See Exhibit 3.2, from the index to *American Jurisprudence Second.* Spending time perusing an index is a wise investment.[3]

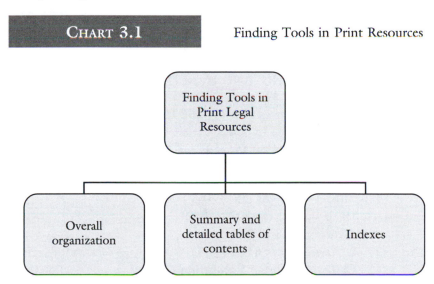

| CHART 3.1 | Finding Tools in Print Resources |

---

3. If you are using an encyclopedia or treatise after you already have a lead on a primary authority, you may use an additional access tool: the tables of authorities. These tables list statutes, cases, or other authorities and point the reader to the place where the authority is discussed.

EXHIBIT 3.1   Encyclopedia Table of Contents

45A Am Jur 2d

B. BONA FIDE OCCUPATIONAL QUALIFICATIONS
    (§§ 254 TO 265)
    1. In General (§ 254)
    2. Particular Characteristics as BFOQs (§§ 255 to
        265)
        a. Sex (§§ 255 to 259)
        b. Age (§§ 260 to 264)
        c. Other Characteristics (§ 265)
C. PERFORMANCE AND OTHER EXCEPTIONS
    RELATED TO JOB QUALIFICATIONS (§§ 266 TO
    267)
D. PREFERENCES AND OTHER EXCEPTIONS (§§ 268
    TO 272)
E. RELIANCE ON ADMINISTRATIVE GUIDANCE
    (§§ 273 TO 278)
    1. Applicable provisions (§§ 273 to 275)
    2. Equal Employment Opportunity Commission
        opinions (§§ 276 to 278)

VI. REGULATED EMPLOYER PRACTICES,
     GENERALLY; TESTING, EVALUATION AND
     SELECTION OF JOB APPLICANTS AND
     EMPLOYEES (§§ 279 TO 599)
     A. SELECTION, SCREENING, AND EVALUATION
         PRACTICES (§§ 288 TO 477)
         1. Tests and Similar Procedures (§§ 288 to 367)
             a. In General (§§ 288 to 300)
             b. Testing and Selection Procedures Regulated by
                 the Americans with Disabilities Act (§§ 301 to
                 304)
             c. Disparate Treatment (§§ 305 to 306)
             d. Disparate Impact (§§ 307 to 312)
             e. Validation (§§ 313 to 345)
                 (1) In General (§§ 313 to 321)
                 (2) Criterion-related Validation (§§ 322 to
                      335)
                 (3) Content Validation (§§ 336 to 342)
                 (4) Construct Validation (§§ 343 to 345)

8

EXHIBIT 3.1   *(continued)*

JOB DISCRIMINATION

    f. Documentation (§§ 346 to 359)
       (1) In General (§§ 346 to 349)
       (2) Evidence of Validity (§§ 350 to 359)
    g. Selection of Apprentices for Registered Programs (§§ 360 to 367)

  2. Proof In Job Requirements Cases, In General (§§ 368 to 370)
  3. Types Of Selection Criteria (§§ 371 to 477)
    a. In General; Subjective Criteria (§§ 371 to 375)
    b. Personal Morality (§§ 376 to 379)
    c. Work History (§§ 380 to 382)
    d. Education, Job Skills, and Experience (§§ 383 to 389)
    e. Health and Physical Fitness (§§ 390 to 405)
       (1) In General (§§ 390 to 393)
       (2) Particular Health, Fitness, or Size Requirements (§§ 394 to 405)
    f. Freedom from Substance Abuse; Consent to Drug Testing (§§ 406 to 432)
       (1) In General (§§ 406 to 409)
       (2) Duty to Maintain a Drug-free Workplace (§§ 410 to 414)
       (3) Public Employer Substance Abuse Policies (§§ 415 to 418)
       (4) Fourth Amendment Considerations in Substance Abuse Testing (§§ 419 to 428)
       (5) Other Constitutional Restraints on Substance Abuse Testing (§§ 429 to 432)
    g. Appearance and Grooming (§§ 433 to 440)
  → h. Marital Status (§§ 441 to 446)
    i. Legal History (§§ 447 to 451)
    j. Military History (§§ 452 to 453)
    k. Financial Condition (§§ 454 to 456)
    l. Personal Associations (§§ 457 to 463)
    m. Union Affiliations and Obligations (§§ 464 to 466)
    n. Availability for Work (§§ 467 to 477)

9

EXHIBIT 3.2	Encyclopedia Index (45 Am. Jur. 2d)

GENERAL INDEX

JOB DISCRIMINATION—*continued*

Lie detector testing—*continued*
sanctions and remedies. Employee Polygraph Protection Act, above in this group
security firms, permissible testing, **JobDiscrim § 872**
service and filing of all documents, civil penalty hearings, **JobDiscrim § 1582**
state laws, effect, **JobDiscrim § 873**
statutory limitations on questioning, **JobDiscrim § 884**
subpoenas, enforcement, **JobDiscrim § 1816**
suspicion, justification of polygraph, **JobDiscrim § 879**
technical assistance and cooperation, **JobDiscrim § 1575**
termination or prevention of examination, examinee's right, **JobDiscrim § 881**
threats to use lie detector test or provide bad references, **JobDiscrim § 870**
time computations, administrative hearings, **JobDiscrim § 1583**
time limitations, judicial proceedings, **JobDiscrim § 1923**
venue, judicial proceedings, **JobDiscrim § 1892**
violations, reporting, **JobDiscrim § 1578**
waiver restrictions, **JobDiscrim § 875**
written notices required, **JobDiscrim § 882, 883**
written statements required, employer's use of polygraph, **JobDiscrim § 880**
Life insurance and death benefits
age restrictions on participation in insurance plan, **JobDiscrim § 727**
permissible age-based reductions in life insurance, **JobDiscrim § 727**
sex discrimination in administration, **JobDiscrim § 727**
Limitation of actions
generally, **JobDiscrim § 1898 to 1973**
affirmative defense, statute of limitations as, **JobDiscrim § 1901**
Age Discrimination in Employment Act (ADEA), above
Civil Rights Acts, above
computation of time limitations
FRCP 6(a), applicability, **JobDiscrim § 1966**
FRCP 6(e), applicability, **JobDiscrim § 1967**
defense, statute of limitations as, **JobDiscrim § 1901**
early Civil Rights Acts. Civil Rights Acts, above
Equal Pay Act, above
FRCP 6(a), applicability, **JobDiscrim § 1966**

JOB DISCRIMINATION—*continued*

Limitation of actions—*continued*
FRCP 6(e), applicability, **JobDiscrim § 1967**
Government Employee Rights Act, **JobDiscrim § 1922**
Rehabilitation Act, **JobDiscrim § 1921, 1947**
removal, **JobDiscrim § 1878**
revival of time-barred suits, **JobDiscrim § 1900**
state statutes of limitations, applicability
personal injury torts under early Civil Rights Acts, **JobDiscrim § 1910**
Title VII, **JobDiscrim § 1902**
Title VI, **JobDiscrim § 1920**
Title VII, below
tolling, below
Liquidated damages
generally, **JobDiscrim § 2545, 2666 to 2672**
availability, generally, **JobDiscrim § 2667**
awareness of law's requirement, effect on willfulness, **JobDiscrim § 2670**
computation, **JobDiscrim § 2672**
factual issue of willfulness, **JobDiscrim § 2671**
front pay, **JobDiscrim § 2647**
motivation and good faith as affecting willfulness standard, **JobDiscrim § 2668**
pretextual excuse for discrimination as willful conduct, **JobDiscrim § 2669**
willfulness standard
applications, **JobDiscrim § 2667**
awareness of law's requirement, **JobDiscrim § 2670**
factual issue, **JobDiscrim § 2671**
motivation and good faith as affecting, **JobDiscrim § 2668**
pretextual excuse for discrimination, **JobDiscrim § 2669**
Local governments. State and local governments, below
Lodging, housing, and other allowances
company housing, **JobDiscrim § 728**
uniform cleaning allowances, **JobDiscrim § 731**
Longshore and Harbor Workers' Compensation Act, **FedEmpComp § 107**
Managerial employees
employment discrimination laws, **JobDiscrim § 58**
hostile work environment, **JobDiscrim § 849**
selection, screening, and evaluation practices, supervisor's ratings, use in criterion-related validation, **JobDiscrim § 324**
sex discrimination in pay, **JobDiscrim § 665, 666**

JOB DISCRIMINATION—*continued*

Managerial employees—*continued*
supervisor's acts. Liability of employer, above
Mandatory retirement. Pensions and retirement, below
Manufacturing, compensation, **JobDiscrim § 686 to 689**
Marital status
generally, **JobDiscrim § 441 to 446**
BFOQ, no-marriage rules as, **JobDiscrim § 442**
competition employing spouse, rules restricting employment based on, **JobDiscrim § 444**
competitor employing spouse, rules restricting employment based on, **JobDiscrim § 444**
federal employment, discrimination, **JobDiscrim § 446**
national origin of spouse, rules restricting employment based on, **JobDiscrim § 443**
no-marriage rules
generally, **JobDiscrim § 441**
bona fide occupational qualification, **JobDiscrim § 442**
bona fide occupational qualifications, as, **JobDiscrim § 442**
no-spouse rules, **JobDiscrim § 445**
race of spouse, rules restricting employment based on, **JobDiscrim § 443**
Maternity leave
generally, **JobDiscrim § 735 to 754**
ability to work as basis of restrictions on, **JobDiscrim § 738**
availability
equal under all leave policies, **JobDiscrim § 740**
obligations of employer, effect, **JobDiscrim § 741**
duration, **JobDiscrim § 744**
equal availability under all leave policies, **JobDiscrim § 740**
extending to child care, **JobDiscrim § 742**
Family and Medical Leave Act of 1993, **JobDiscrim § 746 to 755**
reinstatement, **JobDiscrim § 745**
restrictions on mandatory leaves
ability to work as basis of, **JobDiscrim § 738**
not placed on other leave, **JobDiscrim § 739**
service credit during, rights, **JobDiscrim § 743**
state laws, validity, **JobDiscrim § 737**
treated equally to leaves for other disabilities, **JobDiscrim § 736**
McCarran-Ferguson Act, Title VII not superseded by, **JobDiscrim § 716**
Meals. Rest and meal breaks, below
Medical insurance. Health insurance, above

Consult Correlation Tables in text volumes for references to materials published after this index.

335

Skill Set 2: Updating Print Resources. Recall that another search in the work-flow of legal research is updating. As noted previously, encyclopedias and some treatises are updated. In the law, research must be current to be thorough, so a critical attribute of any resource is its currency. In print legal research resources, as summarized in Chart 3.2, updating is accomplished through supplemental publications: (1) Pocket parts are inserted in the back of a volume. (2) When a volume needs substantial updating, a pocket part may be too small. Supplemental pamphlets are separate publications that are shelved after the volume(s) to which they pertain. (3) For loose-leaf print publications, that is, ones that are published in binders, new pages are issued; they either replace older pages or are filed behind an updating tab.

Thus once you have selected a resource and found the pertinent sections to read, you should check for updating material. You may find nothing, or you may find new references, some additional text, or a complete revision. Some researchers first read the original discussion in the main volume, which is likely to be the major discussion and more coherent than the updating material. Other researchers first check for updating material on the theory that the update could render substantial portions of the original material obsolete. Either way, you often will need to knit the two together to obtain a complete and current discussion. In addition, you should update your research in the table of contents and index as well, to see whether any new sections pertinent to your topic have been added.

When we researched the issue of marital status discrimination in *American Jurisprudence Second*, Exhibits 3.1 and 3.2 pointed us to the text in Exhibits 3.3 and 3.4. Exhibit 3.3 was the discussion in the main, 2002, hardbound volume. Exhibit 3.4, the pocket part for 2011, provided an additional case description. We learned that federal law did not broadly prohibit marital status discrimination.

CHART 3.2	Updating Publications for Print Resources

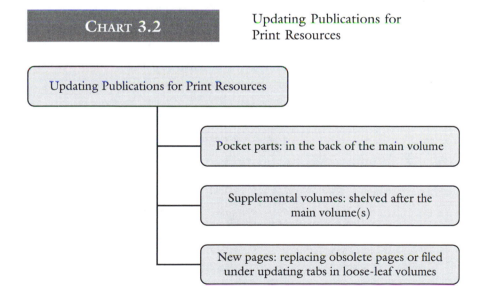

EXHIBIT 3.3   Encyclopedia Main Text

§ 445   45A AM JUR 2d

§ 445   No-spouse rules

Employment policies against hiring or continuing the employment of spouses of employees are lawful under Title VII of the Civil Rights Act of 1964,[1] as long as they are applied equally to male and female employees. An airline's policy of discharging the spouse with the least seniority if the married workers cannot decide between themselves who should leave does not violate the sex discrimination provisions of Title VII under either a discriminatory treatment or a disparate impact theory.[2] Similarly, a school board's decision to transfer the wife of a male department head to a new school under its policy of not employing spouses in the same school does not violate Title VII, where the couple agreed to let the school board pick who would transfer and the choice is based on the best interests of the educational program.[3]

No-spouse rules are valid where they prohibit:

- a husband and wife from working in the same department, with the couple having the choice of who should resign, and if the couple could not agree as to who should resign, then the junior in seniority would have to step down[4]
- a woman in the employer's Washington office from transferring to its New York office after she married a man who worked in the New York office, where the company has offered a number of times to help her obtain other employment in New York and she does not pursue those possibilities[5]
- spouses from working in a supervisor-subordinate relationship[6]
- a university from hiring a female applicant as a chemistry professor, where her husband was already a member of the university's chemistry department and the applicant's research expertise is essentially identical to her husband's[7]

Workers' morale does not justify implementing a facially neutral no-spouse

---

As to Title VII liability, generally, see § 280.

[Section 445]

[1] 42 U.S.C.A. §§ 2000e et seq.

[2] Harper v. Trans World Airlines, Inc., 385 F. Supp. 1001 (E.D. Mo. 1974), judgment aff'd, 525 F.2d 409, 34 A.L.R. Fed. 639 (8th Cir. 1975).

As to Title VII liability, generally, see § 280.

As to discrimination claims based upon disparate treatment, generally, see § 2434.

As to the disparate impact theory of discrimination, generally, see § 2437.

Legal Periodicals: In Order to Form a More Perfect Union: Applying No-Spouse

Rules to Employees Who Meet at Work. 31 Colum J L&SP 1:119 (1998).

[3] Meier v. Evansville-Vanderburgh School Corp., 416 F. Supp. 748 (S.D. Ind. 1975), aff'd, 539 F.2d 713 (7th Cir. 1976).

[4] EQUAL EMPLOYMENT OPPORTUNITY COMMISSION, 2 Fair Empl. Prac. Cas. (BNA) 429, 1970 WL 3501 (E.E.O.C. 1970).

[5] Tuck v. McGraw-Hill, Inc., 421 F. Supp. 39 (S.D. N.Y. 1976).

[6] Smith v. Mutual Ben. Life Ins. Co., 13 Fair Empl. Prac. Cas. (BNA) 252, 11 Empl. Prac. Dec. (CCH) ¶ 10876, 1976 WL 552 (D. N.J. 1976).

[7] Sime v. Trustees of California State University and Colleges, 11 Fair Empl. Prac. Cas. (BNA) 334, 1974 WL 10481 (E.D. Cal. 1974), aff'd, 526 F.2d 1112 (9th Cir. 1975).

523

Exhibit 3.3   *(continued)*

policy where the claimed dissatisfaction does not establish a business necessity for the rule. It is not sufficient that the rule be merely business-related; it must be essential to safety and efficiency and there must be no other available nondiscriminatory alternative to accomplish the legitimate business purpose.[8] A neutral no-spouse policy also violates Title VII where it has the effect of denying employment to a disproportionate number of female applicants, as where the employer's workforce is predominantly male.[9]

No-spouse rules cannot be used as a pretext to discriminate. For example, a company's "sensitive position" policy under which female secretaries who are married to male employees are required to transfer to another division, as a means of preventing disclosure of sensitive management information, violates Title VII, where the policy of protecting confidential information is not evenhandedly applied between men and women in that men who are employed at the same level as supervisors of their spouses are not required to transfer.[10] However, an employer's general conflict of interest regulation that prohibits employment of a person in a job over which a member of that person's immediate family exercises supervisory authority, or who serves on a board or committee with authority to order personnel actions affecting the job, does not violate Title VII, where the regulation applies to immediate family members, even those of the same sex.[11]

§ 446   Discrimination in federal employment

Research References

West's Key Number Digest, Civil Rights ☞158.1, 164

Discrimination on the basis of marital status is prohibited by a federal civil service statute enforced by the Office of Personnel Management.[1] The statute also requires benefits to be provided to a married female employee's spouse and children equal to those provided to a married male employee's spouse and children.[2]

---

[8]E.E.O.C. v. Rath Packing Co., 787 F.2d 318 (8th Cir. 1986).

As to the business necessity defense, generally, see § 311.

[9]EQUAL EMPLOYMENT OPPORTUNITY COMMISSION, 21 Fair Empl. Prac. Cas. (BNA) 1777, 1975 WL 20713 (E.E.O.C. 1975).

[10]EQUAL EMPLOYMENT OPPORTUNITY COMMISSION, 26 Fair Empl. Prac. Cas. (BNA) 1774, 1979 WL 6935 (E.E.O.C. 1979).

[11]Southwestern Community Action Council, Inc. v. Community Services Administration, 462 F. Supp. 289 (S.D. W. Va. 1978).

[Section 446]

[1]5 U.S.C.A. §§ 7204(b), (c).

[2]5 U.S.C.A. § 7202(b).

A retiree failed to establish that the Office of Personnel Management (OPM) engaged in marital status discrimination when it required her to include her husband's income on her financial resources questionnaire (FRQ), for purpose of determining whether she was entitled to waiver of annuity overpayment, absent evidence that the OPM was motivated by an improper intent to discriminate against married annuitants. Hundley v. Office of Personnel Management, 83 M.S.P.R. 632, 1999 WL 804607 (M.S.P.B. 1999), aff'd, 2000 WL 310584 (E.E.O.C. 2000).

| EXHIBIT 3.4 | Encyclopedia Pocket Part |

§ 441

station by United States Postal Service (USPS) did not constitute, under Title VII, an adverse action taken against him due to his marital status, where employee was a part-time flexible employee who only worked 20 hours a week, and after the reassignment, he was guaranteed 40 hours. Cardona v. Potter, 536 F. Supp. 2d 172 (D.P.R. 2008).

§ 444 Rules restricting employment based on spouse's employment by competitor

Cases

County had legitimate concern about employee's ability to perform her job as prenatal program manager in health department, as required before county could require employee to undergo psychiatric evaluation under ADA; employee's primary job duty was to manage and deliver advanced and comprehensive prenatal nursing care for clients, in particular, high-risk patients, but employee was not focused on her job, failed to complete sufficient amount of work on protocols that were required for state accreditation of prenatal program, spent too much time away from office, worked too many hours, sent rambling, bizarre, and inappropriate e-mails, and stated that she was suffering from exhaustion and chronic fatigue syndrome. Conrad v. Board of Johnson County Com'rs, 237 F. Supp. 2d 1204 (D. Kan. 2002).

§ 445 No-spouse rules

Cases

Genuine issues of material fact existed as to whether state corrections department's policy of requiring medical certification with general diagnosis after absence of four or more days was necessary to determine whether returning employee could safely perform functions of corrections officer, or to determine whether employee's absence was due to legitimate medical reasons, precluding summary judgment as to whether department established business necessity defense to ADA's prohibition against inquiries into disability. Conroy v. New York State Dept. of Correctional Services, 333 F.3d 88 (2d Cir. 2003).

§ 446 Discrimination in federal employment

Cases

Former federal agency employee who was discharged during probationary period of employment was not entitled under applicable regulation to appeal her discharge, since she did not allege that she was discriminated against due to marital status, and she did not support her claim of discrimination based on partisan political reasons with allegations, including allegations of specific facts, showing that the discrimination was based on her affiliation with a political party or candidate. McCall-Scovens v. Merit Systems Protection Bd., 174 Fed. Appx. 569 (Fed. Cir. 2006).

i. Legal History

§ 447 Generally; arrest records

Cases

State police department's proffered legiti-

mate reason for automatically disqualifying African-American cadet applicant, namely applicant's expunged criminal record for theft, was not shown to be pretextual, precluding recovery in applicant's Title VII and § 1983 equal protection action against state police alleging race discrimination; department had official written policy that any cadet applicants were subject to disqualification for "criminal behavior, regardless if arrested," policy had been applied to at least 41 white cadet applicants, and fact that single white applicant allegedly was treated more favorably was insufficient to show pretext. Foxworth v. Pennsylvania State Police, 402 F. Supp. 2d 523 (E.D. Pa. 2005).

j. Military History

§ 452 Generally; Uniformed Services Employment and Reemployment Rights Act

Cases

Under the Uniformed Services Employment and Reemployment Rights Act (USERRA), as amended, a federal district court lacks jurisdiction over a USERRA action brought by an individual against a state as an employer; plain language of statute, as well as its legislative history, showed that Congress intended that actions brought by individuals against a state be commenced in state court, and, by providing that claims against a state "may" be brought in state court, the statute did not evince an unequivocal intent to abrogate the states' sovereign immunity so as to provide for federal court jurisdiction. Townsend v. University of Alaska, 543 F.3d 478 (9th Cir. 2008), cert. denied, 129 S. Ct. 1907 (2009).

Uniformed Services Employment and Reemployment Rights Act (USERRA) does not create an express cause of action against individual state supervisors. Townsend v. University of Alaska, 543 F.3d 478 (9th Cir. 2008), cert. denied, 129 S. Ct. 1907 (2009).

Department of Veterans Affairs (DVA) employee who was not selected for Human Resources Assistant position did not meet his initial burden of showing by preponderance of evidence that his military service or prior Uniformed Services Employment and Reemployment Rights Act (USERRA) actions was a substantial or motivating factor in adverse employment action; no evidence was presented that employee's military service was a motivating factor in DVA's nonselection decision, and there was insufficient evidence that DVA's decision not to offer position to him was based on his prior actions under USERRA. 38 U.S.C.A. § 4311. Becker v. Department of Veterans Affairs, 373 Fed. Appx. 54 (Fed. Cir. 2010).

Civilian employee of United States Department of Transportation was not denied benefit of employment on account of his military service, in violation of Uniformed Services Employment and Reemployment Rights Act (USERRA) antidiscrimination provisions, when agency decided that time he served as cadet at Coast Guard Academy was not creditable for leave accrual purposes. Crawford v. Department of Transp., 373 F.3d 1155 (Fed. Cir. 2004).

Encyclopedias and some treatises are available online. If possible, check to see if an index is available, toggle through the various tables of contents to discern the organization of the source, and page forward and backward to replicate browsing in a book. Online versions have several advantages: they generally are updated seamlessly, with new text incorporated into the older text; they may provide hyperlinks to connect you to the sources to which the text and footnotes refer within the service's other databases; and you can conduct a search for pertinent material by use of key words, a skill covered a little later in this chapter. If you use a sophisticated and extensive service, such as Westlaw or LexisNexis, you may also receive suggestions for other commentary sources the service provides that also cover the topic.

Citation to Encyclopedias and Treatises

Encyclopedias are cited as follows:

BLUEBOOK: 45A Am. Jur. 2d *Job Discrimination* § 445 (2002 & Supp. 2011). [See rules B.8.1 and 15.]

ALWD: 45A Am. Jur. 2d *Job Discrimination* § 445 (2002 & Supp. 2011). [See rule 26.]

The treatise featured in Chapter 1, which is volume 17 of a larger series titled *Minnesota Practice*, is cited as follows:

BLUEBOOK: Stephen F. Befort, *Employment Law and Practice* § 10.11 (Minn. Practice Ser., vol. 17, 2d ed. 2003 & Supp. 2010–2011). [See rules B8.1 and 15.]

ALWD: Stephen F. Befort, *Employment Law and Practice* § 10.11 (Minn. Prac. Ser., vol. 17, 2d ed. West 2003 & Supp. 2010–2011). [See rule 22.]

PERIODICALS: LAW REVIEWS AND A.L.R. ANNOTATIONS

If the term "legal periodical" is used in the broadest sense to encompass any publication that comes out on a more or less regular interval and discusses a legal topic, this category is exceedingly large. For many years, legal newspapers and bar association publications have covered not only events of interest to lawyers but also developments in the law. Commercial publishers have long published newsletters that update lawyers in specific practice areas. Recently, for good or ill, the Internet has become awash with blogs and websites on legal topics written by individuals, law firms, and organizations. As valuable as some of these sources are, they are not the type of publication that should be used to frame legal research. Rather, the periodicals used for framing legal research are law review articles and *American Law Reports Annotations*.

Most law reviews are published by law schools and edited by students.[4] The typical law review publishes several issues a year; each contains a handful or two of papers on a range of topics by experts such as professors, judges, and practitioners (called "articles" or "essays") as well as papers by students (called "notes" or "comments"). Some academic law reviews focus on specific areas of law. In addition, some bar association sections and academic organizations publish journals with articles focused on their areas of interest; these resemble law reviews.

A typical article in a law review provides a detailed discussion of a fairly narrow topic, along with many references. The discussion may cover not only the law as it now stands but also its evolution, nonlegal studies pertinent to the topic, critique of the current law, and recommendations for reform. Indeed, some articles have been the instrument of law reform as courts and legislatures act on their recommendations.

Law reviews have both advantages and disadvantages from a research standpoint. If you find an article on your topic, it may provide a wealth of information and insight and abundant references. If it is written by a respected author, published in a respected law review,[5] or both, it will be highly citable. On the other hand, the analysis may be idiosyncratic, and because articles are not updated, the analysis will be current only to the date the author wrote the text.[6] Furthermore, there may be no article on your research issue. Thus law reviews can either be very helpful or not helpful at all depending on the project. They are uniquely useful in one situation: when the law is either undeveloped or adverse to your client's interests and you are thus working on a matter involving law reform.

American Law Reports Annotations, or A.L.R., is a uniquely legal publication. A.L.R. resembles law reviews in some ways: issues are published throughout the year;[7] each issue contains six to ten articles, or "annotations," on various topics; and each annotation provides an in-depth discussion of its topic with abundant references. A.L.R. is distinctive in that it is published by a commercial publisher. The main version (now in its sixth series) covers state law topics, and A.L.R. Federal (now in its second series) covers federal topics.[8] Compared to law reviews, A.L.R. annotations are only descriptive: each

4. This is highly unusual for academic scholarship. One advantage of this system is that students who serve on the staff of a law review are able to highly refine their research and writing skills; thus many employers prize service on law review.

5. A few law reviews and journals are peer-reviewed, i.e., experts select the articles they publish. These articles are particularly citable.

6. An article may be referred to in later sources, such as articles and cases. While these later sources do not update the article in the traditional sense, they do provide more recent information on the same topic. The two standard ways to find these later sources are KeyCite and Shepard's, which are used to a great extent in case law research and are thus discussed in Chapter 4.

7. Because A.L.R. does not have a fixed publication schedule, its technical category is that of a serial.

8. Even newer, and less commonly used, is A.L.R. International.

consists of some introductory material followed by summaries of cases from around the country on the topic, organized by outcome and important facts.

As with law reviews, A.L.R. has advantages and disadvantages. A.L.R. has a strong index, permitting you to find a pertinent annotation if you use it well. If you do find an annotation on your research issue, it will provide a detailed and comprehensive analysis of the case law, along with abundant references to cases and to other commentary sources on the same subject. The annotations are clearly structured and include tables of contents and jurisdictions, along with indexes, so you will be able to readily find material on your specific issue from your jurisdiction. The material will be quite current because the annotations are regularly supplemented.

On the other hand, because the authors are not well-known experts, A.L.R. annotations are cited only for limited reasons, such as the number of states that take a certain position on an issue. Furthermore, there may be no annotation on your research issue.

Skill Set 3. Using External Finding Tools. A resource that is, in effect, a set of sources needs an external finding tool that directs you to the specific source pertinent to your issue. For example, the tool to find a treatise within a library's collection is its catalog.[9] As noted previously, A.L.R. has an index. Law review articles are covered in several major periodical indexes, including *Index to Legal Periodicals and Books* (through EBSCOhost),[10] *LegalTrac* (through Gale), and *Legal Resource Index* (through Westlaw). These indexes cover over 1,000 legal periodicals (in addition to other law-related publications such as government studies).

Online catalogs and indexes afford several searching options. One option is to identify pertinent subject headings and subheadings and then read the sources listed thereunder. If you do not find a pertinent subject heading at the outset, another option is to enter a key-word search based on your research vocabulary to locate one pertinent source. You can then leverage that find by discerning its subject heading and then perusing the list of sources under that heading.

Whether in a library catalog or periodicals index, you are likely to find a longer list of sources than you would care to read. The listing for a source should provide some information permitting you to winnow the options. For a treatise, the catalog entry likely will provide information about the author, the topics covered, the size of the treatise, its most recent edition or update, and publisher—all indications of its likely utility and credibility. Similarly, for a law review article, you will find at least the title, author, journal, and date; you may also find a brief abstract, or description, of the article. With this information, you may make a judgment about its likely pertinence to your topic, currency, and credibility (based on the author or law review).

---

9. Sophisticated library catalogs now lead to additional sources, including journal and newspaper articles.

10. An earlier *Index to Legal Periodicals* print version covered 1908–1981. It was slated to become *Legal Source* in 2012.

Once you identify a source through a finding tool, the next step is, of course, to read it. As a practical matter, while many libraries have A.L.R. in print, most have only partial collections of the vast number of law reviews in print. Thus these sources are often obtained through an online resource.

Skill Set 4. Key-Word Searching in a Full-Text, Online Database. Some legal research resources are online databases containing many individual sources. Three classic examples are the online databases containing legal periodicals available through HeinOnline, LexisNexis, and Westlaw. A potentially excellent way to identify a pertinent source within such a database is through a key-word search—but only if you craft the search carefully. Drafting key-word searches entails several decisions.

The initial decision is which documents to search within a database. For example, within a periodicals database, you can search the entire database or narrow the search to certain journals or time periods.

A second decision is which components of a document, or fields, to search. In the context of a periodicals database, the standard choices are the titles, authors, and full texts of the articles. The broader the field searched, the more likely a document will be retrieved; that is, the higher the recall the search will provide. On the other hand, a search of a broad field is likelier to yield more documents and less precise results than a search in a narrower field.

A third decision is which words to search for, in which configuration. If you have carefully developed your research terms and issue, you should have some strong candidates for the words to use. Combining them into a workable search, called "Boolean"[11] or "terms-and-connectors" searching in various systems, can involve some trial and error. Adept search writers typically work through these steps as noted in Chart 3.3:

1. Use wildcard characters, such as * or !, to create variants on a stem word.
2. Use a phrase tool, typically quotation marks, to capture words that will appear together in a fixed sequence.
3. Use the *OR* connector to combine words that capture the same concept in the search.
4. Use the various conjunctive connectors to add terms together. Conjunctive connectors include *AND* or *&*; proximity connectors, e.g., */25* calling for the first word to appear within twenty-five words of the second; and grammatical connectors, e.g., */s* calling for the words to be in the same sentence.
5. On rare occasions, use the *NOT* connector to eliminate a document containing a word that often appears with the words of interest but not in pertinent documents. This is a risky option, because the document may be pertinent even so.

11. The name refers to a nineteenth-century mathematician.

6. Use parentheses to control the sequence in which the tasks are pro-
    cessed. Programs have orders of operations in which they generally
    process tasks. Placing a task in parentheses indicates that it should be
    done before others.

All of these matters—selection of portions of a database, fields to search,
and Boolean protocols—operate in unique ways in the various legal research
resources. Thus a critical first step when using a resource for the first time is to
learn how it operates. Otherwise, you may carry out a search that is different
than you intended—and the computer will not so inform you.

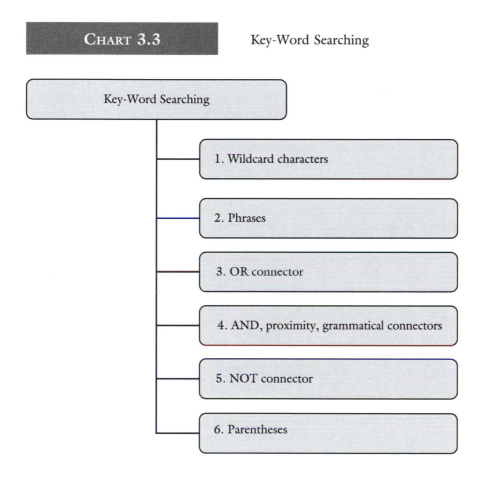

CHART 3.3   Key-Word Searching

Key-Word Searching

1. Wildcard characters

2. Phrases

3. OR connector

4. AND, proximity, grammatical connectors

5. NOT connector

6. Parentheses

As an illustration involving both law reviews and A.L.R. Annotations,
consider this new situation: Our fictional firm represented an employee, Casey
Nichols, who was fired from his job at a grocery store. The factual research to
date indicated that a coworker, who had a personal conflict with Nichols,
reported that Nichols had given food away to friends of his, contrary to the
store's policy. Nichols vehemently denied this. After the store's manager,
Dana Molinaro, talked to the complaining coworker and Nichols, she decided

to believe the coworker. Not only did she fire Nichols, she also told other employees of the store the reason for the termination in an effort to show that the store took the prohibition on pilferage seriously. These events took place in Lawrence, Kansas, in the spring of 2011.

As a bit of reading in an encyclopedia or treatise would reveal, one possible claim was the tort of defamation, also called "libel" or "slander" depending on the mode of the communication. One potential wrinkle was that the publication in Nichols' situation was entirely within the company, possibly failing to satisfy the requirement that the defendant publish the communication to a third party. We explored this issue in both law reviews and A.L.R. Annotations.

We researched law reviews in HeinOnline's Law Library Journal database. We chose HeinOnline because it has an extensive database of law reviews, is a cost-effective subscription service, and has strong Boolean search options.

We searched the full text of all journals. We could have used *defam** to search for defame, defamation, defamatory, etc., but we chose to use *defamation* because the word was very likely to be stated that way. We added *libel* and *slander* through *OR* connectors. Two approaches to capture the factual setting—*employer* and *workplace*—proved too imprecise. Rather, we added *intra-corporate OR intracorporate* through the basic *AND* connector as a way of capturing the specific publication issue. The search yielded fifty-nine results, arrayed by probable relevance.

One article, excerpted in Exhibit 3.5, covered a full range of issues on the subject of defamation in the workplace, was written by a professor, ran over eighty pages, and was published in the University of Dayton Law Review in 1999. The article provided an overview of the law on our issue, revealing that courts differed on whether communication within a corporation constituted the publication required for defamation. The article also provided references to various sources on the topic in the footnotes, including several cases and other commentary; unfortunately, the article did not provide references to Kansas authorities. While the article did not critique the law much, it did set out various practices for employers to follow to avoid defamation—which were not followed in the Nichols situation.

We also researched the same issue in A.L.R. Annotations, a sensible strategy given the indication in the article that courts took different positions on our research issue. We researched in the Westlaw A.L.R. database to take advantage of key-word searching, seamless updating, and links to the cases within the Westlaw case law databases.

There we chose a field search focused on the titles of annotations, which tend to be lengthy and specific, and entered a variety of related terms for each of the two main concepts: *defamation libel slander & employee employer workplace corporation company*. This search yielded twenty-eight documents, including one titled "Defamation: publication by intracorporate communication of employee's evaluation."

Exhibit 3.5	Law Review Text (University of Dayton Law Review)

stated that plaintiff had a "mental problem."[147] Plaintiff thereupon sued the supervisor and her employer for defamation, but the district court disposed of the plaintiff's defamation claim on summary judgment, in part explaining:

> As for the second allegedly libelous statement, found by [plaintiff] when she was accessing [her supervisor's] computer, [plaintiff] must show that the defamatory matter was published by proof that it was communicated to someone other than herself.[148] There is no evidence in the record that this document was ever communicated to a third party.[149]

Accordingly, because there was no publication of the document, the court ruled in favor of defendants.[150]

Any third person should suffice to satisfy the publication requirement, regardless of his or her relationship to the plaintiff or defendant, so long as the defamatory import of the transmitted communication is understood.[151] Consequently, the defamatory statement may be communicated to "a member of the plaintiff's family, including [one's spouse], or to the plaintiff's agent or employee. It may be made to the defendant's own agent, employee or officer, even where the defendant is a corporation."[152] However, "[w]hen the publication of defamatory matter has been invited, instigated or procured by the one defamed, or by someone acting on his behalf, he generally cannot be heard to complain of the resulting injury, particularly, when it is elicited for the purposes of predicating an action thereon."[153]

In the employment context, communications among officers, managers, and supervisors regarding an employee, or between employees and their superiors, at times called intra-corporate communications, may be

---

[147] *Mills*, 991 F. Supp. at 1387-88.

[148] *Id.* (citations omitted).

[149] *Id.*

[150] *Id.* at 1388.

[151] RESTATEMENT (SECOND) OF TORTS § 577 cmts. b & c; KEETON ET AL., *supra* note 1, § 113, at 798-99.

[152] KEETON ET AL., *supra* note 1, § 113, at 798; *accord* RESTATEMENT (SECOND) OF TORTS § 577 cmts. e, f, h, & i; *Bochenek*, 18 F. Supp. 2d at 971-72.

[153] *Beck*, 711 A.2d at 959 (quoting from *Mick v. American Dental Ass'n*, 139 A.2d 570 (N.J. Super. Ct. App. Div. 1958). In *Beck*, the plaintiff employee was concerned that the president of the defendant company was giving plaintiff negative references, and thereupon concocted a scheme where two friends would pose as prospective employers in order to elicit comments from defendant's president, which were forthcoming. *Id.* at 954. The *Beck* court nonetheless ruled: "These statements . . . do not form the basis for a slander claim because they were not published." *Id.* at 959.

| EXHIBIT 3.5 | *(continued)* |

432   *UNIVERSITY OF DAYTON LAW REVIEW*   [Vol. 24:3

construed as "published" communications.[154] Some courts, however, maintain that intra-corporate communications or disclosures made solely among the firm's employees are not "published."[155] These jurisdictions "treat all employees of a corporation acting within the scope of their employment as one entity for agency purposes."[156] In a corporate context, accordingly, "[t]he rationale for the intra[-]corporate immunity rule is that a corporation can communicate only through its employees: that what they say to one another in the ordinary course of business . . . does not constitute publication to third persons; the corporation is communicating with itself."[157] "To hold otherwise," the Georgia Court of Appeals noted, "could impede legitimate inquiries by employers into employee conduct."[158] Statements, however, between managers and prospective employers of the employee that slander or libel the plaintiff employee clearly are published defamation.[159]

---

[154] RESTATEMENT (SECOND) OF TORTS § 577 cmts. e, f, h, & i; PANARO, *supra* note 1, § 2.01[2][b] (2d ed. 1993); *id.* at S2-12 (Supp. 1997) (examining employment cases and indicating that "probably a minority [of courts] have ruled that communications to any third party not the plaintiff, regardless of whether it is a coemployee, constitute publication. Intracorporate communications, these courts hold, satisfy the publication requirement . . . no less than telling the world."); Bennett et al., *supra* note 53, at 864 ("A large number of jurisdictions follow this *Restatement* view and hold that purely intracorporate communications can give rise to actionable publications."). *See, e.g., Bochenek,* 18 F. Supp. 2d at 971-72. In *Bochenek,* the "communication [accusing plaintiff employee of theft] was published when Walgreen's agents told other employees that she was fired for theft." *Id.* The court held that communicating employee evaluation information to management personnel may be considered published for purposes of a defamation action. *Id.*

[155] RESTATEMENT (SECOND) OF TORTS § 577 cmts. e, f, h & i; PANARO, *supra* note 1, § 2.03[2][b], at 2-48 to -54 (2d ed. 1993); *id.* at S2-12 (Supp. 1997) (examination of employment cases indicating that communications among corporation's management personnel or among firm's employees does not constitute "publication"); Bennett et al., *supra* note 53, at 863-63. *See, e.g., Garcia,* 961 S.W.2d at 604 (issue as to whether an employee evaluation co-authored by plaintiff employee and communicated to two high-level supervisors would be regarded as a publication); *Luckey,* 496 S.E.2d at 541 (hospital ER nurse, who accused physician of "patient dumping," sued hospital contract physician, her immediate supervisor, for libel, based on statements he made in a letter accusing nurse of erroneous documentation "to the point of fabrication," unprofessional conduct, and "betraying the essence of her profession–integrity and trust"; physician sent letter to hospital administrator who then passed on letter to hospital's human resources director; hospital terminated nurse six weeks after letter; court held "the publication of allegedly defamatory information in the course of an employer's investigation of an employee's job performance, when made to persons in authority, is not 'publication'").

[156] Bennett et al., *supra* note 53, at 863.

[157] PANARO, *supra* note 1, § 2.03[2][b], at 2-49; *accord Luckey,* 496 S.E.2d at 541 (stating:

It is absolutely undisputed that . . . [defendant physician], who was . . . [nurse plaintiff's] immediate supervisor at the time of the incident, provided the letter only to . . . the [h]ospital administrator, who communicated it only to . . . the director of human resources. The record is devoid of any evidence that the letter at issue was shown to anyone who did not need to see it for employment purposes.).

[158] *Luckey,* 496 S.E.2d at 541.

[159] RESTATEMENT (SECOND) OF TORTS § 577 cmts. e, f, h, & i.

Exhibit 3.6 was the first page of that annotation as found in Westlaw. The annotation first discussed cases holding that intra-corporate communication did not or did constitute publication, then presented cases according to particular circumstances, e.g., statements by supervisors, letters, and personnel files. We used the table of cases, laws, and rules, which listed cases by state, to find summaries of two Kansas cases within the annotation. Exhibit 3.7, the summary of *Luttrell v. United Tel. System, Inc.*, provided the facts of the case, the court's analysis, the outcome, and a reference to various places we could find the case itself. One option was to link directly to the case in Westlaw. The A.L.R. also provided references to additional A.L.R.s, the encyclopedia Am. Jur. 2d, a law review article, and several practice guides.

As illustrated by the detailed description of *Luttrell* in Exhibit 3.7, some commentary sources provide extensive descriptions of legal authorities. It may be tempting to rely on such a description in lieu of reading the authority itself. This is not permissible in legal research for several reasons: First, commentary authors are human and make mistakes. Second, they are not thinking about your client's situation and may omit a nuance that is important to your client's situation. Third, legal analysis should be based on the authority itself; it is thus unethical to cite to an authority you have not actually read.

Citation to Law Reviews and A.L.R. Annotations

The law review article featured in this chapter is cited as follows:

BLUEBOOK: Frank. J. Cavico, *Defamation in the Private Sector: The Libelous and Slanderous Employer*, 24 U. Dayton L. Rev. 407 (1998–1999). [See rules B.9.1 and 16 along with table T13.]

ALWD: Frank. J. Cavico, *Defamation in the Private Sector: The Libelous and Slanderous Employer*, 24 U. Dayton L. Rev. 407 (1998–1999). [See rule 23 along with appendix 5.]

The A.L.R. Annotation featured in this chapter is cited as follows:

BLUEBOOK: Jane M. Draper, Annotation, *Defamation: Publication by Intracorporate Communication of Employee's Evaluation*, 47 A.L.R.4th 674 (1986). [See rule 16.7.6.]

ALWD: Jane M. Draper, *Defamation: Publication by Intracorporate Communication of Employee's Evaluation*, 47 A.L.R.4th 674 (1986). [See rule 24.]

EXHIBIT 3.6   A.L.R. Annotation Opening Page

Westlaw.

47 A.L.R.4th 674   Page 1
47 A.L.R.4th 674 (Originally published in 1986)

American Law Reports ALR4th
The ALR databases are made current by the weekly addition of relevant new cases.

Defamation: publication by intracorporate communication of employee's evaluation

Jane M. Draper, B.C.L.

TABLE OF CONTENTS

EXHIBIT 3.7   A.L.R. Annotation Text

47 A.L.R.4th 674   Page 19
47 A.L.R.4th 674 (Originally published in 1986)

self-publication; defendant's motion for summary judgment was denied as to plaintiffs' claim for slander where, although conditional privilege existed as to statements communicated to plaintiff's supervisors, plaintiff produced evidence which may establish abuse of that privilege by publishing alleged defamatory statement to non-supervisory employees. Quinn v Limited Express, Inc. (1989, WD Pa) 715 F Supp 127 (applying Pa law).

[Top of Section]

[END OF SUPPLEMENT]

§ 4[a] Particular circumstances under which publication has been found or held supportable-Statements by supervisory personnel

[Cumulative Supplement]

In the following cases involving defamation claims based on statements, in regard to an employee's evaluation, by corporate supervisory personnel to other corporate employees, the courts found that such statements constituted publication to a third person as required by the law of defamation.

A statement by a supervisor, an employee of the defendant corporation, acting within the scope of his employment, to the defendant corporation's managing agent to the effect that a former employee who was reapplying for employment had misused company funds, constituted publication, the court ruled in Kelly v General Telephone Co. (1982, 2d Dist) 136 Cal App 3d 278, 186 Cal Rptr 184, rejecting the defendant corporation's argument that the plaintiff had not alleged publication of the statements because he had alleged only that the statements were made by one of the defendant corporation's employees to other employees of the defendant. Publication occurs when a statement is communicated to any person other than the party defamed, the court explained, adding that publication might involve internal corporate statements. The order of dismissal was reversed with directions to the trial court to overrule the demurrer to the slander action.

Remarks communicated by one corporate employee to another concerning the job performance of a third employee were publication for the purposes of a defamation action against the employer, the court ruled in Luttrell v United Tel. System, Inc. (1984) 9 Kan App 2d 620, 683 P2d 1292, 47 ALR4th 669, affd 236 Kan 710, 695 P2d 1279, 102 CCH LC ¶55495. The court explained that one of the defendant corporation's employees had informed the plaintiff employee's supervisor that the plaintiff had been engaging in illegal activities and the supervisor had communicated this information to two other corporate employees. Noting that this issue of first impression was whether interoffice communications between supervisory employees of a corporation, acting within the scope and course of their employment, regarding the work of another employee of the corporation, constituted publication to a third person sufficient for a defamation action, the court pointed out that damage to one's reputation within a corporate community might be just as devastating as that effected by defamation spread to the outside, and that thus, the injury caused by intracorporate defamation should not be disregarded simply because the corporation could be sued as an individual entity. The defendant corporation had argued that corporate employers must be free to evaluate and comment on their employees' work performance and that this freedom would be unduly restrained if they were liable for intracorporate defamation. Seeing no reason for greater freedom from liability for defamation to be accorded a corporate employer than that already available to all employers through the qualified privilege, the court reversed the judgment of the trial court sustaining the defendant corporation's motion to dismiss for failure to state a claim upon which relief might be granted.

Statements by an insurance company's area supervisor to his supervisor, regarding the manner in which the plaintiff conducted his insurance agency, which resulted in the termination of the plaintiff's agency contract constituted publication, the court ruled in Brewer v American Nat. Ins. Co. (1980, CA6 Ky) 636 F2d 150 (applying Kentucky law), reversing the judgment of the court below. After reviewing the apparent conflict in regard to the

RESTATEMENTS OF THE LAW AND JURY INSTRUCTIONS

Restatements of the Law and jury instructions differ from encyclopedias, treatises, and periodicals both in how they are generated and how they are formatted. Both are the outcome of a deliberative process involving a group of experts and are formatted as legal rules followed by explanatory material. Both are highly credible and citable sources.

The Restatements are created by the American Law Institute (ALI), an organization of 4,000 elected members from elite positions in the legal profession around the country. Each Restatement begins as a draft written by a preeminent scholar in the subject and proceeds through rounds of review by a panel of experts, the ALI Council, the public, and the entire ALI membership. The original purpose of the Restatements—the first was promulgated in 1932—was to capture the law generated by the many court rulings on important legal subjects around the country. More recently, some Restatements have sought to present what the authors believe the law should be.

Chart 3.4 lists the various Restatements, which cover a wide range of legal subjects but by no means all legal subjects. Some subjects have been covered in more than one Restatement over time, as the law has evolved. Note that the series designation depends on the date of adoption rather than the number of versions on a subject.

Each Restatement consists of many sections, carefully sequenced and organized to reflect the structure of the subject. Each section consists of (1) the rule itself; (2) comments, which discuss the scope, meaning, and rationale of the rule; (3) illustrations, which are short stories showing how the rule applies; and (4) for recent Restatements, reporter's notes, which provide the history of the rule and references. See Exhibit 3.8.

As a consequence of both their origins and format, the Restatements are, in general, the most citable form of commentary. However, as much as it resembles one, a Restatement rule is not itself law. On the other hand, many courts rely on the Restatements as they build the law on a new subject for their own jurisdictions, sometimes adopting rules and even incorporating illustrations into their decisions. Thus it is important to know when researching in Restatements whether a particular pertinent section has been adopted by your jurisdiction or, more generally, has been cited favorably by the courts. The ALI publishes summaries of those cases in various Restatement publications.

Restatements are not the best place to begin to research an issue about which you know fairly little. Most obviously, there may be no Restatement on the subject. Even if there is, the format is not as easy to read as the discussion in other sources discussed in this chapter. Rather, you are most likely to use the Restatement to discern the most respected rule—which could be the standard rule or the more progressive rule—on your research issue, either when your jurisdiction has not yet taken a position on the issue or its current position is contrary to your client's interests. For example, a classic use of a Restatement is to urge a court to recognize a claim it has not yet addressed.

Jury instructions are similar to Restatements in that they are generated through a deliberative process, consist of statements resembling rules followed by discussion and references, and cover some but not all subjects. They differ from Restatements in that they focus on the law of a particular state or federal law, represent the law as it currently stands, and are designed for a very specific

CHART 3.4	Restatements of the Law

First Series (1930s and 1940s)
Agency, Conflict of Laws, Contracts, Judgments, Property, Restitution, Security, Torts, Trusts

Second Series (1950s through 1980s)
Agency, Conflict of Laws, Contracts, Foreign Relations, Judgments, Property: Landlord and Tenant, Property: Donative Transfers,[12] Torts, Trusts

Third Series (1990s to date)
Agency, Foreign Relations,[13] Law Governing Lawyers, Property: Mortgages, Property: Servitudes, Property: Wills & Other Donative Transfers, Restitution and Unjust Enrichment, Suretyship & Guaranty, Torts: Apportionment of Liability, Torts: Products Liability, Trusts, Trusts: Prudent Investor Rule, Unfair Competition

Currently in Development
Employment Law, Property: Wills & Other Donative Transfers, The U.S. Law of International Commercial Arbitration, Torts: Liability for Economic Harm, Torts: Liability for Physical and Emotional Harm, Trusts

situation: stating the instructions to be read to a jury after it has heard the evidence and arguments in a case and before it deliberates. They are useful, however, at earlier stages in the handling of a client's problem as well. That is, knowing how a case would be framed before a jury is important when framing a claim to present to the opponent at the outset of litigation or in negotiating a settlement.[14]

As an illustration involving both the Restatements and jury instructions, consider this new client situation: Our fictional firm's client, the Acme Balloon Company, was contacted after a car accident involving one of the company's employees. When the accident occurred, the employee was driving his own car to work but was stopping to pick up doughnuts for the company's weekly staff meeting. The employee was talking on his cell phone and ran into the other driver. Fortunately the other driver was not hurt, but her car was heavily damaged, so she contacted a lawyer, who contacted Acme, which contacted the firm. The events occurred in Santa Barbara, California, in August 2011.

One issue in the case was whether the client would be liable for an activity the employee engaged in while commuting to, but not yet at, work, although on an errand related to work. This issue fell within the subject of agency law as an employee is one type of agent.

---

12. The last volume of this Restatement was adopted in 1990.
13. The last volume of this Restatement was adopted in 1986.
14. Very few of the many cases filed every year make it to trial, much less a jury trial. According to data published at www.uscourts.gov/statistics, only one percent of cases reached trial in the twelve-month period ending September 2010.

| EXHIBIT 3.8 | Restatement Rule, Comment, and Illustration |

---

§ **7.06**   AGENCY   Ch. 7

Inc., 863 F.Supp. 159, 162 (S.D.N.Y. 1994). Courts in other circuits, however, continue to hold ship owners vicariously liable for crew members' willful misconduct against passengers. See, e.g., Doe v. Celebrity Cruises, Inc., 394 F.3d 891 (11th Cir. 2004), cert. denied, 126 S. Ct. 548 (2005); Morton v. De Oliveira, 984 F.2d 289 (9th Cir.1993); Muratore v. M/S Scotia Prince, 845 F.2d 347 (1st Cir.1988); Jackson Marine Corp. v. M/V Blue Fox, 845 F.2d 1307 (5th Cir.1988).

§ **7.07 Employee Acting Within Scope of Employment**

(1) **An employer is subject to vicarious liability for a tort committed by its employee acting within the scope of employment.**

(2) **An employee acts within the scope of employment when performing work assigned by the employer or engaging in a course of conduct subject to the employer's control. An employee's act is not within the scope of employment when it occurs within an independent course of conduct not intended by the employee to serve any purpose of the employer.**

(3) **For purposes of this section,**

(a) **an employee is an agent whose principal controls or has the right to control the manner and means of the agent's performance of work, and**

(b) **the fact that work is performed gratuitously does not relieve a principal of liability.**

Comment:

a. Scope and cross-references. Subsection (1) repeats the basic doctrine of respondeat superior stated in § 2.04 as a basis on which legal consequences of one person's actions may be attributed to another person. Subsection (2) states when an employee's tortious conduct occurs within the scope of employment for purposes of subjecting the employer to liability. Comment *b* discusses the rationale for the formulation in subsection (2), contrasting it with its counterparts in Restatement Second, Agency § 228 and in cases. Comment *c* discusses employee conduct that constitutes performance of work and is within the scope of employment. Comment *d* discusses other employee conduct that is subject to an employer's control. Comment *e* examines employees' peregrinations, that is, their travel necessitated by or otherwise in connection with their work. Comment *f* discusses the definition of employee in subsection (3).

For general discussion of respondeat superior, see § 2.04, Comment *b*.

198

EXHIBIT 3.8   *(continued)*

§ 7.07   AGENCY   Ch. 7

Moreover, if an employer exercises control over an employee's personal acts while the employee is off the employer's premises and not otherwise engaged in work, the employee's conduct remains within the scope of employment because it is subject to the employer's control. However, an employee's conduct is not within the scope of employment, although the employee is physically present on the employer's premises, when the employee's actions are far removed in purpose from work assigned by the employer. In some circumstances, even multitasking at an employee's assigned work station may remove the employee's conduct from the scope of employment because it may provide an employee with an occasion to commit a tort motivated solely by the employee's own purposes.

Illustrations:

10. P Insurance Co. furnishes telephones to its office staff with the direction that they may be used only when necessary to an employee's work. A, a claims processor, uses the telephone P Insurance Co. provides to make statements defamatory of T, a personal enemy of A's. The recipients of A's defamatory statements are unrelated to P Insurance Co.'s business. P Insurance Co. is not subject to liability to T. A's conduct in defaming T was not within the scope of A's employment. A acted only for A's own purposes.

11. Same facts as Illustration 10, except that P Insurance Co. permits its employees to make personal use of the telephones that it furnishes. Same result. By permitting employees to make personal use of its telephones, P Insurance Co. did not expand A's scope of employment to encompass defamation of A's personal enemies.

e. Peregrinations. In general, travel required to perform work, such as travel from an employer's office to a job site or from one job site to another, is within the scope of an employee's employment while traveling to and from work is not. However, an employer may place an employee's travel to and from work within the scope of employment by providing the employee with a vehicle and asserting control over how the employee uses the vehicle so that the employee may more readily respond to the needs of the employer's enterprise. An employee's travel to and from work may also be within the scope of employment if the employee does more than simply travel to and from work, for example by stopping for the employer's benefit to accomplish a task assigned by the employer.

An employee's travel during the work day that is not within the scope of employment has long been termed a "frolic" of the employee's own. De minimis departures from assigned routes are not "frolics." A

EXHIBIT 3.9	Restatement Case Citation

Custom ID : - **No Description** - ▾ | Switch Client | Preferences | Help | LiveSupport |

Search	Get a Document	*Shepard's®*	More		History	Alerts

FOCUS™ Terms [   ]   Search Within Original Results (1 - 35)   ▢ ▮   View
Advanced...   Tutorial

Source: **Legal > / . . . / > Restatement of the Law 1st, 2d & 3d, Agency - Case Citations** ⓘ
Terms: **(LexisNexis Provided Search)**

☞Select for FOCUS™ or Delivery

Restatement of the Law, Third, Agency § 7.07

Restatement of the Law, Third, Agency
Copyright (c) 2007, The American Law Institute

View Rule

Case Citations to the Third Restatement

Chapter 7 - Torts--Liability of Agent and Principal

Topic 2 - Principal's Liability

Restat 3rd of Agency, § 7.07

§ 7.07 Employee Acting Within Scope of Agency

CASE: Patterson v. Blair (2005)

CITATION: 172 S.W.3d 361, 369-371

COURT: The Supreme Court of Kentucky

DATE: 2005

TREATMENT: Quoted in support, comments (b) and (c) quoted in support (Tentative Draft No. 5, 2004)

SUMMARY: Dealership's customer, who refused to return a car he had purchased or to pay the balance he owed on the transaction, sued dealership and its employee under a variety of tort theories, after employee, in an effort to repossess the car, fired a pistol at the car's tires while customer was in the vehicle. The trial court entered a jury verdict for customer, and the court of appeals reversed. Reversing and remanding, this court held, inter alia, that employee was acting within the scope of his employment for vicarious-liability purposes; the relevant inquiry was whether employee's tortious conduct was intended to serve the purposes of employer, not the foreseeability of such conduct.

The Restatement Third of Agency was recently published in 2006. Citations below are still to Tentative Drafts.

Source: **Legal > / . . . / > Restatement of the Law 1st, 2d & 3d, Agency - Case Citations** ⓘ

For a national perspective, we researched in the Restatements, starting with the print version to take advantage of the clear structure and browsing capacity of a book. (Another good option was HeinOnline, the same source used for law reviews.) The Restatement (Third) of Agency, promulgated in 2005, provided a general rule in section 7.07 Employee Acting Within Scope of Employment, excerpted in Exhibit 3.8. That rule focused on whether the work was within the scope of employment, in a course of conduct subject to the employer's control versus conduct not intended to serve the employer's purposes. Moreover, one comment addressed the subject of "peregrinations," including commuting, noting that while commuting to work would not be within the scope of employment, stopping to accomplish an assigned task would be.

To learn whether that section had been adopted in California, we switched to LexisNexis, where we could retrieve the section by citation and link to the case citations. This stage of Restatements research is more easily accomplished online than in a series of print volumes. As shown in Exhibit 3.9, we found only one case referring to the section, from Kentucky; this was not surprising given its relative newness. A follow-up option would be to research in the Restatement (Second) of Agency to discern whether the rule in that Restatement was the same and followed in California.

As an alternative, for more focused research in California law, we researched in the California Civil Jury Instructions, available on the California court system's website. We easily found the pertinent instruction in Series 3700 Vicarious Responsibility, namely 3724. Going-and-Coming Rule, excerpted in Exhibit 3.10. There we found much the same rule as in the Restatement, along with references to both California cases and commentary focused on California law. The case references would be important to pursue in developing an analysis based on the law itself.

Citation to Restatements of the Law and Jury Instructions

The Restatement section, along with its comment, featured in this chapter is cited as follows:

BLUEBOOK: Restatement (Third) of Agency § 7.07 cmt. e (2006). [See rule 12.9.5.]

ALWD: *Restatement (Third) of Agency* § 7.07 cmt. e (2006). [See rule 27.]

The jury instruction featured in this chapter is cited as follows:

BLUEBOOK: Judicial Council of Cal., California Civil Jury Instructions § 3724 (2011). [See rule 12.9.5, by analogy.]

ALWD: Cal. Civ. Jury Instr. § 3724 (2011). [See rule 17.6.]

| EXHIBIT **3.10** | Jury Instruction (California Civil Jury Instructions) |

3724. Going-and-Coming Rule

In general, an employee is not acting within the scope of employment while traveling to and from the workplace. But if the employee, while commuting, is on an errand for the employer, then the employee's conduct is within the scope of his or her employment from the time the employee starts on the errand until he or she returns from the errand or until he or she completely abandons the errand for personal reasons.

New September 2003

Sources and Authority

- " 'An offshoot of the doctrine of respondeat superior is the so-called "going and coming rule." Under this rule, an employee is not regarded as acting within the scope of employment while going to or coming from the workplace. . . . This is based on the concept that the employment relationship is suspended from the time the employee leaves work until he or she returns, since the employee is not ordinarily rendering services to the employer while traveling. . . .' " (*Jeewarat v. Warner Brothers Entertainment, Inc.* (2009) 177 Cal.App.4th 427, 435 [98 Cal.Rptr.3d 837].)

- " 'A well-known exception to the going-and-coming rule arises *where the use of the car gives some incidental benefit to the employer*. Thus, the key inquiry is whether there is an incidental benefit derived by the employer. [Citation.]' This exception to the going and coming rule . . . has been referred to as the 'required-vehicle' exception. The exception can apply if the use of a personally owned vehicle is either an express or implied condition of employment, or if the employee has agreed, expressly or implicitly, to make the vehicle available as an accommodation to the employer and the employer has 'reasonably come to rely upon its use and [to] expect the employee to make the vehicle available on a regular basis while still not requiring it as a condition of employment.' " (*Lobo v. Tamco* (2010) 182 Cal.App.4th 297, 301 [105 Cal.Rptr.3d 718], original italics, internal citations omitted.)

- "If the employer requires or reasonably relies upon the employee to make his personal vehicle available to use for the employer's benefit and the employer derives a benefit from the availability of the vehicle, the fact that the employer only rarely makes use of the employee's personal

727   (Pub. 1283)

EXHIBIT 3.10   *(continued)*

CACI No. 3724   VICARIOUS RESPONSIBILITY

vehicle should not, in and of itself, defeat the plaintiff's case." (*Lobo, supra*, 182 Cal.App.4th at p. 303.)

- "When an employee is engaged in a 'special errand' or a 'special mission' for the employer it will negate the 'going and coming rule.' An employee ' "coming from his home or returning to it on a special errand either as part of his regular duties or at a specific order or request of his employer . . . is considered to be in the scope of his employment from the time that he starts on the errand until he has returned or until he deviates therefrom for personal reasons." ' The employer is 'liable for torts committed by its employee while traveling to accomplish a special errand because the errand benefits the employer. . . .' " (*Jeewarat, supra,* 177 Cal.App.4th at p. 436, internal citations omitted.)

- One specific exception to the going-and-coming rule is when the employer compensates the employee for travel time to and from work. (See *Hinman v. Westinghouse Electric Co.* (1970) 2 Cal.3d 956, 962 [88 Cal.Rptr. 188, 471 P.2d 988].)

- Some examples of the special-errand exception include: (1) where an employee goes on a business errand for his employer, leaving from his workplace and returning to his workplace; (2) where an employee is called to work to perform a special task for the employer at an irregular time; and (3) where the employer asks an employee to perform a special errand after the employee leaves work but before going home. (*Felix v. Asai* (1987) 192 Cal.App.3d 926, 931–932 [237 Cal.Rptr. 718].)

- "Plaintiffs contend an employee's attendance at an out-of-town business conference authorized and paid for by the employer may be a special errand for the benefit of the employer under the special errand doctrine. [Defendant] asserts that the special errand doctrine does not apply to commercial travel. We conclude that a special errand may include commercial travel such as the business trip in this case." (*Jeewarat, supra,* 177 Cal.App.4th at p. 436.)

- The employee is still within the scope of employment after the errand is completed. (*Trejo v. Maciel* (1966) 239 Cal.App.2d 487, 495 [48 Cal.Rptr. 765].)

Secondary Sources

3 Witkin, Summary of California Law (10th ed. 2005) Agency and Employment, §§ 181–184

2 Levy et al., California Torts, Ch. 20, *Motor Vehicles*, § 20.42[3] (Matthew Bender)

2 California Employment Law, Ch. 30, *Employers' Tort Liability to Third*

PRACTICE GUIDES

This book uses the term "practice guides" to refer to commentary sources that are less citable and less focused on providing an exposition of the law than the sources discussed earlier. Rather, the primary purpose of a practice guide is to assist the lawyer in carrying out some task in which the legal analysis developed through other sources is put into play, such as drafting documents for a transaction or litigating a case.

Practice guides are published by commercial publishers in various formats. Some cover only one subject; others cover many subjects. Some focus on transactions; others focus on litigation. Some operate at a fairly general level; others are highly specialized. Some examples are *Causes of Action, American Jurisprudence Legal Forms, 2d*, and *American Jurisprudence Pleading and Practice Forms Annotated*. Selecting a useful guide is similar to selecting a treatise: Asking a more senior colleague or librarian is a very good idea.[15]

A classic tool provided by a practice guide is a sample form. Of course, using a form in a practice guide without adapting it for the client's situation is exceedingly unwise; by definition the form was not created to fit the specific client's situation and indeed may not have been based on the law of the jurisdiction of the client's situation. Nonetheless, forms can be useful as starting points, in particular as ways to check for the topics a document should include.

Researching the defamation claim for Casey Nichols (discussed earlier in the context of legal periodicals) in *American Jurisprudence Pleading and Practice Forms Annotated*, we found Exhibit 3.11, a sample pleading for a lawsuit challenging an employee's termination, including a claim, or "cause of action," of defamation. While the sample was written for a different factual dispute (a conflict of interest due to a social relationship with a former employee), it nonetheless provided a framework for the legal points to allege, e.g., publication of the statements, their defamatory meaning, lack of privilege to publish them, injury to the plaintiff, and damages.

SUMMARY OF COMMENTARY RESEARCH

As explained in this chapter, every form of commentary research has its own role to play. Optimal options will change over time as resources develop; a skilled researcher continually updates his or her research practices in light of new options. As presented in the discussion of the illustrations, we favor some particular strategies for researching in each form of commentary. Chart 3.5 presents our preferences as of mid-2011, when this book was written.

15. Many law offices in effect create their own practice guides when they maintain files of documents they have created for various client matters. To the extent a new client's matter resembles that of a previous client, this is an efficient practice. To the extent the new client's lawyer does not think through the document in light of that client's situation, this is a problematic practice.

EXHIBIT 3.11	Sample Pleading

Westlaw

AMJUR PP MASTERSER § 70   Page 1
17A Am. Jur. Pl. & Pr. Forms Master and Servant § 70

American Jurisprudence Pleading and Practice Forms Annotated
Database updated April 2011

Master and Servant
II. Contract of Employment
C. Wrongful Discharge

Topic Summary References Correlation Table

§ 70. Complaint, petition, or declaration—Wrongful discharge—Discharge of employee because of romantic relationship with manager of competitor—Breach of contract—Tortious breach of covenant of good faith and fair dealing— Libel and slander—Sex discrimination

[Caption, see § 5]

COMPLAINT

Plaintiff alleges:

1. Plaintiff is now, and at all times mentioned was, a resident of *[name of city]*, *[name of county]*, *[name of state]*.

2. Defendant, *[name of corporation]*, is now, and at all times mentioned was, a corporation organized and existing under the laws of the State of *[name of state]*, with its principal place of business at *[street address of business]*, in *[name of city]*, *[name of county]*, *[name of state]*.

3. Defendant, *[name of branch manager]*, is now, and at all times mentioned was, a resident of *[name of city]*, *[name of county]*, *[name of state]*, and was an employee of defendant corporation. Defendant branch manager was on *[date of employment]*, employed by defendant corporation as a branch manager, and was, in that capacity, the immediate supervisor of plaintiff. As branch manager, defendant branch manager had the authority and power to discharge and discipline plaintiff.

4. Defendant, *[name of regional manager]*, is now, and at all times mentioned was, a resident of *[name of city]*, *[name of county]*, *[name of state]*, and an employee of defendant corporation. Defendant regional manager, on *[date of employment]*, was employed by defendant corporation as regional manager. In that capacity, defendant regional manager supervised defendant branch manager and exercised general authority over the persons under the supervision of defendant branch manager.

5. Defendant, *[name of resident director]*, is now, and at all times mentioned was, a resident of *[name of city]*, *[name of county]*, *[name of state]*, and an employee of defendant corporation. Defendant resident director was employed by defendant corporation on *[date of employment]* as a resident director, whose responsibilities included, but were not limited to, assistance in resolving grievances between and among employees of defendant corporation.

Exhibit 3.11   *(continued)*

AMJUR PP MASTERSER § 70   Page 4
17A Am. Jur. Pl. & Pr. Forms Master and Servant § 70

[number of years]-year commitment to a lifetime career with defendant corporation. Plaintiff further suffered great emotional and physical distress as a consequence of the bad faith of defendant corporation and its agents, and the breaches of defendant corporation.

19. Plaintiff has been generally and specially damaged in an amount in excess of the jurisdictional minimum of this court, which exact amount will be specifically pleaded when determined.

20. Defendant corporation intentionally and maliciously breached its duty and its implied covenant of good faith and fair dealing, and subjected plaintiff to oppression and cruel and unjust hardship in conscious disregard of plaintiff's rights by committing the acts alleged. Plaintiff is therefore entitled to punitive damages in the amount of $*[dollar amount of punitive damages]*.

Third Cause of Action

21. Plaintiff repeats and realleges as though fully set forth every allegation contained in Paragraphs 1 through 14.

22. On *[date of allegation 1]*, and *[date of allegation 2]*, and on other dates and times not yet ascertained, defendants intentionally and maliciously stated to other persons, including persons not employed by defendant corporation, that plaintiff was involved in a direct conflict of interest because of plaintiff's social relationship with *[name of former employee]*, and that this conflict of interest was the reason plaintiff was removed from *[his/her]* position.

23. Defendants' statements were and are libelous and slanderous because they wrongfully and untruthfully impute to plaintiff the traits of disloyalty, dishonesty, and general unfitness for employment at the managerial level. The acts, conduct, and statements of defendants were not privileged.

24. Defendants' false statements about plaintiff have also injured plaintiff in *[his/her]* profession, occupation, and calling, in that it has been and will be assumed by others in *[the office products industry/[type of industry]]*, particularly other potential employers, that plaintiff was in fact guilty of maintaining conflicting interests, disloyalty, and dishonesty, or was otherwise unfit for employment as a managerial employee.

25. As a proximate result of the described libelous and slanderous statements, plaintiff has been injured in her profession and in reputation in a sum as yet unknown.

26. As a further proximate result of the complained of statements, acts, conduct, and publications, plaintiff has suffered humiliation and shame and has suffered severe emotional distress and injury, and special damages in an amount in excess of the jurisdictional minimum of this court, which amount will be specifically pleaded when finally determined.

27. The described statements, acts, conduct, and publications were done and said by defendants because of defendants' malice, ill will, and intent to oppress plaintiff, and to make plaintiff an example to deter other of defendant corporation's employees from freely associating with employees of defendant corporation's competitors. An award of punitive damages in the amount of $*[dollar amount of punitive damages]* against defendant is therefore justified.

Fourth Cause of Action

CHART 3.5	Optimal Options for Commentary Research	

Source	Advantages and Disadvantages	Optimal Options
Encyclopedias	Broad updated coverage of nearly all legal topics. But very general discussion and low citability.	Use state version if available. Research in print. Use various finding tools, browse, and update.
Treatises	In-depth coverage of subject, possibly updated. Some variability in quality.	Use most credible treatise available. Research in print. Use various finding tools, browse, and update to extent possible.
Legal Periodicals	Very in-depth coverage of narrow topic, possibly with law-reform slant. Possibly idiosyncratic analysis and not updated. Do not cover all topics.	Select recent articles in credible journals by credible authors. Use various methods to find articles, e.g., index and key-word search in full-text database. Try HeinOnline.
A.L.R. Annotations	Very in-depth description of cases on subject, with strong updating. Limited citability. Do not cover all topics.	Use various methods to find annotation, e.g., index, full-text key-word searching. Use print or Westlaw or LexisNexis.
Restatements of the Law	Highly credible and citable statement of current or best rules, with information on adoption in various states. Do not cover all topics.	Use print or HeinOnline to identify and read pertinent sections; browse within general topic. Use online case summaries on LexisNexis and Westlaw to track adoption.
Jury Instructions	Highly credible and citable statement of rule in specific jurisdictions, with supporting references. Do not cover all topics.	Use library catalog or Internet search engine to locate set and table of contents to locate specific instructions.
Practice Guides	Practical guidance for creating documents and managing legal processes. Less utility in providing legal framework or references. No citability.	Use sources recommended by more senior colleague. Use for general approach, not details. Adapt in light of jurisdiction's specific rules and client's situation.

PLAN YOUR RESEARCH IN LEGAL AUTHORITIES

If you have researched thoughtfully and thoroughly in commentary, by the end of that process, you should have both an overview of the legal framework into which your research issue fits and some references to legal authorities. It is the latter that should ultimately drive your analysis of your client's situation. Thus the next step is to take stock of what you know and develop a plan as you turn to researching legal authority.

First, monitor your research: Record the rules you have derived thus far, noting not only what the sources represent the law to be but also how they phrase it and how they organize the various pieces, or "elements," of the law. Look for similarities and differences across commentary sources. Carefully note where you derived each rule. Then return to your summary of your client's situation and your research terms and issues, and revise them as needed. In particular, consider whether you have learned of additional terms or issues and whether you can create sub-issues within your issues.

Second, plan your next research phase: Identify which categories of law, according to commentary, appear to govern your research issues. If nothing else, commentary research should clue you in to which law-making body governs the research issue. Two dimensions are important: the level of government and the law-making body. That is, consider where in the matrix shown in Chart 3.6 the research issue resides.

As explained in more detail in the chapters that follow, many issues reside in more than one box. Two very typical patterns are overlap of federal and state law and the interaction of case law and statutory law.

| CHART 3.6 | Legal Authority Matrix |

	Common Law	Constitutions or Statutes	Administrative Law	Rules of Procedure
Federal				
State				
Local				

Third, engage in your preliminary search for legal authorities: List the solid leads you have on authorities from your jurisdiction. While each form of authority has means of locating pertinent materials (pertinent cases within a court's entire collection of cases, pertinent sections within a state's entire set of statutes), following up on leads from commentary is an excellent way to start. Discern whether the various commentary sources pointed you to the same authorities.

With this information in hand, you are ready to turn to the ultimate goal of your research: the law that will help you resolve your client's problem.

TEST YOUR UNDERSTANDING

Reflection Questions

1. For any particular research project, you are unlikely to use all of the commentary sources discussed in this chapter. So why is it not enough for you to learn how to use only one or two of the sources and disregard the rest?

2. As noted in this chapter and shown in Chapter 1's demonstration of Google, you can easily find an individual lawyer's discussion of the law. Indeed, through tools discussed in Chapter 4 on case law, you can find copies of briefs filed by lawyers on behalf of their clients in some courts. Why, then, does this chapter focus on the sources discussed here? What makes them worthy of your research time?

Your Scenario

Refer again to the client situation in Chapter 2: Your client, Elaine Wilson, who has PTSD, wants to keep a companion animal in her apartment, and her landlord is opposed. The events take place in West Virginia. Your client and the landlord view the situation quite differently; the landlord apparently sees your client as breaching a term of the lease; your client sees the landlord as discriminating against her because she has PTSD.

- Research this situation in the various commentary sources discussed in this chapter.
- Did you find one form of commentary easier to use or more helpful?
- Compare your results. Did you find the same information as to the legal rule and references?

CASE LAW RESEARCH

Contents

This chapter explores the topic of defamation in the workplace (also covered in Chapter 3).

Key Concepts and Tools in This Chapter

- common law, precedents, and stare decisis
- motions, trials, and appeals

(continued)

- judicial decisions
- holding, dictum, rule of law, and public policy
- split decision: majority, plurality, concurrence, dissent
- case brief
- court systems
- types of jurisdiction
- mandatory versus persuasive precedent
- good law: subsequent history and treatment
- unpublished cases
- seminal cases
- retrospectivity of cases
- factors affecting choice of cases
- factors affecting choice of resources
- slip opinions
- official reporters
- West Reporter System
  - regional, state, and federal reporters
  - headnotes
  - topics and key numbers
  - digests
  - Descriptive Word Index
- Westlaw research in case law
  - Find
  - database selection
  - terms and connectors, natural language, key number, KeySearch
  - field and date constraints
  - Westlaw Next
  - KeyCite
- LexisNexis research in case law
  - Get a Document
  - database selection
  - terms and connectors, natural language, Search by Topic, Search by Headnote
  - Shepard's

- Google Scholar
- Loislaw, Fastcase, CASEMaker
- Court websites
- PACER

The United States has a common law legal system following the principle of stare decisis. In the simplest of terms, this means that the decisions of the courts, also called "precedents," have the force of law. The full Latin phrase is "stare decisis et non quieta movere," which means "to adhere to precedent and not to unsettle things which are settled." Stare decisis provides justice, in that similar situations are treated similarly, and predictability, in that people know how to conduct their affairs within the law.

In some areas of law, the law derives entirely from judicial decisions. In most areas, the courts render decisions that interact with other legal authorities, such as statutes and agency rules, to create the law governing a client's situation. In either context, to properly assist a client, proficiently researching the decisions of the courts is imperative.

A few notes about vocabulary: Lawyers use the word "case" in various ways: (1) to refer to a client's matter, especially if it involves a dispute; (2) to refer to a dispute in litigation; and (3) to refer to a decision of a court. The words "decision" and "opinion" refer to the text a court writes when it decides a case. "Case law" is the term used for a set of cases that together constitute the law on a topic.

This chapter first briefly discusses how a dispute yields a decision of a court that constitutes legal authority and how a decision in someone else's case from some time ago is used to guide the resolution of a current client's situation. The chapter then discusses court structures and the key principles of the common law system that determine which of the many decisions one could find on a topic actually govern a client's situation. With this background set, the chapter turns to the many resources for researching case law, featuring those that are most useful in the most common situations in which case law research occurs.

As the illustration for this chapter, consider the case of Casey Nichols. Nichols was fired from his job at a grocery store after a coworker, who had a personal conflict with Nichols, reported that Nichols had given food away to friends of his, contrary to the store's policy. Although Nichols vehemently denied this, the store's manager decided to believe the coworker and fired Nichols. She also told other employees of the store the reason for the termination in an effort to show that the store took the prohibition on pilferage seriously. These events took place in Lawrence, Kansas, in the spring of 2011. According to our research in commentary, one possible claim was the tort of defamation.

LITIGATED DISPUTES, JUDICIAL DECISIONS, AND GUIDANCE FOR YOUR CLIENT

Litigated disputes and judicial decisions. Although American lawyers have no lack of disputes to resolve for clients, very few make law. Rather, most disputes are settled by the lawyers or resolved through informal means of dispute resolution, such as mediation or arbitration, in which a private individual assists the parties to come to a negotiated resolution or makes a decision for them. Some disputes do become lawsuits, enter the judicial system, and get resolved by judges, with the potential of making law to govern similar situations in the future.

At the risk of significant oversimplification, a case resolved through litigation starts in a trial court. Most cases in litigation are resolved by a judge by grant of a motion. That is, the judge decides that he or she can apply the law to the facts without a trial and render a decision. When the facts of a case or the application of the law to the facts is less clear, the case proceeds to trial before a judge or a jury, at which witnesses testify and documents and other items are viewed. At points throughout the proceedings in the trial court, the lawyers may make various motions, asking the judge to handle the case in certain ways; examples are bringing in another party as a defendant and seeking to exclude certain evidence from the jury. Indeed, much of an American litigator's practice is devoted to motions, not trials.

After a final result is obtained in the trial court, a party that is dissatisfied may appeal. The appeal may encompass motions granted or denied along the way as well as the final outcome. An appeal is decided by several or more judges, and the focus is on correcting errors that could have led to the wrong outcome, not redoing the work of the trial court. Hence appeals are presented through written briefs and oral arguments by lawyers, along with transcripts of the proceedings in the trial court in some situations. Because there are so many ways that decisions are made in the trial courts, courts of appeals use various standards of review; for example, they defer more to jury decisions on matters of fact than to judges' rulings on how to read the law. A fairly small number of important cases are reviewed by a system's highest court, as described in the next section.

As a case makes its way through the courts, judges write decisions. These decisions draw heavily on the written and oral arguments presented by the parties' lawyers; thus lawyers are deeply involved in making the common law in the United States. The decisions have two distinct purposes. First, a decision resolves the case before the court. Second, the decision sets out a roadmap for people with similar situations in the future so they may deduce how their situations would be handled by the courts and act accordingly.

As an example, consider the case of *Luttrell v. United Telephone System, Inc.*, found in Exhibit 4.1. In Nichols' situation, a possible wrinkle was that the publication was entirely within the company, possibly failing to satisfy the defamation requirement that the defendant publish the communication to a third party. The court addressed this issue in *Luttrell*.

EXHIBIT 4.1	Case from West Reporter

1292   Kan.   683 PACIFIC REPORTER, 2d SERIES

a defectively acknowledged and recorded deed imparts constructive notice if the defect in the acknowledgment is entirely latent. *Mills v. Damson Oil Corp.*, 437 So.2d 1005, 1006 (Miss.1983).

We recognize that there is a division of authority on this question, but we are persuaded that the better reasoning supports the majority rule.

In view of our ruling, we need not discuss other issues raised by the parties. The trial court did not err in holding that the original deed was a valid conveyance as between the parties, that it was properly received for record, and that it imparted constructive notice to subsequent purchasers and encumbrancers, including the defendant.

Affirmed.

Marvin G. LUTTRELL, Appellant,

v.

UNITED TELEPHONE SYSTEM, INC., Appellee.

No. 56031.

Court of Appeals of Kansas.

July 19, 1984.

Review Granted Sept. 6, 1984.

Employee brought action against employer alleging that statements by managerial employees concerning employee's job performance constituted defamation. The District Court, Johnson County, Phillip L. Woodworth, J., granted employer's motion to dismiss for failure to state claim upon which relief may be granted, and employee appealed. The Court of Appeals, Parks, J., held that remarks communicated by one corporate employee to another concerning job performance of third employee are publication for purposes of defamation against

employer; thus, claim was improperly dismissed.

Reversed and remanded.

HEADNOTES

1. Libel and Slander ⟐1
   Tort of defamation includes both libel and slander.

2. Libel and Slander ⟐1
   Elements of defamation include false and defamatory words communicated to a third person which result in harm to the reputation of the person defamed.

3. Corporations ⟐423
   Corporation may be liable for defamatory utterances of its agent which are made while acting within scope of his authority.

4. Libel and Slander ⟐117
   Laws of libel and slander protect reputation.

5. Libel and Slander ⟐45(2)
   Communication made within work situation is qualifiedly privileged if it is made in good faith on any subject matter in which person communicating has an interest, or in reference to which he has a duty, if it is made to a person having corresponding interest or duty.

6. Libel and Slander ⟐44(3)
   Employer who is evaluating or investigating employee in good faith and within bounds of employment relationship is protected from threat of defamation suits by requirement that employee prove that employer acted with knowledge of falsity or reckless disregard for the truth.

7. Libel and Slander ⟐23
   Remarks made in course and scope of employment by one corporate employee and communicated to second corporate employee concerning job performance of third employee are publication for purposes of defamation action against corporate employer. K.S.A. 60-212(b)(6).

8. Libel and Slander ⟐80
   Allegation by employee that managerial employees of corporate employer had

EXHIBIT 4.1   *(continued)*

LUTTRELL v. UNITED TELEPHONE SYSTEM   Kan.   **1293**
Cite as 683 P.2d 1292 (Kan.App. 1984)

made false statements about his job performance was sufficient to state defamation action.

Syllabus by the Court

Remarks made in the course and scope of employment by one corporate employee and communicated to a second corporate employee concerning the job performance of a third employee constitute publication for the purposes of a defamation action against the corporate employer.

———————

Richard M. Smith of Smith & Winter-Smith, Mound City, for appellant.

Paul Hasty, Jr. of Wallace, Saunders, Austin, Brown & Enochs, Chartered, Overland Park, for appellee.

Before FOTH, C.J., and PARKS and SWINEHART, JJ.

> COURT'S OPINION

PARKS, Judge:

Plaintiff Marvin G. Luttrell appeals the dismissal of his defamation action against the defendant, United Telephone System, Inc.

Plaintiff alleges in his petition that several managerial employees of defendant maliciously communicated defamatory remarks about him between themselves while acting within the scope of their employment. Particularly, he alleges that on or about April 6 or 7 of 1982, Mr. R.H. Baranek, an employee of defendant, stated to Mr. R.L. Flint, plaintiff's supervisor, that plaintiff was illegally taping telephone conversations on April 1 and that Baranek had requested him to stop but plaintiff persisted in this illegal activity the rest of the afternoon despite the direct order given him to stop by his supervisor. He further alleged that the communication of the same defamatory information was made by Mr. Flint to Mr. T.V. Tregenza and by Mr. Tregenza to Mr. W. Soble, all while acting within the scope of their employment. Defendant filed a motion to dismiss pursuant to K.S.A. 60–212(b)(6) on the grounds that intracorporate communications did not con-

stitute "publication." The trial court sustained the motion to dismiss for failure to state a claim upon which relief may be granted.

[1–3] The tort of defamation includes both libel and slander. The elements of the wrong include false and defamatory words (*Hein v. Lacy*, 228 Kan. 249, 259, 616 P.2d 277 [1980]) communicated to a third person (*Schulze v. Coykendall*, 218 Kan. 653, 657, 545 P.2d 392 [1976]) which result in harm to the reputation of the person defamed. *Gobin v. Globe Publishing Co.*, 232 Kan. 1, 6, 649 P.2d 1239 (1982) (*Gobin III*). A corporation may be liable for the defamatory utterances of its agent which are made while acting within the scope of his authority. *Bourn v. State Bank*, 116 Kan. 231, 235, 226 P. 769 (1924).

In this case, the defendant argued and the district court agreed that there can be no communication to a third person, or "publication," when the defamatory words are exchanged by agents of a single corporate defendant. This issue of first impression is more precisely whether interoffice communications between supervisory employees of a corporation, acting within the scope and course of their employment, regarding the work of another employee of the corporation, constitute publication to a third person sufficient for a defamation action.

There is a considerable division of authority concerning this issue. For example, courts recently considering the laws of Nevada, Missouri, Arkansas, Georgia and Louisiana have all accepted the assertion that intracorporate defamation is simply the corporation talking to itself and not publication. See *e.g., Jones v. Golden Spike Corp.*, 97 Nev. 24, 623 P.2d 970 (1981); *Ellis v. Jewish Hospital of St. Louis*, 581 S.W.2d 850 (Mo.App.1979); *Halsell v. Kimberly-Clark Corp.*, 683 F.2d 285 (8th Cir.1982); *Monahan v. Sims*, 163 Ga. App. 354, 294 S.E.2d 548 (1982); *Commercial Union Ins. Co. v. Melikyan*, 424 So.2d 1114 (La.App.1982). The contrary conclusion has been reached in courts applying the laws of Kentucky, Massachusetts, New

Exhibit 4.1 *(continued)*

York and California. See *e.g., Brewer v. American Nat. Ins. Co.*, 636 F.2d 150 (6th Cir.1980); *Arsenault v. Allegheny Airlines, Inc.*, 485 F.Supp. 1373 (D.Mass.), *aff'd* 636 F.2d 1199 (1st Cir.1980); *Pirre v. Printing Developments, Inc.*, 468 F.Supp. 1028 (S.D.N.Y.), *aff'd* 614 F.2d 1290 (2d Cir.1979); *Kelly v. General Telephone Co.*, 136 Cal.App.3d 278, 186 Cal.Rptr. 184 (1982). The latter opinions have held that while communications between supervisory employees of a corporation concerning a third employee may be qualifiedly privileged, they are still publication. Prosser also favors the view that such communications are publication and dismisses those cases holding otherwise as confusing publication with privilege. Prosser, Law of Torts § 113, p. 767 n. 70 (4th ed. 1971).

[4] Undeniably, the district court's holding in this case is not without support or technical appeal; however, we believe it ignores the nature of the civil injury sought to be protected in a defamation action. Damage to one's reputation is the essence and gravamen of an action for defamation. It is reputation which is defamed, reputation which is injured, reputation which is protected by the laws of libel and slander. *Gobin III*, 232 Kan. at 6, 649 P.2d 1239. Certainly, damage to one's reputation within a corporate community may be just as devastating as that effected by defamation spread to the outside. Thus, the injury caused by intracorporate defamation should not be disregarded simply because the corporation can be sued as an individual entity.

[5] Defendant argues that corporate employers must be free to evaluate and comment on their employees' work performance and that this freedom will be unduly restrained if they are liable for intracorporate defamation. However, the law in this state has already extended protection to comments made within a work situation by means of a qualified privilege. A communication is qualifiedly privileged if it is made in good faith on any subject matter in which the person communicating has an interest, or in reference to which he has a duty, if it is made to a person having a corresponding interest or duty. The essential elements of a qualifiedly privileged communication are good faith, an interest to be upheld, a statement limited in its scope to the upholding of such interest and publication in a proper manner only to proper parties. *Dobbyn v. Nelson*, 2 Kan. App.2d 358, 360, 579 P.2d 721, *aff'd* 225 Kan. 56, 587 P.2d 315 (1978). Thus, in *Dobbyn* the Court held that a letter written by an employee of the Kansas State University library concerning the conduct of another employee and transmitted to the second employee's superior was qualifiedly privileged. *Dobbyn*, 2 Kan.App.2d at 361, 579 P.2d 721. As a result, the plaintiff was required to prove that the defendants acted with knowledge of falsity or reckless disregard for the truth before the privilege could be overcome. See also *Scarpelli v. Jones*, 229 Kan. 210, 216, 626 P.2d 785 (1981).

[6] By virtue of the qualified privilege, the employer who is evaluating or investigating an employee in good faith and within the bounds of the employment relationship is protected from the threat of defamation suits by the enhanced burden of proof which the plaintiff would have to bear. We see no reason for greater freedom from liability for defamation to be accorded the corporate employer than that already available to all employers through the qualified privilege.

[7, 8] We conclude that remarks communicated by one corporate employee to another concerning the job performance of a third employee are publication for the purposes of a defamation action against the employer. Since the dismissal motion was granted in this case prior to the commencement of any discovery, we make no findings concerning the possible application of qualified privilege to the communications alleged.

RULE

The dismissal for failure to state a claim upon which relief may be granted is reversed and the case is remanded for further proceedings.

The first page of Exhibit 4.1 is editorial matter written by the publisher; the second and third pages comprise the judicial decision. As explained in the first two paragraphs of the decision, in April of 1982, Marvin Luttrell worked for United Telephone and alleged that various managers, including his supervisor, stated that he was illegally taping telephone conversations. As plaintiff, he sued United Telephone, and the company filed a motion to dismiss the complaint for failure to state a claim.[1] The trial court granted this motion.

Luttrell appealed to the Court of Appeals of Kansas, which wrote the decision in Exhibit 4.1. As stated in the last paragraph, the court of appeals reversed the trial court, ruling for Luttrell, and sent the case back to the trial court for further proceedings. Had the court simply been concerned about the dispute between Luttrell and United Telephone, it could have issued just that single paragraph. Rather, the court wrote a fairly extensive explanation of why it made that decision, in the third through ninth paragraphs (the paragraphs preceded by bracketed numbers). That explanation was the guidance we found for Casey Nichols' case.

Guidance for your client. When reading a decision for guidance for your client's situation, you should glean as much as possible from it. Some decisions are more extensive, better reasoned, and more easily read than others, of course. Nonetheless, with some effort you should be able to draw out the following:

1. What rule did the court use to decide the case before it? A rule is a statement connecting a set of facts to a legal outcome. The rule may be one the court makes in the decision or one it draws from an earlier case, some other legal authority such as a statute, or a combination of authorities.
2. How did the court apply the rule to the facts of the case before it? That is, what was the outcome, and why? The decision the court renders in the case is called the "holding." Rules tend be generally framed, so it is always helpful to know how they work in specific settings. Furthermore, to the extent the facts of the case before the court resemble the client's situation, considerable guidance can come from analogizing the client's situation to the case before the court.
3. What public policies are discussed in the decision? Lawyers use the term "public policy" to refer to considerations that go beyond the particular facts of the parties. It encompasses how other people will be affected by the decision in the future and what social goals the law is intended to accomplish.
4. What lessons can be drawn for your client's situation in light of the first three points?
5. What authorities did the court rely on that merit reading?

---

1. This motion comes very early in litigation; it asserts that even if the plaintiff's factual allegations are true, the law does not provide a claim.

6. In addition to the issue for which you originally identified the case, what other issues, if any, did the court address that merit consideration as you continue your research and analysis?

Sometimes, judges write more than is needed to actually decide the case. This material may provide useful insight into how the law evolves, so it also merits careful consideration. First, "dictum"[2] arises when a decision discusses a situation not before the court in order to provide additional insight into the court's thinking on the general issue. Because the dictum is not necessary to resolve the case, it is not as authoritative as the points that actually decide the case.

Second, in a split decision the judges on an appellate panel do not agree on one opinion. A split court may yield a majority opinion, which garners more than half of the votes; a plurality opinion, which garners the most votes, although not a majority, and operates as the court's opinion; a concurrence, which agrees in the majority result but not its reasoning; and a dissent, which disagrees with the majority outcome as well as its reasoning.

Given the wealth of information to draw from a pertinent case and its centrality in your legal analysis of a client's situation, you should strongly consider capturing this information two ways. First, save a copy of the case. As noted in Chapter 1, a wise process is to read the case in print form, which facilitates careful study better than reading online. Second, take careful notes, capturing the material answering the questions listed here; lawyers call these notes "case briefs." This step serves not only as a means of monitoring your research by processing your sources—one of the steps of the work-flow of legal research—but also as a bridge to your analysis of your client's problem.

For example, we created the case brief of *Luttrell* in Example 4.1 for purposes of Nichols' possible defamation claim.

EXAMPLE 4.1	Case Brief

Luttrell v. United Telephone System, Inc., Kans. Ct. App. 1984, 683 P.2d 1292

RULE: Remarks communicated by one corporate employee to another re job performance of third employee/plaintiff are publication for purposes of defamation action against employer.

APPLICATION TO FACTS AND HOLDING: Plaintiff alleged managers and supervisor falsely stated within workplace that he illegally taped phone conversations. Plaintiff sued employer for defamation. Trial court granted motion to dismiss on grounds there was no publication. Court of appeals reversed on this issue—publication requirement was met. (Remanded on privilege issue.)

(continued)

---

2. The full phrase is "obiter dictum," which means "something said in passing."

POLICIES: Damage to reputation within corporation can be as devastating as damage outside corporation. On other hand, employers have need for free evaluation and comment on work performance. This need is protected through qualified privilege and need not also be protected by deeming intra-corporate communication not published.

NO NON-MAJORITY OPINION.

LESSON: Publication by supervisor to other employees of store as to Nichols' performance probably was publication for purposes of defamation (though *Luttrell* involved managers speaking to each other, versus manager speaking to employees).

AUTHORITIES: On publication topic, court relied on cases from out of state, so no need to follow up on them. However—

ADDITIONAL ISSUES: Communication may be qualifiedly privileged if made in good faith, to serve interest of speaker, limited in scope to that interest, and published properly only to proper parties. This applies in employment setting. Check out *Dobbyn v. Nelson*, 579 P.2d 721, *aff'd* 587 P.2d 315; *Scarpelli v. Jones*, 626 P.2d 785.

THE COMMON LAW SYSTEM

Hundreds, if not thousands, of courts in the United States decide cases every week on an amazingly wide array of subjects, and they have been doing so for hundreds of years.[3] Thus researching the common law may seem to be a daunting prospect, and to a certain extent it should be. However, the common law system has a structure and follows key principles that together provide a framework that simplifies the process considerably. The framework enables you to answer two main questions: Whose law governs? And which cases matter most?

Whose law governs? The American legal system is a federal system, i.e., a collection of jurisdictions each with its own court system. Covering the entire country is a system of federal courts. Each state also has its own court system.

Most court systems have many trial courts, a single intermediate appellate court sitting in multiple panels or a number of appellate courts, and a highest court, as well as a few courts that hear only a narrow range of cases.[4] In the federal system, there are nearly one hundred trial courts (one to four per state and territory); twelve regional courts of appeals—eleven numbered courts of

---

3. Indeed, one principle of the American common law system is that the case law of England is incorporated into American law—a more important point early in our history than today.
4. Examples are courts that hear international trade disputes, claims against the government, or tax matters, at the initial or appellate level.

appeals, each covering a set of states, and one for the District of Columbia (as shown in Chart 4.1); and the U.S. Supreme Court. Appeal to an intermediate appellate court is typically as of right; that is, the court must hear the case if the appeal is properly brought. Appeal to a highest court is typically discretionary; that is, the highest court selects the cases it hears based on their importance to the development of the law.[5] As you would expect, court systems operate hierarchically: trial courts are bound by decisions of the two higher courts to which their decisions may be appealed, intermediate courts are bound by decisions of the highest court, and each court also takes into account decisions at its level.

Every court has jurisdiction over certain matters. "Jurisdiction" is used by lawyers for several closely related concepts. The key concept is power: When a court has jurisdiction over a case, it may render an enforceable decision in the case. This is partly a function of the court's geographic jurisdiction.

Jurisdiction is also a function of the law that governs the case. As a general matter, federal courts enforce federal laws, and state courts enforce their own state laws. In some situations, the pattern is more complex. A federal court can enforce state law when the parties are citizens of different states and the amount involved is sufficiently high (diversity jurisdiction). A federal court can enforce state law when the case also involves a claim under federal law (supplemental jurisdiction). Congress has given state courts the power to enforce some federal laws, along with the federal courts (concurrent jurisdiction). In our national economy, contracts that are used in many states often identify the law of a particular state as the law to be applied, wherever the case arises and is handled.

CHART 4.1	Federal Appellate Court Map

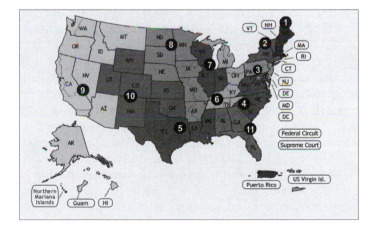

5. There are exceptions, which vary by court system. For example, a state high court may be required to review the most serious criminal cases.

Given this structure, knowledge of the place of a client's situation and of which law (federal or state) governs your research issue permits you to answer the first critical question in case law research: whose decisions govern? If the issue is one of federal law, the governing decisions—called "binding" or "mandatory precedents"—are from the U.S. Supreme Court, the court of appeals that covers the state, and the federal trial court where the case is filed, in descending order of importance. If the issue is one of state law, the governing decisions are from the state's highest court, the state's court of appeals (either the single court of appeals or the court for the circuit where the case is filed), and the state trial court where the case is filed, again in descending order of importance. Decisions from other courts are called "persuasive precedent" and are considered useful but not binding, to the extent there is no binding precedent on your issue or you are seeking a different legal rule than that provided by binding precedent.

In some situations, a court in one system is bound to follow the law of a court in a different system. In the most common example, when a federal court has diversity jurisdiction over a claim arising under state law, it will follow the precedent from the state's highest court. As another example, when a state court has concurrent jurisdiction over a federal claim, it will look to federal cases, not cases from the state courts.

For example, Nichols' case occurred in Kansas, so his potential defamation claim, which in this situation is a tort defined by state law, would be governed by state law. The binding precedents would be decisions of the Kansas Supreme Court and the Court of Appeals of Kansas, and decisions of the trial courts would merit consideration. Decisions of federal courts (the U.S. District Court for the District of Kansas and the U.S. Court of Appeals for the Tenth Circuit[6]) applying the Kansas state law of defamation would be persuasive precedents. Decisions from other states would also be persuasive precedents.

Which decisions matter most? Generally a strong legal analysis draws on at least several cases; a group of decisions provides more complete insight than one or two cases. Often you will find many binding cases on your research issue, and you will need to decide which handful to use. First, any case you choose to use must be what lawyers call "good law." Second, you should select cases that are considered "published." Third, various factors can be used to select from among a large set of published cases that are good law.

There are three main ways in which a case ceases to be good law, as shown in Chart 4.2. The first is a matter of the case's subsequent history. A decision of a lower court that is appealed to a higher court may be affirmed on appeal; the case remains good law. However, if the decision of the lower court is reversed or modified on appeal, it ceases to be good law to that extent. In a case involving various issues, one holding of the lower court may be affirmed, and another may be reversed, so a very careful reading of the

---

6. The U.S. Supreme Court rarely elects to hear cases of state law and does so only when state and federal law are intertwined. For example, a defamation claim against the press raises federal constitutional concerns, and the Supreme Court has addressed those concerns.

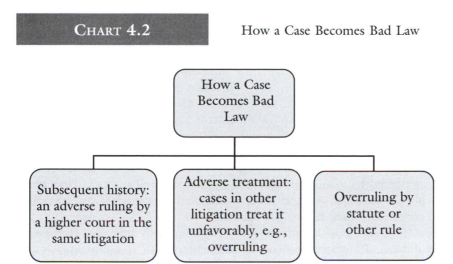

CHART 4.2 How a Case Becomes Bad Law

decisions is necessary. Thus this obvious point: most of the time, you will rely on the decision of the highest court in a case.

The second way in which a case ceases to be good law is through adverse treatment by later cases involving different parties. The common law evolves by accretion, as one case on a topic is overlaid on other earlier cases on the same topic. Generally, the cases take the same approach over time. Sometimes, however, the law changes because social policy has changed in some way. This happens in various ways. In the clearest example, a court, almost always the highest court, overrules an earlier case and replaces its rule with the rule in the new case. Less obviously, newer cases criticize the older case, decline to follow it, or distinguish it, such that its impact is diminished. To have an impact, this adverse treatment occurs within the jurisdiction of the case; what courts in other jurisdictions think of a case has little bearing on its authoritativeness.

Finally, some other form of law, typically a statute, may change the rule developed by the courts, as discussed in more detail in later chapters.

Although every decision matters to the litigants, not all decisions involve significant application or development of the law. Most courts other than the highest courts in a system identify some of their cases as not being of particular significance beyond the parties and so designate them as not to be "published." Before online databases, this distinction had functional significance; unpublished decisions were difficult for nonparties to find. Now it is very easy to find unpublished decisions. Even so, the distinction continues and should firmly guide your judgment about whether to consider a decision a significant one in your analysis. Courts differ on how citable their unpublished decisions are; you should know what the rule is in your jurisdiction.[7]

---

7. For example, Federal Rule of Appellate Procedure 32.1 prohibits a court from restricting the citation of recent unpublished decisions, so long as the party citing the unpublished case provides the other party a copy if the decision is not in a publicly accessible database.

Once you have identified the published cases that are good law and you have sorted them by position in the hierarchy of the courts in your jurisdiction, if the number is still high, you may need to consider some additional factors. One factor is age. Age by itself does not erode the weightiness of a case. On the other hand, a new case best reflects the court's current thinking. If a case was decided more recently than the client's events occurred, it still governs the client's case; case law is effective when the decision issues and is retrospective.[8]

A second factor is the degree of similarity between a case and the client's situation. This is a matter of both their legal issues and their factual situations. A case that is highly similar is called "on all fours"; these are rare. More often the best you will find is a case that is similar in major ways factually and raises the same legal issues; this case is called "on point."

A third factor is the quality of the decision, including how clearly reasoned it is and how comprehensively it discusses your research issue. A case that is often and favorably cited in later cases is called a "seminal case," is highly citable, and almost always merits consideration even if it is not a recent or highly similar case factually.

On occasion, you may consider persuasive cases, possibly because the courts in your jurisdiction have not yet addressed your client's issue or your client's factual context, or because they did so some time ago and the law elsewhere is shifting. In selecting persuasive cases to focus on, you should take into account all of the factors just stated as to mandatory precedents. Additional factors include which court is considered a leader in the area of law and which courts tend to rule similarly to yours on related topics.

For example, we chose to work with the *Luttrell* case as we analyzed Nichols' potential defamation claim for several reasons. It was decided in 1984 and designated for publication by the Court of Appeals of Kansas. As you will see later in this chapter, it was good law; indeed, it qualified as a seminal case. Nichols' facts were very similar to those of Luttrell, and we found the decision clear and comprehensive.

OVERVIEW OF CASE LAW RESEARCH OPTIONS

Given the centrality of cases in the American legal system, it is not surprising that resources for case law research abound. Choosing which resources to use in a specific situation has a significant impact on the second element of FEAT—the efficiency of your research. Note the use of the plural "resources"; you will use more than one resource to research cases. The key attributes of each resource are the size of its collection, its searching tools, its updating tools, and its cost.

---

8. On occasion, when a court issues a decision that changes the law significantly, it may soften its retrospectivity, such as limiting the damages the defendant must pay.

As a general proposition, the more cases from a jurisdiction a resource includes, the better. However, as previously noted, some cases are weightier than others, so a lack of unpublished cases, very old cases, and decisions from trial courts may not be problematic.

So too, as a general proposition, the stronger the search tools the resource affords, the better. Search tools vary significantly from resource to resource, in part as a function of media, but not entirely. The premier print resource, the West National Reporter System, has one of the best search tools, whereas some online resources are weaker on this score.

Somehow or other, as previously detailed, you must discern whether each case you plan to rely on is good law. Some resources include means for updating cases; others do not. This is one reason case law research involves use of more than one resource.

Perhaps the most difficult factor to consider is cost. In part, cost is a function of the cost of the resource. Using a print resource provided by a public law library, obtaining cases from a court database, or using an online service provided through a bar association are all less expensive than paying a fee to one of the major commercial online services. Cost is also a function of the time it takes to conduct the research and to do so properly. Thus the best means of containing costs is to become very adept at whatever resources are available to you and selecting the low-cost option when it will do the job as well as more expensive options.

As you consider the available resources, consider as well your specific research context. If you follow the process covered in Chapter 3, you will begin case law research with a significant idea of what you are looking for and perhaps even a reference to a leading case or two in your jurisdiction. On other occasions, you may not have such a reference and will be starting from scratch. On yet other occasions, you may be updating nearly complete research or simply obtaining a known case on your research issue. Experienced researchers likely would choose different resources for these different situations, as detailed next.

THE CLASSIC APPROACH: THE WEST REPORTER SYSTEM IN PRINT

Understanding the West system. In the pre-digital era (and to a certain extent still today), when a court issued a decision, called a "slip opinion," it sent print copies to the parties and also to a government publishing office. That office collected the slip opinions and published them in hardbound volumes, called "official reporters." Each volume contained the decisions from one or more courts in a specific timeframe on a wide range of topics. This system was better designed for collecting than researching cases.

The West Reporter System began in the late 1800s as a means of improving on the many official reporters being published around the country.

A commercial resource published by West (a business owned by Thomson Reuters), the West Reporter System provides federal and state court decisions in a set of reporters, as set out in Chart 4.3. To provide prompt publication, new cases appear first in soft-cover pamphlets, called "advance sheets"; once there are enough pages in a set of advance sheets, a hardbound volume is published. Each series contains hundreds of volumes, and many reporters are now in their second or third series.

The pattern of publication for state court decisions varies somewhat from state to state. The typical pattern is that the decisions of the state's intermediate court of appeals and highest court appear in a West regional reporter. A fairly small number of states do not have an intermediate court of appeals. Another variation is that a few states' decisions are published in West reporters focused on just that state. The West system has been so successful that many states no longer publish official reporters; rather, the West reporter serves as the official print reporter. Table 1 in *The Bluebook* and Appendix 1 of the *ALWD Citation Manual* provide state-by-state details.

As for federal cases, West publishes decisions of the U.S. Supreme Court in the *Supreme Court Reporter*; the U.S. Supreme Court publishes the official *United States Reports*. The West reporters are the official print reporters for the lower federal courts, with the *Federal Reporter* containing decisions of the courts of appeals and the *Federal Supplement* containing trial court decisions. West also publishes some federal court of appeals decisions not designated by the courts as published in the *Federal Appendix*.

Each case in a West reporter includes more than the decision itself. As shown in Exhibit 4.1, a case published in a West reporter is preceded by a several-sentence summary and then a series of what are called "headnotes." Each headnote consists of a sentence, with each sentence being a point stated in the court's decision. That sentence is preceded by two pieces of information. The first piece is the headnote's number within the case, which permits you to move from the headnote to the place in the decision—identified by a number in brackets—from which the West editor drew the point stated in the headnote.

The second piece of information is the genius of the West system. West has divided all of American law into over 400 topics and further divided each topic into, in most instances, hundreds of subtopics, each assigned a "key number." The key-number system cuts across all West reporters; thus, through this system, West topically and precisely categorizes the case law from around the country as it publishes the cases in the various reporters.

West's reporters are accompanied by the West digests, which serve as a highly sophisticated external finding tool for the West reporters. As detailed in Chart 4.3, each state court and the various federal courts are covered by one or more digests; there is a rough alignment between reporters and digests. A West digest typically consists of many volumes, organized alphabetically by topic. For each topic there appear pages of what are called "digest paragraphs," each followed by a reference to the case it describes, arrayed according to the numbered subtopics. The digest paragraphs are identical to the headnotes found at the beginning of the cases in the reporters. Exhibits 4.2 and 4.3 are from a digest, showing a partial table of contents for a topic and a page of headnotes, respectively.

| CHART 4.3 | | West National Reporter System |

Cases from these courts	appear in these West reporters (current series)	and are covered in these West digests (current series)
U.S. Supreme Court	*Supreme Court Reporter*	*United States Supreme Court Digest*; *Federal Practice Digest* (4th); older cases in *Modern Federal Practice Digest* and *Federal Digest*
Federal courts of appeals	*Federal Reporter* (3d) and *Federal Appendix*	*Federal Practice Digest* (4th); older cases in *Modern Federal Practice Digest* and *Federal Digest*
Federal district (trial) courts	*Federal Supplement* (2d); older cases in *Federal Reporter*	*Federal Practice Digest* (4th); older cases in *Modern Federal Practice Digest* and *Federal Digest*
Connecticut, Delaware, District of Columbia, Maine, Maryland, New Hampshire, New Jersey, Pennsylvania, Rhode Island, Vermont	*Atlantic Reporter* (3d)	*Atlantic Digest* (2d); state digests, except for Delaware, including federal cases from state
Illinois, Indiana, Massachusetts, New York, Ohio	*North Eastern Reporter* (2d); also *New York Supplement* (2d)	State digests, including federal cases from state
Iowa, Michigan, Minnesota, Nebraska, North Dakota, South Dakota, Wisconsin	*North Western Reporter* (2d)	*North Western Digest* (2d); state digests (North Dakota and South Dakota are merged), including federal cases from state
Alaska, Arizona, California, Colorado, Hawaii, Idaho, Kansas, Montana, Nevada, New Mexico, Oklahoma, Oregon, Utah, Washington, Wyoming	*Pacific Reporter* (3d); also *California Reporter* (3d)	*Pacific Digest* (2d); state digests, except Nevada and Utah, including federal cases from state
Georgia, North Carolina, South Carolina, Virginia, West Virginia	*South Eastern Reporter* (2d)	*South Eastern Digest* (2d); state digests (Virginia and West Virginia are merged), including federal cases from state
Arkansas, Kentucky, Missouri, Tennessee, Texas	*South Western Reporter* (3d)	State digests, including federal cases from state
Alabama, Florida, Louisiana, Mississippi	*Southern Reporter* (3d)	State digests, including federal cases from state

EXHIBIT 4.2　　　　Table of Contents for Digest Topic

LIBEL & SLANDER

20B Kan D 2d—30

I. WORDS AND ACTS ACTIONABLE, AND LIABILITY THEREFOR.—Continued.

II. PRIVILEGED COMMUNICATIONS, AND MALICE THEREIN.

EXHIBIT 4.3	Digest Paragraphs

20B Kan D 2d—51

·LIBEL & SLANDER ☞25

For references to other topics, see Descriptive-Word Index

publication of matter that is both defamatory and false; where defendant establishes truth of matter charged as defamatory, defendant is justified in law, and exempt from all civil responsibility.

> Walker v. Couture, 804 F.Supp. 1408.

Kan. 1987. For there to be liability for defamation there must be publication of matter that is both defamatory and false; where published statements are substantially true, there is no liability and motion for summary judgment is proper.

> Ruebke v. Globe Communications Corp., 738 P.2d 1246, 241 Kan. 595.

Kan.App. 2001. Intentional or negligent communication of the defamatory matter is called "publication," and the person making the communication is called the "publisher." Restatement (Second) of Torts § 577(1).

> Wright v. Bachmurski, 29 P.3d 979, 29 Kan.App.2d 595, review denied.

Kan.App. 1984. Remarks made in course and scope of employment by one corporate employee and communicated to second corporate employee concerning job performance of third employee are publication for purposes of defamation action against corporate employer. K.S.A. 60–212(b)(6).

> Luttrell v. United Telephone System, Inc., 683 P.2d 1292, 9 Kan.App.2d 620, 47 A.L.R.4th 669, affirmed 695 P.2d 1279, 236 Kan. 710.

☞**24. ——— Slander.**

D.Kan. 1995. Remarks communicated by one corporate employee to another concerning job performance of third employee are publication for purposes of defamation action against employer.

> Deghand v. Wal-Mart Stores, Inc., 904 F.Supp. 1218.

Kan. 1985. Interoffice communications between supervisory employees of a corporation, acting within scope and course of their employment, regarding work of another employee of corporation constituted publication to a third person sufficient to support maintenance of defamation action against corporation.

> Luttrell v. United Telephone System, Inc., 695 P.2d 1279, 236 Kan. 710.

Kan.App. 2004. Hotel operator's alleged refusal to rent rooms to church youth group because members would "make too much noise" would not support slander claim without evidence of publication to third party, and, thus, personal injury coverage for slander in hotel operator's commercial general liability (CGL) insurance policy did not apply; there was no evidence that anyone but the group members

heard the comments about the potential for noise from the group.

> Rockgate Management Co. v. CGU Ins., Inc./PG Ins. Co. of New York, 88 P.3d 798.

An indispensable element of slander is the communication of the defamation to at least one person other than the person defamed.

> Rockgate Management Co. v. CGU Ins., Inc./PG Ins. Co. of New York, 88 P.3d 798.

Kan.App. 2001. Litigant could not recover for defamation based on a statement that adverse party's attorney made to him, absent any allegation that the statement was communicated to a third party.

> Gatlin v. Hartley, Nicholson, Hartley & Arnett, P.A., 26 P.3d 1284, 29 Kan.App.2d 318.

☞**25. ——— Libel.**

D.Kan. 1986. Intragovernmental communication of accusation that former city employee engaged in unprofessional conduct constituted "communication," for purposes of city employee's defamation claim against city and city personnel director, under Kansas law. K.S.A. 75–6103(a).

> Polson v. Davis, 635 F.Supp. 1130, affirmed 895 F.2d 705.

"Communication" element of defamation under Kansas law was satisfied by alleged conduct of city and city personnel director in granting press access to former city employee's personnel notebook and notice of termination in notebook, which accused employee of unprofessional conduct.

> Polson v. Davis, 635 F.Supp. 1130, affirmed 895 F.2d 705.

Kan. 1906. Where a person writes a defamatory letter, and sends it in a sealed envelope through the mail to the person defamed, who receives and reads the contents thereof to a third person, such reading is not a publication of the libel by the writer for the purposes of a civil action.

> Lyon v. Lash, 88 P. 262, 74 Kan. 745, 11 Am.Ann.Cas. 424.

Kan.App. 2001. Under the "single publication rule," a single issue or single edition of a periodical or book constitutes a single publication. Restatement (Second) of Torts § 577A.

> Wright v. Bachmurski, 29 P.3d 979, 29 Kan.App.2d 595, review denied.

Kan.App. 1989. Employee could not recover on defamation claim in connection with termination of his employment, where there was no evidence of publication or communica-

† This Case was not selected for publication in the National Reporter System

For example, the *Luttrell* case was published in the *Pacific Reporter*,[9] second series, volume 683, beginning at page 1292, shortly after it was decided in 1984. The West editor who prepared the case decided that it provided eight points of law, most falling within the topic of Libel and Slander, one falling within Corporations. The seventh headnote captured the point for which we read *Luttrell*.

Using the West system. Because the West system has so dominated publishing of American cases for so many years, when you find a reference to a case in some other source, such as commentary, it is likely to include its location in a West reporter. In this situation, finding the case is easy enough: simply locate the proper reporter, series, and volume on the shelf, and turn to the right page number.

The power of the West system is in the digest. That is, once you identify the topic and key numbers that pertain to your research issue, in the digest you will find headnotes and references to the cases in the West reporters. Using a digest to its fullest entails four steps sketched in Chart 4.4.

1.   Select a digest that covers your jurisdiction. If you can use a state digest for researching state law, this is more efficient than using a regional digest, which encompasses various states. When researching federal law, you generally will use the *Federal Practice Digest*.

2.   Identify the pertinent topic and key numbers. Almost always, you will want to explore more than one key number within the topic. In some situations, you will want to explore more than one topic as well. One way to accomplish this task is to work off of a case you have already identified, such as through commentary research. Another option is to scan the list of digest topics found at the beginning of a digest volume. A third option is to use the Descriptive Word Index, which is an index to the West digest system. See Exhibit 4.4.[10] However you begin, it is always wise to scan the table of contents for the topic to identify all potentially pertinent key numbers and to obtain the editor's view of the legal framework into which your research issue fits.

3.   Read the headnotes listed under the key numbers you have identified in the main, bound volume. Then look for newer entries in any pocket part or supplementary pamphlet to the digest. Also check the digest pages in the volumes and advance sheets whose cases are not covered in the most recent update to the digest. Depending on how many cases this research yields, consider looking at entries in an older series of the digest, if indeed there is one that is not incorporated into the current one.[11]

9. Created over a hundred years ago, the *Pacific Reporter* covers a huge geographical region, including (yes) Kansas.

10. The topics and subtopics are the same across reporters, so any Descriptive Word Index should yield the same information.

11. From time to time, West updates a topic by reconfiguring the key numbers. The old numbers remain with the cases in the reporters. A conversion table in the digest facilitates working with the old and new configurations.

EXHIBIT 4.4   Descriptive Word Index

37B Minn D 2d–13   **LIBEL**

References are to Digest Topics and Key Numbers

LIBEL AND SLANDER—Cont'd
PROFESSION or business—Cont'd
Words injuring in—Cont'd

Ministers, Libel ☞ 9(4)
Newspapers, Libel ☞ 9(8)
Physician and surgeons, Libel ☞ 9(2)
Professors, Libel ☞ 9(5)
Storekeepers, Libel ☞ 9(7)
Teachers, Libel ☞ 9(5)
Tradesmen, Libel ☞ 9(7)
Written or printed words, Libel ☞ 18

PROFESSORS, words injuring in profession,
Libel ☞ 9(5)

PROSTITUTION, imputation of, Libel
☞ 7(19)

PROVOCATION,
Mitigation grounds, Libel ☞ 63
Qualified privilege, Libel ☞ 47

PUBLIC,
Duty, discharge of as qualified privilege,
Generally, Libel ☞ 43
Malice, effect on privilege, Libel ☞ 51(4)
Employees, privileged communications. See
subheading EMPLOYEES under this
heading.
Matters or figures, privilege in criticism or
comment. See subheading
PRIVILEGED communications under
this heading.
Officers. See subheading OFFICERS under
this heading.

PUBLICATION of words or acts,
Generally, Libel ☞ 23.1-25
Complaint, declaration or petition, Libel
☞ 84
Criminal responsibility,
Generally, Libel ☞ 146
Furnishing libelous information for
publication, Libel ☞ 147
Evidence,
Admissibility, Libel ☞ 106
Burden of proof, Libel ☞ 101(3)
Other publications, admissibility. See
Other publications, admissibility,
generally, under subheading
PUBLICATION of words or acts.
Presumptions and inferences, Libel
☞ 101(3)
Indictment and information, criminal
proceedings, Libel ☞ 152(4)
Justification, publication by others as facts
constituting, Libel ☞ 56(3)
Libel, Libel ☞ 25
Mitigation grounds, publications by others,
Libel ☞ 64

LIBEL AND SLANDER—Cont'd
PUBLICATION of words or acts—Cont'd

News, privileged communications,
Generally, Libel ☞ 49
Malice, effect on privilege, Libel ☞ 51(5)
Other publications, admissibility,
Inducement and extrinsic matter, Libel
☞ 105(2)
Intent and malice, Libel ☞ 104(3-5)
Retraction. See subheading RETRACTION,
generally, under this heading.
Slander, Libel ☞ 24

PUNITIVE damages. See subheading
EXEMPLARY damages, generally, under
this heading.

QUALIFIED privilege. See subheading
PRIVILEGED communications under
this heading.

QUASI-judicial proceedings, absolute
privilege, Libel ☞ 36

RAPE, imputation of, Libel ☞ 7(18)

RECKLESSNESS, exemplary damages for,
Libel ☞ 120(2)

RECORDS, absolute privilege of official
records, Libel ☞ 39

RELIGIOUS societies, qualified privilege,
Common interest of members, Libel
☞ 45(3)
Reports of proceedings, Libel ☞ 42(3)

REPARATION, grounds for mitigation, Libel
☞ 66

REPETITION of words or acts,
Generally, Libel ☞ 26.1-29
By others, Libel ☞ 28
By same person, Libel ☞ 27
Hearsay or rumors, as, Libel ☞ 29

REPLICATION or reply and subsequent
pleadings, Libel ☞ 96

REPORTS,
Absolute privilege, official reports, Libel
☞ 39
Qualified privilege,
Generally, Libel ☞ 42(.5-3)
Association proceedings, Libel ☞ 42(3)
Credit reports, Libel ☞ 44(4)
Executive proceedings and investigations,
Libel ☞ 42(2)
Judicial proceedings, Libel ☞ 42(1)
Legislative proceedings and
investigations, Libel ☞ 42(2)
Mercantile standing, Libel ☞ 44(4)
Religious proceedings, Libel ☞ 42(3)

4. As you read the various headnotes, look for points that most clearly pertain to your research issue. Also categorize the cases according to the factors discussed in this chapter. That is, if you are researching an issue of state law in a state digest, it will include both state court cases and federal cases in which the court applied state law. The most important cases are from the state's highest court, then the state's intermediate court of appeals, then the federal courts.

By way of example, had we not had a lead on *Luttrell* from a commentary source, we could have found it as follows: The list of topics revealed that, while defamation was not a topic, Libel & Slander was. Alternatively, in the Descriptive Word Index, the entry for "defamation" provided a cross-reference to the heading "libel and slander," under which was a subheading for "publication," which pointed to Libel 23.1–25, as shown in Exhibit 4.4. As shown in Exhibit 4.2, the table of contents for the Libel & Slander topic confirmed that key numbers 23–25 were the most pertinent. Looking at the digest paragraphs under key number 23, shown in Exhibit 4.3, in the left column we found a digest paragraph setting out the point about intra-corporate publication drawn from *Luttrell*, followed by a reference to the case. We also noted that the *Polson* case described in the right column of Exhibit 4.3 pertained to publication about an employee within the company; however, as a federal trial court case (as evidenced by "D. Kan." and the reference to "F. Supp."), it was not as weighty.

An important limitation of the West reporter system is true of all reporters: once a case appears in a reporter, it stays there, even though the law may move beyond it. That is, reporters are not themselves updated. To update the law in a reporter, you use a case citator, described in the next section.

CHART 4.4   Use of West Digests

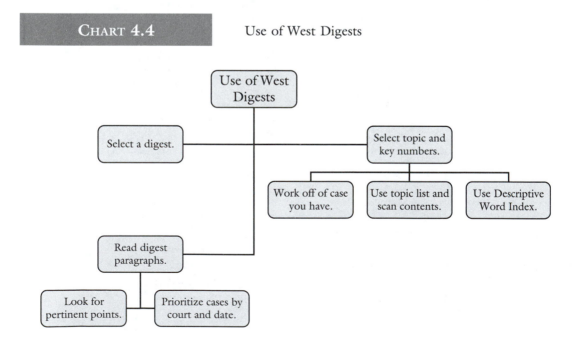

THE MAJOR COMMERCIAL ONLINE SERVICES: WESTLAW AND LEXISNEXIS

For about forty years, two commercial online services—Westlaw and Lexis-Nexis—have competed to provide the most extensive and elaborate online resource for case law research. Both provide extensive collections of federal and state cases, generally extending back to the starting dates of each court, encompassing just-issued decisions, and including many unpublished cases. Both package the cases into various databases so that you can choose to search cases by issuing court, for example. Both provide various ways to search for cases within the databases. Finally, both provide sophisticated updating tools.

Not surprisingly, many lawyers think of these two services as the gold standard for online case law research. A gold-standard product can be expensive, so it is important to be aware of the pricing structure for all research you conduct in these services. In addition, proficiency is key to using either in an efficient way. Most lawyers become proficient in one service or the other, depending on availability. Because the services change on a regular basis, proficiency is something of a moving target; it is important to stay up to date on the innovations each offers. Accordingly, the following discussion is somewhat general; consulting the service's current training materials should provide any needed details.

Westlaw. Westlaw can be used for various research purposes. For example, to obtain a copy of a known case, simply enter its citation in the Find function. The following discussion focuses on using Westlaw to find not-yet-identified pertinent cases. Proficient use of Westlaw in this setting involves careful selection of a database; skilled drafting of some type of search; systematic collection of pertinent cases; and use of Westlaw's citator, KeyCite.

Westlaw packages cases into many databases. You should select the database that contains what you need and little else, to avoid an overwhelming number of cases. Ordinarily, you will choose the database containing the cases from your jurisdiction's courts. An alternative is to select a database containing cases from various jurisdictions discussing a particular practice area. When you first research in a new database, it pays to read its identifying information by clicking on the database information icon.

Westlaw offers many means of searching a database. The classic is the terms-and-connectors (Boolean) search, in which you tightly control the search by specifying the words and their relationships; Westlaw offers additional terms to incorporate. See the results list for our illustrative problem in Exhibit 4.5. A second option is a natural-language search, in which the program weights your terms and presents the cases in order of descending probable pertinence. Two other options take advantage of West's significant editorial work. One is using a West key number as a search term. Another is KeySearch, which entails drilling down through topic/subtopic choices provided by Westlaw, thereby tapping into searches already written by West editors. Finally, searches can be honed by specifying the dates of decisions or fields to search, such as the headnotes or case titles.

Westlaw recently introduced a new platform, WestlawNext. Researching in WestlawNext entails selecting a jurisdiction and entering a "plain language" search, i.e., any combination of search terms. The search runs in Westlaw's vast collection of documents.[12] Unless you specify otherwise, your results span over a dozen categories of sources: cases; other legal authorities, such as statutes and regulations; commentary; and practitioner documents, such as briefs actually filed in litigation. The search operates through a sophisticated technology that builds not only on key numbers but also on patterns of searches West has identified. (These two features have prompted many observers to see WestlawNext as similar to Google.) The results are arrayed with the documents identified as most likely to be pertinent listed first, within each category. See the results list in Exhibit 4.6. The Westlaw search options are summarized in Chart 4.5.

However you search for cases, and you may want to run more than one search, you are likely to amass quite a list of cases. From the results list, you generally can discern which cases to read by reading the excerpt of text in which your research terms appear, and you can sort the cases by court, date, and publication status. See Exhibits 4.5 and 4.6.

The next step is to link to the cases—one of the clear advantages of online research in a cases database.

CHART 4.5	Westlaw Search Options

Find	Retrieve a known case by citation.
Terms and connectors	Find cases that fit requirements of your Boolean search.
Natural language	Find cases the program identifies as most likely to be pertinent based on weighting of terms you enter.
Key number	Find cases that have headnotes falling under topics and key numbers you specify.
KeySearch	Find cases obtained through search written by West editors, identified by selecting from topic/subtopic choices.
WestlawNext	Find cases (and other documents) through plain-language search you enter that taps into various analyses of West editors.

12. When the service launched, West indicated that its collection numbered over 2 billion documents.

EXHIBIT 4.5	Results List from Westlaw

Westlaw.

QUERY - EMPLOYEE EMPLOYER /S DEFAM!   DATABASE(S) - KS-CS-ALL
LIBEL SLANDER /S PUBLISH! PUBLICA-
TION

1.   **C**   Lindemuth v. Goodyear Tire and Rubber Co.,
19 Kan.App.2d 95, 864 P.2d 744, 1993 WL 504450, 148 L.R.R.M. (BNA) 2571, Kan.App.,
December 10, 1993 (NO. 69,604)

...2d at 622, 683 P.2d 1292 The Luttrell court further stated: "We conclude that remarks communicated by one corporate employee to another concerning the job performance of a third employee are publication for the purposes of a defamation action against the employer." Luttrell, 9
Kan.App.2d at 623, 683 P.2d 1292 [7] When a conditional or qualified privilege exists, a
plaintiff...

2.   **H**   Batt v. Globe Engineering Co., Inc.,
13 Kan.App.2d 500, 774 P.2d 371, 1989 WL 53248, Kan.App., May 19, 1989 (NO. 62,739)

...appealed. The Court of Appeals, Rulon, P.J., held that: (1) trial court properly excluded tran-
script from unemployment compensation hearing; (2) employee could not recover on defamation
claim, where there was no evidence of publication or communication of contents of separation
notice beyond management personnel; (3) employee could not recover on breach of contract
claim, where employee failed to present sufficient evidence of an implied employment contract
and his testimony established that he had been discharged for ...

...237 106 k. Publication. 237 Libel and Slander 237IV Actions 237IV(C) Evidence 237 102 Admissibility 237 109 k. Privilege. Employee could not use his supervisor's testimony at unemployment compensation hearing to demonstrate either supervisor's actual malice or publication of alleged defamatory statements, although arguably supervisor's alleged statements at the hearing
were, at least in part, the basis for his defamation claim. [8] 13 Action 13I Grounds and Conditions Precedent 13 6 k. Moot, Hypothetical or Abstract Questions. Issue whether allowing ...

...12] 237 Libel and Slander 237I Words and Acts Actionable, and Liability Therefor 237 23 Publication 237 25 k. Libel. Employee could not recover on defamation claim in connection with termination of his employment, where there was no evidence of publication or communication of
contents of separation notice beyond management personnel. [13] 231H Labor and Employment
231HI In General 231H 37...

3.   **H**   Luttrell v. United Telephone System, Inc.,
236 Kan. 710, 695 P.2d 1279, 102 Lab.Cas. P 55,495, Kan., March 02, 1985 (NO. 56031)

...P.2d 1292, reversed and remanded. Review was granted. The Supreme Court, Prager, J., held
that interoffice communications between supervisory employees of a corporation, acting within
scope and course of their employment, regarding work of another employee of corporation constituted publication to a third person sufficient to support maintenance of defamation action
against corporation. Judgment of district court reversed and remanded; judgment of Court of Appeals affirmed. West Headnotes 237 Libel ...

EXHIBIT 4.6	Results List from WestlawNext

WestlawNext™

Overview (14)

Set Default

VIEW:

Overview	14
Cases	122
Statutes	47
Regulations	3,364
Administrative Decisions & Guidance	3,647
Trial Court Orders	20
Secondary Sources	1,586
Forms	32
Briefs	143
Pleadings, Motions & Memoranda	79
Expert Materials	1,145
Jury Verdicts & Settlements	580
Proposed & Enacted Legislation	1,386
Proposed & Adopted Regulations	5,741
All Results	17,892

☐ Select all items   No items selected

Cases   View all 122

☐   **Luttrell v. United Telephone System, Inc.**
Court of Appeals of Kansas.   July 19, 1984   9 Kan.App.2d 620

Employee brought action against employer alleging that statements by managerial employees concerning employee's job performance constituted **defamation**.   The District Court, Johnson...

...Remarks made in the course and scope of **employment** by one corporate employee and communicated to a second corporate employee concerning the job performance of a third employee constitute **publication** for the purposes of a **defamation** action against the corporate employer...

...[7][8] We conclude that remarks communicated by one corporate employee to another concerning the job performance of a third employee are **publication** for the purposes of a **defamation** action against the employer...

☐   **Gertz v. Robert Welch, Inc.**
Supreme Court of the United States   June 25, 1974   418 U.S. 323

Libel action was brought against **publisher** of magazine article describing plaintiff as a 'Communist-fronter,' 'Leninist' and participant in various...

...'a vindicatory function by enabling the plaintiff publicly to brand the defamatory **publication** as false...

...At the very least, the rule allowed the recovery of nominal damages for any defamatory **publication** actionable per se and thus performed...

Statutes   View all 47

☐   **60-514.   Actions limited to one year**
KS ST 60-514   West's Kansas Statutes Annotated

West's Kansas Statutes Annotated
    Chapter 60. Procedure, Civil
        Article 5. Limitations of Actions
            Personal Actions and General Provisions

...Under Kansas law, as predicted by federal district court, statute of limitations for **defamation** based on oral statement regarding individual's **employment** history does not begin to run until discovery of the **publication**...

...Under Kansas law, plaintiff must bring suit for **defamation** within one year of **publication** of alleged defamatory statement....

Regulations   View all 3,364

☐   **Appendix to Part 600--Commentary on the Fair Credit Reporting Act**
16 C.F.R. Pt. 600. App.   Code of Federal Regulations

...A consumer reporting agency that furnishes public record information for **employment** purposes must comply with either subsection (1) or (2), but need not comply with both....

...When a consumer reporting agency furnishes public record information in reports "for **employment** purposes," it must follow the procedure set out in section 613....

Administrative Decisions & Guidance   View all 3,647

☐   **In re Beverly Health and Rehabilitation Services, Inc.**
N.L.R.B.   August 08, 2000   331 NLRB No. 121

...The judge further observed that, to be actionable under Linn, labor speech must be defamatory, false, and **published** with malice...

...The alleged **defamation** is that false and defamatory statements **published** with malice accused Respondent of providing substandard care to the patients and residents in its nursing homes...

Trial Court Orders   View all 20

☐   **Paul F. HOFER, et al., Plaintiffs, v. STAN CRAMER, et al., Defendants.**
District Court of Kansas, Wyandotte County   September 16, 1999   No. 99C 00914.

...To qualify as defamatory, a statement must "tend to expose another living person to public hatred, contempt or ridicule."...

A case obtained through Westlaw has the same content, including the headnotes, as the print version, although it has a bit of a different look. See Exhibit 4.7. From the digital version, you can extend your research by linking to the references to older, potentially pertinent cases.

A major advantage of conducting case law research on Westlaw is Key-Cite, its citator. Indeed, you may well use KeyCite even if you research primarily in some other resource because it serves the critical updating function so effectively. Recall that you must verify that a case you find remains good law. In citator jargon the case you have read and are updating is the "cited case." KeyCite provides three kinds of information about the cited case: (1) its history, i.e., decisions in the same litigation preceding and following the cited case; (2) its treatment in decisions in other litigation, which are called "citing cases"; and (3) references to sources other than cases, such as commentary, that discuss the cited case. See Exhibit 4.8. KeyCite has various features that permit you to process the citing references efficiently, including symbols that capture whether a cited case is indeed good law, and an indication of the extent of the discussion of the cited case in the citing case. See Chart 4.6.

CHART 4.6	KeyCite Symbols and Labels[13]

Red flag	Cited case is no longer good law for at least one cited point.
Yellow flag	Cited case has some adverse treatment but has not been reversed or overruled.
Blue H	Cited case has history that gives rise to neither red flag nor yellow flag.
Green C	Cited case has citing references but no direct or indirect negative history.
**** Examined, preceding list of citing cases	Discussion of cited case in citing cases is extended, running a page or more.
*** Discussed, preceding list of citing cases	Discussion of cited case in citing cases runs more than a paragraph but less than a page.
** Cited, preceding list of citing cases	Discussion of cited case in citing cases runs a paragraph or less.
* Mentioned, preceding list of citing cases	Citing cases only briefly refer to cited case.
"	Citing case quotes cited case.
HN #	Number of headnote in cited case for which citing case refers to cited case.

13. WestlawNext uses a somewhat different format, but the content is the same.

EXHIBIT 4.7   Case from WestlawNext

WestlawNext™

Luttrell v. United Telephone System, Inc.
See Original Image of 236 Kan. 710 (PDF)
Supreme Court of Kansas   March 2, 1985   236 Kan. 710   695 P.2d 1279
695 P.2d 1279
Supreme Court of Kansas.

Marvin G. LUTTRELL, Appellant,

v.

UNITED TELEPHONE SYSTEM, INC., Appellee.

No. 56031.   March 2, 1985.

Employee of corporation brought defamation action against corporation. The District
Court, Johnson County, Phillip L. Woodworth, J., dismissed action for failure to state a
claim upon which relief could be granted, and employee appealed. The Court of
Appeals, 9 Kan.App.2d 620, 683 P.2d 1292, reversed and remanded. Review was
granted. The Supreme Court, Prager, J., held that interoffice communications between
supervisory employees of a corporation, acting within scope and course of their
employment, regarding work of another employee of corporation constituted publication
to a third person sufficient to support maintenance of defamation action against
corporation.

Judgment of district court reversed and remanded; judgment of Court of Appeals
affirmed.

West Headnotes (1)

Change View

1   **Libel and Slander** 🔑   Slander
     Interoffice communications between supervisory employees of a corporation,
     acting within scope and course of their employment, regarding work of
     another employee of corporation constituted publication to a third person
     sufficient to support maintenance of defamation action against corporation.

     25 Cases that cite this headnote

**1279 *710 Syllabus by the Court
Remarks made in the course and scope of employment by one corporate employee and
communicated to a second corporate employee concerning the job performance of a
third employee constitute publication for the purposes of a defamation action against the
corporate employer.

Attorneys and Law Firms

Richard M. Smith, of Smith & Winter-Smith, Mound City, argued the cause and was on
the brief, for appellant.

Paul Hasty, Jr., of Wallace, Saunders, Austin, Brown & Enochs, Chartered, Overland
Park, argued the cause, and James L. Sanders, Overland Park, of the same firm, was
with him on the brief, for appellee.

Wendell F. Cowan, Jr., of Cowan, Jarboe & Korte, Topeka, was on the brief amicus
curiae for IBP, Inc.

Opinion

PRAGER, Justice:

EXHIBIT 4.7   *(continued)*

Luttrell v. United Telephone System, Inc. - WestlawNext

This case is before the court on a petition for review of a decision of the Court of
Appeals in *Luttrell v. United Telephone System, Inc.,* 9 Kan.App.2d 620, 683 P.2d 1292
(1984). The facts are fully set forth in the opinion of the Court of Appeals and need not
be repeated here. The trial court sustained the motion of the defendant to dismiss for
failure to state a claim upon which relief may be granted. The Court of Appeals reversed
and remanded the case for further proceeding. We granted review. The Court of
Appeals fully discussed the facts and applicable law. We have carefully examined the
record, the briefs of the parties, the reported cases in Kansas and other jurisdictions,
and the commentary on the subject. We find no reason to disturb the judgment of the
Court of Appeals.

The issue presented is strictly one of law and, simply stated, is whether interoffice
communications between supervisory employees of a corporation, acting within the
scope and course of their employment, regarding the work of another employee of *711
the corporation, constitute publications to a third person sufficient for a defamation
action.

The opinion of Judge Parks points out there is considerable division of authority
concerning this issue. The various cases supporting each position are cited. The opinion
points out that Professor Prosser favors the view that such communication **1280
constitutes a publication and rejects those cases that hold otherwise as confusing
publication with privilege. Prosser, Law of Torts § 113, p. 767 n. 70 (4th ed. 1971).

In addition, we note that Restatement (Second) of Torts § 577, comment *i* (1977),
adopts the position that a communication within the scope of his employment by one
agent to another agent of the same principal is a publication not only by the first agent
but also by the principal and this is true whether the principal is an individual, a
partnership or a corporation.

We adopt the opinion of the Court of Appeals.

The judgment of the district court is reversed and the case is remanded to the trial court
for further proceedings. The judgment of the Court of Appeals is affirmed.

Parallel Citations

695 P.2d 1279, 102 Lab.Cas. P 55,495

End of Document   © 2011 Thomson Reuters. No claim to original U.S. Government Works.

Preferences   My Contacts   Getting Started   Help   Sign Off

WestlawNext. © 2011 Thomson Reuters   Privacy   Accessibility   Contact Us   1-800-REF-ATTY (1-800-733-2889)   Improve WestlawNext

 THOMSON REUTERS

EXHIBIT 4.8	KeyCite Report for Case

Westlaw.

Date of Printing: Jun 14, 2011

KEYCITE

▷ Luttrell v. United Telephone System, Inc., 9 Kan.App.2d 620, 683 P.2d 1292, 47 A.L.R.4th 669 (Kan.App.,Jul 19, 1984) (NO. 56,031)

History

Direct History

=>   1 **Luttrell v. United Telephone System, Inc.,** 9 Kan.App.2d 620, 683 P.2d 1292, 47 A.L.R.4th 669 (Kan.App. Jul 19, 1984) (NO. 56,031)

Judgment Affirmed by

→H   2 Luttrell v. United Telephone System, Inc., 236 Kan. 710, 695 P.2d 1279, 102 Lab.Cas. P 55,495 (Kan. Mar 02, 1985) (NO. 56031)

Negative Citing References (U.S.A.)

Declined to Follow by

▶   3 Bals v. Verduzco, 564 N.E.2d 307, 6 IER Cases 54 (Ind.App. 3 Dist. Dec 19, 1990) (NO. 64A03-9006-CV-218) *

C   4 Charleswell v. Bank of Nova Scotia, 2001 WL 1464759 (Terr.V.I. May 01, 2001) (NO. 605/96) * * **HN: 7 (P.2d)**

EXHIBIT 4.8   *(continued)*

Westlaw.

Date of Printing: Jun 14, 2011

KEYCITE

▷ Luttrell v. United Telephone System, Inc., 9 Kan.App.2d 620, 683 P.2d 1292, 47 A.L.R.4th 669 (Kan.App. Jul 19, 1984) (NO. 56,031)

Citing References: limited to Headnotes = 7(P.2d), selected document types

Negative Cases (U.S.A.)

Declined to Follow by

C 1 Charleswell v. Bank of Nova Scotia, 2001 WL 1464759, *4 (Terr.V.I. May 01, 2001) (NO. 605/96) * * HN: 7 (P.2d)

Positive Cases (U.S.A.)

★ ★ ★ ★   Examined

▷ 2 Naab v. Inland Container Corp., 1994 WL 70268, *1+, 129 Lab.Cas. P 57,768, 57768+ (D.Kan. Feb 28, 1994) (NO. 93-1501-PFK) HN: 6,7,8 (P.2d)

★ ★ ★   Discussed

C 3 Lindemuth v. Goodyear Tire and Rubber Co., 864 P.2d 744, 750+, 19 Kan.App.2d 95, 102+, 148 L.R.R.M. (BNA) 2571, 2571+ (Kan.App. Dec 10, 1993) (NO. 69,604) " HN: 5,6,7 (P.2d)

H 4 Etzel v. Musicland Group, Inc., 1993 WL 23741, *7+, 8 IER Cases 483, 483+ (D.Kan. Jan 08, 1993) (NO. 91-4231-SAC) " HN: 2,7,8 (P.2d)

H 5 Polson v. Davis, 635 F.Supp. 1130, 1146+, 51 Fair Empl.Prac.Cas. (BNA) 307, 307+ (D.Kan. Apr 25, 1986) (NO. CIV. A. 84-2211) " HN: 2,6,7 (P.2d)

C 6 Hagebak v. Stone, 61 P.3d 201, 205+, 133 N.M. 75, 79+, 2003-NMCA-007, 007+ (N.M.App. Dec 09, 2002) (NO. 22,486) " HN: 6,7 (P.2d)

★ ★   Cited

H 7 Batt v. Globe Engineering Co., Inc., 774 P.2d 371, 375+, 13 Kan.App.2d 500, 504+ (Kan.App. May 19, 1989) (NO. 62,739) HN: 1,2,7 (P.2d)

C 8 Auld v. Value Place Property Management LLC, 2010 WL 610690, *5 (D.Kan. Feb 19, 2010) (NO. 09-1139-EFM) HN: 7 (P.2d)

H 9 Sunlight Saunas, Inc. v. Sundance Sauna, Inc., 427 F.Supp.2d 1032, 1071+, 2006-1 Trade Cases P 75,252, 75252+ (D.Kan. Apr 17, 2006) (NO. CIV.A. 04-2597-KHV) HN: 2,7 (P.2d)

H 10 Ali v. Douglas Cable Communications, 929 F.Supp. 1362, 1384+ (D.Kan. May 24, 1996) (NO. 94-1146-SAC) HN: 1,2,7 (P.2d)

H 11 Deghand v. Wal-Mart Stores, Inc., 904 F.Supp. 1218, 1223+, 34 Fed.R.Serv.3d 247, 247+ (D.Kan. Oct 12, 1995) (NO. 94-4172-SAC) " HN: 5,7 (P.2d)

In addition, a KeyCite entry identifies for which of the cited case's headnotes the citing case cites the cited case.[14]

KeyCite is fairly seamlessly integrated into cases on Westlaw. That is, a case's symbol appears at the beginning of the case when you pull it up from a database, and you can link directly to the KeyCite report from the case. In addition, you can link from a listing in KeyCite to the citing case or other document.

For example, we researched the intra-corporate communication issue in the Casey Nichols case in Westlaw four different ways. We used the KS-CS-ALL database, containing decisions of the Kansas state and federal courts. Our Boolean search, *employee employer/s defam! libel slander/s publish! publication,* yielded sixty cases. See Exhibit 4.5 for the results list for this search. Our natural-language search was *Is an intra-corporate statement a publication for defamation purposes?;* we obtained the pre-programmed 100 cases. A search for the key number we found through the digest yielded twenty cases, and a KeySearch search focused on defamation and publication yielded eighteen cases. We also researched in WestlawNext, focusing on Kansas state and federal courts as our jurisdiction and using *defamation publication employment* as our search. See Exhibit 4.6 for the results list for this search.

Not surprisingly all of our searches yielded the *Luttrell* case—not only the 1984 decision from the Kansas Court of Appeals, but also the 1985 decision by the Kansas Supreme Court affirming the court of appeals decision. See Exhibit 4.7. You may wonder why the supreme court decision did not surface in the research conducted in print resources discussed earlier. One half of the answer is: it did, but not as obviously. The digest referred to the supreme court decision ("affirmed 695 P.2d 1279"), and the copy of the court of appeals decision in the print reporter noted "Review Granted" below the title. The second half of the answer is that the supreme court adopted the reasoning and outcome of the court of appeals decision, rendering that decision unusually weighty for a court of appeals decision in a case that has been reviewed by the highest court.

All of this was revealed as well in the KeyCite report for the court of appeals decision, shown in Exhibit 4.8. The first page provided information about the case's direct history. That page covered its affirmance by the supreme court (item number 2) and two negative references from courts in Indiana and the Virgin Islands (items 3 and 4)—thus establishing that the case was good law. The second page of Exhibit 4.8 listed cases that discussed *Luttrell* for the point of interest to us; we confined the printout to documents citing *Luttrell* for the point in headnote 7 (the headnote discussing intra-corporate publication). The full printout listed forty-three cases, from Kansas state and federal courts as well as nine other states and thirty-five commentary sources—evidence that *Luttrell* was a seminal case on this topic.

Based on the KeyCite report, we decided that we should read the supreme court decision revealed in the first KeyCite page as well as *Lindemuth*

---

14. KeyCite also functions in reverse in a table-of-authorities mode. This program indicates whether the authorities on which the cited case relies remain good law.

and *Batt*, the two Kansas Court of Appeals cases listed on the second page.[15] Here is what the *Lindemuth* entry (the third citing case) told us: (1) The case was named *Lindemuth v. Goodyear Tire and Rubber Co.* (2) It appeared in various reporters, including 864 P.2d, where *Luttrell* was cited at page 750 and following. It also appeared in other reporters, including the official *Kansas Appellate 2d*. (3) It was decided by the Kansas Court of Appeals on December 10, 1993, as docket number 69,604. (4) Because *Lindemuth* was listed under *** Discussed and its entry included "and HN: 7, it provided a significant discussion of the point of interest in *Luttrell* and quoted *Luttrell*. (5) The C in the left-hand margin was the symbol for *Lindemuth*, signifying that it had been cited but did not have negative history.

As noted previously and seen in Exhibit 4.7, the supreme court adopted the court of appeals' ruling in *Luttrell*. Neither *Lindemuth* nor *Batt* provided significant additional insight on the topic of intra-corporate communication. Thus we determined that, as to that issue at least, Nichols' defamation claim looked solid.

LexisNexis. As you might expect, Westlaw and LexisNexis share many features, although the names differ. For example, LexisNexis packages cases into various databases based on jurisdiction and area of law.

LexisNexis offers various search options, summarized in Chart 4.7. To obtain a copy of a known case, you would use the Get a Document feature on LexisNexis permitting you to obtain a document by citation, party name, or court's docket number. LexisNexis offers terms-and-connectors and natural-language searching.

A third option, Search by Topic, entails searching for or selecting a broad topic, toggling into narrower and narrower subtopics, selecting the jurisdiction and sources to search, and adding some search terms if desired. This search resembles Westlaw's KeySearch.

A fourth option, Search by Headnote somewhat resembles Westlaw's topic and key number search. This option builds on headnotes the LexisNexis editors have written for cases in its database. This search is identical to a Search by Topic until you come to the screen that gives you the choice between the two searches. At this screen you need only enter a jurisdiction for a headnotes search. A search by headnote retrieves all headnotes classified to the topic and cases that discuss the topic even if they do not have a specific headnote.

The list of results from a LexisNexis search generally displays not only the name and location of cases but also some basic information permitting you to discern whether a case is indeed likely to be pertinent. See Exhibit 4.9.

A case obtained through LexisNexis has the same decision written by the court as a case obtained through a West resource. However, the editorial matter differs, of course. See Exhibit 4.10, a case obtained through Lexis-Nexis. At the beginning of the case, LexisNexis provides editorial matter, including a summary (with procedural posture, overview, and outcome); core terms used in the case; and headnotes with topics and pertinent sentences

---

15. Recall that on an issue of state law, state court authority is mandatory. Cases from the federal court ("D. Kan.") are not as weighty.

EXHIBIT 4.9	Results List from LexisNexis

Search	Get a Document	*Shepard's®*	More		History	Alerts

FOCUS™ Terms supervisor or co-worker or job w/p d¦ Search Within Original Results (1 - 5)   View Tutorial
Advanced...

Source: **Legal > States Legal - U.S. > Kansas > Find Cases > KS State Cases, Combined** ⓘ

Terms: **supervisor or co-worker or job w/p defam! or libel or slander w/p privilege** (Edit Search | Suggest Terms for My Search | Feedback on Your Search)

🖝Select for FOCUS™ or Delivery

☐ ❖   1. Dominguez v. Davidson, No. 80,175, SUPREME COURT OF KANSAS, 266 Kan. 926; 974 P.2d 112; 1999 Kan. LEXIS 118; 14 I.E.R. Cas. (BNA) 1567, March 5, 1999, Opinion Filed

  OVERVIEW: Plaintiff was not entitled to relief because he failed to make out claims for defamation and false light/invasion of privacy.

  CORE TERMS: summary judgment, baseball, playing, defamation, malice, actual malice, work restrictions, false light, defamatory, reputation ...

☐ ❶   2. Mitchell v. Thorman & Wright Motel Corp., No. 65,353, Supreme Court of Kansas, 807 P.2d 161; 1991 Kan. LEXIS 32, March 1, 1991, Filed , NOT DESIGNATED FOR PUBLICATION

  OVERVIEW: In a former employee's retaliatory discharge action against a former employer, the clear and convincing burden of proof properly was applied in conformance with the relevant Kansas statute authorizing the award of punitive damages.

  CORE TERMS: doctor, work release, clear and convincing evidence, retaliation, defamation, summary judgment, work-related, workers compensation, burden of proof, good faith ...

  ... was held that an employee can be **defamed** by false remarks about his work when uttered by his **supervisors,** even though those words are not heard ...
  ... within the corporate setting receive a qualified **privilege** if the following elements are met: The ...
  ... 9 Kan. App. 2d at 622. To overcome this qualified **privilege**, plaintiff must prove that defendants acted with ...
  ... to the treating physician received a qualified **privilege** because it was made in good faith ...
  ... one corporate employee to another about the **job** performance of a third employee were publication for purposes of a **defamation** action against the employer, but would be entitled to a qualified **privilege** if the employer was evaluating or investigating ...
  ... findings about the possibility of a qualified **privilege**. 9 Kan. App. 2d at 623. In *Munsell,* 208 Kan. at 910-11 ...

☐ ❖   3. Lindemuth v. Goodyear Tire & Rubber Co., No. 69,604, COURT OF APPEALS OF KANSAS, 19 Kan. App. 2d 95; 864 P.2d 744; 1993 Kan. App. LEXIS 141; 148 L.R.R.M. 2571, December 10, 1993, Filed

  OVERVIEW: The LMRA did not preempt employee's state claims of intentional infliction of emotional distress, defamation, and tortious interference with contract

EXHIBIT 4.9	*(continued)*

because no statement attributed to employer was made during grievance or disciplinary proceedings.

CORE TERMS: defamatory, preempted, collective-bargaining, defamation, emotional distress, matter of law, grievance, outrage, summary judgment, outrageous ...

... be affirmed.IF MATERIALS AND STATEMENTS WERE **DEFAMATORY**, WERE THEY SUBJECT TO A QUALIFIED **PRIVILEGE**? Lindemuth argues that Goodyear is liable, through respondeat superior, for several allegedly **defamatory** incidents, including statements made by **supervisors** and employees, the posting of various materials ...

☐ ◆   4. Luttrell v. United Tel. System, Inc., No. 56,031, Court of Appeals of Kansas, 9 Kan. App. 2d 620; 683 P.2d 1292; 1984 Kan. App. LEXIS 352; 47 A.L.R.4th 669, July 19, 1984, Opinion Filed , Affirmed 236 Kan. 710, 695 P.2d 1279 (1985).

OVERVIEW: Remarks communicated by one corporate employee to another concerning the job performance of a third employee constituted publication for the purposes of a defamation action against the employer.

CORE TERMS: defamation, reputation, defamation action, qualified privilege, intracorporate, qualifiedly, privileged, good faith, communicated, defamatory ...

... one corporate employee to another concerning the **job** performance of a third employee are publication for the purposes of a **defamation** action against the employer. Since the dismissal ...
... findings concerning the possible application of qualified **privilege** to the communications alleged. The dismissal for ...

☐ ⚠   5. Dobbyn v. Nelson, No. 48,946, Court of Appeals of Kansas, 2 Kan. App. 2d 358; 579 P.2d 721; 1978 Kan. App. LEXIS 192, June 9, 1978, Opinion Filed , Affirmed, 225 Kan. 56.

OVERVIEW: Defendants in a defamation action did not lose a qualified privilege protecting a letter circulated about plaintiff when the letter was written in the course of their employment duties and without proof of any malice.

CORE TERMS: good faith, summary judgment, qualifiedly, grievance committee, qualified privilege, actual malice, librarian, privileged communication, conditional privilege, reckless disregard ...

Source: **Legal > States Legal - U.S. > Kansas > Find Cases > KS State Cases, Combined** ⓘ
Terms: **supervisor or co-worker or job w/p defam! or libel or slander w/p privilege** (Edit Search | Suggest Terms for My Search | Feedback on Your Search)
View: Cite
Date/Time: Wednesday, July 13, 2011 - 2:44 PM EDT

* Signal Legend:
● - Warning: Negative treatment is indicated
Ⓠ - Questioned: Validity questioned by citing refs
⚠ - Caution: Possible negative treatment
◆ - Positive treatment is indicated
Ⓐ - Citing Refs. With Analysis Available
ⓘ - Citation information available
* Click on any *Shepard's* signal to *Shepardize*® that case.

CHART 4.7	LexisNexis Search Options[16]

Get a Document	Retrieve a known case by citation, party name, or docket number.
Terms and connectors	Find cases that fit the requirements of your Boolean search.
Natural language	Find cases the program identifies as most likely to be pertinent based on weighting of terms you enter.
Search by Topic	Find cases that fall within topics and subtopics you choose by toggling through list.
Search by Headnote	Find headnotes classified to a topic and subtopic and pertinent cases.

drawn from the case. Because LexisNexis databases are not the official resource for cases and other versions are preferred for citation, a LexisNexis decision contains numbers in brackets permitting you to track the page breaks in official and West reporter versions (a system called "star pagination" after the asterisks that also appear in the brackets).[17]

As with Westlaw, a major advantage of conducting case law research on LexisNexis is its citator, Shepard's. Indeed you may well use Shepard's for this purpose even if you research primarily in some other resource. As with KeyCite, Shepard's provides the following information about the cited case: (1) its history, i.e., decisions in the same litigation preceding and following the cited case; (2) its treatment in decisions in other litigation; and (3) references to sources other than cases, such as commentary, that discuss the cited case. See Exhibit 4.11. Shepard's has symbols that permit you to quickly discern whether the cited case is good law. See Chart 4.8. The report begins with a summary of the case's status. Shepard's then lists the references in this order: the cited case's history, citing cases from the jurisdiction's higher then lower courts, citing cases from persuasive jurisdictions, and commentary. Each reference to a citing case is preceded by a phrase indicating how the court used the cited case. Furthermore, Shepard's indicates which of the cited case's LexisNexis headnotes is pertinent to the discussion in the citing case.[18]

Shepard's is seamlessly integrated into cases on LexisNexis. That is, a case's symbol appears at the beginning of the case when you pull it up from a database, and you can link directly to the Shepard's report from the case. In addition, you can link from a listing in Shepard's to the citing case.

16. When this text was written, LexisNexis was working on a new platform that would parallel WestlawNext, with the name Lexis Advance.

17. If there is more than one reporter covered, LexisNexis uses pairs and trios of asterisks.

18. Shepard's also has a table-of-authorities function, which indicates whether the authorities on which the Shepardized case relies are good law.

EXHIBIT 4.10	Case from LexisNexis

Custom ID : - No Description - ▾ | Switch Client | Preferences | Help | LiveSupport |

Search	Get a Document	Shepard's®	More		History	Alerts

FOCUS™ Terms supervisor or co-worker or job w/p d Search Within Original Results (1 - 5)   View Tutorial

Advanced...

Source: **Legal > States Legal - U.S. > Kansas > Find Cases > KS State Cases, Combined** i

Terms: **supervisor or co-worker or job w/p defam! or libel or slander w/p privilege** (Edit Search | Suggest Terms for My Search | Feedback on Your Search)

✏Select for FOCUS™ or Delivery

☐

2 Kan. App. 2d 358, *; 579 P.2d 721, **;
1978 Kan. App. LEXIS 192, ***

> Margaret L. Dobbyn, Appellant, v. Margene Nelson, G. Jay Rausch and Virginia Quiring, Appellees

No. 48,946

Court of Appeals of Kansas

2 Kan. App. 2d 358; 579 P.2d 721; 1978 Kan. App. LEXIS 192

June 9, 1978, Opinion Filed

SUBSEQUENT HISTORY: [***1] Affirmed, 225 Kan. 56.

PRIOR HISTORY: Appeal from Riley District Court; Ronald D. Innes, Judge.

DISPOSITION: Affirmed.

CASE SUMMARY

PROCEDURAL POSTURE: Plaintiff employee appealed a decision from the Riley District Court (Kansas), which granted summary judgment to defendants, an employee, plaintiff's supervisor, and a library director, in her libel action.

OVERVIEW: Plaintiff worked as a **supervisor** in a university library. The other employee, a library assistant, was conducting a tour of the library for a student orientation group. Two students complained of the conduct of a member of the library staff. The assistant wrote down the complaint, describing the rude and sarcastic conduct of a member of the staff. The assistant identified the speaker as plaintiff based on the description given by the students. Plaintiff sued defendants for **libel** after the assistant's letter was used by the **supervisor** to give her a poor **job** evaluation. On appeal from summary judgment for defendants, the court held that defendants had no duty to investigate the truth of the accusations contained within the letter when there were no circumstances sufficient to notify defendants that the accusations might be false and that the letter was therefore subject to a qualified **privilege.** The court held that plaintiff failed to introduce any evidence except for her own conclusory statements to show that defendants acted with malice and that summary judgment for defendants was proper.

OUTCOME: The court affirmed the decision of the trial court.

EXHIBIT 4.10	*(continued)*

CORE TERMS: good faith, summary judgment, qualifiedly, grievance committee, qualified privilege, actual malice, librarian, privileged communication, conditional privilege, reckless disregard, ill feelings, conditionally, defamatory, privileged, patrons', state of mind, absolute privilege, subject matter, corresponding, discovery, malice, intent to injure, reasonably sufficient, independent investigation, orientation, transmittal, supervisor, imputation, sarcastic, ascertain

LEXISNEXIS® HEADNOTES   - **Hide**

Torts > Intentional Torts > Defamation > Defenses > Privileges > Absolute Privileges ⬑

Torts > Intentional Torts > Defamation > Defenses > Privileges > Qualified Privileges ⬑

HN1 ⬇ In defamation actions, two classes of privilege are recognized: absolute privilege and conditional or qualified privilege. There is no liability on a conditionally or qualifiedly privileged communication absent the existence of actual malice. Proof of actual malice when a conditional privilege is found to exist requires a plaintiff to prove that the publication was made with knowledge that the defamatory statement was false or with reckless disregard of whether it was false or not. Ordinarily a publication is qualifiedly or conditionally privileged if it is made under circumstances and in a manner which repel, preclude or rebut the inference of malice arising prima facie from a statement prejudicial to the character of the plaintiff. A communication is qualifiedly privileged if it is made in good faith on any subject matter in which the person communicating has an interest, or in reference to which he has a duty, if it is made to a person having a corresponding interest or duty. The essential elements of a qualifiedly privileged communication are good faith, an interest to be upheld, a statement limited in its scope to the upholding of such interest and publication in a proper manner only to proper parties. The determination of whether a conditional privilege exists is a matter of law for the court when the facts upon which such a determination must stand are undisputed. More Like This Headnote | *Shepardize:* Restrict By Headnote

Torts > Intentional Torts > Defamation > Defenses > Privileges > Qualified Privileges ⬑

HN2 ⬇ The law imposes upon one publishing derogatory information, even for laudatory purposes, the responsibility of exercising due care in knowing whereof he speaks, and that a conditional privilege may be destroyed by a failure to exercise reasonable care and diligence to ascertain the truth of the defamatory matter. More Like This Headnote | *Shepardize:* Restrict By Headnote

Torts > Intentional Torts > Defamation > Defenses > Privileges > Qualified Privileges ⬑

HN3 ⬇ If there are no circumstances that are reasonably sufficient to put the defendant on notice that an imputation, which he reasonably believes to be true, is false, qualified privilege is not lost because he does not conduct an independent investigation to determine the truth or falsity of the imputation. More Like This Headnote

Civil Procedure > Summary Judgment > Burdens of Production & Proof > General Overview ⬑

Civil Procedure > Summary Judgment > Motions for Summary Judgment > General Overview ⬑

Civil Rights Law > Practice & Procedure > Civil Rights Commissions > Complaints ⬑

EXHIBIT 4.10	*(continued)*

HN4↓ On motion for summary judgment the pleadings are not controlling as summary judgment contemplates piercing the allegations of the pleadings by affidavits and discovery. More Like This Headnote

Civil Procedure > Summary Judgment > Standards > General Overview ↰

HN5↓ In considering a motion for summary judgment a trial court must give to a litigant against whom judgment is sought the benefit of all inferences that may be drawn from the admitted facts under consideration. A court should be cautious in granting a motion for summary judgment when resolution of the dispositive issue necessitates a determination of the state of mind of one or both of the parties. Whether a party acts in good faith depends not only on the facts and circumstances but also on his state of mind. More Like This Headnote

HEADNOTES / SYLLABUS   ⌐ Hide

SYLLABUS

SYLLABUS BY THE COURT

1. LIBEL AND SLANDER -- *Privileged Conduct in Defamation Action*. In defamation actions, two classes of privilege are recognized -- absolute privilege and conditional or qualified privilege.

2. LIBEL AND SLANDER -- *Conditional Privilege -- Proof of Actual Malice*. Proof of actual malice when a conditional privilege is found to exist requires a plaintiff to prove that the publication was made with knowledge that the defamatory statement was false or with reckless disregard of whether it was false or not.

3. LIBEL AND SLANDER -- *Qualified Privilege -- Elements of Qualified Privileged Communication*. A communication is qualifiedly privileged if it is made in good faith on any subject matter in which the person communicating has an interest, or in reference to which he has a duty, if it is made to a person having a corresponding interest or duty. The essential elements of a qualifiedly privileged communication are good faith, an interest to be upheld, a statement limited in its scope to the upholding of such interest and publication [***2] in a proper manner only to proper parties. Following *Senogles v. Security Benefit Life Ins. Co.*, 217 Kan. 438, Syl. 3, 536 P.2d 1358 (1975).

4. LIBEL AND SLANDER -- *Conditional Privilege -- Matter of Law*. The determination of whether a conditional privilege exists is a matter of law for the court when the facts upon which such a determination must stand are undisputed.

5. LIBEL AND SLANDER -- *Qualified Privilege -- Independent Investigation to Determine Truth or Falsity of Imputation*. If there are no circumstances that are reasonably sufficient to put the defendant on notice that an imputation, which he reasonably believes to be true, is false, qualified privilege is not lost because he does not conduct an independent investigation to determine the truth or falsity of the imputation.

COUNSEL: *Charles S. Scott* of Scott, Scott, Scott & Scott, of Topeka, for the appellant.

Richard H. Seaton, university attorney, of Manhattan, and *Howard Harper* of Harper & Hornbaker, Chartered, of Junction City, for the appellees.

EXHIBIT 4.10   *(continued)*

JUDGES: Foth, C.J., Spencer and Swinehart, JJ.

OPINION BY: SPENCER

OPINION   STAR PAGINATION TO WEST REPORTER

[*358] [722]** In an action for damages based upon libel, summary **[***3]** judgment was entered for defendants on the grounds of qualified privilege with no showing of malice. Plaintiff appeals.

During the years 1974 and 1975, plaintiff was employed as supervisor of the Social Sciences Division of the Kansas State University Library in Manhattan, Kansas. Defendant Margene **[*359]** Nelson was employed as a library assistant in the General Records Division of the library. Defendant G. Jay Rausch was the library director and defendant Virginia Quiring was assistant to the director. Quiring was plaintiff's immediate superior.

On September 25, 1974, Nelson had conducted a tour of the library for a freshman orientation group. Two of the students in the tour group complained of the conduct of a member of the library staff. Nelson reported this complaint to Rausch, who requested that she reduce it to writing and deliver it to him. She did so as follows:

"September 26, 1974

"Dear Dr. Rausch:

"While giving a tour to a Freshman Orientation group yesterday, a very distressing occurrence was related to me. When I asked if any of the students had yet used the library, one of the girls indicated she had. I then asked if she had found the materials she was **[***4]** seeking. She said she had had difficulty, so she had asked a librarian to help her. This librarian replied 'If you don't know how to use the library by now, well it's too late.' Another girl in the group indicated she was present when this statement was made, and that the librarian was very sarcastic and refused to help them in any way. Since the student had told the other group members about it, I felt I should pursue the matter and try to determine if the person in question were indeed a librarian, and if so, who it was.

"From the physical description given me: female, middle-aged, gray hair pulled back away from her face, sarcastic, abrupt manner, I believe they were referring **[**723]** to Margaret Dobbyn. If this is indeed the case, and from other reports I have had from students who have been refused their requests for help on the second floor, I tend to believe it is, I am extremely upset that this is the image we are projecting to our student body and other patrons. I don't know what can be done about the situation, but I thought someone should inform you of the complaints we are receiving at the General Reference desk.

"Sincerely,

/s/ Margene Nelson

"Margene Nelson"

The **[***5]** letter remained in Rausch's files for some months. In early 1975, plaintiff filed a grievance with the internal Kansas State University library grievance committee protesting her job evaluation for the year 1974 as given by her immediate supervisor Quiring. The hearing on her complaint was held February 6, 1975. A few days prior to that date, Rausch delivered the Nelson letter to Quiring for her use at the hearing in support of her job evaluation of plaintiff. Quiring submitted the letter for that purpose.

EXHIBIT 4.10   *(continued)*

Plaintiff alleges that the contents of the Nelson letter were false **[*360]** and defamatory and that Nelson maliciously composed and published the letter. She further alleges that transmittal of the letter by all defendants was with "actual malice with willful intent to injure . . . ." After issues were joined and discovery completed, defendants by their motion to dismiss were granted summary judgment. The trial court found that the Nelson letter was qualifiedly privileged and that there was no evidence of actual malice.

HN1 In defamation actions, two classes of privilege are recognized -- absolute privilege and conditional or qualified privilege. There is no liability on **[***6]** a conditionally or qualifiedly privileged communication absent the existence of actual malice. *Bradford v. Mahan*, 219 Kan. 450, 548 P.2d 1223 (1976). Proof of actual malice when a conditional privilege is found to exist requires a plaintiff to prove that the publication was made with knowledge that the defamatory statement was false or with reckless disregard of whether it was false or not. *Schulze v. Coykendall*, 218 Kan. 653, 545 P.2d 392 (1976). There is no claim here of absolute privilege.

Ordinarily a publication is qualifiedly or conditionally privileged if it is made under circumstances and in a manner which repel, preclude or rebut the inference of malice arising prima facie from a statement prejudicial to the character of the plaintiff. *Schulze v. Coykendall*, supra. The concept has been further defined:

"A communication is qualifiedly privileged if it is made in good faith on any subject matter in which the person communicating has an interest, or in reference to which he has a duty, if it is made to a person having a corresponding interest or duty. The essential elements of a qualifiedly privileged communication are good faith, an interest to be upheld, a **[***7]** statement limited in its scope to the upholding of such interest and publication in a proper manner only to proper parties." *Senogles v. Security Benefit Life Ins. Co.*, 217 Kan. 438, Syl. 3, 536 P.2d 1358 (1975).

The determination of whether a conditional privilege exists is a matter of law for the court when the facts upon which such a determination must stand are undisputed. *Schulze v. Coykendall*, supra.

There is no claim that the subject matter of the letter (courtesy in dealing with library patrons and such patrons' complaints of the lack thereof) is not one in which all of the parties who transmitted the letter, as well as those who received it, had a duty or interest. Nelson, whose job to a large extent dealt with public **[*361]** relations, obviously had a duty and interest in reporting the matter to the director of the library, Rausch. Rausch in turn had a duty and interest in receiving such information. The conduct of plaintiff as reported in the letter was relevant to her job evaluation and, therefore, Quiring had a duty and interest in receiving the letter from Rausch and transmitting it to the grievance committee. **[**724]** The letter was limited **[***8]** in its scope to upholding the interest involved and publication of the letter was limited to the parties named, *i.e.*, Nelson, Rausch, Quiring, and the grievance committee.

Plaintiff argues that the publication was not made in "good faith." She claims that Nelson lacked good faith because she (Nelson) failed to ascertain the identity of the students who reported receiving discourteous treatment and failed to verify the truth of their allegation. Plaintiff denotes such failure as "negligence" and claims that it defeats the privilege.

Noting that the definition of qualified privilege stated by our Supreme Court in *Senogles*, supra, was adopted essentially from what is now 50 Am. Jur. 2d, *Libel and Slander* § 195, pp. 698-699, plaintiff points to 50 Am. Jur. 2d, *Libel and Slander* § 198, which provides in part:

"It has been held that *HN2* the law imposes upon one publishing derogatory information, even for laudatory purposes, the responsibility of exercising due care in knowing whereof he speaks, and that a conditional privilege may be destroyed by a failure to exercise reasonable care and diligence to ascertain the truth of the defamatory matter. . . ." (pp. 704-705.)

Exhibit 4.10   *(continued)*

[***9] Plaintiff fails to note that the section continues:

"On the other hand, there is authority to the effect that *HN3* if there are no circumstances that are reasonably sufficient to put the defendant on notice that an imputation, which he reasonably believes to be true, is false, qualified privilege is not lost because he does not conduct an independent investigation to determine the truth or falsity of the imputation . . . ." (p. 705.)

Is there any evidence that any of the defendants were motivated by ill will or a lack of good faith in publishing the letter? The petition can be read as so alleging. It speaks of the "ill feelings" of the defendants toward plaintiff because of her complaints to the Kansas Commission on Civil Rights and the Equal Employment Opportunity Commission. However, *HN4* on motion for summary judgment the pleadings are not controlling as summary judgment contemplates piercing the allegations of the pleadings **[*362]** by affidavits and discovery. *Meyer, Executor v. Benelli*, 197 Kan. 98, 415 P.2d 415 (1966).

Nelson testified that she was not even aware of the complaints. When pressed to state what she felt demonstrated ill will on the part of Nelson, plaintiff **[***10]** could say only that writing the letter itself showed ill will. Later she stated that she thought Nelson had written the letter to gain favor from Rausch. Rausch and Quiring testified that they "might" have known of the complaints. Quiring stated that she knew plaintiff was active in women's political awareness and that she objected to this only because plaintiff spent working time on private matters.

Plaintiff is not specific in her testimony as to what she feels demonstrates ill will or lack of good faith on the part of defendants in publishing the letter. She testified at some length regarding her feelings that all of the defendants had ill feelings toward her in general. She states that she was met with hostility by the library as a whole; that groups would gather and tell untrue gossip; and that Quiring demonstrated ill feelings from the moment she became assistant to the director. She refers to events occurring after transmittal of the letter. For instance, she feels that ill will by Rausch is shown by the fact that he affirmed her poor job evaluation and by his attitude in an interview she had with him after affirmance by the grievance committee. She feels the very fact **[***11]** Rausch gave Quiring the letter to pass onto the grievance committee shows ill will.

It is clear that each of the defendants had a duty and a corresponding interest in the publication of the Nelson letter, imposed upon each of them by the nature of their employment. In the absence of circumstances reasonably sufficient to put them on notice that the contents of the letter were false, they were not obliged to **[**725]** conduct an independent investigation to determine the truth or falsity of those statements.

We hold that the Nelson letter was a conditionally privileged communication for which there can be no liability on the part of the defendants unless publication of that letter was with knowledge that the statements contained therein were false or with reckless disregard as to whether they were false. Our review of the record reveals nothing to indicate that any of the defendants had actual knowledge that the contents of the Nelson letter were false. In support of the position that the publication was not with **[*363]** "reckless disregard," Rausch stated in his deposition that he had received several similar complaints of plaintiff's performance prior to the Nelson letter. **[***12]** He referred specifically to complaints from others of the library staff, faculty members and students. Plaintiff expresses only her opinion that defendants should have known the letter was false.

We are mindful of *Bowen v. Westerhaus*, 224 Kan. 42, 578 P.2d 1102 (1978), wherein it is stated:

HN5 "In considering a motion for summary judgment a trial court must give to a litigant against whom judgment is sought the benefit of all inferences that may be drawn from the admitted facts under consideration. (*Timi v. Prescott State Bank*, 220 Kan. 377, Syl. para. 2,

EXHIBIT **4.11**   Shepard's Report for Case

 LexisNexis®

Copyright 2011 SHEPARD'S(R) - 28 Citing references

Dobbyn v. Nelson, 2 Kan. App. 2d 358, 579 P.2d 721, 1978 Kan. App. LEXIS 192 (1978)

Restrictions: *Unrestricted*
FOCUS(TM) Terms: *No FOCUS terms*
Print Format: *FULL*
Citing Ref. Signal Legend:
     🔴{Warning} -- Negative treatment is indicated
     ⚠{Warning} -- Negative case treatment is indicated for statute
     🅠{Questioned} -- Validity questioned by citing references
     △{Caution} -- Possible negative treatment
     ◆{Positive} -- Positive treatment is indicated
     🅐{Analysis} -- Citing Refs. With Analysis Available
     🅒{Cited} -- Citation information available

SHEPARD'S SUMMARY

Unrestricted *Shepard's* **Summary**
No negative subsequent
appellate history.
Citing References:
△   Cautionary Analyses: **Distinguished (1)**
    Positive Analyses: Followed (3)
    Neutral Analyses: Dissenting Op. (1)
    Other Sources: Law Reviews (3), Restatements (2), Treatises (2), Court Documents (1)

LexisNexis Headnotes: HN1 (17), HN2 (1)

PRIOR HISTORY   (0 citing references)

     (CITATION YOU ENTERED):
     Dobbyn v. Nelson, 2 Kan. App. 2d 358, 579 P.2d 721, 1978 Kan. App. LEXIS 192 (1978)

SUBSEQUENT APPELLATE HISTORY   (1 citing reference)

   1.   **Affirmed by:**
      Dobbyn v. Nelson, 225 Kan. 56, 587 P.2d 315, 1978 Kan. LEXIS 409 (1978)🅐

CITING DECISIONS   (19 citing decisions)

KANSAS SUPREME COURT

   2.   Cited by:
      Hall v. Kan. Farm Bureau, 274 Kan. 263, 50 P.3d 495, 2002 Kan. LEXIS 452 (2002) ❯ **LexisNexis**
      Headnotes HN1
        274 Kan. 263 *p.278*

ЕХHIBIT **4.11**   *(continued)*

SHEPARD'S® - 2 Kan. App. 2d 358 - 28 Citing References

50 P.3d 495 *p.505*

3.   **Cited in Dissenting Opinion at:**
      Turner v. Halliburton Co., 240 Kan. 1, 722 P.2d 1106, 1986 Kan. LEXIS 388 (1986)△ **LexisNexis**
      Headnotes HN1
           240 Kan. 1 *p.18*
           722 P.2d 1106 *p.1119*

4.   **Distinguished by, Cited by:**
      Hanrahan v. Horn, 232 Kan. 531, 657 P.2d 561, 1983 Kan. LEXIS 233, 9 Media L. Rep. (BNA) 1216
      (1983)△ **LexisNexis Headnotes HN1**
           Distinguished by:
           232 Kan. 531 *p.535*
           657 P.2d 561 *p.565*

           Cited by:
           232 Kan. 531 *p.532*
           657 P.2d 561 *p.563*

5.   **Cited by:**
      Scarpelli v. Jones, 229 Kan. 210, 626 P.2d 785, 1981 Kan. LEXIS 184, 7 Media L. Rep. (BNA) 1284
      (1981)△ **LexisNexis Headnotes HN1**
           229 Kan. 210 *p.216*
           626 P.2d 785 *p.790*

6.   **Cited by:**
      Dobbyn v. Nelson, 225 Kan. 56, 587 P.2d 315, 1978 Kan. LEXIS 409 (1978)🅐

KANSAS COURT OF APPEALS

7.   **Cited by:**
      Lindemuth v. Goodyear Tire & Rubber Co., 19 Kan. App. 2d 95, 864 P.2d 744, 1993 Kan. App. LEXIS 141,
      148 L.R.R.M. (BNA) 2571 (1993)▷ **LexisNexis Headnotes HN1**
           19 Kan. App. 2d 95 *p.102*
           864 P.2d 744 *p.750*

8.   **Cited by:**
      Daniels v. Church of God, 791 P.2d 752, 1990 Kan. App. LEXIS 245 (Kan. Ct. App. 1990)🅘 **LexisNexis**
      Headnotes HN1

9.   **Cited by:**
      Wallace v. Rural Water Dist., 1988 Kan. App. LEXIS 41 (Kan. Ct. App. Jan. 21, 1988) **LexisNexis**
      Headnotes HN1

10.   **Cited by:**
      Luttrell v. United Tel. System, Inc., 9 Kan. App. 2d 620, 683 P.2d 1292, 1984 Kan. App. LEXIS 352, 47
      A.L.R.4th 669 (1984)▷ **LexisNexis Headnotes HN1**
           9 Kan. App. 2d 620 *p.622*
           683 P.2d 1292 *p.1294*

| EXHIBIT **4.11** | *(continued)* |

Page 3

SHEPARD'S® - 2 Kan. App. 2d 358 - 28 Citing References

11.   **Cited by:**
     Knight v. Neodesha, Kansas, Police Dep't, 5 Kan. App. 2d 472, 620 P.2d 837, 1980 Kan. App. LEXIS 320
     (1980) **LexisNexis Headnotes HN1**
       5 Kan. App. 2d 472 *p.480*
       620 P.2d 837 *p.845*

10TH CIRCUIT - U.S. DISTRICT COURTS

12.   **Followed by:**
     D'Souza-Klamath v. Cloud County Health Ctr., Inc., 2009 U.S. Dist. LEXIS 27881 (D. Kan. Mar. 31,
     2009) **LexisNexis Headnotes HN1**
       2009 U.S. Dist. LEXIS 27881

13.   **Followed by:**
     Parker v. Life Care Ctrs. of Am., Inc., 2006 U.S. Dist. LEXIS 16865 (D. Kan. Mar. 31, 2006)
     LexisNexis Headnotes HN1
       2006 U.S. Dist. LEXIS 16865

14.   **Cited by:**
     Castleberry v. Boeing Co., 880 F. Supp. 1435, 1995 U.S. Dist. LEXIS 4450 (D. Kan. 1995) **LexisNexis
     Headnotes HN1**
       880 F. Supp. 1435 *p.1443*

15.   **Cited by:**
     Naab v. Inland Container Corp., 877 F. Supp. 546, 1994 U.S. Dist. LEXIS 18743 (D. Kan. 1994)
     LexisNexis Headnotes HN1
       877 F. Supp. 546 *p.551*

16.   **Cited by:**
     Weathers v. American Family Mut. Ins. Co., 1988 U.S. Dist. LEXIS 9969 (D. Kan. Aug. 12, 1988)
     LexisNexis Headnotes HN1

17.   **Cited by:**
     Polson v. Davis, 635 F. Supp. 1130, 1986 U.S. Dist. LEXIS 26277, 51 Fair Empl. Prac. Cas. (BNA) 307 (D.
     Kan. 1986) **LexisNexis Headnotes HN1**
       635 F. Supp. 1130 *p.1148*

18.   **Cited by:**
     WIGGINS v. WHIRLPOOL CORP., 1985 U.S. Dist. LEXIS 14851 (D. Kan. Oct. 16, 1985) **LexisNexis
     Headnotes HN1**

OHIO COURT OF APPEALS

19.   **Cited by:**
     McCartney v. Oblates of St. Francis deSales, 80 Ohio App. 3d 345, 609 N.E.2d 216, 1992 Ohio App.
     LEXIS 2745 (Ohio Ct. App., Lucas County 1992) **LexisNexis Headnotes HN1**

EXHIBIT **4.11**   *(continued)*

SHEPARD'S® - 2 Kan. App. 2d 358 - 28 Citing References

80 Ohio App. 3d 345 *p.360*
609 N.E.2d 216 *p.226*

UTAH SUPREME COURT

20.   **Followed by:**
         Ferguson v. Williams & Hunt, Inc., 2009 UT 49, 221 P.3d 205, 2009 Utah LEXIS 159, 635 Utah Adv. 73
         (2009) ◆ **LexisNexis Headnotes HN2**
         2009 UT 49
         221 P.3d 205 *p.213*

LAW REVIEWS AND PERIODICALS (3 Citing References)

21.   61 J. Bar Assoc. Kan. 1
         61 J. Bar Assoc. Kan. 1 *p.27*

22.   54 J. Bar Assoc. Kan. 258
         54 J. Bar Assoc. Kan. 258 *p.269*

23.   27 U. Kan. L. Rev. 321
         27 U. Kan. L. Rev. 321 *p.360*

RESTATEMENTS (2 Citing Restatements)

24.   *Restat 2d of Torts, @ 596*

25.   *Restat 2d of Torts, @ 600*

TREATISE CITATIONS (2 Citing Sources)

26.   *11-46 Personal Injury--Actions, Defenses, Damages @ 4*

27.   *11-46 Personal Injury--Actions, Defenses, Damages @ 46.16*

MOTIONS (1 Citing Motion)

28.   *TILLEY v. EQUIFAX INFORMATION SERVS.*, 2006 U.S. Dist. Ct. Motions 913824, 2007 U.S. Dist. Ct.
         Motions LEXIS 86727 (D. Kan. Dec. 26, 2007)

CHART 4.8	Shepard's Symbols

Red stop sign	Negative treatment is indicated, e.g., the cited case is overruled or reversed.
Orange square with Q	Validity is questioned by citing reference.
Yellow triangle	There is possible negative treatment, e.g., the cited case is distinguished or questioned.
Green diamond with +	There is only positive treatment, e.g., the cited case is followed or affirmed.
Blue circle with A	There is treatment that is neither positive nor negative, e.g., the cited case is explained.
Blue circle with I	There are citing references without treatment, e.g., the cited case is merely cited.

As the illustration for the discussion of LexisNexis, consider this second issue in the Casey Nichols case, alluded to in *Luttrell*: Was the communication by Nichols' boss to his coworkers privileged and thus legally protected from a defamation claim?

We searched in the KS State Cases Combined database. Our terms-and-connectors search, *supervisor or co-worker or job w/p defam! or libel or slander w/p privilege*, yielded five cases. Those results overlapped significantly with the first ten cases obtained through this natural-language search: *Are communications by supervisors or bosses privileged from defamation claims?* We obtained similar results by searching under the topic *Torts > Intentional Torts > Defamation > Defenses > Privileges > Qualified Privileges*.

Among the various cases we read, we found *Dobbyn v. Nelson*, decided by the Kansas Court of Appeals in 1978, most helpful. See Exhibit 4.10. *Dobbyn* was affirmed and adopted by the Kansas Supreme Court. See Exhibit 4.11. It was distinguished in one case, but this would not undermine its authority.

As is often the situation, the facts in *Dobbyn* were similar but not totally parallel to Nichols' facts. In Nichols' case, the disputed communication was made by a supervisor to coworkers to explain a termination of employment. Dobbyn complained that a coworker committed defamation in complaining in a letter about her performance to her supervisor and that her supervisors also did so in further disseminating the letter, which led to an adverse job evaluation.

Nonetheless, the *Dobbyn* court applied rules that were broad enough to cover Nichols' case. That is, a communication was qualifiedly privileged if it was made in good faith on a subject in which the person communicating had an interest or a duty to a person having a corresponding interest or duty. The statement had to be accordingly limited in scope, recipients, and manner of communication. As for good faith, absent an indication that a communication was questionable, a defendant did not have to investigate its truth. Also pertinent was any ill will toward the plaintiff that motivated the defendant.

This decision provided various avenues to explore with Nichols before deciding to bring a claim for defamation: Was there good reason to communicate the statement to his coworkers, and how limited in scope was the statement? How credible was the statement on which Molinaro acted? Did the coworker or Molinaro have ill will toward him? The law was clear enough; the facts needed developing.

THE ALTERNATIVE COMMERCIAL ONLINE SERVICES

While Westlaw and LexisNexis constitute the gold standard of online services for case research, it is important to remember that other online options may also accomplish the needed task.

As of mid-2011, Google was becoming a credible resource for researching in cases. Within Google Scholar is a collection of legal opinions (the legal opinions and journals collection), encompassing U.S. Supreme Court opinions dating back to 1791, lower federal court cases dating back to 1923, and state cases dating back to 1950. Working with the options presented on the Advanced Search page, you can select courts to focus on and run basic Boolean searches, whether the name of the case if you already know this or your research terms.

In some ways the yield of a Google Scholar search resembles the yield of a Westlaw or LexisNexis search. As shown in Exhibit 4.12, Google provides a citation list with some text showing your research terms in response to the search (our search was for the terms *defamation privilege* in Kansas Supreme Court and Court of Appeals decisions). As shown in Exhibit 4.13, Google also provides the case itself. And as shown in Exhibit 4.14, it provides information about where the case you select has been cited and links to related documents.

At the same time, Google Scholar does not provide the editorial insights embedded in Westlaw and LexisNexis. Researching in Google Scholar does not bring with it the headnotes written by Westlaw and LexisNexis editors or the legal framework the headnotes represent. Nor does Google Scholar provide advanced searches that build on the insights of the Westlaw and LexisNexis editors. Finally, while the listing of documents in which the case is cited is useful, it is not as refined or complete as the report generated by KeyCite or Shepard's. This is not surprising, of course. Google Scholar is free and newer to the market than Westlaw and LexisNexis.

EXHIBIT 4.12	Results List from Google Scholar

Search Images Videos Maps News Shopping Gmail More

Sign in

My Citations

Google scholar

defamation OR privilege

[Search]   Advanced Scholar Search

Scholar   Kansas courts   anytime   include citations   Create email alert   Results **21 - 30** of about **1,730**. (0.08 sec)

Clear Water Truck Co., Inc. v. M. Bruenger & Co., Inc.
519 P. 2d 682, 214 Kan. 139 - Kan: Supreme Court, 1974 - Google Scholar
... IX Columbia Law Review entitled "Absolute Immunity in **Defamation**: Judicial Proceedings,"
pp. 463-490. The author credits the origin of the absolute **privilege** rule to Lord Mansfield and
points out that the publication, as Lord Mansfield said, must be made: "... ...
Cited by 35 - How cited - Related articles

Knudsen v. Kansas Gas and Electric Co.
807 P. 2d 71, 248 Kan. 469 - Kan: Supreme Court, 1991 - Google Scholar
... 30, 33, 716 P.2d 168 (1986). Certain communications are recognized as privileged and as
such are not within the rules imposing liability for **defamation**. The defense of **privilege** is
a matter of public policy in the furtherance of the right of free speech. ...
Cited by 51 - How cited - Related articles

State v. Newman
680 P. 2d 257, 235 Kan. 29 - Kan: Supreme Court, 1984 - Google Scholar
... The trial court suppressed this evidence in its entirety, holding that the marital **privilege** applied. ...
The other spouse or either his or her guardian or conservator may claim the **privilege** on
behalf of the spouse having the **privilege**." (Emphasis supplied.). ...
Cited by 48 - How cited - Related articles

Alseike v. Miller
412 P. 2d 1007, 196 Kan. 547 - Kan: Supreme Court, 1966 - Google Scholar
... production also is made subject to the scope of examination permitted by 60-226(b) and to the
provisions of 60-230(b). Under this latter proviso if significant countervailing considerations appear,
such as, for example, something in the nature of a qualified **privilege** as mentioned ...
Cited by 73 - How cited - Related articles

State v. Durrant
769 P. 2d 1174, 244 Kan. 522, 244 Kan. 2d ... - Kan: Supreme ..., 1989 - Google Scholar
... 79-5201 et seq., unconstitutional as violating the Fifth Amendment **privilege** against
self-incrimination. ... 79-5201 et seq. (the Kansas drug tax act), contending, among other things,
that the act violates the Fifth Amendment **privilege** against compelled self-incrimination. ...
Cited by 69 - How cited - Related articles

Lindemuth v. Goodyear Tire & Rubber Co.
864 P. 2d 744, 19 Kan. App. 2d 95 - Kan: Court of Appeals, 1993 - Google Scholar
... matters are remanded for further findings consistent with this opinion, focusing on our reversal
of the court's finding that § 301 and/or absolute **privilege** preempted Lindemuth's claims of
intentional infliction of emotional distress, tortious interference with contract, and **defamation**. ...
Cited by 50 - How cited - Related articles

Dobbyn v. Nelson
579 P. 2d 721, 2 Kan. App. 2d 358, 2 Kan. ... - Kan: Court of ..., 1978 - Google Scholar
... In **defamation** actions, two classes of **privilege** are recognized — absolute **privilege** and conditional
or qualified **privilege**. There is no liability on a conditionally or qualifiedly privileged communication
absent the existence of actual malice. Bradford v. Mahan, 219 Kan. ...
Cited by 24 - How cited - Related articles

State v. Crumm
654 P. 2d 417, 232 Kan. 254 - Kan: Supreme Court, 1982 - Google Scholar
... Mr. Kreamer, met in chambers and took up a motion in limine filed by the State, in which the State
sought to have the court instruct defense counsel not to ask Mrs. Hobson about any matters which
might incriminate her and which might be within her Fifth Amendment **privilege**. ...
Cited by 19 - How cited - Related articles

Hein v. Lacy
616 P. 2d 277, 228 Kan. 249 - Kan: Supreme Court, 1980 - Google Scholar
... "Proof of actual malice in **defamation** actions when a conditional **privilege** is found to exist requires
a plaintiff to prove that the publication was made with knowledge that the defamatory statement
was false or with reckless disregard of whether it was false or not. ...
Cited by 45 - How cited - Related articles

State v. Humphrey
537 P. 2d 155, 217 Kan. 352 - Kan: Supreme Court, 1975 - Google Scholar

EXHIBIT 4.13	Case from Google Scholar

Search Images Videos Maps News Shopping Gmail More   Sign in

Google scholar

defamation OR privilege   [Search]   Advanced Scholar Search

Read this case	How cited	**Dobbyn v. Nelson, 579 P. 2d 721 - Kan: Court of Appeals 1978**

Highlighting **defamation OR privilege** Remove highlighting

2 Kan. App. 2d 358 (1978)
579 P.2d 721

MARGARET L. DOBBYN, Appellant,
v.
MARGENE NELSON, G. JAY RAUSCH and VIRGINIA QUIRING, Appellees. Affirmed, 225 Kan. 56.

No. 48,946

Court of Appeals of Kansas.

Opinion filed June 9, 1978.

Charles S. Scott of Scott, Scott, Scott & Scott, of Topeka, for the appellant.

Richard H. Seaton, university attorney, of Manhattan, and *Howard Harper* of Harper & Hornbaker, Chartered, of Junction City, for the appellees.

Before FOTH, C.J., SPENCER and SWINEHART, JJ.

SPENCER, J.:

In an action for damages based upon libel, summary judgment was entered for defendants on the grounds of qualified **privilege** with no showing of malice. Plaintiff appeals.

During the years 1974 and 1975, plaintiff was employed as supervisor of the Social Sciences Division of the Kansas State University Library in Manhattan, Kansas. Defendant Margene *359 Nelson was employed as a library assistant in the General Records Division of the library. Defendant G. Jay Rausch was the library director and defendant Virginia Quiring was assistant to the director. Quiring was plaintiff's immediate superior.

359

On September 25, 1974, Nelson had conducted a tour of the library for a freshman orientation group. Two of the students in the tour group complained of the conduct of a member of the library staff. Nelson reported this complaint to Rausch, who requested that she reduce it to writing and deliver it to him. She did so as follows:

"September 26, 1974

"Dear Dr. Rausch:

"While giving a tour to a Freshman Orientation group yesterday, a very distressing occurrence was related to me. When I asked if any of the students had yet used the library, one of the girls indicated she had. I then asked if she had found the materials she was seeking. She said she had had difficulty, so she had asked a librarian to help her. This librarian replied 'If you don't know how to use the library by now, well it's too late.' Another girl in the group indicated she was present when this statement was made, and that the librarian was very sarcastic and refused to help them in any way. Since the student had told the other group members about it, I felt I should pursue the matter and try to determine if the person in question were indeed a librarian, and if so, who it was.

"From the physical description given me: female, middle-aged, gray hair pulled back away from her face, sarcastic, abrupt manner, I believe they were

| Exhibit 4.14 | "How Cited" Report from Google Scholar |

Search Images Videos Maps News Shopping Gmail More   Sign in

Google scholar

defamation OR privilege   [Search]   Advanced Scholar Search

[Read this case] | [How cited]   **Dobbyn v. Nelson, 579 P. 2d 721 - Kan: Court of Appeals 1978**

How this document has been cited

When a conditional or qualified **privilege** exists, a plaintiff must demonstrate actual malice, requiring the plaintiff to prove that the publication was made with knowledge that the defamatory statement was false or was made with reckless disregard of whether it was false or not.
- in Lindemuth v. Goodyear Tire & Rubber Co., 1993 and 3 similar citations

The Court of Appeals defined a qualifiedly privileged communication as one "made in good faith on any subject matter in which the person communicating has an interest, or in reference to which he has a duty, if it is made to a person having a corresponding interest or duty. The essential elements of a qualifiedly privileged communication are good faith, an interest to be ...
- in Hall v. Kansas Farm Bureau, 2002 and 2 similar citations

—inating any significance for a conditional **privilege** under the rule of § 601 in the first Restatement), a substantial majority of the courts have followed Clause (b).
- in Restatement of the law, second, torts 2d and one similar citation

When a communication is qualifiedly privileged, unless the defendants act with knowledge of falsity or reckless disregard for truth or falsity, lack of reasonable care to investigate will not defeat the **privilege**.
- in Scarpelli v. Jones, 1981 and one similar citation

Further, although the majority opinion contains no direct authority applying the **privilege** to an occasion involving communications between school teachers and/or officials and parents of a student on matters pertaining to their common interest in the student, it is clear that such an occasion would generally warrant application of the **privilege**.
- in McCartney v. Oblates of St. Francis deSales, 1992 and one similar citation

Thus, in Dobbyn the Court held that a letter written by an employee of the Kansas State University library concerning the conduct of another employee and transmitted to the second employee's superior was qualifiedly privileged.
- in Luttrell v. United Telephone System, Inc., 1984 and one similar citation

The determination of whether a qualified **privilege** exists "is a matter of law for the court when facts upon which a determination must stand are undisputed
- in D'SOUZA-KLAMATH v. CLOUD COUNTY HEALTH CENTER, 2009 and one similar citation

They were made about a subject matter in which the defendants had an interest and made to a person with a corresponding interest or duty.
- in Scarpelli v. Jones, 1981 and one similar citation

Defendants contend any feelings of ill will between Miller and Naab do not satisfy a showing of actual malice.
- in Naab v. Inland Container Corp., 1994 and one similar citation

On motion for summary judgment, pleadings are not controlling as summary judgment contemplates piercing allegations of pleadings by affidavits and discovery.
- in West's Pacific Digest, Beginning 367 P. 2d

Cited by

Hall v. Kansas Farm Bureau
50 P. 3d 495 - Kan: Supreme Court 2002

Luttrell v. United Telephone System, Inc.
683 P. 2d 1292 - Kan: Court of Appeals 1984

Dobbyn v. Nelson
587 P. 2d 315 - Kan: Supreme Court 1978

Ferguson v. Williams & Hunt, Inc.
221 P. 3d 205 - Utah: Supreme Court 2009

Hanrahan v. Horn
657 P. 2d 561 - Kan: Supreme Court 1983

all 24 citing documents »

Related documents

Dobbyn v. Nelson
587 P. 2d 315 - Kan: Supreme Court 1978

Schulze v. Coykendall
545 P. 2d 392 - Kan: Supreme Court 1976

Scarpelli v. Jones
626 P. 2d 785 - Kan: Supreme Court 1981

Senogles v. Security Benefit Life Ins. Co.
536 P. 2d 1358 - Kan: Supreme Court 1975

Bradford v. Mahan
548 P. 2d 1223 - Kan: Supreme Court 1976

all related documents »

About Google Scholar - All About Google - My Citations

©2012 Google

A third set of commercial options can be seen as occupying the middle territory between the gold-standard services and Google. Examples are Lois-law, Fastcase, and CASEMaker. As a very general proposition, these services provide more cases and searching sophistication than Google Scholar but fewer editorial insights and sophisticated search options than Westlaw and LexisNexis. You may have access to one of these as a member of a state bar association, which makes it a cost-effective option. The features of each of these services change periodically, so your best strategy is to learn the details of whichever service is most accessible to you.

COURT RESOURCES

Many courts now publish their cases on their websites. These web-based resources typically have two disadvantages from a research standpoint: They do not reach far back in time, and they do not permit searching for cases by research terms or issues. On the other hand, they are an excellent and generally free or very low-cost means of obtaining recent decisions you learn about some other way.

A unique federal resource, PACER, which stands for Public Access to Court Electronic Records, provides detailed information about cases filed in federal courts and documents related to those cases. PACER covers all district and appellate courts;[19] as of mid-2011, PACER provided access to over 500 million documents. It is used heavily by lawyers who litigate in federal court. You may search for a case by name, number, or nature of lawsuit.

For example, as we were writing this book in the summer of 2011, we came across a reference to a decision from the U.S. District Court for the Western District of Kentucky that we thought would be interesting to read. The case addressed the lawyer's approach to research. We obtained the decision through PACER. We found the following footnote worth quoting here, as a word to the wise:

> The court notes here that defense counsel appears to have cobbled much of his statement of the law . . . by cutting and pasting, without citation, from the Wikipedia website. . . . The court reminds counsel that such cutting and pasting, without attribution is plagiarism. The court also brings to counsel's attention Rule 8.4 of the Kentucky Rules of Professional Conduct, which states that it is professional misconduct for an attorney to "engage in conduct involving dishonesty, fraud, deceit or misrepresentation." . . . Finally, the court reminds counsel that Wikipedia is not an acceptable source of legal authority in the United States District Court.[20]

---

19. It also covers the federal bankruptcy courts.
20. *United States v. Sypher*, No. 3:09-CR-00085, 6 (W.D. Ky. Feb. 9, 2011).

Citation to Cases

The basic elements of a citation to a case are:

1. the case name;
2. its location, e.g., reporter, volume, and first page number;
3. the page number where the specific information of interest is located (a "pinpoint cite");
4. the court and date; and
5. in some situations, the case's subsequent history.

As to each element, the details can be complicated. Both *the Bluebook* and *ALWD Citation Manual* have precise rules and tables covering which words to include in a case name and how to abbreviate them, which of the various resources in which a case can be found to cite, how to identify the court, how much information to provide about the date of decision, and which subsequent history to include. See *Bluebook* rules B4 and 10 and tables 1, 6, 7, and 8; *ALWD* rule 12 and appendices 1 through 4.

From a research standpoint, a key question is which of the many resources containing cases to cite. If you are writing to a court, follow the court's rules. For example, a state court may require a citation to its official reporter as well as the West regional reporter. Otherwise, U.S. Supreme Court decisions are cited to its official reporter, and the decisions of other courts are typically cited to West reporters. Cases not appearing in West reporters are cited to Westlaw, Lexis-Nexis, or court websites, depending on their availability.

Following are some sample citations for the cases featured in this chapter.

Luttrell cited to the West regional reporter, with a pinpoint cite to page 1294:

BLUEBOOK: *Luttrell v. United Tel. Sys., Inc.,* 683 P.2d 1292, 1294 (Kan. Ct. App. 1984), *aff'd*, 695 P.2d 1279 (Kan. 1985).

ALWD: *Luttrell v. United Tel. Sys., Inc.,* 683 P.2d 1292, 1294 (Kan. App. 1984), *aff'd*, 695 P.2d 1279 (Kan. 1985).

(continued)

> *Dobbyn*, cited for purposes of illustration to the LexisNexis database with a pinpoint cite to pages 6 and 7, without the subsequent history:
>
> BLUEBOOK: *Dobbyn v. Nelson*, No. 48,946, 1978 Kan. App. LEXIS 192, at *6-7 (Kan. Ct. App. June 9, 1978).
>
> ALWD: *Dobbyn v. Nelson*, 1978 Kan. App. LEXIS 192, at *6-7 (Kan. App. June 9, 1978).

SUMMARY

At the risk of oversimplification, Chart 4.9 presents the optimal options for use of the many case law resources. The key to researching cases well is to be aware not only of the topic you are researching but also of the posture of your research: your present knowledge, the degree of challenge it presents, and your ability to incur costs to use a resource.

CHART 4.9   Optimal Options for Case Law Research

If you have the name or citation of a case and need only to retrieve the case—	Pull the print West reporter; retrieve the case from the court's website or pull the case off Google Scholar, depending on its age; pull the case off a commercial online service available to you.
If you have the name or citation of a case and need to research further from that case—	Pull the case from the West print reporter and work from its headnotes into the digest system; pull the case in Westlaw or LexisNexis and leverage it into other searches, e.g., a key-number search.
If you are beginning your focused case law research—	Use the West print digests; as resources permit, use an online search building on the editor's work, e.g., Search by Topic or Headnote in LexisNexis.
If you are fairly far along in your research and want to expand your collection of cases or are looking for a case with very specific features—	Run a Boolean or natural-language search in the least expensive service and narrowest database available.
To check whether a case is good law and to find additional sources—	Use KeyCite or Shepard's.

TEST YOUR UNDERSTANDING

Reflection Questions

1. Deciding which cases to work with when you find quite a few requires considerable judgment. What practical methods can you develop to not only keep track of what you are finding but also prioritize among cases, so your research is cost-effective?

2. Online resources provide access to an enormous body of case law. Is this a good thing? These days, it is easy to believe that a case on all fours must be out there and to spend a lot of time looking for it. Compare this to pre-online research, when lawyers focused on selecting the most pertinent cases from a smaller number of possibilities and—perhaps—analyzed their clients' cases more deeply.

Your Scenario

Review the scenario stated in Chapter 2. Assume that there is case law pertinent to the dispute between your client, Elaine Wilson, and her landlord. He is seeking to evict her because her companion dog, which helps with her PTSD, violates the no-pets policy.

- Research in West Virginia state case law at least three different ways. Compare the results and processes.
- Read and brief an important case you find.
- Cite the case. Is it good law?

RESEARCH IN ENACTED LAW

Contents

This chapter explores an employer's liability for an employee's car accident (also covered in Chapter 3).

Key Concepts and Tools in This Chapter

- bill, law, and statute
- relationships between cases and statutes
- legislative process
- prospective application and effective date

(continued)

- amendment, repeal, and sunset dates
- hierarchy of federal, state, and local law
- statutory components: opening, operative, implementation, and technical sections
- judicial interpretation and review of statutes
- legislative intent
- tools of statutory interpretation
- model and uniform laws
- slip law and session laws
- print and online official codes
- print and online annotated unofficial codes
- KeyCite and Shepard's
- sources of newly enacted law
- constitutions
- local laws: ordinances and charters

Much of American life is governed by enacted law of one form or another. This is due in part to the sheer number of legislative bodies: not only the federal Congress but also state legislatures and local government units such as city councils. It is also due in part to the capacity of legislative bodies both to identify, on their own, topics to address through legislation and to respond to the requests of constituents. Many citizens and organizations tend to see law as a solution to social and economic problems, large and small.

Thus when you undertake a research project, you should assume that enacted law is involved until you determine otherwise. You also should assume that judicial decisions and perhaps administrative agency law are involved as well. In many areas, the law is a composite of law from all three branches.

A few notes about vocabulary: "Enacted law" is used here to encompass various forms of laws passed by legislative bodies. "Bill" is the term used for a proposed law that has not yet passed; "law" is the term for a bill that has passed and become law. "Statute" is the term used for a law passed by the federal Congress or a state legislature. "Ordinance" is the term used for a law passed by a unit of local government. Some enacted laws, created through a more elaborate process than statutes and ordinances, create the powers of the government and the fundamental rights of citizens; these are termed "constitutions" at the federal and state levels and "charters" at the local level.

This chapter first discusses how statutes are created and how they are interpreted—key information to understand as you research them. With this background set, the chapter then turns to the many resources for researching statutes, featuring those that are most useful in the common situations in which statutory research occurs and focusing on state statutes. The chapter then briefly addresses constitutions and local laws, including charters and ordinances. In some situations, when the meaning of a statute as applied to a client's situation is particularly difficult to determine, you may research the documents created by the legislature as it considered the statute; these legislative history materials are complicated enough that they are covered in their own chapter, Chapter 6, which focuses on federal statutes.

The first part of this chapter returns, for its illustration, to a case introduced in Chapter 3. The fictional firm's client, Acme Balloon, was contacted after a car accident involving a company employee who, while driving his own car to work, detoured to pick up doughnuts for the weekly staff meeting. When the crash occurred, the employee was talking on his cell phone. The other driver sought compensation for damages to her car. The events occurred in Santa Barbara, California, in August 2011.

THE STATUTORY SYSTEM

Legislative process. To understand enacted law, it is useful to understand the legislative process, which differs from the judicial process. Legislatures are more autonomous bodies than courts. They can identify topics to address on their own,[1] and they may also respond to concerns of constituents. Sometimes the legislature acts in response to judicial decisions, whether to adopt the court's rule, modify it, or create a new rule. In this respect the legislature is superior to the judiciary, reflecting our system of checks and balances.

The legislative process is more varied than the litigation process. The formal process[2] entails introduction of a bill by one or more legislators, committee hearings and deliberations, full-chamber debates, votes in both houses of the legislature,[3] and approval by the executive. This formal process is accompanied by the political processes of lobbying by constituents and deal-making between legislators.

Statutes are understood to create law in a different manner than judicial decisions. Case law is considered to state law as it already exists, so it operates retrospectively; the court applies the law it states to the dispute before it. Statutory law is considered to create law that did not exist before, so it generally operates prospectively. It does not apply until a future date, known as the statute's "effective date." Often the legislature designates the effective

---

1. There are a few requirements on legislatures, most obviously funding government activities.

2. This process is covered in more depth in Chapter 6.

3. Congress and almost all of the state legislatures have two chambers.

date in a statute. If a statute lacks an express effective date, the statute takes effect on the default effective date for that legislature.[4]

Once a statute becomes effective, it remains in effect until one of several things happens. Many statutes are amended. Just as a legislature can choose to take up a topic and enact a statute, so it can return to a topic and amend a statute, whether to address changes in circumstances or to refine the language, perhaps in response to judicial decisions interpreting the statute. When a statute has been amended, identifying the language in effect at the time of your client's situation is a necessary step in properly analyzing your client's legal position.

Statutes may cease to have effect in several situations. A statute may contain a sunset provision stating that the statute expires on a specified date unless renewed. A legislature may repeal a statute, even though it did not include a sunset provision when enacting the statute. Finally, a court may declare a statute unconstitutional and of no effect. In this respect, the judiciary is superior to the legislature, again reflecting our system of checks and balances.

Chart 5.1 depicts the actions of the legislature and judiciary in creating, modifying, and nullifying statutes.

One of the more complicated facets of the American statutory system is the interplay between Congress, state legislatures, and local governments. Each has its own sphere of permitted legislative activity. Congress may act

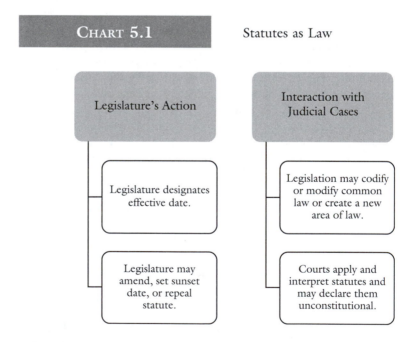

CHART 5.1   Statutes as Law

Legislature's Action

Interaction with Judicial Cases

Legislature designates effective date.

Legislation may codify or modify common law or create a new area of law.

Legislature may amend, set sunset date, or repeal statute.

Courts apply and interpret statutes and may declare them unconstitutional.

4. For federal statutes, the default date is the date of the president's approval.

to preserve its national sovereignty or to address topics granted to it by the U.S. Constitution. State legislatures may address matters of state concern as well as matters delegated by Congress or not expressly assigned to the federal government. Local governments, as creatures of the state, may exercise the powers explicitly granted by the state and powers implied by the explicit grants. Some topics fall into more than one legislature's sphere. The system is hierarchical, with Congress having the power to determine whether its law preempts state law or coexists with state law.[5]

In many areas, more than one law on a subject exists. For example, a federal law may regulate large, interstate companies' employment relations, while a state statute regulates smaller companies. Thus, early in your research, you should seek to determine which enacted laws—federal, state, or local— may govern your client's situation. Commentary can provide important insight on this matter.

Statutory texts and guidance for your client. Statutes read quite differently from cases in that all language is rule language; there is no description of a real-life story or its legal outcome. Rather, all sections of a statute state who or what is encompassed by the statute; what conduct by that person or entity is permitted, required, or prohibited; and how the statute is enforced, such as a suit by a harmed party or prosecution by the government.

Statutes take various forms. Some are only a paragraph long; others consist of many sections, some containing many paragraphs. A fairly standard format used for many statutes is:

- opening sections: the statute's name, purpose, definitions of terms used throughout the statute, and scope;
- operative sections: the statute's general rule and exceptions to the rule;
- implementation sections: the consequences of violating the rule and its method of enforcement;[6] and
- technical sections: the statute's effective date, severability provision (stating that if part is declared unconstitutional, the rest is meant to continue in effect), and possibly a sunset provision.

Exhibit 5.1 is a California statute pertaining to the Acme Balloon situation. A fairly short statute, Vehicle Code section 23123 addresses one facet of the client's situation: that the employee was talking on a cell phone when the crash occurred. It became effective on July 1, 2011, so it governed the employee's conduct in August 2011.

---

5. Unfortunately, Congress does not always exercise this power, leaving the issue to the courts to determine.

6. Some statutes lack implementation sections, leaving the issue of how it is to be enforced to the courts.

EXHIBIT 5.1	State Statute from Legislature's Website (California Vehicle Code)

administrative charges authorized under Section 22850.5 and any parking fines, penalties, and administrative fees incurred by the registered owner.

(h) The law enforcement agency and the impounding agency, including any storage facility acting on behalf of the law enforcement agency or impounding agency, shall comply with this section and shall not be liable to the registered owner for the improper release of the **vehicle** to the legal owner or the legal owner's agent provided the release complies with the provisions of this section. The legal owner shall indemnify and hold harmless a storage facility from any claims arising out of the release of the **vehicle** to the legal owner or the legal owner's agent and from any damage to the **vehicle** after its release, including the reasonable costs associated with defending any such claims. A law enforcement agency shall not refuse to issue a release to a legal owner or the agent of a legal owner on the grounds that it previously issued a release.

23120. No person shall operate a motor **vehicle** while wearing glasses having a temple width of one-half inch or more if any part of such temple extends below the horizontal center of the lens so as to interfere with lateral vision

23123. (a) A person shall not drive a motor **vehicle** while using a **wireless** telephone unless that telephone is specifically designed and configured to allow hands-free listening and talking, and is used in that manner while driving.

(b) A violation of this section is an infraction punishable by a base fine of twenty dollars ($20) for a first offense and fifty dollars ($50) for each subsequent offense.

(c) This section does not apply to a person using a **wireless** telephone for emergency purposes, including, but not limited to, an emergency call to a law enforcement agency, health care provider, fire department, or other emergency services agency or entity.

(d) This section does not apply to an emergency services professional using a **wireless** telephone while operating an authorized emergency **vehicle**, as defined in Section 165, in the course and scope of his or her duties.

(e) This section does not apply to a person driving a schoolbus or transit **vehicle** that is subject to Section 23125.

(f) This section does not apply to a person while driving a motor **vehicle** on private property.

(g) This section shall become operative on July 1, 2011.

23123.5. (a) A person shall not drive a motor **vehicle** while using an electronic **wireless** communications device to write, send, or read a text-based communication.

(b) As used in this section "write, send, or read a text-based communication" means using an electronic **wireless** communications device to manually communicate with any person using a text-based communication, including, but not limited to, communications referred to as a text message, instant message, or electronic mail.

(c) For purposes of this section, a person shall not be deemed to be writing, reading, or sending a text-based communication if the person reads, selects, or enters a telephone number or name in an electronic **wireless** communications device for the purpose of making

When reading a statute to obtain guidance for your client's situation, you should attend carefully to every word chosen by the legislature and work through the statute several times.

1. Read the entire statute to discern its general structure and how the various sections fit together.
2. Discern which sections pertain to your client's situation and which sections do not.
3. Combine the sections that pertain to your client's situation into a rule of law, using the precise language selected by the legislature as you do so. In particular, if the statute defines words used in the statute (which may appear at the beginning of the chapter), use those definitions for the words, even if outside of the statute you can imagine a different meaning for the words.
4. Note any cross-references in the statute to other statutes, and review those statutes. In particular, an implementation section may be identified by cross-reference.
5. Record what you have thus gleaned into a complete rule incorporating references to the sections where you found the key language.

This latter step serves not only as a means of monitoring your research by processing your sources—one of the steps of the work-flow of legal research—but also serves as a bridge to your analysis of your client's situation.

For example, we created the summary of the cell-phone driving statute in Example 5.1 for purposes of analyzing the conduct of Acme Balloon's employee. Note that the summary incorporates a provision of the Vehicle Code that is not referred to there but defines a term used in the section.

| EXAMPLE 5.1 | Summary of Statute |

Vehicle Code section 23123

GENERAL RULE: "(a) A person shall not drive a motor vehicle while using a wireless telephone unless that telephone is specifically designed and configured to allow hands-free listening and talking, and is used in that manner while driving."

EXCEPTIONS: (c) Possible exception is "a person using a wireless telephone for emergency purposes, including, but not limited to, an emergency call to a law enforcement agency, health care provider, fire department, or other emergency services agency or entity."

(f) Possible exception is "a person while driving a motor vehicle on private property." See section 490 of Vehicle Code, defining "private road or driveway" for entire code as a "way or place in private ownership and used for vehicular travel by the owner and those having express or implied permission from the owner but not by other members of the public."

ENFORCEMENT: (b) Infraction punishable by base fine of $20 for first offense or $50 for each subsequent offense.

CONNECTION TO CLIENT SITUATION: Need to confirm that he was driving. Learn what type of phone he was using, whom he was calling and why (potential emergency call exception), where he was (potential private property exception). Probable outcome: fines against employee.[7]

Statutory interpretation. Sometimes, a statute alone may govern a client's situation. There may be no other authorities related to the statute, and its application to the situation may be clear. Thus, statutory research and analysis ends with the statute. Much more often, research in statutes also involves research in other sources.

In many situations, researching a statute also entails researching cases.[8] When an issue arises under a statute, it is not the legislature but rather the courts that handle the dispute. In doing so, courts incorporate the statute into their judicial decisions. Cases interpreting statutes operate as precedent, at a minimum providing an example of how the statute applies, often also providing judicial gloss—that is, elaboration upon the statutory language. On occasion, courts do more than interpret and apply statutes; they evaluate them for compliance with constitutional requirements[9] and invalidate them if found lacking. A court may strike down some or all of a statute depending on the extent of the concern.

For some statutes, as shown in Chart 5.2, an ongoing dialogue develops between the legislature and the courts. That is, the legislature may enact a statute, the court may strike some or all of it or interpret it in a way that the legislature disfavors, and the legislature may amend the statute. Given the principles that statutes are prospective and court rulings are retrospective, it is critical to understand this dialogue to discern the statutory language in effect as of the time of your client's situation.

7. Often breach of a duty imposed by statute also gives rise to a claim by the injured party against the breachor on the theory of negligence per se. On the other hand, an employer might argue that it should not be liable when an employee commits a criminal activity. Additional research into these topics would be necessary.

8. If the subject is regulated by an agency, research must also include the law made by that agency.

9. See the discussion of constitutions later in this chapter for examples of constitutional constraints on the government.

CHART 5.2	Statute/Case Law Timeline

```
1├─────/────────────/────────────2├───────/───────3│
```

Statute is enacted.	Court rules statute is unconstitutional.		Legislature reenacts statute to meet court's concerns.

Client's events arose at time 1.	Statute is inapplicable: not yet in effect.
Client's events arose at time 2.	Statute is inapplicable: has been ruled unconstitutional.
Client's events arose at time 3.	New statute is applicable.

In some situations involving statutes, you may lack interpreting cases, or they may not address an issue arising out of your client's situation, and you may need to expand your research realm. The goal of this research is to reveal a broader context for the statute from which you can infer the legislature's intent behind the statutory language.[10] As depicted in Chart 5.3, among the sources used in this setting are:

- related statutes incorporating similar or identical language from your jurisdiction, on the theory that the legislature uses language in the same manner from statute to statute within the same general context;
- case law predating the statute, which may serve as a backdrop against which the legislature acted, whether to codify or modify it;
- dictionaries providing definitions of specific terms and commentary discussing the topic of the statute;
- canons of construction, that is, principles by which all statutes are to be read, some based on linguistics, some based on policy matters; and
- cases interpreting similar or identical laws in other jurisdictions.

As to the latter, if you are working with a little-interpreted state law, one possibility is to examine how a parallel federal law has been interpreted. Another is to look to interpretation of a different state's law on the topic, especially when the two laws are derived from the same model law or uniform law. Model and uniform laws are not really laws but suggestions for laws developed by such organizations as the National Conference of Commissioners on Uniform State Laws,[11] the

---

10. The notion of "intent" on the part of a body made up of tens if not hundreds of individuals, with varying interests, may be unrealistic, but it nonetheless guides statutory analysis.

11. The most widely known example of such a law is the NCCUSL's Uniform Commercial Code, which is the law in some form in nearly every state.

| CHART 5.3 | Tools of Statutory Interpretation |

Cases
- Cases in your jurisdiction interpreting your statute
- Cases in your jurisdiction predating the statute
- Cases from other jurisdictions interpreting similar statutes

Statutory Materials
- Other statutes in your jurisdiction with same language
- Statute's legislative history materials

Other Sources
- Dictionaries and commentary
- Canons of construction

American Law Institute, the Council of State Governments, and sections of the American Bar Association. The aim of these organizations is to develop a sample law that is so well drafted that many state legislatures adopt it, verbatim or nearly so, thus unifying law around the country.

As an example, consider the exception for "while driving on private property" in the California cell-phone driving statute. How would the statute apply to the Acme Balloon situation if the employee were backing out of the doughnut shop's parking lot, which could be private property, and ran into the other driver's car on the street, certainly public property? The first step would be to look for a case on point in California; we found none. Without such a case, we could then look at how California courts had handled similar situations under other driving statutes; how courts in other states had applied their cell-phone driving statutes; and canons of construction, including the principle that criminal statutes are to be interpreted to favor the defendant.

OVERVIEW OF STATUTORY RESEARCH OPTIONS

Not surprisingly, resources for researching statutes abound. Choosing which to use in a specific situation has a significant impact on the second element of FEAT—the efficiency of your research. Understanding the options starts with understanding the various compilations in which statutes are published.

When a bill becomes law, it is published as a slip law. The various laws passed during a legislative session are compiled into a set of session laws for that session, with the laws appearing in the order passed rather than any logical order. This compilation is useful in a limited range of circumstances for research purposes.

By contrast, a code is a compilation of laws currently in effect, whether enacted decades ago or during the last legislative session.[12] Codes are highly organized according to some topical scheme. Some codes have subject titles for the various major units, which typically are called "chapters" or "titles"; other codes use title numbers. Within a major unit, the sections are logically arrayed and designated by number.

Official codes are published under the authority of the legislature by the government itself or a commercial publisher. Unofficial codes are published by commercial companies. Official codes typically include the language of the statutes and little else, while unofficial codes include significant editorial matter, called "annotations," facilitating research in sources related to the statutes. Codes are available online as well as in print. The codes available for each jurisdiction are listed in Table 1 of *The Bluebook* and Appendix 1 of the *ALWD Citation Manual*. Codes are generally much more useful for researching current law than session laws.

As you consider which of the various codes to use, keep in mind several factors: The more up-to-date and extensive the information it provides, the better. The search methods should be adequate for what you need given your research context. And the lower the cost to use the resource, the better.

Because there is no single best choice, the following discussion proceeds from the simplest type of code to the most complex: unannotated official codes in paper and legislative websites, annotated codes in print, and commercial online research in statutes. It concludes with session laws, which are used for limited purposes.

UNANNOTATED OFFICIAL CODES

Traditionally, unannotated official codes are published in print by a state publisher and come out on a fairly slow schedule, e.g., every two years with perhaps an update in-between.

Using an unannotated code is fairly straightforward. If you already know the citation to the pertinent statute, you would simply locate that section. If you do not already know the citation for the pertinent statute through (for example) commentary research, you would use the code's internal finding tools: the index, the list of chapters, and the list of sections within a chapter. Once you locate the pertinent statute, you would be able to read the most authoritative codified version of the language and generally learn the statute's derivation, i.e., which laws created or amended the statute.

---

12. Generally only public, permanent laws appear in a code, not private laws (relating to a specific person or situation) or temporary laws (such as funding of government agencies), which do appear in session laws.

Recently, many legislative websites have come to contain the legislature's statutes in codified form. Online versions vary somewhat. As of this writing in mid-2011, it was fair to expect that a legislative website would be current to the most recently concluded legislative session, permit you to peruse the list of chapters and sections within chapters, and offer basic Boolean searching by section numbers or key words. The online statutes may or may not be designated the official code.

Exhibit 5.1, the California cell-phone driving statute, was found via the California legislature's website, leginfo.ca.gov. California does not have an official print code.

ANNOTATED CODES IN PRINT

Either after you have used an unannotated official code or as you begin your statutory research, you are likely to research in an annotated code. Annotated codes contain the same statutory language in the same configuration as in an unannotated official code. The major advantage of an annotated code is the annotation: material that can include a detailed explanation of the statute's initial enactment and amendments, references to commentary discussing the topic of the statute, and synopses of cases interpreting the statute. Furthermore, annotated codes are frequently updated. You may have a choice of researching in an annotated code in print or online.

Many lawyers prefer print codes because they provide a clear impression of the structure of the chapter and its various subparts, finding pertinent material works well through the code's internal finding tools, and it is desirable to avoid the costs of online research. A print annotated code is a large source with many volumes and components. As shown in Chart 5.4, using it properly entails several steps:

1. Identify which statutory section(s) are potentially pertinent. Options include following up on a lead from some other source, such as commentary, and using the code's own finding tools, such as the index and lists of chapters and sections. Indeed, it often makes sense to check out the index and table of chapters, even if you have a reference from another source, to avoid missing something.

2. Once you have located a pertinent section, look at the list of sections within the chapter containing that section so you are sure that you have identified all pertinent sections. What can seem to be a small and entirely self-contained statute may intersect in some important way with other sections, especially definitions sections that may be applicable to an entire chapter.

3. Once you have identified the pertinent sections, work through the statute itself by following the process described earlier in this chapter.

4. With your research situation and statutory analysis in mind, explore the annotations; start with the notes of decisions. Look for cases that hold

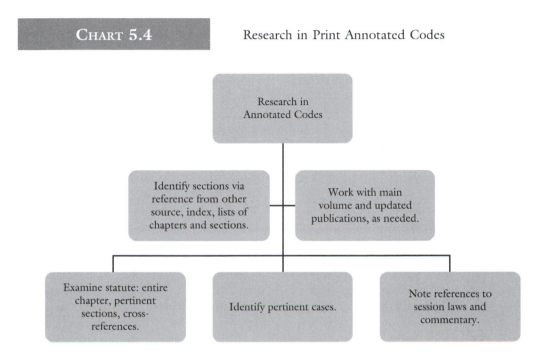

CHART 5.4   Research in Print Annotated Codes

Research in Annotated Codes

Identify sections via reference from other source, index, lists of chapters and sections.

Work with main volume and updated publications, as needed.

Examine statute: entire chapter, pertinent sections, cross-references.

Identify pertinent cases.

Note references to session laws and commentary.

the statute unconstitutional, address points raised in your client's situation, or state the court's general approach to the statute. Focus on the most binding cases, e.g., recent cases from a state's highest court.

5.   Consider next the additional references in the annotation, such as session law references or commentary sources, should you need to continue to expand your research realm beyond cases.

More likely than not, you will need to conduct this process in more than one volume. The typical situation is a bound volume and a pocket part; indeed, a supplementary pamphlet may also be involved. A good process is to take a look at the pocket part before delving too deeply into the main volume, once to check for any changes in the language of the statute, again before looking for cases.

For purposes of illustration, consider a second dimension of the potential Acme Balloon case. Acme was concerned that a claim would be brought against it as the employer of the employee involved in the crash. At the time of the accident, the employee was commuting to work yet also on an errand for Acme. One issue was whether the employee was "acting within the scope of employment," a requirement that the claimant would need to meet to hold Acme liable.[13] A California statute governed this issue.

13. The claimant would also, of course, have to prove that the employee-driver acted with some degree of fault, most likely negligence, which could be based on driving while talking on a cell phone.

Exhibits 5.2 through 5.5 are from the print version of *West's Annotated California Codes*, a typical print code.[14] Before we turned to the California statutes, we had learned about the key concept of agency through research in commentary. Exhibit 5.2, the index page for Agents, directed us, under sub-heading "Liability—Principals" to CC 2330 et seq. Exhibit 5.3 was from the Civil Code, showing various layers of its organization: Title 9 Agency, Chapter 1 Agency in General, Article 3 on Mutual Obligations of Principals and Third Persons.

Exhibit 5.4 was the pertinent section, section 2338, which stated that a principal (i.e., the employer) was responsible to third parties for the negligence of the agent (i.e., the employee) "in the transaction of the business of the agency." Immediately following the statutory language was identification of the statute's origin: it was enacted in 1872 and had not been amended. For more recent statutes, one would also find the session law numbers for the original law and amendments. We then found a reference to a formbook, related statutory sections, and law review articles. On the next page, we found references to a West key number and the encyclopedia *Corpus Juris Secundum*. Finally, the West editors provided synopses of cases, called "Notes of Decisions," filed under 532 different topics (preceded by an outline and index). One of those topics was "Going to or from work, scope of employment." Under that heading we found descriptions of various cases, including those listed in Exhibit 5.5, which was from the 2011 pocket part supplementing the 1985 main volume.

Because we found the language of the statute unclear as applied to the Acme Balloon facts, we read cases, including one synopsized in the 2011 pocket part, *Jeewarat v. Warner Bros. Entertainment, Inc.*, a 2009 decision of the California Court of Appeals.[15] The employee there was involved in a crash as he drove home from the airport upon his return from a business trip. The case provided an extensive discussion of scope of employment, including the general principle that an employee is not acting within the scope of employment when going to or coming from the workplace. An exception exists, however, when the trip involves "a special errand either as part of his regular duties or at a specific order or request of his employer."[16]

Thus we determined that we would need to inquire into how it was that the employee came to take on the task of picking up doughnuts before we could know whether Acme Balloon would likely be liable for the employee's driving.

---

14. In addition, LexisNexis publishes *Deering's California Codes Annotated*.
15. *Jeewarat v. Warner Bros. Entm't, Inc.*, 98 Cal. Rptr. 3d 837 (Cal. Ct. App. 2009).
16. *Id.* at 844. The court ruled that the business trip qualified as a special errand.

EXHIBIT 5.2   Index from Print Annotated Code
(*West's Annotated California Code*)

AGENTS

AGENTS—Cont'd

Food and agriculture department, **Food & A 104**

Foreign Banking Corporations, this index

Foreign Corporations, this index

Forestry department, agency for state, urban forestry, **Pub R 4799.10**

Fox Canyon groundwater management agency, **Water App 121–102 et seq.**

Fraud, **CC 2306**

Frauds, statute of, real estate sales, **CC 1624**

Fraudulent transfers, principles supplementing, **CC 3439.10**

Funds transfers, transfer system, **Com 11206**

Fur agents, licenses, **Fish & G 4032 et seq.**

General agent, definitions, **CC 2297**

Good faith, principal bound by acts under ostensible authority, **CC 2334**

Government agencies. Public Agencies, generally, this index

Group life insurance, **Ins 10203.7**

Health care service plans,
  Compensation and salaries, disclosure, **Health & S 1367.08**
  Contracts, sales, leases, transfers, **Bus & P 511.3; Health & S 1375.7**

Hearsay rule, exception, **Evid 1222**

Home equity sales contracts, equity purchasers, liability, **CC 1695.15 et seq.**

Home improvement business, **Bus & P 7150 et seq.**

Horse Racing, this index

Horses, sales, dual agency, **Bus & P 19525**

Hospital districts, voluntary area health planning agency, **Health & S 32221**

Hospitals,
  Referral agencies, **Health & S 1400 et seq.**
  Report of personal injury inflicted by weapons, **Pen 11160 et seq.**

Housing Finance Agency, generally, this index

Incapacity, termination of agency, **CC 2355, 2356**

Income Tax—State, this index

Indemnity and indemnification, **CC 2775; Corp 317**

Independent wholesale sales representatives, **CC 1738.10 et seq.**

Industrial Loan Companies, this index

Informing principal, **CC 2020**

Instructions by principal, disobedience, **CC 2320**

Instrument within scope of authority, binding principal, **CC 2337**

Insurance Agents, Solicitors or Brokers, generally, this index

AGENTS—Cont'd

International Banking Corporations, this index

Investment Securities, this index

Job training and placement services, **Un Ins 9000 et seq.**

Joint powers agencies, grand jury investigations, **Pen 925a**

Joint stock associations, criminal liability, **Corp 22001, 22002**

Kern County water agency, **Water App 99–1 et seq.**

Landlord and Tenant, this index

Landscape architecture, state board, **Bus & P 5629**

Liability, **CC 2342 et seq.**

Principals, **CC 2330 et seq.**

Limitation of actions, stolen art or artifacts, **CCP 338**

Limited liability companies, fraud, **Corp 17656**

Limited partnership, general partners, **Corp 15904.02**

Limits of authority, **CC 2019**

Liquidation, credit unions, **Fin 15251**

Local Agency Allocation, generally, this index

Local Agency Formation Commission, generally, this index

Long term health care facilities, sale or gift to residents property, **Health & S 1289**

Marine insurance, acts of insurers agents subsequent to loss, **Ins 1980**

Mariposa County water agency, **Water App 85–1 et seq.**

Masters of vessels,
  Cargo owners, authority, **Harb & N 812**
  Shipowners, **Harb & N 810, 812**

Measure of authority, **CC 2315**

Meat and poultry inspection, adulteration, crimes, **Food & A 18933**

Mechanics liens, **CC 8066**

Medi Cal Program, this index

Medical Care and Treatment, this index

Military base reuse authority, purchase, sale or lease of property, **Gov 67842**

Mobilehomes and Mobilehome Parks, this index

Mojave water agency, **Water App 97–1 et seq.**

Money transmission, **Fin 2060 et seq.**

Mortgages,
  Agent of mortgagee, collection, notice of default, **CC 2924.3**
  Trustees payments, **CC 2924d**

Motor Clubs, this index

Motor vehicle fuel, licenses and permits, information, **Rev & T 7520**

Motor vehicle repair dealers, estimates, **Bus & P 9884.9**

<table>
<tr><td>EXHIBIT 5.3</td><td>List of Titles, Chapters, Articles, and Sections from Print Annotated Code (West's Annotated California Code)</td></tr>
</table>

Title 9
AGENCY

Chapter 1
AGENCY IN GENERAL

Article 1
DEFINITION OF AGENCY

Section

2295. Agent defined.
2296. Capacity to appoint agent; capacity to be agent.
2297. General and special agents defined.
2298. Actual or ostensible agency.
2299. Actual agency defined.
2300. Ostensible agency defined.

Cross References

Partner as agent of partnership, see Corporations Code § 15009.
Provisions of this title as subordinate to intention of parties and waiver of benefit thereof,
        see § 3268.

§ 2295.   Agent defined

AGENCY, WHAT. An agent is one who represents another, called the principal, in dealings with third persons. Such representation is called agency.

(Enacted 1872.)

EXHIBIT 5.4

Statute with Annotation from Print
Annotated Code (*West's Annotated
California Code*)

MUTUAL OBLIGATIONS   § 2338
Pt. 4

only. McDonald v. Bear River and Auburn Water & Mining Co. (1859) 13 C. 220.

If, on the face of an instrument not under seal, executed by an agent, with competent authority, signing his own name simply, it appears that the agent executed it in behalf of the principal, the principal, and not the agent, is bound. Haskell v. Cornish (1859) 13 C. 45.

§ 2338. Responsibility for agent's negligence or omission

PRINCIPAL'S RESPONSIBILITY FOR AGENT'S NEGLIGENCE OR OMISSION. Unless required by or under the authority of law to employ that particular agent, a principal is responsible to third persons for the negligence of his agent in the transaction of the business of the agency, including wrongful acts committed by such agent in and as a part of the transaction of such business, and for his willful omission to fulfill the obligations of the principal.

(Enacted 1872.)

Forms

See West's California Code Forms, Civil.

Cross References

Damages for torts, see § 3333.
Negligence, see § 1714.
Negligence of pilot and persons employed in navigation, see Harbors and Navigation Code § 820.

Law Review Commentaries

Allegations of defendant's breach of duty in negligence actions, requirements. (1947) 35 C.L.R. 267.

Assault by barkeeper, liability of owners of saloon. (1919) 7 C.L.R. 457.

Automobiles, liability of owner for injuries caused by reckless and incompetent driver. (1923) 12 C.L.R. 61.

Charitable corporations, liability for torts. (1951) 3 Hast.L.J. 81.

Charitable institutions, liability for negligence of agents with reference to operation of automobiles. (1951) 39 C.L.R. 455.

Contract provision restricting representations made by agent to those set forth in contract, effect. (1938) 26 C.L.R. 622.

Employer's liability for assault by employee. (1947) 35 C.L.R. 126.

Executors and administrators, liability for torts occurring while conducting estate business. (1947) 35 C.L.R. 586.

Foreseeability as test of scope of employment, applied to baseball player throwing ball in anger. (1955) 28 So.Cal.L.R. 314.

Independent contractor, liability of employer where work is inherently dangerous. (1935) 9 So.Cal.L.R. 47.

Landlord and tenant, liability to tenant for negligence of independent contractor. (1945) 19 So.Cal.L.R. 141.

Liability of labor unions for picket line assaults. (1973) 21 U.C.L.A. Law Rev. 600.

Master and servant, criminal liability of master for unauthorized acts of servant. (1947) 35 C.L.R. 583.

Liability of master for injuries to third persons. (1929) 17 C.L.R. 582.

Liability of master for servant's assault upon third person. (1929) 17 C.L.R. 185.

Tort liability of master for negligent act of employee while engaged contemporaneously in the performance of his own and his employer's business. (1921) 9 C.L.R. 166.

Obligation to defend under liability insurance. Leslie L. Roos, (1961) 13 Hast.L.J. 206.

EXHIBIT 5.4   *(continued)*

---

§ 2338   **AGENCY**
                                                                                             Div. 3

Presumption of fraud and damages arising from secret payments to known agent.
(1950) 2 Stan.L.R. 574.

Rescission for fraudulent misrepresenta-
tions by agent. (1935) 8 So.Cal.L.R. 146.

Scope of employment as question of fact
or law. (1945) 33 C.L.R. 646.

Scope of employment of servant, use of
unauthorized instrumentality. (1938) 11 So.
Cal.L.R. 377.

Service station torts; oil companies' responsibility. (1974) 10 C.W.L.R. 382.

Special police officer, liability of persons
obtaining appointment and paying compen-

sation for acts of officer. (1930) 18 C.L.R.
705.

Taxicab owner, liability for negligence of
chauffeur operating taxicab in violation of
instructions. (1923) 12 C.L.R. 27.

Vicarious liability of franchisor. (1970) 5
U.S.F.L.Rev. 122.

Vicarious municipal liability: Local
government violations of civil rights.
(1980) 16 C.W.L.R. 58.

Wanton acts of agent, liability of principal. (1939) 12 So.Cal.L.R. 197.

Library References

Principal and Agent ⬤159.
C.J.S. Agency § 423 et seq.

Notes of Decisions

I.   **IN GENERAL   1–80**
II. **ASSAULT   81–150**
III. **FORGERY   151–210**
IV. **FRAUD   211–270**
V.   **LIBEL   271–330**
VI. **MALICIOUS PROSECUTION   331–390**
VII. **NEGLIGENCE   391–470**
VIII. **THEFT, EMBEZZLEMENT AND CONVERSION   471–530**
IX. **TRESPASS   531, 532**

In general 1–80
Actions and proceedings 22
   Assault 89
Acts for which principal is liable, scope of
   employment 10
   Negligence 402
Acts of agent in his own behalf, scope of
   employment 11
   Assault 85
   Forgery 153
   Fraud 215
   Negligence 403
Agent under control of third person, rela-
   tionship of parties 7
   Negligence 399
Agreements to avoid agency relationship,
   liability of principal 395
Assault 81–150
Building and construction contracts, lia-
   bility for acts of independent contrac-
   tor, negligence 407
Burden of proof, assault 90
Control or interference by principal, lia-
   bility for acts of independent contrac-
   tor, negligence 409

Criminal acts of agent, scope of employ-
   ment 17
Damages 26
   Assault 93
Damages in general, negligence 418
Defective means or appliances, liability
   for acts of independent contractor, neg-
   ligence 412
Defective plans or methods, liability for
   acts of independent contractor, negli-
   gence 411
Deviation from instructions, scope of em-
   ployment 9
   Assault 84
   Negligence 401
Evidence 23
   Assault 91
Evidence in general, negligence 416
Foreseeability, scope of employment, as-
   sault 88
Forgery 151–210
Fraud 211–270
Fraudulent and deceitful acts of agent,
   scope of employment 16

620

EXHIBIT 5.5

Notes of Decisions from Print
Annotated Code (*West's Annotated
California Code*)

CIVIL CODE   **§ 2338**
                                                                      Note 12

Employee was not within scope of employment when he injured plaintiff in automobile accident while returning home after taking his children to school and, thus, employer was not vicariously liable for employee's alleged tort, although employee's job required him to be on call at all hours every day, employee wore pager, he was reimbursed when he used his automobile for business travel, and employee intended to make business telephone call at home; purpose of employee's trip was purely personal activity and trip was substantial deviation from employment duties. Le Elder v. Rice (App. 4 Dist. 1994) 26 Cal.Rptr.2d 749, 21 Cal.App.4th 1604, as modified. Automobiles ⬅ 197(2)

In determining whether employee's activity was within scope of employment for respondeat superior purposes, it is necessary to determine main purpose of injury-producing activity; if it was pursuit of employee's personal ends, employer is not liable. Le Elder v. Rice (App. 4 Dist. 1994) 26 Cal.Rptr.2d 749, 21 Cal.App.4th 1604, as modified. Labor And Employment ⬅ 3061(1)

For respondeat superior purposes, totality circumstances is of no legal significance when employee is engaged in purely personal activity when his or her tort causes injury to third party. Le Elder v. Rice (App. 4 Dist. 1994) 26 Cal.Rptr.2d 749, 21 Cal.App.4th 1604, as modified. Labor And Employment ⬅ 3061(1)

12. —— Going to or from work, scope of employment

Assuming that employee's attendance at an out-of-town business conference was a "special errand" for the employer and thus within the scope of employment for purposes of tort liability under respondeat superior doctrine, the "special errand" did not terminate when employee drove past his office on the way from the airport to his home and resumed his regular commute route at approximately his usual time. Jeewarat v. Warner Bros. Entertainment, Inc. (App. 2 Dist. 2009) 98 Cal. Rptr.3d 837, 177 Cal.App.4th 427. Labor And Employment ⬅ 3046(3)

The "special errand" exception to the "going and coming rule" may be applicable to the employee who is called to work to perform a special task for the employer at an irregular time, causing the employee to be within the scope of his employment during the entire trip from his home to work and back to his home, for purposes of respondeat superior doctrine. Jeewarat v. Warner Bros. Entertainment, Inc. (App. 2 Dist. 2009) 98 Cal.Rptr.3d 837, 177 Cal.App.4th 427. Labor And Employment ⬅ 3046(2)

An employee coming from his home or returning to it on a special errand either as part of his regular duties or at a specific order or request of his employer is considered to be in the scope of his employment, for purposes of respondeat superior doctrine, from the time that he starts on the errand until he has returned or until he deviates therefrom for personal reasons. Jeewarat v. Warner Bros. Entertainment, Inc. (App. 2 Dist. 2009)

98 Cal.Rptr.3d 837, 177 Cal.App.4th 427. Labor And Employment ⬅ 3046(2)

Exceptions will be made to the "going and coming rule" that an employee is not acting within the scope of employment while going to or coming from the workplace, for purposes of respondeat superior doctrine, where the trip involves an incidental benefit to the employer, not common to commute trips by ordinary members of the work force. Jeewarat v. Warner Bros. Entertainment, Inc. (App. 2 Dist. 2009) 98 Cal.Rptr.3d 837, 177 Cal.App.4th 427. Labor And Employment ⬅ 3046(2)

An employee who is going to work, or coming from work, is within the scope of employment if the employee is on a special errand, either as part of his or her regular duties or at a specific order or request of the employer; when engaging in a special errand, the employee is considered to be in the course and scope of employment from the time that he or she starts on the errand until returning, unless he or she deviates from the errand in such a material manner as to constitute a departure from the course of employment. Kephart v. Genuity, Inc. (App. 3 Dist. 2006) 38 Cal.Rptr.3d 845, 136 Cal.App.4th 280, rehearing denied, review denied. Labor And Employment ⬅ 3046(2)

Under the going-and-coming rule in a respondeat superior case, an employee is considered not to be in the scope of employment while going to or coming from work. Kephart v. Genuity, Inc. (App. 3 Dist. 2006) 38 Cal.Rptr.3d 845, 136 Cal.App.4th 280, rehearing denied, review denied. Labor And Employment ⬅ 3046(1)

Restaurant employee's work schedule, under which he worked double shift lasting 17.5 hours, was off for 16 hours, and then worked six hours more did not create special risk that employee would fall asleep while driving home after six-hour shift and rear-end another vehicle; thus, imposition of respondeat superior liability on employer for death of other motorist was not warranted. Depew v. Crocodile Enterprises, Inc. (App. 2 Dist. 1998) 73 Cal.Rptr.2d 673, 63 Cal.App.4th 480. Automobiles ⬅ 197(2)

Under "going-and-coming rule," employee is generally not considered to be acting within scope of employment when going to or coming from place of work, for purposes of employer's potential liability for employee's torts under respondeat superior. Depew v. Crocodile Enterprises, Inc. (App. 2 Dist. 1998) 73 Cal.Rptr.2d 673, 63 Cal.App.4th 480. Labor And Employment ⬅ 3046(1)

Exception to rule that employee is not acting in scope of employment when going to or coming from place of work will be found, for purposes of vicarious liability, when employer derives some incidental benefit from employee's trip. Depew v. Crocodile Enterprises, Inc. (App. 2 Dist. 1998) 73 Cal.Rptr.2d 673, 63 Cal.App.4th 480. Labor And Employment ⬅ 3046(2)

In determining whether employment created special risk so as to permit respondeat superior

Additions or changes indicated by <u>underline</u>; deletions by asterisks * * *

COMMERCIAL ONLINE RESEARCH IN STATUTES

Researching in a commercial online resource can provide some advantages, which, depending on the situation, may merit the cost of doing so. Westlaw and LexisNexis are the gold standards of statutory online research. One way to think of their statutory resources is as print annotated codes[17] delivered online and supplemented with citators. Researching in them resembles researching in print annotated codes, as shown in Chart 5.5.

One advantage over the print option is that these online resources provide search methods, such as key-word searching, not available in print resources. Many statutes are written in general language, which is reflected in the internal finding tools of a print resource. However, if you have a quite specific research term, perhaps a factual term, that would appear in a case synopsis but not the statute, key-word searching would be helpful. This advantage is, of course, only as real as your search is well drafted. On the other hand, some commercial online codes do not include indexes.

Two additional advantages of online codes stem from the consolidation of resources online. The online codes provide links to many of the sources referred to in the text and annotations, in particular the cases. And the online codes are seamlessly updated, so you are less likely to miss something important by failing to check a pocket part.

As with cases, you may cite a statute in Shepard's and KeyCite to find sources that potentially affect its status or refer to it in some other way. A statutory citator report resembles a report on a case with a variation or two. A statutory report may include information about the statute's legislative history and information about pending legislation that would affect the statute. The former could be useful in understanding how the statute read at various times in the past or how it came to be. The latter could be helpful in advising a client whose conduct in the future may be governed by any amendments that may be enacted. Citing a statute is a wise follow-up to research in print annotated codes.

By way of example, consider again the cell-phone driving statute. We researched this topic in the LexisNexis Deering's California Codes Annotated database. Our simple search *driv!/s telephone*[18] yielded section 23123, among others. Exhibit 5.6 is the LexisNexis version of section 23123. Note that this result was current into the 2011 special session. LexisNexis also provided various potentially useful items of information: fairly extensive information about the laws that created and amended the statute, a reference to a law review article, and a reference to a LexisNexis survey of laws on this topic

---

17. Many of the print annotated codes are either West or Lexis products.
18. Note that a search for "cell phone" or a variant of this term would not have succeeded; the statute uses the term "wireless."

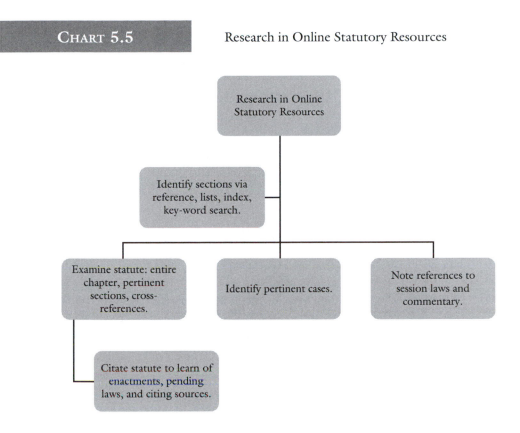

CHART 5.5   Research in Online Statutory Resources

from the fifty states. The annotation's lack of cases was attributable to the newness of the statute.

As shown in Exhibit 5.7, we also cited the statute through Shepard's. The report proved very interesting. First, we saw that the statute carried a yellow triangle indicating that legislation to amend the statute was pending. When we linked to that legislation, we learned that the main purpose of the bills was to raise the penalties for violation of the statute.

Second, we saw a fairly lengthy list of cases citing to the statute, including cases predating its enactment. Puzzled, we checked out these cases and learned that they cited an older statute with the same section number; thus the report was technically correct, but the supplanting of that statute by the cell-phone driving statute had rendered the report confusing.[19] We did find two cases (listed on a page not excerpted here) citing the current section 23123, although neither shed light on our client's situation. Revealing the scope of Shepard's, one case was an unreported federal trial court case from California, the other an unreported appellate state court case from New Jersey.[20]

19. The same pattern occurred on Westlaw.
20. *Le v. Hilton Hotel*, No. C 09-4871 PJH, 2010 U.S. Dist. LEXIS 6346 (N.D. Cal. Jan. 11, 2010). *State v. Malone*, No. A-6176-09T4, 2011 N.J. Super. Unpub. LEXIS 1738 (N.J. Super. Ct. App. Div. July 1, 2011).

EXHIBIT 5.6   Statute from Online Annotated Code

DEERING'S CALIFORNIA CODES ANNOTATED
Copyright (c) 2011 by Matthew Bender & Company, Inc.
a member of the LexisNexis Group.
All rights reserved.

*** This document is current through urgency Chapter 745 & Extra. Sess. Ch. 16 ***
of the 2011 Session, and the 2011 Governor's Reorganization Plan No. 1.

VEHICLE CODE
Division 11.   Rules of the Road
Chapter 12.   Public Offenses
Article 1.   Driving Offenses

GO TO CALIFORNIA CODES ARCHIVE DIRECTORY

Cal Veh Code § 23123 (2011)

§ 23123.   Use of wireless telephone while driving, Infraction; Exceptions

(a) A person shall not drive a motor vehicle while using a wireless telephone unless that telephone is specifically designed and configured to allow hands-free listening and talking, and is used in that manner while driving.

(b) A violation of this section is an infraction punishable by a base fine of twenty dollars ($20) for a first offense and fifty dollars ($50) for each subsequent offense.

(c) This section does not apply to a person using a wireless telephone for emergency purposes, including, but not limited to, an emergency call to a law enforcement agency, health care provider, fire department, or other emergency services agency or entity.

(d) This section does not apply to an emergency services professional using a wireless telephone while operating an authorized emergency vehicle, as defined in Section 165, in the course and scope of his or her duties.

(e) This section does not apply to a person driving a schoolbus or transit vehicle that is subject to Section 23125.

(f) This section does not apply to a person while driving a motor vehicle on private property.

(g) This section shall become operative on July 1, 2011.

HISTORY:

Added Stats 2006 ch 290 § 5 (SB 1613), effective January 1, 2007, operative July 1, 2011; Amended Stats 2007 ch 214 § 3, (SB 33), effective January 1, 2008.

NOTES:

Former Sections:

Former Veh C § 23123, similar to the present section, was added Stats 2006 ch 290 § 4 (SB 1613), effective January 1, 2007, operative July 1, 2008, amended Stats 2007 ch 214 § 2, (SB 33), effective January 1, 2008, and repealed July 1, 2011, by its own provisions.

Exhibit **5.6**   *(continued)*

Page 2

Cal Veh Code § 23123

Amendments:

2007 Amendment:

Amended subd (b) by (1) deleting "Notwithstanding subdivision (a) of Section 42001 or any other provision of law," at the beginning; and (2) substituting "section" for "sections".

Law Review Articles:

How Hands-On Will Regulation of Hands-Free Be? An Analysis of SB 1613 and the Effectiveness of Its Proposed Regulation. 31 Hastings Comm. & Ent. L.J. 463.

Hierarchy Notes:

Div. 11, Ch. 12 Note

Div. 11, Ch. 12, Art. 1 Note

LexisNexis 50 State Surveys, Legislation & Regulations

Distracted Driving and Cell Phones

EXHIBIT 5.7	Statutory Citator Report

Copyright 2011 SHEPARD'S(R) - 16 Citing references

Cal. Veh. Code sec. 23123

Restrictions: *Comprehensive Report Unrestricted*
FOCUS(TM) Terms: *No FOCUS terms*
Print Format: *FULL*
Citing Ref. Signal Legend:

● {Warning} -- Negative treatment is indicated
① {Warning} -- Negative case treatment is indicated for statute
▣ {Questioned} -- Validity questioned by citing references
▲ {Caution} -- Possible negative treatment
◆ {Positive} -- Positive treatment is indicated
Ⓐ {Analysis} -- Citing Refs. With Analysis Available
❶ {Cited} -- Citation information available

SHEPARD'S SUMMARY

Unrestricted *Shepard's* Summary			
Citing References:			𝒱 - Pending Legislation
❶ Citing Decisions:	**Citing decisions with no analysis assigned (15)**	
Other Sources:	**Law Reviews (1)**	

HISTORY Legislative History could not be retrieved.

CITING DECISIONS (15 citing decisions)

CALIFORNIA COURTS OF APPEAL

1.   **Cited by:**
     People v. Mack, 66 Cal. App. 3d 839, 136 Cal. Rptr. 283, 1977 Cal. App. LEXIS 1183 (Cal. App. 3d Dist.
     1977)Ⓐ
        66 Cal. App. 3d 839 *p.847*
        136 Cal. Rptr. 283 *p.284*

2.   **Cited by:**
     Stackhouse v. Municipal Court, 63 Cal. App. 3d 243, 133 Cal. Rptr. 694, 1976 Cal. App. LEXIS 2007 (Cal.
     App. 2d Dist. 1976)❶
        63 Cal. App. 3d 243 *p.245*
        133 Cal. Rptr. 694 *p.695*

3.   **Cited by:**
     Frederick v. Justice Court, 47 Cal. App. 3d 687, 121 Cal. Rptr. 118, 1975 Cal. App. LEXIS 1059 (Cal. App.
     2d Dist. 1975)▲

This experience proves a critical point about research in general: to research competently, you must be something of a skeptic. As expansive and sophisticated as the resources available to you are, especially those delivered online, no resource is infallible. If you use various search methods, you likely will retrieve some information; you must examine it carefully to determine whether it is indeed pertinent and accurate.

Furthermore, you must consider what you retrieve to determine whether it is all that you need. Research is vexing: you know what you have found, but you do not know what you have *not* found. To reduce the possibility that the unfound is substantial and significant, practice reasonable redundancy, such as both reading annotations to a statute and citing it.

NEWLY ENACTED LAWS AND SESSION LAWS

As noted previously, as laws are enacted, they are collected into a compilation called "session laws," because each such compilation contains the laws from one session. Lawyers research in session laws for several reasons.

First, you may need to find a recent law not yet appearing in the jurisdiction's code.[21] Most lawyer's now conduct this research online. An online annotated code may provide a link to the law as it passed the legislature, and many legislatures post new laws on their websites.

Your interest in session laws may pertain to an older statute. First, your client's situation may have occurred in the past when the law was different than it is now; session laws, unlike current codes, are historical repositories of laws. Second, a statute that proves unclear in its application to a client's situation may be understood in part by how it came to be and how it has evolved over time.[22] Most statutory codes provide a good start by providing session law citations. Indeed, some codes provide significant editorial material explaining the various versions of a statute over time.

As with codes, session laws are available in print and online, in official and unofficial publications. Official print session laws issue at the end of a session. Annotated codes include session law pamphlets and databases as part of their updating process, typically under the designation "legislative service." Session laws are not annotated.

For example, Exhibit 5.8 is chapter 214 of the laws passed during the 2007 regular session of the California Legislature, which enacted section 23123. We obtained it through a link when researching on LexisNexis.

---

21. Some lawyers track not only new laws but also pending bills so that they can keep their clients up to date for planning purposes and, indeed, seek to persuade legislators to pass laws favoring their clients.
22. On rare occasions, there may be a question about the exact wording of a law. The version in the session law is the original version and generally governs.

EXHIBIT 5.8   Law as Enacted from Online Resource

2007 REGULAR SESSION
CHAPTER 214 (Senate Bill No. 33)

BILL TRACKING SUMMARY FOR THIS DOCUMENT

2007 Cal ALS 214; 2007 Cal SB 33; 2007 Cal Stats. ch. 214

Approved by Governor September 13, 2007. Filed with Secretary of State September 13, 2007.

Urgency legislation is effective immediately, Non-urgency legislation will become effective January 1, 2008

To view the next section, type .np* and TRANSMIT.
To view a specific section, transmit p* and the section number.   E.g. p*1

DIGEST: Vehicles: wireless telephones and mobile service devices.

. (1) Under existing law, on and after July 1, 2008, it will be an infraction for any person to drive a motor vehicle while using a wireless telephone, unless that telephone is designed and configured to allow hands-free listening and talking operation, and is used in that manner while driving, except as otherwise provided. A violation point is not given for a violation. A violation is punishable by a base fine of $20 for a first offense and $50 for each subsequent offense.

This bill, on and after July 1, 2008, would prohibit a person under the age of 18 years from driving a motor vehicle while using a wireless telephone, even if equipped with a hands-free device, or while using a mobile service device, as defined. The prohibition would not apply to such a person using a wireless telephone or a mobile service device for emergency purposes. By creating a new infraction, the bill would impose a state-mandated local program.

The bill would prohibit a law enforcement officer from stopping a vehicle for the sole purpose of determining whether the driver is violating the above prohibition, but would not prohibit a law enforcement officer from stopping a vehicle for the purpose of determining whether the driver is using a wireless telephone without a hands-free device. The bill would prohibit a violation point from being given for a conviction of violating the above prohibition. A violation would be punishable by a base fine of $20 for a first offense and $50 for each subsequent offense.

(2) The California Constitution requires the state to reimburse local agencies and school districts for certain costs mandated by the state. Statutory provisions establish procedures for making that reimbursement.

This bill would provide that no reimbursement is required by this act for a specified reason.

SYNOPSIS: An act to amend Sections 12810.3 and 23123 of, and to add Section 23124 to, the Vehicle Code, relating to vehicles.

NOTICE: [A> Uppercase text within these symbols is added <A]
        * * * indicates deleted text

TEXT: The people of the State of California do enact as follows:

EXHIBIT 5.8   *(continued)*

2007 Cal ALS 214, *; 2007 Cal SB 33;
2007 Cal Stats. ch. 214

[*1]   SECTION 1.
Section 12810.3 of the Vehicle Code is amended to read:

§ 12810.3.

(a) Notwithstanding subdivision (f) of Section 12810, a violation point shall not be given for a conviction of a violation of subdivision (a) of Section 23123   [A>OR SUBDIVISION (B) OF SECTION 23124<A] .

(b)   * * *   [A>THIS<A]   section shall become operative on July 1, 2008.

[*2]   SEC. 2.
Section 23123 of the Vehicle Code, as added by Section 4 of Chapter 290 of the Statutes of 2006, is amended to read:

§ 23123.

(a) A person shall not drive a motor vehicle while using a wireless telephone unless that telephone is specifically designed and configured to allow hands-free listening and talking, and is used in that manner while driving.

(b)   * * * A violation of this section is an infraction punishable by a base fine of twenty dollars ($20) for a first offense and fifty dollars ($50) for each subsequent offense.

(c) This section does not apply to a person using a wireless telephone for emergency purposes, including, but not limited to, an emergency call to a law enforcement agency, health care provider, fire department, or other emergency services agency or entity.

(d) This section does not apply to an emergency services professional using a wireless telephone while operating an authorized emergency vehicle, as defined in Section 165, in the course and scope of his or her duties.

(e) This section does not apply to a person when using a digital two-way radio that utilizes a wireless telephone that operates by depressing a push-to-talk feature and does not require immediate proximity to the ear of the user, and the person is driving one of the following vehicles:

(1)   (A) A motor truck, as defined in Section 410, or a truck tractor, as defined in Section 655, that requires either a commercial class A or class B driver's license to operate.

(B) The exemption under subparagraph (A) does not apply to a person driving a pickup truck, as defined in Section 471.

(2) An implement of husbandry that is listed or described in Chapter 1 (commencing with Section 36000) of Division 16.

(3) A farm vehicle that is exempt from registration and displays an identification plate as specified in Section 5014 and is listed in Section 36101.

(4) A commercial vehicle, as defined in Section 260, that is registered to a farmer and driven by the farmer or an employee of the farmer, and is used in conducting commercial agricultural operations, including, but not limited to, transporting agricultural products, farm machinery, or farm supplies to, or from, a farm.

(5) A tow truck, as defined in Section 615.

(f) This section does not apply to a person driving a schoolbus or transit vehicle that is subject to Section 23125.

(g) This section does not apply to a person while driving a motor vehicle on private property.

(h) This section shall become operative on July 1, 2008, and shall remain in effect only until July 1, 2011, and, as of July 1, 2011, is repealed.

[*3]   SEC. 3.
Section 23123 of the Vehicle Code, as added by Section 5 of Chapter 290 of the Statutes of 2006, is amended to read:

§ 23123.

(a) A person shall not drive a motor vehicle while using a wireless telephone unless that telephone is specifically designed and configured to allow hands-free listening and talking, and is used in that manner while driving.

EXHIBIT 5.8   *(continued)*

Page 3

2007 Cal ALS 214, *; 2007 Cal SB 33;
2007 Cal Stats. ch. 214

(b)   * * * A violation of this   * * *   [A>SECTION<A]   is an infraction punishable by a base fine of twenty dollars ($20) for a first offense and fifty dollars ($50) for each subsequent offense.

(c) This section does not apply to a person using a wireless telephone for emergency purposes, including, but not limited to, an emergency call to a law enforcement agency, health care provider, fire department, or other emergency services agency or entity.

(d) This section does not apply to an emergency services professional using a wireless telephone while operating an authorized emergency vehicle, as defined in Section 165, in the course and scope of his or her duties.

(e) This section does not apply to a person driving a schoolbus or transit vehicle that is subject to Section 23125.

(f) This section does not apply to a person while driving a motor vehicle on private property.

(g) This section shall become operative on July 1, 2011.

[*4]   SEC. 4.
Section 23124 is added to the Vehicle Code, to read:

§ 23124.

(a) This section applies to a person under the age of 18 years.

(b) Notwithstanding Section 23123, a person described in subdivision (a) shall not drive a motor vehicle while using a wireless telephone, even if equipped with a hands-free device, or while using a mobile service device.

(c) A violation of this section is an infraction punishable by a base fine of twenty dollars ($20) for a first offense and fifty dollars ($50) for each subsequent offense.

(d) A law enforcement officer shall not stop a vehicle for the sole purpose of determining whether the driver is violating subdivision (b).

(e) Subdivision (d) does not prohibit a law enforcement officer from stopping a vehicle for a violation of Section 23123.

(f) This section does not apply to a person using a wireless telephone or a mobile service device for emergency purposes, including, but not limited to, an emergency call to a law enforcement agency, health care provider, fire department, or other emergency services agency or entity.

(g) For the purposes of this section, "mobile service device" includes, but is not limited to, a broadband personal communication device, specialized mobile radio device, handheld device or laptop computer with mobile data access, pager, and two-way messaging device.

(h) This section shall become operative on July 1, 2008.

[*5]   SEC. 5.

No reimbursement is required by this act pursuant to Section 6 of Article XIII B of the California Constitution because the only costs that may be incurred by a local agency or school district will be incurred because this act creates a new crime or infraction, eliminates a crime or infraction, or changes the penalty for a crime or infraction, within the meaning of Section 17556 of the Government Code, or changes the definition of a crime within the meaning of Section 6 of Article XIII B of the California Constitution.

Citation to Statutes

The basic elements of a citation to a statute are:

1. the name of the code;
2. the information needed to locate the section, including the name of the title, chapter name or title, and section numbers, depending on the design of the code;
3. the date the code was published (not the date the statute was enacted), in parentheses; and
4. the publisher of the code, if the code that is cited is not the official code, also in parentheses.

Not surprisingly, the citation manuals prefer citation to the official code. See *Bluebook* rules B5 and 12 and tables 1 (United States jurisdictions) and 16 (subdivisions); *ALWD* rules 3(c) and 14 and appendix 1 (primary sources by jurisdiction). Thus, the statute featured in this chapter's discussion of print statutes would be cited to the West code as follows:

BLUEBOOK: Cal. Civ. Code § 2338 (West 1985).
ALWD: Cal. Civ. Code Ann. § 2338 (West 1985).

The citation to statutes drawn from an online resource varies, depending on the resource, under *Bluebook* rule 12.5 and *ALWD* rule 14.5. The general principle is to supplement the information with the name of the database and its currency.

SUMMARY OF STATUTORY RESEARCH

At the risk of oversimplification, Chart 5.6 presents the optimal options for use of the many statutory research resources. The key to researching well is to be aware not only of the topic you are researching but also the nature of your research: your present knowledge, the degree of challenge the client's problem presents, the resources available to you, and your ability to incur costs to use a resource.

Chart 5.6	Optimal Options for Statutory Research

If you already have the citation of a statute and want to read only the statute—	Use the legislature's website or a print code.
If you want to focus on the language of the statute itself and have sufficient grounding in the area—	Use the official code, whether on the legislature's website or in print.
If you need to research the statute more deeply—	Use an annotated code, in print or online, depending on your reading preferences, the utility of key-word searching, and cost considerations.
If the situation does not point in a different direction—	Use the resource preferred by *The Bluebook* and the *ALWD Citation Manual* for citation purposes.
To update and expand your research once you have found a pertinent statute—	Check a collection of newly enacted laws; cite the statute in Shepard's or KeyCite.
To research the language of a law as it passed the legislature—	Use a session law publication.

CONSTITUTIONS

The U.S. Constitution, as interpreted by the U.S. Supreme Court, is the highest form of law in the United States. Its articles and amendments set out the roles of the various branches of government, the interaction between the federal government and the states, and the rights of citizens against the government. For example, Article 1, Section 8 gives Congress the power to regulate interstate commerce. As another example, the First Amendment protects citizens from government action that infringes on free speech and free exercise of religion.

States have constitutions as well. They serve analogous functions within their states; indeed, some have provisions tracking provisions of the U.S. Constitution. Some also address matters not addressed in the U.S. Constitution.[23]

---

23. Indeed, some state constitutions run to hundreds of provisions.

Constitutions differ from statutes. They are enacted through more elaborate procedures, including ratification by the states of an amendment to the U.S. Constitution and referenda by the electorate for a state constitutional amendment. The language of a constitutional provision typically is much more general than that of a statute. As a result of this breadth of language and the significance of constitutional provisions, much of constitutional law is found in judicial opinions interpreting the constitutional text.

State courts and federal courts are both called upon to interpret the U.S. Constitution. The U.S. Supreme Court, of course, issues the key precedents. Also important are mandatory precedents from the federal appellate courts for your client's jurisdiction. Federal district court opinions from your client's jurisdiction, federal appellate opinions from other circuits, and state court opinions can provide persuasive authority.

When it comes to state constitutions, state courts have the final interpretive word, although sometimes a federal court may be asked to review whether a state constitution is consistent with the U.S. Constitution. Even when this happens, the federal court generally accepts the state court's explanation of what the state constitution means.

Resources for researching constitutional law are the same as the resources used to research cases, as discussed in Chapter 4, and the resources used to research statutes, discussed in this chapter.

CHARTERS AND ORDINANCES

A surprising amount of law is neither federal nor state but local, created by bodies such as city councils and commissions. These entities typically are created by state law. As with the federal and state governments, their laws may include charters, which are parallel to constitutions, and ordinances, codes, or regulations, which are parallel to statutes. Furthermore, the latter may be enforced by a local enforcement entity.

Historically, the standard means of finding a local government's law was to visit its offices. Now many local governments post their laws on their websites.

Consider again the Acme Balloon situation, in which the employee was pulling out of a private parking lot into traffic, while talking on a cell phone, and ran into another driver. This event occurred in Santa Barbara, California. On the website for Santa Barbara, we found not only its city charter but also its municipal code, including its transportation and parking regulations. Exhibit 5.9 is a potentially pertinent traffic regulation.

EXHIBIT 5.9	Local Regulation (Santa Barbara, California Municipal Code)

Chapter 10.16

STOP AND YIELD REGULATIONS

Sections:

10.16.010   Stop Signs - Transportation Engineer to Erect.

The Transportation Engineer shall erect or cause to be erected, boulevard stop signs complying with provisions of the Vehicle Code at the entrance to every intersection of two (2) or more streets which he has determined is an intersection at which there is special hazard to life or property by reason of the volume of traffic upon such street, or at such intersections, or because of the number of reported accidents or the apparent probability thereof, or by reason of physical conditions which render any such streets or intersections exceptionally dangerous or hazardous to life or property, and where the factors creating the special hazard are such that according to the principles and experience of traffic engineering the installation of stop signs is reasonably calculated to reduce the expectancy of accidents, and that the use of warning signs would be inadequate. (Ord. 2713 §1(part), 1959; prior Code §31.35.)

10.16.020   Obedience to Stop Signs at Intersections.

When stop signs are erected as provided, at the entrance to any intersection, every driver of a vehicle shall stop at every such sign, before entering the intersection. (Ord. 2713 §1(part), 1959; prior Code §31.36.)

10.16.030   Exceptions to Stops at Intersections.

No stop need be made at any such intersection where:
(1)   A Police Officer is on duty and directs traffic to proceed.
(2)   A traffic signal is in operation and indicates that traffic may proceed.
(3)   The operator turns right into a highway from a separate right turn lane which lane is delineated by buttons, markers, or channelization, and no stop sign is in place at the intersection of such separate right turn lane and such highway. (Ord. 2713 §1(part), 1959; prior Code §31.37.)

10.16.040   Emerging from Alley or Private Driveway.

The driver of a vehicle emerging from an alley, driveway or building shall stop such vehicle immediately prior to driving onto a sidewalk or into the sidewalk area extending across any alley-way, yielding the right-of-way to any pedestrian as may be necessary to avoid collision, and upon entering the roadway shall yield the right-of-way to all vehicles approaching on said roadway. (Ord. 2713 §1(part), 1959; prior Code §31.38.)

10.16.050   Obedience to Signal Indicating Approach of Railroad Train.

Whenever any person driving a vehicle approaches a railroad grade crossing under any of the following circumstances stated in this section, the driver of such vehicle shall stop within fifty feet (50') but not less than ten feet (10') from the nearest rail of such railroad, and shall not proceed until he can do so safely. The foregoing requirements shall apply when:
(1)   A clearly visible electric or mechanical signal device gives a warning of the immediate approach of a railroad train.
(2)   A crossing gate is lowered or when a human flagman gives or continues to give signal of the approach or passage of a railroad train.
(3)   An approaching railroad train is plainly visible and is in hazardous proximity to such crossing.
(4)   No person shall drive any vehicle through, around, or under any crossing gate or barrier at a railroad grade crossing while such gate or barrier is closed or is being opened or closed. (Ord. 2713 §1(part), 1959; prior Code §31.39.)

Test Your Understanding

Reflection Questions

1. It is in statutory law that the limits of imagination on the part of lawmakers is the most obvious. That is, legislators likely do their best to create a workable law when they enact it, but its full application is hard to foresee. If you were a legislator drafting a statute, what steps could you take to write workable language?

2. Does it make sense to have three levels of legislatures governing the same topic? Now that the United States has a true national identity, would it be wise to provide that any federal statute in an area precludes state or local laws in the same area?

Your Scenario

As detailed in Chapter 2, your client, Elaine Wilson, is seeking to keep her companion animal in her apartment to assist her with her PTSD. Assume that one approach is to bring a claim of disability discrimination in housing based on West Virginia state law.

- Find the pertinent statute at least three different ways.
- Read and summarize it.
- Discern whether it has been interpreted by the West Virginia courts.
- Discern whether any potential changes are pending in the legislature.

Chapter 6

Research in Legislative History Materials

Contents

This chapter explores the issue of whether an employee is eligible for the protections of the federal Family and Medical Leave Act (also covered in Chapter 7).

Key Concepts and Tools in This Chapter

- authority of legislative history materials
- legislative process, including committee, chamber, and presidential stages

(continued)

- bills
- committee materials: hearings, prints, committee
  prints, documents, reports
- floor debates and proceedings
- *Congressional Record*
- presidential messages
- *United States Code, United States Code Annotated,*
  United States Code Service
- public law number
- *Statutes at Large*
- purpose provision
- *United States Code Congressional and Administrative News*
- compiled legislative histories
- THOMAS
- ProQuest Congressional
- HeinOnline resources
- LexisNexis resources
- Westlaw resources, including Graphical Statutes
- bill-tracking tools

As noted in Chapter 5, a statute, even a fairly lengthy one, is spare; the language is all rule language, without elaboration to guide lawyers in applying it to clients' situations. One aid to interpretation of a statute is its legislative history. Statutes are to be applied according to the legislature's intent; legislative history sheds light on legislative intent.

This chapter begins with an overview of the legislative process and the materials it generates. It then covers the major resources for researching federal legislative history, especially for recent statutes. Materials generated by state legislative processes typically are fewer and much more difficult to locate, especially for old laws.

As the illustration for this chapter, consider the case of Irene Fey. Fey worked for the Colby Sugar Beet Transportation Company, which operates two facilities, one in Duluth, Minnesota, where Fey worked, and another in Sartell, Minnesota. The Sartell plant was 75.7 surface (driving) miles from Duluth, but only 74 linear (as the crow flies) miles away. Throughout 2010, the Duluth facility had forty-five employees; the Sartell facility had six.

In July 2010, Fey requested and was granted a leave of absence under the federal Family and Medical Leave Act (FMLA) to care for her newly adopted daughter. A week before her leave expired, Colby's human resources director notified Fey that her position had been eliminated and that the company had no other position for her.

Fey asked our fictional firm to evaluate whether she had a claim under the FMLA. The FMLA exempted from its coverage employers with fewer than fifty employees within seventy-five miles of the employee's worksite: "The term 'eligible employee' does not include . . . any employee of an employer who is employed at a worksite at which such employer employs less than 50 employees if the total number of employees employed by that employer within 75 miles of that worksite is less than 50."[1] Thus one issue was whether Fey was an eligible "employee" under FMLA.

OVERVIEW OF LEGISLATIVE HISTORY MATERIALS

In its broadest sense, legislative history consists of all the background and events giving rise to the enactment of a law. In a narrower sense, "legislative history" refers to the materials created or considered by the legislature at each stage of the legislative process. The statute itself is the authority; because of their unique relationship to that authority, legislative history materials are "quasi-authority."

The legislative process. The process of enacting a statute is similar at the federal and state levels; this review focuses on the federal Congress.

The legislative process typically begins with the introduction of a bill by a member of Congress.[2] When a bill is introduced, it is given a number, which reflects the order in which it was introduced. A Senate bill number begins with "S" for Senate, a House bill number with "H.R." for House of Representatives.[3] The exact same bill may be introduced in both the House and Senate; the bill then has two bill numbers, and the two bills are companion bills.

After a bill is introduced, it may be referred to one or more committees. A committee may refer a bill to a subcommittee. The committee or subcommittee may hold a hearing on the bill. The bill's sponsors, experts on the topic, representatives of the executive branch, groups affected by the proposed legislation, and public interest groups, as well as others, may testify or submit written comments or supplementary materials for the hearing record.

After the hearing, or at any time if there is no hearing, the subcommittee or the full committee may meet to consider and mark up the bill. If the subcommittee approves the bill, with or without changes, it forwards the bill to the full committee. If the full committee approves the bill, with or without changes, it prepares a committee report, setting forth its analysis and recommendations, and reports the bill to its parent body.[4]

---

1. 29 U.S.C. § 2611(2)(B)(ii) (2006). Incidentally, a state statute covers smaller employers. Minn. Stat. § 181.92 (2010).

2. Some bills have multiple sponsors.

3. Because bill numbering starts over again in each Congress, a complete bill number also includes the number of the Congress in which a bill was introduced.

4. If the committee has approved extensive amendments, it may decide to report a new bill incorporating all the amendments. This is known as a "clean bill"; it will have a new number.

Next the bill goes to the floor of the House or Senate for debate. Floor managers explain the bill and respond to questions about it. Members may offer arguments for and against the bill, and amendments may be offered and either passed or defeated.

If the bill passes in one chamber, it is sent to the other chamber, which may pass the bill without change, or it may amend the bill and return it to the first chamber. The first chamber may accept the amendment, or it may amend the amendment and return the bill to the other chamber, or it may insist on its version of the bill and request a conference committee to resolve the differences.

If the second chamber agrees to a conference committee, leaders of both chambers appoint conferees. If the conferees reach agreement, they prepare a conference committee report with the text of the compromise bill and an explanation. If both chambers vote to accept the compromise bill, it is sent to the president.

The president has ten days, excluding Sundays, in which to sign or veto a bill. If the president signs a bill, the bill becomes effective upon signing, unless a different date is specified in the bill. If the president vetoes a bill, the bill and the president's objections are returned to Congress, where the bill dies unless two-thirds of each chamber vote to override the veto. If the president does not act on a bill within ten days and Congress is still in session, the bill becomes law without the president's signature. If Congress has adjourned, however, the bill dies; this is called a "pocket veto."

Chart 6.1 synopsizes this legislative process. For some statutes, the process proceeds smoothly and quickly; other statutes are the product of years of intense lobbying and heated debate.

CHART 6.1	Legislative Process

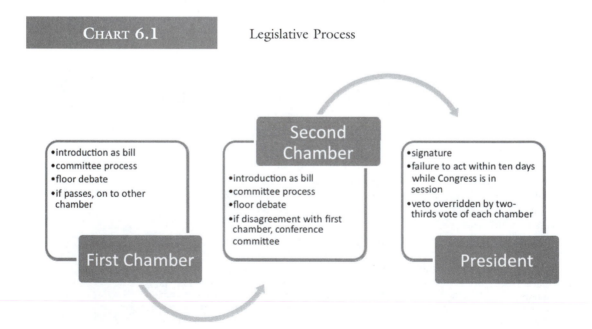

First Chamber
- introduction as bill
- committee process
- floor debate
- if passes, on to other chamber

Second Chamber
- introduction as bill
- committee process
- floor debate
- if disagreement with first chamber, conference committee

President
- signature
- failure to act within ten days while Congress is in session
- veto overridden by two-thirds vote of each chamber

Legislative history materials. The federal legislative process generates seven categories of materials. First, *bills* are printed at various stages: as they are introduced, reported out of committee, and passed by each chamber.[5] In addition, the process may generate amendments that were introduced but did not pass. Exhibit 6.1 is the first page of an introduced bill; Exhibit 6.2 is a proposed amendment.

Second, when a committee or subcommittee holds a hearing on a bill, it may publish the record of the hearing. Published *committee hearings* may include witnesses' oral and written statements, committee questions and answers, statements and exhibits submitted by interested parties, and supplemental material added to the hearing record by committee members and staff. See Exhibit 6.3 for an example of hearing testimony.

Third, a committee may rely on research reports prepared by committee staff or others. These reports, published as *committee prints*, may contain statistics, scientific and social studies, historical data, bibliographies, compilations of statutes, bill comparisons, and other analyses.

Fourth, a communication from the president or an executive agency, such as a message proposing legislation, may appear as a *House or Senate document*. Reports of committee activities, the texts of committee-sponsored studies, background information reports, and other miscellaneous materials may also be issued as House and Senate documents.

Fifth, *committee reports* typically include a description and analysis of the bill, a discussion of its background, the committee's findings and its recommendations, the text of the recommended bill, any minority views, and an estimate of the costs or revenues produced by the bill. Of particular importance are conference committee reports, which contain the text of the compromise bill and an analysis of how the compromise was reached. See Exhibit 6.4.

Sixth, *floor debates and proceedings* include statements made and actions taken in a chamber of Congress. The *Congressional Record* contains more or less verbatim transcripts of floor debates and reports of proceedings, including remarks by members of Congress, their votes, proposed amendments, conference committee reports, messages from the president, and on occasion the texts of bills under consideration.[6] See Exhibit 6.5.

Seventh, *presidential messages* include signing statements and veto messages. See Exhibit 6.6.

Some of these materials are weightier than others. The key factors are who generated the materials, how the materials were generated, and how closely they relate to the law as enacted (rather than prior versions).

Four categories of materials are especially important. First, the various versions of a bill and rejected and adopted amendments may be very persuasive evidence of legislative intent. Second, committee reports are key

5. The term "engrossed bill" refers to the official copy of a bill as it has passed a particular chamber. Other technical terms are defined at the Senate's website, http://www.senate.gov.

6. The *Congressional Record* is not a completely accurate account of what transpired because members of Congress may revise their remarks and may add extended remarks, that is, comments never made on the floor.

documents because they are formally prepared and adopted by the committee that has expertise on the topic and was charged with making a recommendation on the bill. Conference committee reports are especially important because they arise late in the legislative process and explain the resolution of differences between the House and Senate. Third, floor debates are controversial because legislators sometimes seek to use them to establish a reading of the legislation that they were unable to incorporate into the statute itself. Nevertheless, courts do rely on such statements, particularly when they are made by the bill's sponsors. Fourth, hearing records typically have less weight. Although they may contain useful information, much of the testimony is not given by those who vote on the bill and may reflect the biased positions of those testifying.

As for the others, committee prints are less commonly used but may contain factual background information from which you can infer the concerns of the legislature. House and Senate documents also are less commonly used, but reports of the executive branch may discuss the problems that a law was designed to remedy. The executive's action in approving or vetoing a bill may provide indirect evidence of legislative intent, particularly for legislation passed over a veto. Chart 6.2 summarizes typical legislative history documents.

CHART 6.2		Legislative History Materials

Document	Stage of Process	Weightiness
Bills	Various stages, e.g., introduced, reported out of committee, passed by a chamber	Very weighty
Committee hearing	Hearing or subcommittee consideration	Influential
Committee prints	Hearing or subcommittee consideration	Potentially useful for factual background
House or Senate document, e.g., message from executive agency, text of committee studies	Hearing or subcommittee consideration	Potentially useful for factual background
Committee reports	Conclusion of hearing process	Very weighty
Floor debates and proceedings	Chamber debate	Potentially weighty
Presidential messages	Signing or veto statements	Indirect evidence of legislative intent

EXHIBIT 6.1   House Bill (H.R.1 from GPO)

I

103D CONGRESS
1ST SESSION

H. R. 1

To grant family and temporary medical leave under certain circumstances.

IN THE HOUSE OF REPRESENTATIVES

JANUARY 5, 1993

Mr. FORD of Michigan (for himself, Mr. CLAY, Mr. MILLER of California, Mr. MURPHY, Mr. KILDEE, Mr. WILLIAMS, Mr. MARTINEZ, Mr. OWENS, Mr. SAWYER, Mr. PAYNE of New Jersey, Ms. UNSOELD, Ms. MINK, Mr. ANDREWS of New Jersey, Mr. REED, Mr. ROEMER, Mr. ENGEL, Mr. BECERRA, Mr. SCOTT, Mr. GENE GREEN of Texas, Ms. WOOLSEY, Mr. ROMERO-BARCELO, Mr. KLINK, Ms. ENGLISH of Arizona, Mr. STRICKLAND, Mrs. SCHROEDER, Mrs. ROUKEMA, Ms. SNOWE, Mr. SWETT, Mr. FORD of Tennessee, Mr. MATSUI, Mr. BONIOR, Mr. SANDERS, Mrs. KENNELLY, Mr. GORDON, and Mr. WELDON) introduced the following bill; which was referred jointly to the Committees on Education and Labor, Post Office and Civil Service, and House Administration

JANUARY 21, 1993

Additional sponsors: Mr. GEPHARDT, Mr. ACKERMAN, Mr. BACCHUS of Florida, Mr. BAESLER, Mr. BARRETT of Wisconsin, Mr. BERMAN, Mr. BILBRAY, Mr. BORSKI, Mr. BROWN of California, Ms. BYRNE, Mr. CHAPMAN, Mr. CLYBURN, Mr. CONYERS, Mr. COSTELLO, Mr. DEFAZIO, Ms. DeLAURO, Mr. DELLUMS, Mr. DE LUGO, Ms. ESHOO, Mr. ESPY, Mr. FALEOMAVAEGA, Mr. FAZIO, Mr. FLAKE, Mr. FOGLIETTA, Mr. FRANK of Massachusetts, Mr. GIBBONS, Ms. HARMAN, Mr. HINCHEY, Mr. HOLDEN, Mr. HYDE, Mr. JOHNSTON of Florida, Mr. KOPETSKI, Mr. LEHMAN, Ms. LONG, Mr. McCLOSKEY, Mr. McDERMOTT, Mr. MACHTLEY, Ms. MALONEY, Mr. MANTON, Mr. MARKEY, Mr. MAZZOLI, Mr. MEEHAN, Mr. MINETA, Mrs. MORELLA, Mr. MURTHA, Ms. NORTON, Mr. OLVER, Mr. PANETTA, Mr. PASTOR, Ms. PELOSI, Mr. PETERSON of Minnesota, Mr. PETERSON of Florida, Mr. POMEROY, Mr. RAHALL, Mr. REYNOLDS, Ms. SCHENK, Mr. SCHUMER, Mr. SHAYS, Mr. STARK, Mr. STUDDS, Mr. STUPAK, Mr. SWIFT, Mr. VENTO, Mr. WASHINGTON, Mr. WAXMAN, Mr. WISE, Mr. WYNN, Ms. BROWN of Florida, Mr. BLACKWELL, Mr. DOOLEY, Mr. COLEMAN, Mrs. COLLINS of Illinois, Mr. EVANS, Mr. FISH, Mr. LEVIN, Ms. MOLINARI, Mr. NEAL of Massachusetts, Mr. OBERSTAR, Mr. POSHARD, Mr. SABO, Ms. SLAUGHTER, Mr. SMITH of New Jersey, Ms. WATERS, Mr. WHEAT, Mr. DIXON, Mr. SERRANO, Mr. RANGEL, Mr. PALLONE, Mr. TRAFICANT, Mr. CARDIN,

EXHIBIT 6.1   *(continued)*

2

Mr. ANDREWS of Maine, Mr. SANGMEISTER, Mr. WILSON, Mr. EDWARDS of California, Mr. RAVENEL, Mr. KLECZKA, and Mr. DURBIN

A BILL

To grant family and temporary medical leave under certain circumstances.

1   *Be it enacted by the Senate and House of Representa-*

2   *tives of the United States of America in Congress assembled,*

3   **SECTION 1. SHORT TITLE; TABLE OF CONTENTS.**

4   (a) SHORT TITLE.—This Act may be cited as the

5   "Family and Medical Leave Act of 1993".

6   (b) TABLE OF CONTENTS.—The table of contents is

7   as follows:

Sec. 1. Short title; table of contents.
Sec. 2. Findings and purposes.

TITLE I—GENERAL REQUIREMENTS FOR LEAVE

Sec. 101. Definitions.
Sec. 102. Leave requirement.
Sec. 103. Certification.
Sec. 104. Employment and benefits protection.
Sec. 105. Prohibited acts.
Sec. 106. Investigative authority.
Sec. 107. Enforcement.
Sec. 108. Special rules concerning employees of local educational agencies.
Sec. 109. Notice.
Sec. 110. Regulations.

TITLE II—LEAVE FOR CIVIL SERVICE EMPLOYEES

Sec. 201. Leave requirement.

TITLE III—COMMISSION ON LEAVE

Sec. 301. Establishment.
Sec. 302. Duties.
Sec. 303. Membership.
Sec. 304. Compensation.
Sec. 305. Powers.
Sec. 306. Termination.

•HR 1 SC

Exhibit 6.2	Proposed Amendment (*Congressional Record* from Westlaw)

Under the rule, it is now in order for the gentleman from Pennsylvania <Mr. GOODLING> to offer his second **amendment**.

AMENDMENT OFFERED BY MR. GOODLING

Mr. **GOODLING**.

Madam Chairman, I offer an **amendment**.

The CHAIRMAN.

The Clerk will designate the **amendment**.

The text of the **amendment** is as follows:

Amendment offered by Mr. GOODLING: Amend section 101(2)(B) to add a new clause as follows:

(iii) any employee of an employer whose absence during leave would clearly result in substantial and grievous economic injury to the operations of the employer or substantial endangerment to the health and safety of other employees of the employer or the public.

Amend section 101(2)(C) to read as follows:

(c) DETERMINATION.-

(A) CLAUSE (ii).-For purposes of determining whether an employee meets the hours of service requirement specified in subparagraph (A)(ii), the legal standards established under section 7 of the Fair Labor Standards Act of 1938 (29 U.S.C. 207) shall apply.

(B) CLAUSE (iii).-The exception in subparagraph (A)(iii) shall apply only if-

(i) the employer notices the employee of intent of the employer to deny leave on such basis at the time the employer determines that such injury or endangerment would occur; and

(ii) in any case in which the leave has commenced, the employee elects not to return to employment after receiving such notice.

In section 104, strike out subsection (b) and redesignate subsection (c) as subsection (b).

The CHAIRMAN.

The gentleman from Pennsylvania <Mr. GOODLING> will be recognized for 10 minutes, and the gentleman from Michigan <Mr. FORD> will be recognized for 10 minutes.

The Chair recognizes the gentleman from Pennsylvania <Mr. GOODLING>.

Mr. **GOODLING**.

Madam Chairman, I yield myself such time as I may consume.

Madam Chairman, I would like to take some time on this one, because it is a very important **amendment** if we are going to try to improve the bill at all.

What we are talking about here is allowing the employer to deny leave in very critical, limited circumstances when the employee in question is crucial to the ongoing operation of the employer, but only in those circumstances. Again, it is very tightly drawn so that it cannot be abused.

H.R. 1 appears to recognize an employer's right to deny leave in such a situation, but let us look at it carefully. If we turn to section 104(b) of the bill where the so-called key employee exemption is to be found, first the employee must be in the top-paid 10 percent of the employer's work force at the worksite in question, or within 75 miles thereof. Then if the employee's reinstatement would cause substantial and grievous economic harm, the employer need not reinstate the employee.

Note that the focus, strangely, is not on the impact of the employee's absence, but on the reinstatement. Let us read the text of the bill and then the Members will understand what it is all about. Maybe if he or she was making $500,000 a year, reinstatement might lead to grievous harm but when else?

I realize this is strange language that is in this bill, and it may have been structured this way in order to require

EXHIBIT 6.3	Hearing Testimony (from ProQuest Congressional)

71

TESTIMONY OF MICHAEL R. LOSEY, SPHR

Dear Mr. Chairman:

Good morning. My name is Mike Losey, and I am President and CEO of the Society for Human Resource Management (SHRM). I am pleased to be here today to present testimony on behalf of the Society on the subject of family and medical leave legislation. SHRM is the leading voice of the human resource profession, representing the interests of more than 50,000 individual professional and student members from around the world. SHRM provides its membership with education and information services, conferences and seminars, government and media representation, and publications that equip human resource professionals to become leaders and decision makers within their organizations.

As you know, the family and medical leave issue has been before Congress for the last eight years. Throughout that time, SHRM has expressed concerns over specific provisions of the legislation. We have also expressed our concern that government mandates of workforce policies which were previously arranged between employers and employees will result in administrative, statutory and competitiveness challenges. Throughout this long debate on this issue, our nation has experienced changes. We have witnessed changes in the composition of the workforce, changes in employment practices and, now, even political change.

1

EXHIBIT 6.4	Committee Report (from U.S.C.C.A.N.)

FAMILY AND MEDICAL LEAVE ACT OF 1993

P.L. 103–3, see page 107 Stat. 6

DATES OF CONSIDERATION AND PASSAGE

House: February 3, 4, 1993

Senate: February 4, 1993

Cong. Record Vol. 139 (1993)

House Report (Education and Labor Committee) No. 103–8(I), Feb. 2, 1993
[To accompany H.R.1]

House Report (Post Office and Civil Service Committee) No. 103–8(II), Feb. 2, 1993
[To accompany H.R.1]

Senate Report (Labor and Human Resources Committee) No. 103–3, Jan. 27, 1993
[To accompany S.5]

The House bill was passed in lieu of the Senate bill after amending its language to contain the text of the Senate bill. The Senate Report (this page) is set out below and the President's Signing Statement (page 54) follows.

SENATE REPORT NO. 103–3

[page 1]

The Committee on Labor and Human Resources, to which was referred the bill (S. 5) to entitle employees to family and medical leave in certain cases involving a birth, an adoption, or a serious health condition of an employee, a child, a spouse or a parent, with adequate protection of the employees' employment and health benefit rights, having considered the same, reports favorably thereon and recommends that the bill do pass.

CONTENTS

3

EXHIBIT 6.4   *(continued)*

LEGISLATIVE HISTORY
SENATE REPORT NO. 103–3
I. SUMMARY OF THE BILL

Title I of S. 5, the Family and Medical Leave Act of 1993, makes available to eligible employees up to 12 weeks of unpaid leave per

[page 2]

year under particular circumstances that are critical to the life of a family. Leave may be taken (1) upon the birth of the employee's child, (2) upon the placement of a child with the employee for adoption or foster care, (3) when the employee is needed to care for a child, spouse or parent who has a serious health condition, or (4) when the employee is unable to perform the functions of his or her position because of a serious health condition.

The act exempts small businesses and limits coverage of private employers to employers who employ 50 or more employees for each working day during 20 or more calendar weeks in the current or preceding calendar year. To be eligible for leave, an employee of a covered employer must have been employed by the employer for at least 12 months and must have worked at least 1,250 hours during the 12-month period proceeding the commencement of the leave. The employer must, in addition, employ at least 50 people within a 75-mile radius of the employee's worksite.

If the employer provides paid leave for which the employee is eligible, the employee may elect or the employer may require the employee to substitute the paid leave for any part of the 12 weeks of leave to which the employee is entitled under the act. When the need for leave is foreseeable, the employee must provide reasonable prior notice, and make efforts to schedule leave so as not to disrupt unduly the employer's operations. An employer may also require an employee to report periodically during the leave period on the employee's leave status and intention to return to work. Spouses employed by the same employer are limited to a total of 12 weeks of leave for the birth or adoption of a child or for the care of a sick parent.

An employer may require medical certification to support a claim for leave for an employee's own serious health condition or to care for a seriously ill child, spouse or parent. For the employee's own medical leave, the certification must include a statement that the employee is unable to perform the functions of his or her position. For leave to care for a seriously ill child, spouse or parent, the certification must include an estimate of the amount of time the employee is needed to care for the child or parent. An employer may require a second medical opinion and periodic recertification at its own expense. If the first and second opinions differ, the employer, again at its own expense, may require the binding opinion of a third health care provider, approved jointly by the employee and the employer.

An employee needing leave because of his or her own serious health condition or the serious health condition of a child or parent may, if medically necessary, take leave intermittently or on a reduced leave schedule that reduces the employee's usual number of hours per workweek or per workday. However, if an employee requests leave on such a basis, the employer may require the employee to transfer temporarily to an alternative position which better

4

Exhibit 6.5	Floor Debate (*Congressional Record* from Westlaw)

In fact, the United States is the only industrial country without it.

Taxpayers will be better off. Why? Because they do not have to pay unemployment or welfare for workers who have been fired.

But let us put the emphasis where it belongs, on the benefit that makes this bill not just good policy and sound politics, but a compelling moral issue.

Families will be better off. That is what this is about, making families better off. After all, do we really want an America where workers can be fired because they need to take cancer-ridden children for chemotherapy? Do we really want an America where workers can be fired because they need some time off to care for an aging parent who may have Alzheimer's disease? Is that the kind of America that we want, an America that gives lip service to family values but turns it back at the very moment they are the most vulnerable?

For 7 years, this bill has been blocked. Now the roadblocks are removed. The road is clear. Thanks to the likes of the gentleman from Michigan <Mr. FORD>, the gentleman from Missouri <Mr. CLAY>, the gentlewoman from New Jersey <Mrs. ROUKEMA>, and the gentleman from the other body, CHRIS DODD, who have worked tirelessly to make sure this bill hits the President's desk.

Let us get it to the President's desk this week, to the President who not only believes in family values but who values families. Let us move together on this bill that keeps families together.

Mr. MYERS of Indiana.

Madam Chairman, I yield 3 minutes to the gentleman from Kentucky <Mr. BUNNING>.

Mr. BUNNING.

Madam Chairman, I rise in opposition to H.R. 1, the Federal Government-Knows-Best-Act of 1993.

I have nine kids. I know the importance of spending time with newborn infants and children when they are seriously ill. We all understand that. But this bill is not the way to do it.

This bill basically says that the U.S. Congress knows better than the marketplace. This bill says that Congress knows better than the Nation's employers and employees about what kind of benefits our Nation's workers want and need.

It plucks a magic number of 12 weeks a year out of a hat, and says this is what we need.

This kind of one-size-fits-all mandate from on high just does not make sense. It does not matter if your employees want it. It does not matter if it damages your business. This is the one benefit that Congress is going to single out and insist that you provide.

Not only does it reduce flexibility in the kind of benefit programs employers can offer, but like any Government mandate, it also imposes very real costs on small business.

It is another layer of regulation that does nothing to promote economic growth. It will actually destroy job opportunities and damage productivity.

Just yesterday, the owners of a small business in my district explained to me that, if this bill passes, they will just make sure that they do not grow to the point that they have 50 employees. They will hire part-time workers. They will contract out. They will do what is necessary to stay under the 50-employee trigger.

So, this bill-compassionate as it may sound-is going to create a ceiling-a very artificial ceiling that limits growth and slows job creation. And anything that slows job growth is not compassionate in my book. The first and foremost need of American families-any family-is a job. And this bill destroys jobs.

Make no mistake about it, if this bill was as harmless and as inexpensive as its supporters pretend, they would not have had to exempt 95 percent of all businesses from its coverage to get it to the floor.

But, what is even more frightening is that we all know what happens to small business exemptions. They tend to erode over the years. We know that this bill is just the beginning. We know that if we enact this bill, it is just the first step to paid leave and other mandated benefits for all American businesses, large and small alike.

Madam Chairman, this is a bad bill. It is a bad precedent. It is bad economic policy. And it should be rejected.

EXHIBIT 6.6   Presidential Signing Statement (from U.S.C.C.A.N.)

SIGNING STATEMENT
P.L. 103–3

STATEMENT BY PRESIDENT OF THE UNITED STATES

STATEMENT BY PRESIDENT WILLIAM J. CLINTON
UPON SIGNING H.R. 1

29 Weekly Compilation of Presidential Documents 144,
February 8, 1993

Today, I am pleased to sign into law H.R. 1, the "Family and Medical Leave Act of 1993." I believe that this legislation is a response to a compelling need—the need of the American family for flexibility in the workplace. American workers will no longer have to choose between the job they need and the family they love.

This legislation mandates that public and private employers with at least fifty workers provide their employees with family and medical leave. At its core is the provision for employees to take up to 12 weeks of unpaid leave for the care of a newborn or newly adopted child, for the care of a family member with a serious medical condition, or for their own illness. It also requires employers to maintain health insurance coverage and job protection for the duration of the leave. It sets minimum length of service and hours of work requirements before employees become eligible.

The need for this legislation is clear. The American workforce has changed dramatically in recent years. These changes have created a substantial and growing need for family and medical leave for working Americans.

In 1965, about 35 percent of mothers with children under 18 were labor force participants. By 1992, that figure had reached 67 percent. By the year 2005, one of every two people entering the workforce will be women.

The rising cost of living has also made two incomes a necessity in many areas of this country, with both parents working or looking for work in 48 percent, or nearly half, of all two parent families with children in the United States.

Single parent families have also grown rapidly, from 16 percent of all families with children in 1975 to 27 percent in 1992. Finally, with America's population aging, more working Americans have to take time off from work to attend to the medical needs of elderly parents.

As a rising number of American workers must deal with the dual pressures of family and job, the failure to accommodate these workers with adequate family and medical leave policies has forced too many Americans to choose between their job security and family emergencies. It has also resulted in inadequate job protection for working parents and other employees who have serious health conditions that temporarily prevent them from working. It is neither fair nor necessary to ask working Americans to

54

OVERVIEW OF OPTIONS FOR RESEARCHING LEGISLATIVE HISTORY

Researching legislative history entails two closely linked tasks: (1) identifying the particular public law to research and the steps that law took en route to enactment and (2) obtaining and reading the documents created at the various steps.

This chapter discusses five options for researching federal[7] legislative history: (1) using statutory codes, (2) using *United States Code Congressional and Administrative News*, (3) finding a compiled legislative history, (4) researching in a government website, and (5) researching in a commercial service. Some of these options point you to the documents you need, some contain the documents, and still others do both. Most of these options are available only for relatively recent laws.

As you work with legislative history material, keep in mind that the legislature may not have had any intent as to your client's situation. Legislators may not have thought about the situation, or circumstances may have changed since the statute's enactment. Even if you find a legislative statement on point, the statement may be as ambiguous or inconclusive as the statute. You may even find conflicting statements. Thus, to use legislative history materials properly, you must acquaint yourself thoroughly with a law's full legislative history. Otherwise you risk relying on unrepresentative fragments.

STATUTORY CODES

A statutory code is a good beginning point for legislative history research because it contains the text of the statute, useful historical information, and sometimes a reference to another resource. Federal statutes appear in three codes: the official *United States Code*, West's *United States Code Annotated* (U.S.C.A.), and LexisNexis' *United States Code Service* (U.S.C.S.).

First review the text of the statute. Some statutes include a purpose provision, typically in the first or second section of the statute. Because this provision is part of the statute, it is highly authoritative.

Next examine the citations immediately following the text of the statutory section on which you are focusing. Those citations note the public law that created the statute and every law that amended it, providing for each its public law number, date of passage, and a citation to *Statutes at Large* where you will find it. *Statutes at Large* is the federal session law publication, in which the laws passed in a two-year Congressional session appear in the order they passed.

---

7. For guidance researching state legislative history, consult a state-specific legal research guide or a law librarian.

Finally, look at the history information following the citations. That information will help you determine which public law to research when the statutory section you are researching has been amended.[8] If you are researching in U.S.C.A., you will find a reference to one or more documents printed in *United States Code Congressional and Administrative News*, a basic legislative history resource.

As relates to our illustrative problem, we researched in U.S.C.A. Section 2601 of Title 29 (which contains labor laws) provided that the purposes of the FMLA included "balanc[ing] the demands of the workplace with the needs of families . . ." and "accomplish[ing] the purposes . . . in a manner that accommodates the legitimate interests of employers." Exhibit 6.7 showed the history information for the FMLA section defining "eligible employee." The history citations and notes showed that the definition of "eligible employee" containing the phrase "within 75 miles of that worksite" had not been amended since it was passed as part of Public Law 103-3 in 1993. The notes also provided a reference to the Senate Report and the signing statement by the president found at 1993 U.S. Code Cong. and Adm. News, p. 3.

UNITED STATES CODE CONGRESSIONAL AND ADMINISTRATIVE NEWS (U.S.C.C.A.N.)

Because it is so accessible, *United States Code Congressional and Administrative News*, published by West, often is a good second source for legislative history research. Each set of bound U.S.C.C.A.N. volumes covers one session of Congress in two sections: one for *Statutes at Large* reprints (the laws themselves), one for selected legislative history documents. Both sections are arranged by public law number.

You can locate the legislative history material for a law by using its public law number, a reference from U.S.C.A., or a set's subject index. The legislative history section for a law begins with a wealth of information about the law, including, as available: (1) its public law number and *Statutes at Large* citation, (2) the dates of consideration and passage of the legislation by both chambers, (3) the numbers of the House and Senate bills, (4) the committees to which the bills were assigned, (5) the numbers and dates of committee and conference committee reports, and (6) the volumes and years of the *Congressional Record* in which debate and action on the bills occurred. This information is useful if you continue your research in other sources. See Exhibit 6.4.

U.S.C.C.A.N. then typically reprints one or more committee reports and perhaps a presidential signing statement for the law. The committee reports are edited to remove duplicative or less helpful information; omissions are shown by asterisks, and official page numbers are in brackets.

---

8. If the statutory notes do not provide enough help, consult *Statutes at Large* to determine which public law enacted the text you are researching.

EXHIBIT 6.7

Legislative History Information
in Annotated Code (*United States Code
Annotated*)

---

29 § 2611　　　　　　　　　　　　　　　　LABOR　Ch. 28

(B) a unit established for the purpose of providing command and control of members of the Armed Forces receiving medical care as outpatients.

(18) Next of kin

The term "next of kin", used with respect to an individual, means the nearest blood relative of that individual.

(19) Serious injury or illness

The term "serious injury or illness", in the case of a member of the Armed Forces, including a member of the National Guard or Reserves, means an injury or illness incurred by the member in line of duty on active duty in the Armed Forces that may render the member medically unfit to perform the duties of the member's office, grade, rank, or rating.

(Pub.L. 103–3, Title I, § 101, Feb. 5, 1993, 107 Stat. 7; Pub.L. 104–1, Title II, § 202(c)(1)(A), Jan. 23, 1995, 109 Stat. 9; Pub.L. 108–271, § 8(b), July 7, 2004, 118 Stat. 814; Pub.L. 110–181, Div. A, Title V, § 585(a)(1), Jan. 28, 2008, 122 Stat. 128.)

HISTORICAL AND STATUTORY NOTES

Revision Notes and Legislative Reports

1993 Acts. Senate Report No. 103–3 and Statement by President, see 1993 U.S. Code Cong. and Adm. News, p. 3.

1995 Acts. Related House Report No. 104–650(Parts I and II) and Related Senate Report No. 104–397, see 1995 U.S. Code Cong. and Adm. News, p. 3.

2008 Acts. Statement by President, see 2008 U.S. Code Cong. and Adm. News, p. S3.

Amendments

2008 Amendments. Pars. (14) to (19). Pub.L. 110–181, § 585(a)(1), added pars. (14) to (19).

2004 Amendments. Par. (4)(A)(iv). Pub.L. 108–271, § 8(b), substituted "Government Accountability Office" for "General Accounting Office".

1995 Amendments. Subsec. (4)(A). Pub.L. 104–1, § 202(c)(1)(A), struck "and" at the end of cl. (ii), struck the period at the end of cl. (iii), and inserted "; and", and added cl. (iv).

Effective and Applicability Provisions

1995 Acts. Amendment by P.L.104–1 effective 1 year after transmission to Congress of the study under section 1371 of Title 2, The Congress, see section 1312(e)(2) of Title 2. The study required under section 1371 of Title 2, dated Dec. 31, 1996, was transmitted to Congress by the Board of Directors of the Office of Compliance on Dec. 30, 1996.

1993 Acts. Section effective 6 months after Feb. 5, 1993, except that, in the case of collective bargaining agreements in effect on that effective date, this section to apply on the earlier of (1) the date of the termination of such agreement, or (2) the date that occurs 12 months after Feb. 5, 1993, see section 405 of Pub.L. 103–3, set out as a note under section 2601 of this title.

CROSS REFERENCES

Congressional accountability and administrative and judicial dispute-resolution procedures including judicial branch coverage study, see 2 USCA § 1434.

Family and medical leave rights and protections provided to Presidential offices, see 3 USCA § 412.

Participants in private, State, local and Federal community service projects, service sponsors, see 42 USCA § 12631.

To address our illustrative problem, we read the Senate Report (Exhibit 6.4) and presidential signing statement (Exhibit 6.6) for Public Law 103-3, which we found in U.S.C.C.A.N. by using the citation from U.S.C.A. We found seven references in the Senate Report to the FMLA language excluding an employee from coverage of the Act based on the number of the employer's employees "within 75 miles of [an employee's] worksite." Four used the words "75-mile radius"; three used "75 miles." The context of the references did not provide further guidance, but the phrase "75-mile radius" suggested the idea of linear miles.

COMPILED LEGISLATIVE HISTORIES

If your research project merits further consideration of a law's legislative materials, a good next step is to determine whether it has a compiled legislative history, that is, a collection of pertinent legislative materials or citations to those materials. As a general rule, compiled legislative histories exist for major laws.

You have several options for finding a compiled legislative history. First, you may search an online library catalog doing a key-word or subject search. These searches sometimes lead you to compilations of documents. Second, you may consult a bibliography of compiled histories, such as Nancy P. Johnson, *Sources of Compiled Legislative Histories: A Bibliography of Government Documents, Periodicals and Books*, a version of which appears in HeinOnline's Federal Legislative History library. These sources provide citations to compiled legislative histories or other legislative history information for many laws. Finally, Westlaw, LexisNexis, and HeinOnline offer some compiled legislative histories.[9]

For our illustrative problem, we first checked the Johnson bibliography in HeinOnline, using the FMLA's public law number. Although we found citations to almost twenty sources discussing and citing primary source documents for the FMLA, we found only two citations to comprehensive collections of documents. The first citation was to the legislative history compiled by the law firm of Arnold and Porter, available on Westlaw. The second citation was to a history compiled by the law firm of Covington and Burling, available on HeinOnline.

Next we explored HeinOnline's Federal Legislative History library, browsing it alphabetically by the name of our act. Again we identified the six-volume legislative history, prepared by Covington and Burling. We browsed the tables of contents for the volumes, finding bills, hearings, committee reports, and floor debates and actions, as reported in the *Congressional Record*, for the law that passed and for related bills from as far back as the 99th

9. The Law Librarians Society of Washington, D.C., maintains a list of those legislative histories at http://www.llsdc.org/Leg-Hist-Commercial/. It also provides at that site a link to free legislative histories on the Internet. The lists are selective.

Congress (1985–86). HeinOnline proved an efficient option. It contained a very comprehensive legislative history, prepared by a reputable firm. Furthermore, it allowed us to search all of the documents simultaneously, highlight our search terms, and browse all of the documents.

On the search template Hein provided, we selected FMLA as the act to search and chose a content search of all document types. Our search *"75 mile"* OR *"75 miles"* retrieved thirty-seven documents; most contained multiple instances of our search terms. We focused first on the documents for Public Law 103-3, then on the documents for related prior bills. Again, we found use of the terms "75 miles" and "75-mile radius," but the discussions did not offer additional guidance.

THOMAS, A GOVERNMENT WEBSITE

If you do not find a compiled legislative history that is cost effective to use, a free government website is often your next step. THOMAS, the Library of Congress website, tracks the history of bills, beginning with bills introduced in 1973. It provides the materials themselves, beginning in 1989 for the *Congressional Record* and in 1995 for committee reports. THOMAS does not include the full text of committee hearings.[10] A particular strength of THOMAS is its coverage of amendments.

THOMAS provides several search options. Often a good first option is to retrieve the Bill Summary & Status table for your law by following the Public Laws link on the home page. The Bill Status & Summary table provides links to various categories of information. Those for All Congressional Actions lead to detailed lists of all events in the law's passage along with links to the full text of the documents available on THOMAS. Another option is a key-word search in one of the document databases, such as committee reports or the *Congressional Record*.

Researching the Fey situation, we first examined Exhibit 6.8, the Bill Summary and Status report for H.R.1, which became the FMLA. We found some references to the *Congressional Record* that we had not previously noted, so we searched the *Congressional Record* for the 103rd Congress. We retrieved nineteen documents with our search term *"75 mile"* or its plural. Looking for our highlighted search terms, we browsed the potentially relevant documents but found nothing relevant.

---

10. The Government Printing Office's Federal Digital System, which includes selective hearings, is another option for finding and searching legislative history documents. It is available at http://www.gpo.gov/fdsys/search/home.action.

| EXHIBIT 6.8 | All Congressional Actions Report from THOMAS |

Bill Summary & Status - 103rd Congress (1993 - 1994) - H.R.1 - All Cong...   Page 1 of 3

The Library of Congress > THOMAS Home > Bills, Resolutions > Search Results

Bill Summary & Status
103rd Congress (1993 - 1994)
H.R.1
All Congressional Actions

NEW SEARCH | HOME | HELP |

○ Back to Bill Summary and Status

Print   Subscribe   Share/Save

H.R.1
Latest Title: Family and Medical Leave Act of 1993
Sponsor: Rep Ford, William D. [MI-13] (introduced 1/5/1993)   Cosponsors (170)
Related Bills: H.RES.58, H.RES.71, S.5
Latest Major Action: 2/5/1993 Became Public Law No: 103-3.

ALL ACTIONS: (Floor Actions/Congressional Record Page References)

1/5/1993:   [+]
    Sponsor introductory remarks on measure. (CR E29)   FEEDBACK
1/5/1993:
    Referred to the House Committee on Education and Labor.
    1/21/1993:
        Executive Comment Requested from Labor.
    1/25/1993:
        Referred to the Subcommittee on Labor-Management Relations.
        1/26/1993:
            Subcommittee Hearings Held.
    1/27/1993:
        Committee Consideration and Mark-up Session Held.
    1/27/1993:
        Ordered to be Reported (Amended) by the Yeas and Nays: 29 - 13.
    1/27/1993:
        Subcommittee on Labor-Management Relations Discharged.
    2/3/1993:
        Executive Comment Received from Labor.
1/5/1993:
    Referred to the House Committee on Post Office and Civil Service.
    1/27/1993:
        Committee Consideration and Mark-up Session Held.
    1/27/1993:
        Ordered to be Reported (Amended) in the Nature of a Substitute.
1/5/1993:
    Referred to the House Committee on House Administration.
    1/19/1993:
        Referred to the Subcommittee on Personnel and Police.
2/2/1993:
    Sponsor introductory remarks on measure. (CR H315-316, H318-319)
2/2/1993 3:06pm:
    Reported (Amended) by the Committee on Education and Labor. H. Rept. 103-8, Part I.
2/2/1993 3:08pm:
    Reported (Amended) by the Committee on Post Office and Civil Service. H. Rept. 103-8, Part II.
2/2/1993 4:10pm:
    Rules Committee Resolution H. Res. 58 Reported to House. Rule provides for consideration of H.R. 1 with 3
    hours and 20 minutes of general debate. Previous question shall be considered as ordered without
    intervening motions except motion to recommit with or without instructions. It shall be in order to consider
    as an original bill for the purpose of amendment under the five-minute rule the amendment in the nature of
    a substitute printed in part 1 of the report of the Committee on Rules accompanying this resolution, modified
    by the amendment printed in section 2 of this resolution. Measure will be considered read. Specified
    amendments are in order.

http://thomas.loc.gov/cgi-bin/bdquery/z?d103:HR00001:@@@X|TOM:/bss/...   9/1/2011

COMMERCIAL ONLINE SERVICES

ProQuest Congressional. This resource is the leading and most comprehensive online resource focused solely on providing legislative process materials.[11] Its scope, including both dates of coverage and availability of full text documents, varies depending on what the buyer purchases. ProQuest includes, at a minimum, a legislative history report for all public laws since 1969; abstracts and indexing for published hearings, committee prints, committee reports, and miscellaneous Congressional publications from 1970; some full text documents; and the *Congressional Record* (daily edition)[12] from 1985. The most complete collection includes searchable PDFs of hearings from 1824, committee prints from 1830, committee reports and House and Senate Documents from 1789, and more.

ProQuest's Get a Document search option (through the Legislative Histories Bills and Laws link) retrieves a law's legislative history report. The report includes the law's title and summary; bill numbers for enacted and related bills; references to debates and actions as reported in the *Congressional Record*; titles, dates, and numbers for committee prints, hearings, and reports; and a reference to presidential remarks, along with links to the available documents. Note that the legislative history report covers not only the session in which the law was enacted but also previous sessions, if any, in which Congress considered related legislation. See Exhibit 6.9.

The Advanced Search option allows you to select the categories of documents to search. You may search a single category or multiple categories simultaneously.[13]

LexisNexis and Westlaw. Both services provide databases with some bills, limited hearing testimony, the *Congressional Record*, and committee reports, although generally only for relatively recent laws. As you may recall, both also provide some compiled legislative histories.

LexisNexis offers the same legislative histories found in ProQuest Congressional.

---

11. It is derived in part from Congressional Information Service (CIS). CIS is an extensive print and microforms resource. For many years, it was the gold standard in legislative history research and remains a useful resource for those without access to ProQuest Congressional.

12. The *Congressional Record* is published in both a daily and permanent edition. The two editions have some variations in content and different page numbering schemes, with the daily edition using an "S" before page numbers reporting Senate content and an "H" before page numbers reporting House content.

13. ProQuest has recently introduced a similar new service, Legislative Insight, on a new search platform. It is growing in comprehensiveness.

| EXHIBIT 6.9 | Legislative History Report from ProQuest Congressional |

ProQuest® Congressional - Document   Page 1 of 8

 **Congressional**

Search Terms: <System Provided Search> - Edit Search   FOCUS™ Search [_____] Go

Result List | Expanded List | KWIC | Full Document

                    Document 1 of 1.

93 CIS PL 1033; 103 CIS Legis. Hist. P.L. 3

LEGISLATIVE HISTORY OF: P.L. **103-3**

TITLE: Family and Medical Leave Act of 1993

CIS-NO: 93-PL103-3
DOC-TYPE: **Legislative History**
DATE: Feb. 5, 1993
LENGTH: 24 p.
ENACTED-BILL: 103 H.R. 1 Retrieve Bill Tracking report
STAT: 107 Stat. 6
CONG-SESS: 103-1

SUMMARY:
"To grant family and temporary medical leave under certain circumstances."

Entitles eligible private sector and government employees to up to 12 weeks of unpaid medical leave for a serious health condition, and up to 12 weeks of unpaid family leaves of absence for childbirth, adoption, and care of infants or seriously ill children, spouses, or parents.

Exempts from leave requirements small businesses with fewer than 50 employees.

Requires that employees who return from family or medical leave be restored to the positions they held before taking leave or to equivalent positions.

Requires employers to continue health benefits for employees during family and medical leave, and provides that other accrued benefits shall not be lost because of such leave.

Authorizes DOL to enforce worker rights with regard to family and medical leave.

http://web.lexisnexis.com/congcomp/document?_m=1e6b970761573ee8240... 8/30/2011

EXHIBIT 6.9 *(continued)*

ProQuest® Congressional - Document Page 2 of 8

Establishes special rules for employees of local educational agencies and other requirements for civil service employees and Congressional employees.

Establishes a Commission on Leave to study existing and proposed family and medical leave policies.

CONTENT-NOTATION: Employee leave of absence for parental and medical reasons

BILLS: 99 H.R. 2020; 99 H.R. 4300; 99 S. 2278; 100 H.R. 284; 100 H.R. 925; 100 S. 249; 100 S. 2488; 101 H.R. 770; 101 S. 345; 102 H.R. 2; 102 S. 5; 102 S. 418; 102 S. 688; 103 S. 5

DESCRIPTORS:
  ADOPTION; AGED AND AGING; CHILDREN; COMMISSION ON LEAVE; CONGRESSIONAL EMPLOYEES; DEPARTMENT OF LABOR; EMPLOYEE BENEFIT PLANS; FAMILIES; FAMILY AND MEDICAL LEAVE ACT; FEDERAL ADVISORY BODIES; FEDERAL EMPLOYEES; GOVERNMENT AND BUSINESS; HEALTH INSURANCE; PREGNANCY; SMALL BUSINESS; 103 PL 3

REFERENCES:

DEBATE:

136 Congressional Record, 101st Congress, 2nd Session - 1990
  May 9, House consideration of H.R. 770, p. H2157.
  May 10, House consideration and passage of H.R. 770, p. H2198.
  June 14, Senate consideration and passage of H.R. 770, p. S8006.
  July 25, House consideration of the Presidential veto message on H.R. 770, p. H5484.

137 Congressional Record, 102nd Congress, 1st Session - 1991
  Oct. 2, Senate consideration and passage of S. 5, p. S14125.
  Nov. 13, House consideration of H.R. 2 , consideration and passage of S. 5 with an amendment, and tabling of H.R. 2, p. H9722.

138 Congressional Record, 102nd Congress, 2nd Session - 1992
  July 28, Senate disagreement to the House amendment to S. 5 , request for a conference, and appointment of conferees, p. S10485.
  Aug. 4, House insistence on its amendment to S. 5 , agreement to a conference, and appointment of conferees, p. H7273.
  Aug. 10, Submission in the House of the conference report on S. 5, p. H7740.
  Aug. 11, Senate agreement to the conference report on S. 5, p. S12093.
  Sept. 10, House agreement to the conference report on S. 5, p. H8238.
  Sept. 24, Senate consideration of the Presidential veto message and passage of S. 5, p. S14841.
  Sept. 30, House consideration of the Presidential veto message on S. 5, p. H9930.

139 Congressional Record, 103rd Congress, 1st Session - 1993
  Feb. 2, Senate consideration of S. 5, p. S985.
  Feb. 3, House consideration and passage of H.R. 1, p. H379.

http://web.lexisnexis.com/congcomp/document?_m=1e6b970761573ee8240... 8/30/2011

EXHIBIT 6.9   *(continued)*

ProQuest® Congressional - Document   Page 3 of 8

Feb. 3, Senate consideration of S. 5, <u>p. S1090</u>.
Feb. 4, Senate consideration and passage of H.R. 1 with an amendment, and indefinite postponement of S. 5, <u>p. S1254</u>.
Feb. 4, House concurrence in the Senate amendment to H.R. 1, <u>p. H557</u>.

REPORTS:

99th Congress

H. Rpt. 99-699, pt. 1 on H.R. 4300, "Parental and Medical Leave Act of 1986," July 21, 1986.
     <u>DIGITAL-PDF: 13704 H.rp.699/1</u>
     CIS NO: <u>86-H623-9</u>
     LENGTH: 21 p.
     SUDOC: Y1.1/8:99-699/pt.1

H. Rpt. 99-699, pt. 2 on H.R. 4300, "Family and Medical Leave Act of 1986," Aug. 8, 1986.
     <u>DIGITAL-PDF: 13704 H.rp.699/2</u>
     CIS NO: <u>86-H343-19</u>
     LENGTH: 57 p.
     SUDOC: Y1.1/8:99-699/pt.2

100th Congress

H. Rpt. 100-511, pt. 1 on H.R. 925, "Family and Medical Leave Act," Mar. 8, 1988.
     <u>DIGITAL-PDF: 13890 H.rp.511/1</u>
     CIS NO: <u>88-H623-2</u>
     LENGTH: 38 p.
     SUDOC: Y1.1/8:100-511/pt.1

H. Rpt. 100-511, pt. 2 on H.R. 925, "Family and Medical Leave Act of 1988," Mar. 9, 1988.
     <u>DIGITAL-PDF: 13890 H.rp.511/2</u>
     CIS NO: <u>88-H343-2</u>
     LENGTH: 71 p.
     SUDOC: Y1.1/8:100-511/pt.2

S. Rpt. 100-447 on S. 2488, "Parental and Medical Leave Act of 1988," Aug. 3, 1988.
     <u>DIGITAL-PDF: 13864 S.rp.447</u>
     CIS NO: <u>88-S543-14</u>
     LENGTH: 75 p. Corrected print.
     SUDOC: Y1.1/5:100-447/corr

101st Congress

H. Rpt. 101-28, pt. 1 on H.R. 770, "Family and Medical Leave Act of 1989," Apr. 13, 1989.
     <u>DIGITAL-PDF: 13950 H.rp.28/1</u>

http://web.lexisnexis.com/congcomp/document?_m=1e6b970761573ee8240... 8/30/2011

Westlaw also offers Graphical Statutes, a unique tool for identifying and retrieving legislative history materials. Graphical Statutes provides a visual display of the prior, current, and enacted but not yet effective versions of a statute; each version's effective dates; some of its legislative history documents; and links to the documents available on Westlaw. It is available for federal laws from 1996 forward via a link from a statutory section.

HeinOnline. HeinOnline has, in addition to its U.S. Federal Legislative History library, a U.S. Congressional Documents library, which is a good resource for the permanent and daily editions of the *Congressional Record* and a *U.S. Statutes at Large* library.

For our illustrative problem, we decided to search ProQuest Congressional as a double check on our earlier work in HeinOnline's compiled legislative history of the FMLA. A full text search of all (but one) of ProQuest Congressional's document collections for the 103d Congress, using the search *"75 mile" OR "75 miles" AND "Family and Medical Leave Act,"* yielded thirteen documents, including three committee reports and one hearing report. We skimmed them using the highlighted search terms, which appeared in the committee reports but not the hearings. We then ran the same search in the *Congressional Record*, which must be searched separately. Looking only for documents we had not reviewed before, we repeated the process for documents of the prior two Congresses, each of which had passed a Family and Medical Leave Act, which had been vetoed.

We found House hearings on H.R. 770, which contained interesting testimony from John J. Motley, Director of Federal Government Relations for the National Federation of Independent Businesses. He said this about the 1989 bill: "The bill also contains a disturbing definition of worksite. The 75 mile radius definition to determine the number of employees for eligibility purposes is difficult to conceptualize, difficult to ensure compliance with and will lead to greater uncertainties. A much simpler approach is to define threshold eligibility by worksite."

As we ended our research, we concluded that the legislative history materials, as is often the case, did not provide a definitive answer to the meaning of the term on which Fey's case depended, although testimony had identified the problem. When those materials used the expression "75-mile radius," it was not clear what the speakers meant. Furthermore, although the materials stressed that the purpose of the relevant exemption was to accommodate employer concerns about difficulties in reassigning workers to geographically separate facilities and to accommodate the needs of families, those purposes did not tell us where the legislature meant to draw the line.

Citation to Legislative Materials

Each type of legislative material has its own citation form, governed by rules 12.4 and 13 of *The Bluebook* and rules 14.7 and 15 of *ALWD Citation Manual*. The basic citation forms for the major materials featured in this chapter are set out here.

Session law citations differ somewhat as between *The Bluebook* and the *ALWD Citation Manual:*

BLUEBOOK: Family and Medical Leave Act of 1993, Pub. L. No. 103-3, 107 Stat. 6.
ALWD: Pub. L. No. 103-3, 107 Stat. 6 (1993).

Bills are cited as follows:

BLUEBOOK: Family and Medical Leave Act of 1993, H.R. 1, 103d Cong. (1993) (enacted).
ALWD: H.R. 1, 103d Cong. (Jan. 5, 1993).

Citations to transcripts of committee hearings are cited as follows:

BLUEBOOK: *The Family and Medical Leave Act: Hearing on H.R. 1 Before the Subcomm. on Labor-Mgmt. Relations of the H. Comm. on Educ. and Labor*, 103d Cong. 71 (1993) (statement of Mike Losey, President and CEO of the Society for Human Resource Management).
ALWD: H. Subcomm. on Lab.-Mgt. Rel. of Comm. on Educ. & Lab. *Legislative Hearing on H.R. 1, the Family and Medical Leave Act.* 103rd Cong. 71 (Jan. 26, 1993) (statement of Mike Losey, President and CEO of the Society for Human Resource Management).

Committee reports are cited as follows:

BLUEBOOK: Family and Medical Leave Act of 1993, S. Rep. No. 103-3 (1993), *reprinted in* 1993 U.S.C.C.A.N. 3.
ALWD: Sen. Rpt. 103-3 (Jan. 27, 1993) (reprinted in 1993 U.S.C.C.A.N. 3).

(continued)

Floor debates are cited to the *Congressional Record*, preferably to the permanent edition, otherwise to the daily version.

BLUEBOOK: 139 Cong. Rec. 2007 (1993) (statement of Rep. Bunning).

ALWD: 139 Cong. Rec. 2007 (1993) (statement of Rep. Bunning).

Finally, presidential signing statements may be cited to the *Public Papers of the President*, the *Weekly* or *Daily Compilation of Presidential Documents*, or U.S.C.C.A.N., according to rule T1 of *The Bluebook* and rule 19.12 of the *ALWD Citation Manual*.

BLUEBOOK: Statement by President on Signing HR. 920, 29 Weekly Comp. Pres. Doc. 355 (Mar. 8, 1993).

ALWD: William J. Clinton, *Statement on Signing H.R. 920*, 29 Wkly Comp. Pres. Doc. 355 (Mar. 8, 1993).

Note that additional information, such as where to find a document, may be appended to many of these citations.

SUMMARY OF LEGISLATIVE HISTORY RESEARCH

The legislative history materials a court may turn to are often voluminous, and your options for finding the materials sometimes overlap. Thus efficiency requires that you choose wisely among the options and track the documents you have researched so you do not unnecessarily duplicate your work. Chart 6.3 can guide you.

	CHART 6.3	Optimal Options for Legislative History Research

Resource	Advantages and Disadvantages	Optimal Options
Codes	Text of statute, history information for determining which public law to research. No legislative history documents.	Only U.S.C.A. provides a reference to U.S.C.C.A.N.
U.S.C.C.A.N	Committee report, possibly a presidential signing statement, but no other documents. Some citation information to other documents.	Use paper, if available, for a cost-effective start.
Compiled Legislative Histories	Different finding tools may provide different leads. Range of documents varies, but typically very comprehensive. Not available for all laws. Online options provide key-word searching.	Use multiple finding tools. Options often depend on availability. Westlaw and LexisNexis may be cost-effective.
THOMAS	Comprehensive bill tracking for post-1972 bills. Full-text coverage of documents very limited before 1995. Good source for amendments. Does not provide hearings. Linking and key-word options. Free.	Use for the references and to obtain and browse documents you cannot research cost-effectively elsewhere.
ProQuest Congressional	Comprehensive bill tracking. For major bills, covers session in which bill passed and prior sessions. Best source for tracking hearings, committee prints, House and Senate documents; good source for those documents, although full-text coverage varies and can be difficult to determine. Best bet for older legislation if your coverage includes it.	If you have a subscription, use it!
LexisNexis	Some compiled legislative histories, bills, hearing testimony, *Congressional Record*, committee reports. Coverage is limited. Some contracts provide the legislative histories.	Use primarily for a compiled legislative history.
Westlaw	Some compiled legislative histories, bills, hearing testimony, *Congressional Record*, committee reports. Coverage is limited. Graphical Statutes tool.	Use primarily for a compiled legislative history.
HeinOnline	U.S. Federal Legislative History library contains many compiled legislative histories and reference guide. U.S. Congressional Documents library provides both daily and permanent editions of the *Congressional Record*. *U.S. Statutes at Large* library provides session laws.	If you have access, use it! Cost-effective source for *Congressional Record* volumes not available on THOMAS.

OPTIONS FOR RESEARCHING PENDING LEGISLATION

Legislative process resources can be used not only to research the history of enacted laws but also to track the status of pending legislation. Lawyers track pending legislation for two purposes: (1) to help clients plan ahead by taking into account the provisions of probable new laws and (2) to influence the introduction, defeat, modification, or passage of a bill through lobbying.

On the federal side, THOMAS, LexisNexis, and ProQuest Congressional offer much the same materials for bills as they do for laws. You can use a bill number, if you have one, or key-word searching to find bills you may not know about, to obtain the text and status report for a bill. See Exhibit 6.10, which is the report for a bill before Congress in fall 2011 that would amend the definition of "eligible employee" in the FMLA.

On Westlaw, you may use the Graphical Statutes feature to identify pending legislation that would affect the statute. Westlaw also provides the text of bills and a bill-tracking function.[14]

TEST YOUR UNDERSTANDING

Reflection Questions

1. Legislative history materials are only quasi-authoritative. As this chapter's illustration suggests, legislative history research can be very time-consuming and yield nothing definitive. In practice, when do you think it might be justified to engage in such research?

2. Some observers, including legislators, believe that enacted laws should speak for themselves; that is, legislative history materials should not be considered when interpreting a statute. If this were so, what would be used instead? Would this be a wise change?

14. Westlaw and LexisNexis offer bill tracking for state legislation as well. Another less expensive option is to visit the state legislature's website.

EXHIBIT 6.10	Federal Bill Tracking Report

2 of 2 DOCUMENTS

Bill Tracking Report

112th Congress, 1st Session

HR 1440

2011 Bill Tracking H.R. 1440; 112 Bill Tracking H.R. 1440

BILL TITLE: Family and Medical Leave Enhancement Act of 2011

LEGISLATIVE CHAMBER: U.S. House of Representatives

SPONSOR: Representative Carolyn B. Maloney, D-NY

SYNOPSIS:

A bill to amend the Family and Medical Leave Act of 1993 and title 5, United States Code, to allow employees to take, as additional leave, parental involvement leave to participate in or attend their children's and grandchildren's educational and extracurricular activities, and to clarify that leave may be taken for routine family medical needs and to assist elderly relatives, and for other purposes

PROPOSED DATE: April 8, 2011

LAST ACTION DATE: October 26, 2011

STATUS:
Introduced in the House, April 8, 2011

TOTAL COSPONSORS: 10

- 10 Democrats /
- 0 Republicans

Display Major Actions Only

ACTIONS:

Committee Referrals:
April 8, 2011	House Committee on Education and the Workforce
April 8, 2011	House Committee on Oversight and Government Reform
April 8, 2011	House Committee on House Administration

EXHIBIT **6.10**   *(continued)*

Page 2

Bill Tracking Report HR 1440

Legislative Chronology:

1st Session Activity:

April 8, 2011	157 Cong Rec H 2569
	Referred to the House Committee on Education and the Workforce.
April 8, 2011	157 Cong Rec H 2569
	Referred to the House Committee on Oversight and Government Reform.
April 8, 2011	157 Cong Rec H 2569
	Referred to the House Committee on House Administration.
April 8, 2011	157 Cong Rec E 673
	Remarks by Rep. Maloney (D-NY)
October 26, 2011	157 Cong Rec E 1943
	Remarks by Rep. Maloney (D-NY)

SUMMARY:
(from the CONGRESSIONAL RESEARCH SERVICE)

Digest:

Family and Medical Leave Enhancement Act of 2011 - Amends the Family and Medical Leave Act of 1993 (FMLA) to cover employees at worksites that employ fewer than 50 employees, but not fewer than 25 employees. Continues to exempt from FMLA coverage employees at worksites that employ fewer than 25 employees (currently 50), if the total number of employees employed by that employer within 75 miles of that worksite is fewer than 25 (currently 50).

Allows an employee covered by FMLA to take upto 4 hours during any 30-day period, and up to 24 hours during any 12-month period, of parental involvement leave to participate in or attend activities that are sponsored by a school or community organization; and (2) relate to a program of the schoolor organization that is attended by the employee's child or grandchild.

Permits the use of such parental involvement leave tomeet routine family medical care needs, including: (1) such employee's medical and dental appointments, or their spouse,child, or grandchild; and (2) the care needs of their related elderly individuals, including visits to nursing homes and group homes.

Allows an employee to elect, or an employer to require, substitution of any of the paid or family leave or paidmedical or sick leave of the employee for any leave provided under this Act.

Declares that nothing in this Act shall require an employer to provide paid sick leave or paid medical leave in situations where such employer would not normally provideany such paid leave.

Imposes on the employee requesting leave certain notification requirements. Allows an employer to require certification supporting such requests.

Applies the parental involvement and family wellnessleave allowance tofederal employees.

CRS Index Terms:

Employee leave
Family relationships
Government employee pay, benefits, personnel management
Labor and employment

Display Co-Sponsors by Name
Display Co-Sponsors by Political Party
Display Co-Sponsors by Date, Descending
Display Co-Sponsors by Date, Ascending

CO-SPONSORS BY DATE
Original Cosponsors:

Your Scenario

As detailed in Chapter 2, your client, Elaine Wilson, is seeking to keep a companion animal in her apartment to assist her with her PTSD disability. Assume that one possibility is to assert a discrimination claim under the federal Fair Housing Act. The Fair Housing Act is found in Title 42 of the United States Code beginning at section 3601. The pertinent language dates to 1988.

- Find the statute in one of the annotated federal codes, and record what you learn there about its legislative process.
- Examine the legislative history materials in U.S.C.C.A.N. First identify the steps the law took en route to becoming law. Then read the documents (other than the law itself) for insight into your research issue.
- Research the statute's legislative history in some other source, again with a focus on your client's issue.

RESEARCH IN ADMINISTRATIVE MATERIALS

Contents

This chapter explores two issues: (1) an employee's eligibility for protections for taking family leave under federal law (also covered in Chapter 6) and (2) employer responses to social media discussions among employees.

Key Concepts and Tools in This Chapter

- Administrative law
- Rules and regulations
- Organic statute
- Administrative Procedure Act
- Formal and informal rulemaking
- *Federal Register*
- *Code of Federal Regulations*
- Annotated statutes references
- Federal Digital System

(continued)

- e-CFR
- *CFR Index and Finding Aids*
- Agency websites
- Updating regulations
- Judicial review of regulations
- Regulatory history: notice of proposed rulemaking, explanatory material, effective date
- HeinOnline, LexisNexis, and Westlaw databases
- Decisions and orders
- Formal and informal case processes
- Judicial review of agency decisions
- Non-legislative rules
- Guidance materials

The previous chapters focused on statutes. In many fields, such as environmental law, immigration, and workplace safety, legislatures adopt statutes with broad policy objectives and then authorize administrative agencies to fill in the details based on their scientific and policy expertise. This body of law building on general statutory requirements is called "administrative law." Understanding how to access this less visible part of the regulatory structure is as important to developing a complete picture of the law as is finding pertinent judicial cases. In fact, in some heavily regulated fields, lawyers spend most of their time working with administrative law rather than statutes and cases.

This chapter examines the three most important kinds of administrative law materials that lawyers should consult to get a complete picture of the law: legislative rules, which are also called "regulations"; decisions and orders; and non-legislative rules and guidance materials. The chapter then covers the major resources for researching federal administrative law. State administrative law parallels federal administrative law in structure.[1]

The illustration for this chapter is the case of Irene Fey, also discussed in Chapter 6. To review, Fey worked for the Colby Sugar Beet Transportation Company, which operated two facilities, one in Duluth, Minnesota, where Fey worked, and another in Sartell, Minnesota. The Sartell plant was 75.7 surface (driving) miles from Duluth, but only 74 linear (as the crow flies) miles away. Throughout 2010, the Duluth facility had forty-five employees; the Sartell facility had six.

In July 2010, Fey requested and was granted a leave of absence under the federal Family and Medical Leave Act (FMLA) to care for her newly adopted

---

1. In some areas, the content of state administrative law parallels that of the corresponding federal agency.

daughter. A week before her leave expired, Colby's human resources director notified Fey that her position had been eliminated and that the company had no other position for her.

Fey asked our fictional firm to evaluate whether she had a claim under the FMLA. The FMLA exempted employers with fewer than fifty employees within seventy-five miles of the employee's worksite as follows: "The term 'eligible employee' does not include . . . any employee of an employer who is employed at a worksite at which such employer employs less than 50 employees if the total number of employees employed by that employer within 75 miles of that worksite is less than 50."[2] Thus one issue was whether Fey was an eligible "employee" under the FMLA.

In Chapter 6, we learned that the FMLA's legislative history did not provide a definitive answer to the meaning of "75 miles." This chapter shows how this issue is more clearly addressed in rules adopted by the U.S. Department of Labor. As is fairly often the situation, administrative law clarifies ambiguous or general statutory requirements.

For the second part of this chapter, we researched a second problem. Fey was a popular employee, and a good number of her coworkers were angry when they learned that she had been terminated after her adoption leave. One posted a message on his Facebook page proposing a petition to take to management in Fey's support; others posted comments to the same effect. The company's human resource manager heard about the posting from a friend outside the company, determined that it was disloyal to the company, and disciplined the employees involved.

RULES AND REGULATIONS

Connections to statutes. In practice, the terms "rule" and "regulation" are used interchangeably to refer to codified law authored by administrative agencies. Regulations are often referred to as "quasi-legislative" because of their similarities to statutes. Like statutes, regulations usually consist of statements spelling out legal requirements or prohibitions that apply generally and prospectively. Some are long, complex, and very technical. A set of regulations is typically organized into titles, chapters, parts, subparts, and sections. Like statutes, regulations emerge from fairly well-defined procedures that generate paper trails that can be useful in understanding the law. Regulations are law: they are as binding on a client's situation as a statute.

Regulations are different from statutes in a key respect: Congress makes laws under the authority of the Constitution, whereas an agency's authority to make law depends on Congress. Generally, administrative agencies are created by Congress to regulate within particular fields; by statute, Congress creates the agency, defines its subject matter, and authorizes it to adopt regulations

2. 29 U.S.C. §2611(2)(B)(ii) (2006).

carrying the force of law. That is, an agency's authority to make regulations generally is found in the agency's "organic statute," meaning the statute that creates the agency.

The procedure that an agency follows to make regulations generally is defined by the Administrative Procedures Act (APA). This federal law might be regarded as the constitution for federal agencies, because it governs the procedures for so much of what agencies do. The APA defines a rule as:

> the whole or a part of an agency statement of general or particular applicability and future effect designed to implement, interpret, or prescribe law or policy or describing the organization, procedure, or practice requirements of an agency [including] the approval or prescription for the future of rates, wages, corporate or financial structures or reorganizations thereof, prices, facilities, appliances, services or allowances therefor or of valuations, costs, or accounting, or practices bearing on any of the foregoing.[3]

Exhibit 7.1 is a regulation of the Department of Labor that pertains to the Fey case.

The rulemaking process. Understanding the procedural steps in rulemaking is important because at each step documents are created that may be helpful in understanding, complying with, or challenging the final rule. Under the APA, most federal regulations are adopted through a process called "informal rulemaking,"[4] also called "notice and comment rulemaking." This process includes three major steps: notice of a proposed rulemaking, an opportunity for public comment on the proposed rule, and publication of the final rule along with the agency's explanation.

The process begins with notice that the agency intends to adopt a rule. Typically, a notice of a proposed rulemaking (NOPR) is published in the *Federal Register*, a voluminous official U.S. government publication available in print and online formats. The NOPR usually includes a draft of the proposed regulations, some explanation of the necessity and authority for adopting the regulations, and information about how the public may comment on the proposal.

Reading the NOPR can be useful in some cases, especially if it reveals differences between the proposed regulation and the final regulation. Such changes may cast light on how the regulation is to be interpreted. For example, if a final regulation is more lenient than the proposed regulation, one might be able to use that fact to contest a stringent interpretation of the final regulation. Additionally, when differences between the proposed and

---

3. 5 U.S.C. § 551(4) (2006).
4. Formal rulemaking is akin to a trial and entails testimony and cross-examination, written proposed findings and conclusions, and the opportunity to file exceptions to the recommended regulations.

Exhibit 7.1 Regulation from FDsys

§ 825.111 29 CFR Ch. V (7–1–11 Edition)

one another, may be considered a single site of employment. On the other hand, there may be several single sites of employment within a single building, such as an office building, if separate employers conduct activities within the building. For example, an office building with 50 different businesses as tenants will contain 50 sites of employment. The offices of each employer will be considered separate sites of employment for purposes of FMLA. An employee's worksite under FMLA will ordinarily be the site the employee reports to or, if none, from which the employee's work is assigned.

(1) Separate buildings or areas which are not directly connected or in immediate proximity are a single worksite if they are in reasonable geographic proximity, are used for the same purpose, and share the same staff and equipment. For example, if an employer manages a number of warehouses in a metropolitan area but regularly shifts or rotates the same employees from one building to another, the multiple warehouses would be a single worksite.

(2) For employees with no fixed worksite, *e.g.*, construction workers, transportation workers (*e.g.*, truck drivers, seamen, pilots), salespersons, *etc.*, the "worksite" is the site to which they are assigned as their home base, from which their work is assigned, or to which they report. For example, if a construction company headquartered in New Jersey opened a construction site in Ohio, and set up a mobile trailer on the construction site as the company's on-site office, the construction site in Ohio would be the worksite for any employees hired locally who report to the mobile trailer/company office daily for work assignments, *etc.* If that construction company also sent personnel such as job superintendents, foremen, engineers, an office manager, *etc.*, from New Jersey to the job site in Ohio, those workers sent from New Jersey continue to have the headquarters in New Jersey as their "worksite." The workers who have New Jersey as their worksite would not be counted in determining eligibility of employees whose home base is the Ohio worksite, but would be counted in determining eligibility of employees whose home base is New Jersey. For transportation employees, their worksite is the terminal to which they are assigned, report for work, depart, and return after completion of a work assignment. For example, an airline pilot may work for an airline with headquarters in New York, but the pilot regularly reports for duty and originates or begins flights from the company's facilities located in an airport in Chicago and returns to Chicago at the completion of one or more flights to go off duty. The pilot's worksite is the facility in Chicago. An employee's personal residence is not a worksite in the case of employees, such as salespersons, who travel a sales territory and who generally leave to work and return from work to their personal residence, or employees who work at home, as under the concept of flexiplace or telecommuting. Rather, their worksite is the office to which they report and from which assignments are made.

(3) For purposes of determining that employee's eligibility, when an employee is jointly employed by two or more employers (*see* § 825.106), the employee's worksite is the primary employer's office from which the employee is assigned or reports, unless the employee has physically worked for at least one year at a facility of a secondary employer, in which case the employee's worksite is that location. The employee is also counted by the secondary employer to determine eligibility for the secondary employer's full-time or permanent employees.

(b) The 75-mile distance is measured by surface miles, using surface transportation over public streets, roads, highways and waterways, by the shortest route from the facility where the employee needing leave is employed. Absent available surface transportation between worksites, the distance is measured by using the most frequently utilized mode of transportation (*e.g.*, airline miles).

(c) The determination of how many employees are employed within 75 miles of the worksite of an employee is based on the number of employees maintained on the payroll. Employees of educational institutions who are employed permanently or who are under contract are "maintained on the payroll" during any portion of the year

786

final regulations are great enough, it may be possible to argue that the agency has made a procedural error by not giving adequate notice of what the final regulation would look like.

During the second phase of rulemaking, the public is invited to submit written comments on the proposed regulation. Comments often are a mix of praise and criticism of proposed regulations. They may address a proposed regulation's underlying scientific or other empirical justifications, the policy solution the agency developed, or related topics that should be brought into the rulemaking.

Comments typically are not published verbatim in the *Federal Register*. Instead, an agency usually summarizes comments (and the agency's responses) when it publishes the final regulation. Until then, comments are held by the proposing agency as part of the rulemaking record. The record is the body of evidence for and against a regulation that the agency considers before deciding whether to adopt it. The record becomes important if there is a subsequent court challenge to the regulation, because in many cases the court will examine whether the record adequately supports the agency's rule-making choices.

At the close of the comment period, the agency takes one of three paths: adopt the regulation as proposed, adopt a regulation with changes reflecting comments received and other newly developed information, or decline to adopt a regulation.

If the agency decides to adopt a final regulation, it usually publishes in the *Federal Register* both the text of the final regulation and some explanation of the policy choices made by the agency in arriving at the final language. This explanation is a bit like the legislative history for the regulation, although in some ways it is more definitive than legislative history that accompanies a statute because regulations are generally adopted by a single agency speaking with a single voice.

In addition to being published in the *Federal Register*, the new regulation is published in the *Code of Federal Regulations* (C.F.R.), which is a codification of federal administrative regulations. If this dual publication seems confusing, an analogy to statutes may be helpful. Statutes are published chronologically as session laws (such as the federal *Statutes at Large*) and are codified topically in a code that contains all statutes currently in effect, whenever enacted (such as the *United States Code*). Similarly, the *Federal Register* serves as the chronological record of administrative actions of different kinds, while the C.F.R. is a codification of regulations currently in effect that is organized by topic. The organization of the C.F.R. roughly parallels the organization of the federal statutory code; for example, labor statutes appear in title 29 of U.S.C., and labor regulations appear in title 29 of the C.F.R.

As this description of the rulemaking process suggests, the rulemaking process leaves a significant paper trail, summarized in Chart 7.1. Knowing how to find the various documents generated by rulemaking is an important part of legal research.

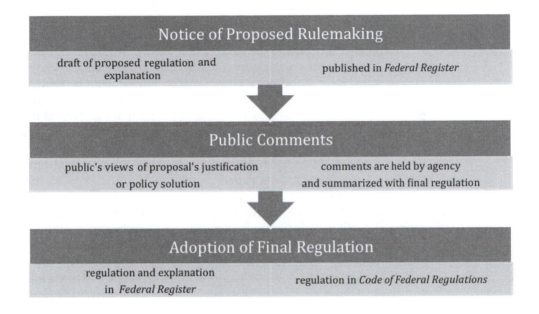

CHART 7.1   Rulemaking Process and Documents

When you research regulations, think in terms of reversing the chronology of rulemaking. Start by locating the final regulations pertinent to your client's situation and updating your research; this material is the law. Then consider whether it makes sense to dig deeper into the backstory for the pertinent regulation by looking for the regulation's history and the statutory authority of the agency to adopt regulations. Both the *Federal Register* and C.F.R. appear in print and online.

Researching the regulation itself. Regulations appear in the print C.F.R. and in databases provided by commercial vendors, including Westlaw, Lexis-Nexis, and HeinOnline. An excellent (and free) alternative is to use the two U.S. Government Printing Office's websites that host the C.F.R.: (1) the Federal Digital System (FDsys) at www.gpo.gov/fdsys and (2) GPO Access' e-CFR, at http://ecfr.gpoaccess.gov. FDsys is an official source supplying PDF versions of the paper C.F.R. pages; these are updated annually (just like the print version). By comparison, e-CFR is an unofficial source but includes online search features and is within a few days of being correct.

Identifying a pertinent rule can be done in various ways. You may obtain a reference through commentary, for example. Often, you will already be aware of the statute creating the agency and setting its rulemaking authority. If so, a good strategy is to examine the statute's annotations for references to pertinent regulations.

If you have a statutory citation but not a citation to the regulation, a good option is to use the Parallel Table of Authorities and Rules in *CFR Index and Finding Aids* that accompanies both paper and FDsys versions of the C.F.R. By looking up your statute in that table, you will find references to corresponding regulations.

If you lack a firm statutory starting point for your research, an option is to look up research terms in the subject index in *CFR Index and Finding Aids*.[5] Or you may skim in that index the List of CFR Titles, Chapters, Subchapters, and Parts, which outlines the C.F.R., and browse those sections that seem promising. Using the name of the agency is a good strategy. One of these methods may be more effective than the others, so be flexible. In general, through these tools you should be able to identify a pertinent title and part, but you may not always locate a specific section immediately. The important thing is to be methodical and patient.

An alternative in some situations is to work through the website of the agency that you have identified as regulating your client's situation. This is more or less difficult depending, of course, on the complexity of the agency involved and the quality of its website. If you know the name of the office within the agency and the name of the specific law or program of interest to you, this may be a fairly direct path. Another possibility is to click on the regulations tab.

Once you have identified and located a potentially pertinent section or part, you should, of course, examine the material carefully. Examine the table of contents for the chapter containing the pertinent material, and identify all pertinent parts and sections. Be sure to look for definitions, which may appear at the beginning of and apply throughout a chapter or part. Read through all sections within a pertinent part, because they are likely to be interconnected. Then take note of the administrative history material in small print at the end of a section or the outline for a part. You may find a reference to the enabling statutes as well as the regulation's date of final promulgation and citation to the *Federal Register*. As with statutes, a good practice, to help you monitor your research and begin your analysis, is to summarize what you have read.

In Irene Fey's case, for example, the annotation to section 2611 of the FMLA in *United States Code Annotated* online included a reference to a series of rule provisions in the C.F.R. starting at 29 C.F.R. §825.100 and continuing from there. See Exhibit 7.2. We found the regulation, Exhibit 7.1, through FDsys. Alternatively, we found the regulation through the Department of Labor's FMLA webpage, which connected to GPO Access. See exhibit 7.3, the overview of the Department of Labor's FMLA webpage.

As stated in Exhibit 7.1, the Department of Labor's regulation specified that seventy-five miles was to be measured based on driving the shortest route by surface transportation, not as the crow flies. Thus the distance by road from Duluth to Sartell was 75.7 miles. If the Department of Labor's rule was valid, then Fey probably did not have a claim.

---

5. An alternative to this index is *West's Code of Federal Regulations General Index.*

| EXHIBIT 7.2 | Regulation Information in Annotated Code (*United States Code Annotated*) |

List of 75 Context & Analysis for § 2611. Definitions

Context and Analysis (75)

Cross References (3)

Congressional accountability and administrative and judicial dispute-resolution procedures including judicial branch coverage study, see 2 USCA § 1434.

Family and medical leave rights and protections provided to Presidential offices, see 3 USCA § 412.

Participants in private, State, local and Federal community service projects, service sponsors, see 42 USCA § 12631.

Code Of Federal Regulations (1)

Applicability of defined terms, see 29 CFR § 825.100 et seq.

Law Review Commentaries (9)

Family and Medical Leave Act of 1993: An overview of the law and regulations (Part I). Gregory W. Guevara, 37 Res Gestae 214 (1993).

Family and Medical Leave Act of 1993: An overview of the law and regulations (Part II). Gregory W. Guevara, 37 Res Gestae 256 (1993).

Federal employment laws and the "integrated enterprise". Richard A. Paschal, 67 Okla.B.J. 3397 (1996).

Issues surrounding family and medical leave. John P. Furfaro and Maury B. Josephson, 215 N.Y.L.J. 3 (Feb. 2, 1996).

Legal ramifications of using independent contractors, temporary agency employees or leased workers. Henry W. Sledz, Jr. and John J. Lynch, 9 CBA Rec. 20 (Nov. 1995).

Overview of the Family and Medical Leave Act. Jeffrey J. Fraser, 70 U.Det.Mercy L.Rev. 691 (1993).

Overview of the Family and Medical Leave Act of 1993. M. Kristen Allman, 67 Fla.B.J. 49 (May 1993).

Parent company liability for discrimination by subsidiary. Robert P. Lewis, 215 N.Y.L.J. 1 (Feb. 20, 1996).

What does it mean to be a salaried employee? The future of pay-docking. Kimberly A. Pace, 21 J.Legis. 49 (1995).

Library References (3)

Labor and Employment ⟜ 337, 343.

Key Number System Topic No. 231H.

CJS Employer-Employee Relationship § 108, Presumptions and Burden of Proof--Public Policy Violation.

ALR Library (11)

35 ALR, Fed. 2nd Series 293, Requirement that Employers Notify Employees of Their Method of FMLA Leave Calculation Under Family and Medical Leave Act, 29 U.S.C.A. §§ 2601 et seq.

190 ALR, Fed. 491, Establishing Employer's Discriminatory Motive in Action to Recover for Employer's Retaliation for Employee's Exercise of Rights Under Family and Medical Leave Act, in Violation of § 105(A) of Act...

184 ALR, Fed. 171, Adequacy of Notice to Employer of Need for Leave Under Federal Family and Medical Leave Act of 1993.

180 ALR, Fed. 579, Immunity of States in Private Actions for Damages Under Family and Medical Leave Act (29 U.S.C.A. §§ 2601 et seq.).

176 ALR, Fed. 591, Award of Damages Under Family and Medical Leave Act (29 U.S.C.A. §§ 2601 et seq.)

EXHIBIT 7.3	Agency Website Overview (U.S. Department of Labor)

Leave Benefits

Family & Medical Leave

DOL Web Pages on This Topic
Laws & Regulations on This Topic

The Family and Medical Leave Act (FMLA) provides certain employees with up to 12 weeks of unpaid, job-protected leave per year. It also requires that their group health benefits be maintained during the leave.

FMLA is designed to help employees balance their work and family responsibilities by allowing them to take reasonable unpaid leave for certain family and medical reasons. It also seeks to accommodate the legitimate interests of employers and promote equal employment opportunity for men and women.

FMLA applies to all public agencies, all public and private elementary and secondary schools, and companies with 50 or more employees. These employers must provide an eligible employee with up to 12 weeks of unpaid leave each year for any of the following reasons:

> for the birth and care of the newborn child of an employee;
>
> for placement with the employee of a child for adoption or foster care;
>
> to care for an immediate family member (spouse, child, or parent) with a serious health condition; or
>
> to take medical leave when the employee is unable to work because of a serious health condition.

Employees are eligible for leave if they have worked for their employer at least 12 months, at least 1,250 hours over the past 12 months, and work at a location where the company employs 50 or more employees within 75 miles. Whether an employee has worked the minimum 1,250 hours of service is determined according to FLSA principles for determining compensable hours or work.

Time taken off work due to pregnancy complications can be counted against the 12 weeks of family and medical leave.

A final rule effective on January 16, 2009, updates the FMLA regulations to implement new military family leave entitlements enacted under the National Defense Authorization Act for FY 2008.

Special rules apply to employees of local education agencies. The Department of Labor administers FMLA; however, the Office of Personnel Management (OPM) administers FMLA for most federal employees.

(▲) **Back to Top**

DOL Web Pages on This Topic

Compliance Assistance: Family and Medical Leave Act (FMLA)
Links to various sources of information about FMLA.

Fact Sheet on FMLA
Covers the major requirements of FMLA and updates to the FMLA regulations.

FMLA Compliance Guide
Summarizes FMLA provisions and regulations and provides answers to the most frequently asked questions.

elaws FMLA Advisor
The FMLA Advisor provides information about employee eligibility under the law; including valid reasons for leave; employee/employer notification responsibilities; and employee rights and benefits.

The FMLA Poster
All covered employers are required to display and keep displayed a poster prepared by the Department of Labor summarizing the major provisions of the FMLA.

Laws & Regulations on This Topic

Regulations

29 CFR Part 825
The Family and Medical Leave Act

Employee Leave Entitlements: Reduced or intermittent leave to care for parent, other family member or servicemember

Subtopics

Family & Medical Leave
Funeral Leave
Government Contracts
Holidays
Jury Duty
Personal Leave
Sick Leave
Vacations

Updating the regulation. Administrative regulations are subject to amend-ment, revision, and repeal just as statutes are. So, once you have located a pertinent regulation, you must make sure it is up-to-date. You can do this most quickly and cost-effectively using the federal government's free online tools. Updating this way involves two steps. First, locate the most current version of the regulation in e-CFR, then look for any changes that may have occurred in the interim by using the official online version of the *Federal Register* at FDsys.

In our example, on January 12, we begin by locating the 75-mile regulation as it appeared on e-CFR. That document was updated last on January 10, 2012. See Exhibit 7.4. Although it seemed unlikely that there would be changes in two days, we needed to check. We went to FDsys, which makes the *Federal Register* available online by year. We selected the entries for 2012, January 11 and 12, and Department of Labor. We found several entries, but none pertained to our issues. See Exhibit 7.5.

If you do not have access to electronic tools, updating is more laborious. You will want to note the publication date for the C.F.R. volume in which your rule is published. The first updating publication is *List of C.F.R. Sections Affected*, which is published monthly (with later issues cumulating material from earlier issues). The second is the *Federal Register*'s Reader Aids Table of Parts Affected, which picks up where L.S.A. leaves off; you must check the last issue for every month since the current L.S.A. and then the most recent issue for the current month. Both tools list *Federal Register* references for actions affecting specific C.F.R. sections.

Furthermore, regulations, like statutes, are applied and interpreted by the courts to specific situations. In some cases, the court's opinion includes judi-cial gloss on the regulatory language. Not infrequently, the party subject to the regulation challenges it as, essentially, not in accord with the statute that led to the regulation or not supported by the evidence gathered in the rule-making process.

Thus, researching case law is a necessary step in updating a statute. The methods described in Chapters 4 and 5 are good options, In addition, citing a regulation through KeyCite or Shepard's is a sound means of locating cases that may undermine a regulation's validity. See Exhibit 7.6.

Our research into case law, which focused on KeyCite, yielded various cases applying our regulation. The *Hackworth* decision (listed first in Exhibit 7.6) provided an extensive analysis of the regulation's validity and upheld the regulation.[6]

---

6. *Hackworth v. Progressive Cas. Ins.*, 468 F.3d 722 (10th Cir. 2006).

EXHIBIT 7.4

Regulation Accessed Through
Agency Website and e-CFR

Electronic Code of Federal Regulations

e-CFR ™

$\longrightarrow$ **e-CFR Data is current as of January 10, 2012**

Title 29: Labor
PART 825—THE FAMILY AND MEDICAL LEAVE ACT OF 1993
Subpart A—Coverage Under the Family and Medical Leave Act

Browse Previous | Browse Next

§ 825.111   Determining whether 50 employees are employed within 75 miles.

(a) Generally, a worksite can refer to either a single location or a group of contiguous locations. Structures which form a campus or industrial park, or separate facilities in proximity with one another, may be considered a single site of employment. On the other hand, there may be several single sites of employment within a single building, such as an office building, if separate employers conduct activities within the building. For example, an office building with 50 different businesses as tenants will contain 50 sites of employment. The offices of each employer will be considered separate sites of employment for purposes of FMLA. An employee's worksite under FMLA will ordinarily be the site the employee reports to or, if none, from which the employee's work is assigned.

(1) Separate buildings or areas which are not directly connected or in immediate proximity are a single worksite if they are in reasonable geographic proximity, are used for the same purpose, and share the same staff and equipment. For example, if an employer manages a number of warehouses in a metropolitan area but regularly shifts or rotates the same employees from one building to another, the multiple warehouses would be a single worksite.

(2) For employees with no fixed worksite, *e.g.* , construction workers, transportation workers (*e.g.* , truck drivers, seamen, pilots), salespersons, *etc.* , the "worksite" is the site to which they are assigned as their home base, from which their work is assigned, or to which they report. For example, if a construction company headquartered in New Jersey opened a construction site in Ohio, and set up a mobile trailer on the construction site as the company's on-site office, the construction site in Ohio would be the worksite for any employees hired locally who report to the mobile trailer/company office daily for work assignments, *etc.* If that construction company also sent personnel such as job superintendents, foremen, engineers, an office manager, *etc.* , from New Jersey to the job site in Ohio, those workers sent from New Jersey continue to have the headquarters in New Jersey as their "worksite." The workers who have New Jersey as their worksite would not be counted in determining eligibility of employees whose home base is the Ohio worksite, but would be counted in determining eligibility of employees whose home base is New Jersey. For transportation employees, their worksite is the terminal to which they are assigned, report for work, depart, and return after completion of a work assignment. For example, an airline pilot may work for an airline with headquarters in New York, but the pilot regularly reports for duty and originates or begins flights from the company's facilities located in an airport in Chicago and returns to Chicago at the completion of one or more flights to go off duty. The pilot's worksite is the facility in Chicago. An employee's personal residence is not a worksite in the case of employees, such as salespersons, who travel a sales territory and who generally leave to work and return from work to their personal residence, or employees who work at home, as under the concept of flexiplace or telecommuting. Rather, their worksite is the office to which they report and from which assignments are made.

(3) For purposes of determining that employee's eligibility, when an employee is jointly employed by two or more employers (*see* §825.106), the employee's worksite is the primary employer's office from which the employee is assigned or reports, unless the employee has physically worked for at least one year at a facility of a secondary employer, in which case the employee's worksite is that location. The employee is also counted by the secondary employer to determine eligibility for the secondary employer's full-time or permanent employees.

| EXHIBIT 7.5 | *Federal Register* Daily Edition
(from FDsys) |

Home | Customers | **Vendors** | Libraries

FDsys > Collection Results

FDsys:
GPO's Federal Digital System
About FDsys
Search Government Publications
Browse Government Publications

Related Resources

Search the Federal Register by Citation.

View Executive Order 13563
Retrospective Review documents in
the Federal Register.

Download multiple issues of the Federal
Register in XML.

Sign up to freely receive the daily
Federal Register Table of Contents via e
-mail.

Find, review, and submit comments on
Federal rules that are open for comment
and published in the Federal Register
using Regulations.gov.

Purchase a subscription to the printed
edition of the Federal Register.

Find issues of the Federal Register
(including issues prior to 1996) at a local
Federal depository library.

FEDERAL REGISTER

Published by the Office of the Federal Register, National Archives and Records Administration (NARA), the Federal
Register is the official daily publication for rules, proposed rules, and notices of Federal agencies and organizations, as
well as executive orders and other presidential documents. About the Federal Register.

Today's Issue of the Federal Register

⊟ 2012

⊟ January
 ⊞ Tuesday, January 3
 ⊞ Wednesday, January 4
 ⊞ Thursday, January 5
 ⊞ Friday, January 6
 ⊞ Monday, January 9
 ⊞ Tuesday, January 10
 ⊞ Wednesday, January 11
 ⊟ Thursday, January 12

View Entire Issue: PDF | XML | Table of Contents | More

  ⊞ Agricultural Marketing Service
  ⊞ Agriculture Department
  ⊞ Centers for Disease Control and Prevention
  ⊞ Centers for Medicare & Medicaid Services
  ⊞ Coast Guard
  ⊞ Commerce Department
  ⊞ Consumer Product Safety Commission
  ⊞ Corporation for National and Community Service
  ⊞ Defense Department
  ⊞ Employment and Training Administration
  ⊞ Energy Department
  ⊞ Environmental Protection Agency
  ⊞ Federal Communications Commission
  ⊞ Federal Emergency Management Agency
  ⊞ Federal Energy Regulatory Commission
  ⊞ Federal Highway Administration
  ⊞ Federal Maritime Commission
  ⊞ Federal Motor Carrier Safety Administration
  ⊞ Fish and Wildlife Service
  ⊞ Foreign Assets Control Office
  ⊞ General Services Administration
  ⊞ Health and Human Services Department
  ⊞ Homeland Security Department
  ⊞ Industry and Security Bureau
  ⊞ Interior Department
  ⊞ International Trade Administration
  ⊞ Justice Department
  ⊟ Labor Department

   Notices
   Notice of Determinations Regarding Eligibility To Apply for Worker Adjustment Assistance
     Pages 1950 - 1952 [FR DOC # 2012-436]   PDF | Text | More

   Investigations Regarding Certifications of Eligibility To Apply for Worker Adjustment Assistance and Alternative Trade
   Adjustment Assistance
     Pages 1952 - 1954 [FR DOC # 2012-437]   PDF | Text | More

   2002 Reopened-Previously Denied Determinations; Notice of Revised Denied Determinations on Reconsideration Under
   the Trade Adjustment Assistance Extension Act of 2011 Regarding Eligibility To Apply for Worker Adjustment Assistance
     Pages 1954 - 1954 [FR DOC # 2012-438]   PDF | Text | More

   2002 Reopened-Previously Denied Determinations; Notice of Negative Determinations on Reconsideration Under the
   Trade Adjustment Assistance Extension Act of 2011 Regarding Eligibility To Apply for Worker Adjustment Assistance
     Pages 1954 - 1955 [FR DOC # 2012-439]   PDF | Text | More

   Agency Information Collection Activities; Submission for OMB Review; Comment Request; Trade Adjustment Assistance
   Community College and Career Training Grant Program Reporting Requirements
     Pages 1949 - 1950 [FR DOC # 2012-449]   PDF | Text | More

   Request for Certification of Compliance-Rural Industrialization Loan and Grant Program
     Pages 1955 - 1955 [FR DOC # 2012-448]   PDF | Text | More

| EXHIBIT 7.6 | Citator Report for Regulation (KeyCite) |

List of 11 Notes of Decisions for § 825.111 Determining whether 50 employees are emp...

Notes Of Decisions (11)

Construction and application

Department of Labor (DOL) regulation reasonably interpreted "50/75 provision" of FMLA, excepting from coverage employee of employer having fewer than 50 employees within "75 miles" of employee's worksite, as referring to surface, not linear miles; interpretation was plausible, furthered provision's purpose in that surface measurement was reasonable proxy for judging employer's ability to relocate employee, and did not unreasonably favor employers over employees. Hackworth v. Progressive Casualty Ins. Co., C.A.10 (Okla.)2006, 468 F.3d 722, certiorari denied 127 S.Ct. 2883, 550 U.S. 969, 167 L.Ed.2d 1153. Labor And Employment ☞ 345

Worksite

Truck driver's "worksite" was in Des Moines, Iowa where corporation's dispatchers were located and at which corporation employed 50 or more workers, meaning driver was not excluded from being an "eligible employee" under FMLA; driver received his work assignments from Des Moines and reported to Des Moines. Cobb v. Contract Transport, Inc., 2006, 452 F.3d 543. Labor And Employment ☞ 345

Both statutory term "worksite" and definition of that term contained in FMLA regulation are based on term "single site of employment" in the Worker Adjustment Retraining and Notification (WARN) Act. Cobb v. Contract Transport, Inc., 2006, 452 F.3d 543. Labor And Employment ☞ 344

Department of Labor (DOL) regulation defining term "worksite" in joint employment situations as primary employer's office from which employee was assigned or reported, as applied to joint employee with fixed place of work, was arbitrary, capricious, and manifestly contrary to FMLA; definition contravened plain meaning of term "worksite", did not effect Congressional purpose underlying FMLA "50/75" provision, and created arbitrary distinction between sole and joint employers. Harbert v. Healthcare Services Group, Inc., 2004, 391 F.3d 1140, certiorari denied 126 S.Ct. 356, 546 U.S. 822, 163 L.Ed.2d 65. Labor And Employment ☞ 345 Labor And Employment ☞ 346

Under first step of Chevron analysis, Congressional intent with respect to meaning of "worksite" in FMLA definition of "eligible employee" for employee who was jointly employed was not sufficiently clear to render invalid Department of Labor (DOL) regulation defining such an employee's worksite as primary employer's office from which employee was assigned to or reported. Harbert v. Healthcare Services Group, Inc., 2004, 391 F.3d 1140, certiorari denied 126 S.Ct. 356, 546 U.S. 822, 163 L.Ed.2d 65. Labor And Employment ☞ 345 Labor And Employment ☞ 346

Central to the reporting element of eligibility requirements for FMLA coverage, under which sales employee with no fixed worksite must report to office with more than 50 employees, is the location of the personnel who are primarily responsible for reviewing sales reports and other information sent by the sales representatives, in order to record sales, assess employee performance, develop new sales strategies, and the like. Conners v. SpectraSite Communications, Inc., 2006, 465 F.Supp.2d 834. Labor And Employment ☞ 345

Genuine issue of material fact, as to whether salesperson's "worksite" was Des Moines office where her supervisor worked, where she maintained mailbox, and where she attended training and sales meetings in addition to orientation but traveled to less than once a month, rather than Sioux City branch office which she utilized once per week, precluded summary judgment for employer on her FMLA claims based on finding she was not an "eligible employee" because her employer did not have 50 or more employees within 75 miles of her worksite. Podkovich v. Glazer's Distributors of Iowa, Inc., N.D.Iowa2006, 446 F.Supp.2d 982. Federal Civil Procedure ☞ 2497.1

Department of Labor (DOL) regulation that was promulgated in conjunction with the FMLA, providing that when joint employment relationship existed employee's "worksite" was primary employer's office from which employee was assigned or reported to, was based on permissible construction of term "worksite" and did not contradict express terms of FMLA. Family and Medical Leave Act of 1993, § 2 et seq., 29 U.S.C.A. § 2601

Researching the regulation's history and statutory basis. If questions arise about how to interpret or apply a regulation, or if your client is considering whether to challenge a regulation, you will want to dig deeper into the regulation's backstory. In particular, you will want to locate the rule's regulatory history (from notice to promulgation) as documented in the *Federal Register* and the statute or statutes outlining the agency's authority to adopt the regulation.

The place to start is the regulation's final-rule publication in the *Federal Register*. The reference for the final-rule publication appears after the outline of the part containing the regulation in the C.F.R. Accompanying the regulation in the *Federal Register* should be explanatory material, which may include descriptions of the comments the agency received, how it analyzed the situation, and previous rules or other agency action on the same topic. In addition, the regulation's effective date is stated. Tracing back through key events as published in the *Federal Register*, such as the notice of proposed rulemaking, can also be revealing.

The entire *Federal Register* is, of course, a very large set. The FDsys site covers back to 1994. Alternatives are the LexisNexis, Westlaw, and HeinOnline databases.

In the example for this chapter, we learned that the pertinent regulations were published in the *Federal Register* on November 17, 2008, in volume 73 beginning at page 68073. They were preceded by nearly 140 pages of explanatory material written by the agency. We learned that the first FMLA rules were adopted in 1993 and were amended in 2008 after the Department of Labor asked stakeholders to comment on their experiences with the FMLA and the implementing regulations. Also included was a summary of the comments made by members of the public during the comment period, another potentially useful source of interpretive and advocacy points.

The language we cared about dated to 1993. FDsys does not carry the *Federal Register* back that far. We switched to the LexisNexis Federal Register database and searched for the term "surface" (as in "surface miles") as well as the issuance date of June 4. We found the explanation of the agency's reasoning, contained in the agency's "Summary and Discussion of Regulatory Provisions" accompanying the original regulation, which provided a sound rationale. See Exhibit 7.7. Completing our excavation, we went back to the original notice of proposed rulemaking for the 1993 regulations, which identified the definitional issue by asking for public comment but did not propose an answer.

A final step in mapping out the rule's backstory is to read (or reread) the statute or statutes that authorized the agency to adopt the regulation at issue. This may include both a general provision in the agency's organic statute authorizing rulemaking and a more specific command by Congress in the same or a subsequent statute to make rules on a specific topic. Chapters 5 and 6 cover statutory research. As you read these statutes, look for the legal standard that the legislature has set for the conduct you are concerned with as well as indications of the agency's authority to promulgate regulations regarding that conduct. These may help clarify the rule or may open avenues to questioning the rule's validity if the agency appears to have misread or overstepped its authority.

EXHIBIT 7.7   Explanatory Material for Regulation

Page 7

58 FR 31794, *

What Is a "Public Agency"? (§ 825.108)

"Public agency" is defined in accordance with section 3(x) of the FLSA, which includes the government of the United States; the government of a State or political subdivision of a State; any agency of the United States (including the United States Postal Service and Postal Rate Commission), a State, or a political subdivision of a State, or any interstate governmental agency. Under the FLSA, States and political subdivisions of States are considered to be single public agency employers, the same test used in these regulations.

While the 50-employee coverage test does not apply to public agencies, the public agency employer must employ 50 employees within a 75-mile area around the worksite in order for an employee to be "eligible" and entitled to FMLA leave (see § 825.110 below). Thus, a State is considered a single public agency employer under FMLA for purposes of counting the number of employees to determine if they are "eligible" for FMLA leave. Likewise, any political subdivision of a State, such as a county or a city, is a single public agency employer for this purpose.

Where there is a question about whether an agency is a single public agency employer (separate from other governmental jurisdictions), the listing in the U.S. Bureau of Census' "Census of Governments" will be conclusive.

Are Federal Agencies Covered by These Regulations? (§ 825.109)

Most Federal executive branch employees are covered by Title II of FMLA, administered by the Office of Personnel Management (OPM). The Department has worked with OPM to determine which executive branch employees are excluded from Title II and, therefore, covered by these regulations. The Federal employees covered by these regulations include: (1) Employees of the U.S. Postal Service, Postal Rate Commission, and Library of Congress; (2) employees of a corporation supervised by the Farm Credit Administration, if private interests elect or appoint a member of the board of directors; (3) part-time employees who do not have an established regular tour of duty during the administrative workweek; (4) employees serving under temporary appointments with a time limitation of one year or less; (5) employees of legislative and judicial branch agencies employed in a unit which has employees in the competitive service (*e.g.*, the Government Printing Office and the U.S. Tax Court); and (6) other Federal executive agencies if they are not covered by Title II of FMLA and OPM jurisdiction. The 50-employees-within-75-miles eligibility test applies to Federal employees covered by these regulations. For employees covered by   [*31798]   these regulations, the U.S. Government constitutes a single employer.

Which Employees Are "Eligible" To Take Leave Under the FMLA? (§ 825.110)

To be "eligible," an employee must have worked for the employer: (1) For at least 12 months and (2) for at least 1,250 hours during the year preceding the start of the leave, and (3) be employed at a worksite where the employer employs at least 50 employees within a 75-mile radius.

In determining whether an employee has 1,250 hours of service, the Act requires that FLSA hours-worked principles be applied. Therefore, all hours which an employer suffers or permits an employee to work are counted towards hours of service (see 29 CFR part 785). For example, on-call time would be hours of service where it meets the FLSA hours-worked requirements (29 CFR part 785.17), as would ground time for flight crews.

The regulations describe how to determine hours of service for this purpose for employees not subject to the minimum wage and overtime requirements of the FLSA, and for whom no record of hours-worked are kept. For purposes of this regulation, FLSA-exempt employees for whom no hours-worked records have been kept and who have worked for the employer for at least 12 months are presumed to have met the 1,250 hours of service requirement for eligibility. For example, in consideration of the time spent at home reviewing homework and tests, full-time teachers in an elementary or secondary school system, or institution of higher education, or other educational establishment or institution, are deemed to meet the 1,250 hour test. An employer must be able to clearly demonstrate that such an employee did not work 1,250 hours during the preceding 12-month period if FMLA leave is to be denied on the basis that the employee is not an "eligible" employee.

In Determining if an employee Is "Eligible" Under FMLA, How Is the Determination Made Whether the Employer Employs 50 Employees Within 75 Miles of the Worksite Where the Employee Requesting Leave Is Employed? (§ 825.111)

The term "single site of employment" from the Worker Adjustment and Retraining Notification Act (WARN) regulations, 20 CFR Part 639, applies in determining what constitutes a "worksite" for purposes of FMLA. Because the

Exhibit 7.7   *(continued)*

Page 8

58 FR 31794, *

purpose of the 75-mile radius limit is to afford employers the opportunity to utilize employees among proximate work-sites when an employee goes on leave, and because of practical difficulties in determining 75 miles "as the crow flies," the regulations provide that 75 miles from the worksite is measured based on surface miles on public roads.

It is important to recognize the distinction made under FMLA between the 50-employees test for determining if a private employer is covered by the Act, and the separate 50-employees-employed-within-75-miles-of-the-worksite test for determining if an employee is "eligible" to take FMLA leave. It is conceivable that a covered employer, employing more than 50 employees at multiple, geographically dispersed worksites, might have no eligible employees if fewer than 50 employees are working within 75 miles of each worksite. For example, an employer that operates a chain of convenience stores with none of the locations within 75 miles of each other could employ hundreds of employees, and be covered by the Act, but still not have any employees who are eligible for FMLA leave if fewer than 50 employees work at each location.

A number of different options were considered for when the count should be made to determine how many employees are employed within 75 miles for eligibility purposes. Commenters variously suggested the point at which an employee requests leave, the point at which an employee begins leave, a fixed year (such as the calendar year or leave year), or at the same time as when employer coverage is determined.

Under FMLA, the purpose of an employee providing notice to an employer of the need for leave is primarily to give the employer an opportunity to plan for handling the work during the employee's absence, such as by reassigning the work among staff in the unit where the employee taking leave is assigned, assigning an employee on temporary duty from another office or worksite, or hiring a temporary replacement. At the same time, the employee needs the opportunity to make plans regarding the leave-for example, to coordinate leave with a spouse so at least one parent can be with a child who is in the hospital, obtain reservations to travel to a distant city to care for a parent, and the like.

Employees should be encouraged to give the employer as much notice as possible so both can make necessary arrangements. Both the employee and the employer benefit from knowing whether or not the employee is going to be entitled to leave so that each can make appropriate plans. It is in their mutual interest to make this determination when the employee requests leave.

If there are not 50 employees employed within 75 miles at that time, the employee may renew his or her request at a later date.

Both the use of a fixed date and the use of the same method used in determining employer coverage were considered inconsistent with the Act's use of the present tense in defining "eligible" employees. In addition, the use of a fixed date could be manipulated to reduce eligibility.

In this regard, the Department also gave serious consideration to an option not suggested by commenters. This option is that where notice is given 30 or more days prior to the commencement of leave, the count would be made on the 30th day preceding the start of leave, or, at the employer's option, as of the date leave is requested; where 30 days notice is not given, the count would be made at the time notice is given or the date leave begins, whichever is earlier. This option might alleviate the inconvenience potentially presented to a seasonal employer who receives a notice for leave during the height of the season, for leave to be taken at a time when the employer's staff is reduced. However, this should not be a significant concern because many seasonal employers may not be covered because of the coverage requirement that an employer employ 50 or more employees in at least 20 workweeks. Comments are specifically invited on whether the problems envisioned for seasonal employers are significant, and whether this or another approach should be considered to address those problems.

Under What Kinds of Circumstances Are Employers Required To Grant Family or Medical Leave? (§ 825.112)

An eligible employee is entitled to FMLA leave for the birth of a child, and to care for such child; for the placement of a child for adoption or foster care; to care for the employee's seriously-ill spouse, child, or parent; and because of a serious health condition that makes the employee unable to perform his or her job functions. Circumstances may require that leave for the birth of a child, or for placement for adoption or foster care, be taken prior to the actual birth or placement. With respect to placement for adoption, the regulations do not require use of licensed adoption agencies. Foster care is defined to require State action, rather than just an informal arrangement to take care of another person's child. [*31799]

Citations to Regulations and Related Materials

Regulations published in C.F.R. are cited under both *Bluebook* rules 13.5.1.4 and 14.2 and *ALWD* rule 19.1 as follows:

29 C.F.R. § 825.111 (2011).

Material published in the *Federal Register* is cited as follows:

BLUEBOOK: Explanation of Regulations Implementing Family and Medical Leave Act, 58 Fed. Reg. 31794, 31796–98 (June 4, 1993) (to be codified at 29 C.F.R. pt. 825). [See rule 14.2.]
ALWD: 58 Fed. Reg. 31794, 31796–8 (June 4, 1993). [See rule 19.3.]

Summary. Thoroughly researching regulations involves more than the regulation itself. Chart 7.2 lists optimal options for each piece of the regulations pie.

| CHART 7.2 | Optimal Options for Regulations Research |

Source	Resources and Finding Tools
Organic statute	Codes
Regulation	C.F.R. online via FDsys, e-CFR, agency website Commercial databases (HeinOnline, LexisNexis, Westlaw) CFR in print Tool: *CFR Index and Finding Aids*
New regulatory action	e-CFR and online *Federal Register* *Federal Register* in print Tool: *List of C.F.R. Sections Affected*
Case law	Case law reporters, databases, court websites Annotated Codes Tools: digests, online searching, citators for regulations
Regulatory history	*Federal Register* in FDsys, HeinOnline, LexisNexis, or Westlaw Tool: C.F.R. reference

DECISIONS AND ORDERS

Parallel to case law. Thus far this chapter has dealt with regulations, which are often described as "quasi-legislative" because of their similarities to statutes. Some agencies also operate in ways that are "quasi-judicial," meaning that they issue orders and make other kinds of decisions involving the application of law to specific facts and issue orders.

These decisions that are the outcome of an agency's case adjudication have the force of law. An agency decision functions as precedent for other similar situations coming within the agency's jurisdiction. In fact, some agencies routinely choose to make law through adjudication rather than rulemaking, resulting in bodies of administrative orders akin to the common law.

Disputes arising under the FMLA are adjudicated by the courts. The agency that governs this chapter's second issue—the issue of discussion among employees—does engage in adjudication. The National Labor Relations Act (NLRA) protects employees who engage in protected concerted activity, whether union-related or not.[7] It also places responsibility for enforcement of the act in the National Labor Relations Board (NLRB). The enforcement system includes investigation of complaints, levying of charges, hearings before and recommendations by administrative law judges, and issuance of orders by the National Labor Relations Board (which are appealable to the federal appellate courts).

Case adjudication procedures. Agency decisions fall into two main categories: formal adjudication and informal adjudication.

A formal administrative adjudication resembles a judicial trial, with parties observing rules of procedure, presenting testimony and documentary evidence before an administrative law judge (ALJ), and making written and oral legal arguments about the final outcome. At the conclusion of a formal adjudication, the ALJ issues a written decision and recommendation about how he or she thinks the case should be decided. The ultimate decision is up to the agency's commissioners or other high-ranking members. Once finalized, a formal agency decision more or less resembles the opinion of a judicial court. It includes a statement of facts as found by the agency, the agency's decision, and its reasoning behind the decision. That reasoning typically includes discussion of the statute, any pertinent regulations, and previous decisions of the agency.[8] Exhibit 7.8 is an excerpt of a decision discussing discipline for Facebook postings under the National Labor Relations Act.

Agencies are not always required to use these formal, court-like procedures. In fact, most agency adjudications are "informal." Although the procedures are less formal, there are some procedural requirements to ensure that parties receive due process of law. For example, an agency may have the authority to decide a dispute based only on written submissions from the parties, without providing the opportunity for a live hearing before an ALJ.

7. 29 U.S.C. § 157 (2006).
8. Some agency decisions substantially incorporate the ALJ's written decision.

EXHIBIT 7.8	Administrative Law Judge Decision and Order

JD-55-11
Buffalo, NY

UNITED STATES OF AMERICA
BEFORE THE NATIONAL LABOR RELATIONS BOARD
DIVISION OF JUDGES

HISPANICS UNITED OF BUFFALO, INC.

and   Case No. 3-CA-27872

CARLOS ORTIZ
    An Individual

Aaron B. Sukert. Esq.
    for the General Counsel.
Rafael 0. Gomez and Michael H Kooshoian, Esqs.,
  (Lo Tempio & Brown. P.C). Buffalo, New York
    for the Respondent.

DECISION

STATEMENT OF THE CASE

ARTHUR 1. AMCHAN, Administrative Law Judge. This case was tried in Buffalo, New York on July 13-15, 2011. Charging Party, Carlos Ortiz, filed the charge on November 18, 2011 and the General Counsel issued the complaint on May 9, 2011 and an amended complaint on May 27.

Respondent, Hispanics United of Buffalo, Inc. (HUB) is a not-for-profit corporation which renders social services to its economically disadvantaged clients in Buffalo, New York. Its services include housing, advocacy for domestic violence victims, translation and interpretation services, a food pantry, senior and youth services and employment assistance.

HUB's Executive Director Lourdes Iglesias terminated the employment of Carlos Ortiz, Mariana Cole-Rivera, Ludimar Rodriguez, Damicela Rodriguez and Yaritza Campos on October 12, 2010. The General Counsel alleges that the five alleged discriminatees were terminated because they engaged in protected concerted activity and that therefore these terminations violated Section 8(a)(1) of the Act.

EXHIBIT 7.8 *(continued)*

JD-55-11

5

II. ALLEGED UNFAIR LABOR PRACTICES

The Alleged Protected Concerted Activity

Relevant events prior to October 9, 2010

10

Respondent hired Lydia Cruz-Moore in May 2010 as a domestic violence (DV) advocate pursuant to a one-year grant from Erie County. Her job was primarily to accompany victims of domestic violence to hearings at the City of Buffalo's Family Justice Center. One day each week Cruz-Moore worked at HUB's offices doing such tasks as finding employment for

15 HUB clients or insuring that their rent was paid. A number of other HUB employees were at the main office every day and generally performed different tasks than Cruz-Moore.

Cruz-Moore and discriminatee Mariana Cole-Rivera communicated very often, normally by sending each other text messages. In these messages Cruz-Moore was often critical

20 about the job performance of other HUB employees, primarily those in Respondent's housing department. Early on the morning of Saturday, October 9, Cruz-Moore told Cole-Rivera that she was going to raise these concerns with Respondent's Executive Director, Lourdes Iglesias.

Several others of the discriminatees also had conversations or text message exchanges

25 with Cruz-Moore, in which Cruz-Moore criticized HUB employees. On August 2, 2010, Cruz-Moore told discriminatee Ludimar Rodriguez that a client had been waiting for Rodriguez for 20 minutes and criticized Rodriguez's job performance.

Discriminatee Damicela Rodriguez had a conversation with Cruz-Moore in late

30 September or early October in which Cruz-Moore complained that HUB staff members were not doing their jobs. Cruz-Moore also complained to Carlos Ortiz about the job performance of employees in Respondent's housing department.

The Facebook postings on which Respondent relies
35 *in terminating the five alleged discriminatees*

On Saturday, October 9, 2010 at 10:14 a.m., Mariana Cole-Rivera posted the following message on her Facebook page from her home:

40 Lydia Cruz, a coworker feels that we don't help our clients enough at HUB I about had it! My fellow coworkers how do u feel?[4]

The following employees responded by posting comments on Cole-Rivera's Facebook page:

---

[4] Respondent argues at page 32 of its brief that this statement is a lie and suggests therefore, the discriminatees are not entitled to protection of the Act. First of all, Cruz-Moore did not testify at the instant hearing, thus, I cannot credit what Respondent's brief characterizes as her "vehement denial." Moreover, I credit Cole-Rivera's testimony, which is corroborated by other discriminatees, that Cruz-Moore had repeatedly criticized the job performance of HUB employees, and Cole-Rivera's testimony, at Tr. 251, that Cruz-Moore had told her that she was going to go to Iglesias with her complaints.

4

EXHIBIT 7.8   *(continued)*

JD-55-11

5   At 10:19, Damicela Rodriguez (also known as Damicela Pedroza Natal) posted the following response:

What the f. .. Try doing my job I have 5 programs

10 At 10:26, Ludimar (Ludahy) Rodriguez posted:

What the Hell, we don't have a life as is, What else can we do???

At 11: 11, Yaritza (M Ntal) Campos posted:

15 Tell her to come do mt [my] fucking job n c if I don't do enough, this is just dum

At 11:41, Carlos Ortiz de Jesus posted:

20 I think we should give our paychecks to our clients so they can "pay" the rent, also we can take them to their Dr's appts, and served as translators (oh! We do that). Also we can clean their houses, we can go to DSS for them and we can run all their errands and they can spend their day in their house watching tv, and also we can go to do their grocery shop and organized the food in their house pantries ... (insert sarcasm here now)

25 Mariana Cole-Rivera posted again at 11:45:

Lol. I know! I think it is difficult for someone that its not at HUB 24-7 to really grasp and understand what we do ..I will give her that. Clients will complain especially when they ask for services we don't provide, like washer, dryers stove and refrigerators, I'm proud to work at HUB and you are all my family and I see what you do and yes, some things may fall thru the cracks, but we are all human :) love ya guys

30 Nannette Dorrios, a member of the Board of Directors at HUB posted at 12:10:

35 Who is Lydia Cruz?

Yaritza Campos posted a second time at 12:11:

40 Luv ya too boo

Mariana Cole-Rivera at 12:12 responded to Dorrios by the following post:

She's from the dv program works at the FJC [Family Justice Center] at hub once a week.

45 Jessica Rivera, the Secretary to HUD Director Iglesias, posted at 1: 10 p.m.

Is it not overwhelming enough over there?

50

5

EXHIBIT 7.8   *(continued)*

JD-55-11

5   At 2:27 Lydia Cruz-Moore posted:

Marianna stop with ur lies about me. I'll b at HUB Tuesday..

Cole-Rivera responded at 2:56:

10

Lies? Ok. In any case Lydia, Magalie [Lomax, HUB'S Business Manager] is inviting us over to her house today after 6:00 pm and wanted to invite you but does not have your number i'll inbox you her phone number if you wish.

15   Carlos Ortiz posted at 10:30 p.m.

Bueno el martes llevo el pop corn [Good, Tuesday, I'll bring the popcorn].

Saturday, October 9, was not a work day for any of HUB's employees. None of the
20   discriminatees used HUB's computers in making these Facebook posts.

Lydia Cruz-Moore complained to HUB Executive Director Lourdes Iglesias about the Facebook posts. Her text messages to Iglesias suggest that she was trying to get Iglesias to terminate or at least discipline the employees who posted the comments on Facebook. She
25   appears to have had a dispute with Mariana Cole-Rivera, which was at least in part work-related. It is not clear why she bore such animosity against the other employees, most of whom did not mention her name in their posts.

Tuesday, October 12, 2010

30

On October 12, Lourdes Iglesias met individually with five of the employees who had made the Facebook posts on October 9 and fired each one of them.[5] She told them that the posts constituted bullying and harassment and violated HUB's policy on harassment. Iglesias did not terminate the employment of her secretary, Jessica Rivera, who had also entered a post on
35   Cole-Rivera's Facebook page on October 9.

Each of the meetings was very short. Iglesias told each of the employees that Cruz-Moore had suffered a heart attack as a result of their harassment and that Respondent was going to have pay her compensation. For these reasons, Iglesias told each one that she would have to
40   fire them. It is not established in this record that Cruz-Moore had a heart attack, nor whether there was any casual relationship between whatever health problems Cruz-Moore may have been experiencing and the Facebook posts. Furthermore, the record establishes that when Iglesias decided to fire the five discriminatees she had no rational basis for concluding that their Facebook posts had any relationship to Cruz-Moore's health.

45

_____

[5] I do not credit Mariana Cole-Rivera's testimony that she attempted to speak to Iglesias on October 12, prior to the meeting in which she was terminated. Iglesias denies any such contact with Cole-Rivera and Carlos Ortiz's testimony leads me not to credit Cole-Rivera's testimony on this point. However, since I find that the October 9 Facebook postings were protected, this finding does not materially affect the outcome of this case.

6

Exhibit 7.8   *(continued)*

JD-55-11

5   It has also not been established why Respondent or its insurance carrier would have had to compensate Cruz-Moore. Typically, a workers compensation claimant has to show some relationship been their physical ailment and their employment. This is often difficult in cases in which the ailment, particularly something like a heart attack or a stroke, manifested itself when the employee was not at work.[6]

10

Several employees were handed termination letters at their meeting with Iglesias; others received them in the mail a few days later. Respondent has not replaced the five alleged discriminatees. It has given their work responsibilities to other employees and has operated with five fewer employees (25 as opposed to 30).

15

Analysis

The Discriminatees engaged in protected concerted activity.
Respondent terminated their employment in violation of Section 8(a)(1) of the Act.

20

Section 8(a)(1) provides that it is an unfair labor practice to interfere with, restrain or coerce employees in the exercise of the rights guaranteed in Section 7. Section 7 provides that, "employees shall have the right to self-organization, to form, join, or assist labor organizations, to bargain collectively through representatives of their own choosing, *and to engage in other*

25   *concerted activities for the purpose of collective bargaining or other mutual aid or protection* ... (Emphasis added)"

In *Myers Industries (Myers 1)*, 268 NLRB 493 (1984), and in *Myers Industries (Myers 11)* 281 NLRB 882 (1986), the Board held that "concerted activities" protected by Section 7 are

30   those "engaged in with or on the authority of other employees, and not solely by and on behalf of the employee himself." However, the activities of a single employee in enlisting the support of fellow employees in mutual aid and protection is as much concerted activity as is ordinary group activity.

35   Individual action is concerted so long as it is engaged in with the object of initiating or inducing group action, *Whittaker Corp.*, 289 NLRB 933 (1988); *Mushroom Transportation Co.*, 330 F.2d 683,685 (3d Cir. 1964). The object of inducing group action need not be express.

Additionally, the Board held in *Amelio's*, 301 NLRB 182 (1991) that in order to present

40   a prima facie case that an employer has discharged an employee in violation of Section 8(a)(1), the General Counsel must establish that the employer knew of the concerted nature of the activity.

---

[6] Under New York Workers Compensation Law, there is a rebuttable presumption that an employee's death from a heart attack or stroke is compensable-if it occurs at work. However, even in cases in which an employee dies of a heart attack while at work, the death is not necessarily compensable in New York State. The presumption may be rebutted by medical evidence, particularly where the decedent had a preexisting medical condition, see, e.g., *Schwartz v. Hebrew Academy of Five Towns*, 39 A.D.3d 1134, 834 N.Y.S. 2d 400, N.Y.A.D. 3 Dept., 2007.

7

EXHIBIT 7.8   *(continued)*

5   Respondent concedes that the sole reason it discharged the five discriminatees is the
October 9 Facebook postings. It also concedes that regardless of whether the comments and
actions of the five terminated employees took place on Facebook or "around the water cooler"
the result would be the same. Thus, the only substantive issue in this case, other than
jurisdiction, is whether by their postings on Facebook, the five employees engaged in activity
10   protected by the Act. I conclude that their Facebook communications with each other, in
reaction to a co-worker's criticisms of the manner in which HUB employees performed their
jobs, are protected.

It is irrelevant to this case that the discriminatees were not trying to change their
15   working conditions and that they did not communicate their concerns to Respondent. A
leading case in this regard is *Aroostook County Regional Ophthalmology Center,* 317 NLRB
218, 220 (1995) enf. denied on other grounds 81 F. 3d 209 (D.C. Cir. 1996),[7] in which the
Board held that employee complaints to each other concerning schedule changes constituted
protected activity. By analogy, I find that the discriminatees' discussions about criticisms of
20   their job performance are also protected.

Likewise in *Parexel International, LLC,* 356 NLRB No. 82 (January 28, 2011) at slip
opinion page 3 and n. 3, the Board found protected, employees' discussions of possible
discrimination in setting the terms or conditions of employment. Moreover, concerted activity
25   for employees' mutual aid and protection that is motivated by a desire to maintain the status
quo may be protected by Section 7 to the same extent as such activity seeking changes in
wages, hours or working conditions, *Five Star Transportation, Inc.,* 349 NLRB 42, 47 (2007).

Other cases similar to the instant matter are *Jhirmack Enterprises,* 283 NLRB 609, 615
30   (1987) and *Akal Security, Inc.,* 355 NLRB No. 106 (2010). In *Akal Security,* the Board
reaffirmed the decision by a 2-member Board at 354 NLRB No. 11 (2009). The Board
dismissed the Complaint allegation that Akal had terminated the employment of two court
security officers in violation of Section 8(a)(1). However, the Board found that the
discriminatees' conversations with a coworker about his job performance constituted concerted
35   activity protected by Section 8(a)(1).

Equally relevant are the Board decisions in *Automatic Screw Products Co.,* 306 NLRB
1072 (1992) and *Triana Industries,* 245 NLRB 1072 (1979). In those cases the Board found
that the employers violated Section 8(a)(1) by promulgating a rule prohibiting employees from
40   discussing their wages. It stands to reason that if employees have a protected right to discuss
wages and other terms and conditions of employment, an employer violates Section 8(a)(1) in
disciplining or terminating employees for exercising this right—regardless of whether there is
evidence that such discussions are engaged in with the object of initiating or inducing group
action.
45

However, assuming that the decision in *Mushroom Transportation, supra,* is applicable
to this case, I conclude that the Facebook postings satisfy the requirements of that decision.
The discriminatees herein were taking a first step towards taking group action to defend

---

[7] The Court of Appeals denied enforcement regarding the termination of Aroostook's employees
primarily on the grounds that their complaints were made in patient care areas.

8

EXHIBIT 7.8   *(continued)*

5   harassment which has no relevance to this case. It also has a policy against harassment of other
     sorts, which states as follows:

>   Hispanics United of Buffalo will not tolerate any form of harassment, joking remarks or
>   other abusive conduct (including verbal, nonverbal, or physical conduct) that demeans
10   or shows hostility toward an individual because of his/her race, color, sex, religion,
>   national origin, age, disability, veteran status or other prohibited basis that creates an
>   intimidating, hostile or offensive work environment, unreasonably interferes with an
>   individual's work performance or otherwise adversely affects an individual's
>   employment opportunity.

15

          There is nothing in this record that establishes that any of the discriminatees were
     harassing Lydia Cruz Moore, and even if there were such evidence, there is no evidence that
     she was being harassed on the basis of any of the factors listed above. Finally, there is no
     evidence that the comments would have impacted Cruz-Moore's job performance. She rarely
20   interacted with the discriminatees. In summary, Lourdes Iglesias had no rational basis for
     concluding that the discriminatees violated Respondent's zero tolerance or discrimination
     policy. For reasons not disclosed in this record, Respondent was looking for an excuse to
     reduce its workforce and seized upon the Facebook posts as an excuse for doing so.

25   The terminations are also not justified by the alleged relationship between the Facebook
     posts and Ms. Moore's health. There is no probative evidence as to the nature of Ms. Cruz-
     Moore's health problem following the Facebook posts nor is there any probative evidence as to
     a causal relationship between Ms. Moore's heart attack (assuming she had one) or other health
     condition and the Facebook posts.

30

                                           REMEDY

          The Respondent, having discriminatorily discharged employees, must offer them
     reinstatement and make them whole for any loss of earnings and other benefits. Backpay shall
35   be computed in accordance with *F. W. Woolworth Co.*, 90 NLRB 289 (1950), with interest at
     the rate prescribed in *New Horizons for the Retarded*, 283 NLRB 1173 (1987), compounded
     daily as prescribed in *Kentucky River Medical Center*, 356 NLRB No.8 (2010).

          On these findings of fact and conclusions of law and on the entire record, I issue the
40   following recommended[9]

                                           ORDER

          The Respondent, Hispanics United of Buffalo, Inc., Buffalo, New York, its officers,
45   agents, successors, and assigns, shall

-----

[9] If no exceptions are filed as provided by Sec. 102.46 of the Board's Rules and Regulations, the
findings, conclusions, and recommended Order shall, as provided in Sec. 102.48 of the Rules, be
adopted by the Board and all objections to them shall be deemed waived for all purposes.

10

EXHIBIT 7.8   *(continued)*

JD-55-11

5   1. Cease and desist from

           (a) Discharging its employees due to their engaging in protected concerted activities.

           (b) In any like or related manner interfering with, restraining, or coercing its employees
10   in the exercise of their rights under Section 7 of the Act.

           2. Take the following affirmative action necessary to effectuate the policies of the Act.

           (a) Within 14 days from the date of the Board's Order, offer Mariana Cole-Rivera,
15   Carlos Ortiz de Jesus, Ludimar Rodriguez, Damicela Rodriguez and Yaritza Campos full
       reinstatement to their former jobs or, if any of those jobs no longer exists, to a substantially
       equivalent position, without prejudice to their seniority or any other rights or privileges
       previously enjoyed.

20   (b) Make Mariana Cole-Rivera, Carlos Ortiz de Jesus, Ludimar Rodriguez, Damicela
       Rodriguez and Yaritza Campos whole for any loss of earnings and other benefits suffered as a
       result of the discrimination against them, in the manner set forth in the remedy section of the
       decision.

25   (c) Within 14 days from the date of the Board's Order, remove from its files any
       reference to the unlawful discharges and within 3 days thereafter notify the employees in
       writing that this has been done and that the discharges will not be used against them in any
       way.

30   (d) Preserve and, within 14 days of a request, or such additional time as the Regional
       Director may allow for good cause shown, provide at a reasonable place designated by the
       Board or its agents, all payroll records, social security payment records, timecards, personnel
       records and reports, and all other records, including an electronic copy of such records if stored
       in electronic form, necessary to analyze the amount of backpay due under the terms of this
35   Order.

           (e) Within 14 days after service by the Region, post at its Buffalo, New York office
       copies of the attached notice marked "Appendix"[10] in both English and Spanish. Copies of the
       notice, on forms provided by the Regional Director for Region 3, after being signed by the
40   Respondent's authorized representative, shall be posted by the Respondent and maintained for
       60 consecutive days in conspicuous places including all places where notices to employees are
       customarily posted. In addition to physical posting of paper notices, the notices shall be
       distributed electronically, such as by email, posting on an intranet or an internet site, and/or
       other electronic means, if the Respondent customarily communicates with its employees by
45   such means. Reasonable steps shall be taken by the Respondent to ensure that the notices are

       _____

       [10] If this Order is enforced by a judgment of a United States court of appeals, the words in the notice
       reading "Posted by Order of the National Labor Relations Board" shall read "Posted Pursuant to a
       Judgment of the United States Court of Appeals Enforcing an Order of the National Labor Relations
       Board."

11

Even though these kinds of decisions do not use court-like procedures, they can still result in decisions that have the force of law.

Formal and informal agency decisions, like agency regulations, are subject to judicial review. The statute creating the agency typically specifies whether the review begins in a trial or appellate court. In either case, the agency's decision is generally reviewed as if it were an appeal from a trial court, because the agency's hearing served as the initial "trial" to determine the facts of the case. Thus the issues before a reviewing court typically are limited to whether there is substantial evidence in the record to support the agency's decision, whether the agency has exceeded its statutory jurisdiction or failed to follow required procedures, and whether the agency has abused its discretion.

Researching agency decisions. Agency decisions involve legal issues governed by statutes or by statutes plus regulations. Thus, as you read the organic statute for the agency, you should look for a description of the agency's authority to adjudicate cases and the process the agency must follow, including any substantive standards governing the case. Also research regulations, as described earlier, that may apply to the issue.

Some agencies publish decisions in print reporters, others in databases made available through public websites, and others in a combination of the two. *Bluebook* Table 1 and *ALWD* Appendix 8 list official reporters of federal agency decisions. Each such compilation has its own particular features. Furthermore, agency decisions appear in HeinOnline's U.S. Federal Agency Documents, Decisions, and Appeals database as well as on LexisNexis and Westlaw. Because agency websites are evolving so rapidly, a good starting point generally is the agency's website, which may itself provide recent decisions and direct you to resources for older decisions.

Of course, you should read with care any decisions you have obtained. As with judicial cases, you should learn the outcome of the decision, discern the rule used by the agency to decide the case, understand the facts of the case and the judge's reasoning about those facts, identify the leading authorities cited in the reasoning, and examine any dissenting and concurring opinions.

As with judicial cases, the law made through agency decisions evolves over time. Later agency decisions may affect the validity of an earlier agency decision in various ways, e.g., overruling, modifying, distinguishing, citing with approval. As noted previously, agency decisions are appealable to courts, so a necessary step is to cite the decision to ascertain whether it has been reviewed on appeal and, if so, to what effect.[9] The standard tools for citing agency decisions are the same as for citing cases: KeyCite and Shepard's.

For example, for many years the National Labor Relations Board has published its decisions in a print reporter system, *Decisions and Orders of the National Labor Relations Board*, accompanied by a classification outline

9. The law involving administrative decisions at times is more complicated than the law created by the courts acting alone. Because agency commissioner positions are political appointments, the views of the commissioners may shift over time; so too may the law they create in their decisions. Furthermore, a decision may be appealable to more than one court, and the various reviewing courts may take different stances on an issue.

and digest. More recently, the Board has provided an online searchable digest of decisions. Now, the NLRB website provides Board decisions, including the ALJ recommendations, online along with various ways to search the database.

We researched the issue of Facebook discussion of working conditions by a group of nonunionized workers on the NLRB website. We learned from *Hispanics United of Buffalo*, excerpted in Exhibit 7.8, that conduct very similar to that of Fey's coworkers was protected under the NLRA, that discipline was therefore not permissible, and that the employer would be ordered to rescind the discipline.

Citation to Agency Adjudications and Orders

An agency adjudication citation parallels the format of a judicial case citation. Assume that the ALJ decision featured in the chapter was affirmed by the NLRB; its citation format (with fabricated numbers) would be:

BLUEBOOK: *Hispanics United of Buffalo, Inc.*, 123 N.L.R.B. 456 (2012). [See rule 14.3.]
ALWD: *Hispanics United of Buffalo, Inc.*, 123 N.L.R.B. 456 (U.S. Natl. Lab. Rel. Bd. 2012). [See rule 19.5.]

Summary. The details of researching agency adjudications differ from agency to agency. The basic structure of this research is similar across agencies: thorough research involves the organic statute, the agency's decision, and citing that decision; regulations and judicial cases may also be involved.

NON-LEGISLATIVE RULES AND OTHER GUIDANCE MATERIALS

Regulations and decisions are law, just as statutes and cases decided by courts are law. In addition, many agencies issue non-legislative rules and other guidance documents, which are intended to help regulated parties better understand and apply the law and how the agency intends to enforce it. Some agencies issue informal documents, sometimes called "advice letters," in which they opine about specific situations, but these documents are not decisions. Documents such as manuals used by agency staff in conducting official inspections may carry weight with courts as they decide difficult statutory interpretation issues. Others are less weighty, such as forms or FAQ (frequently asked questions) documents addressed to the public.

Because these materials are not themselves law, they are not as readily or consistently available as regulations and decisions and orders. Your best resource is usually the agency's website, perhaps followed up with a call to an agency official.

When we researched the Facebook issue, we found on the NLRB website not only the *Hispanics United* decision but also a report from the NLRB's general counsel on the social media issue. The document was addressed to his staff but proved very helpful to employers seeking to avoid charges under the NLRA. See Exhibit 7.9.

LOOSE-LEAF SERVICES

As this chapter has made clear, the law of an area governed by a major federal agency can consist of many moving pieces—not only statutes and judicial cases but also agency regulations, decisions and orders, and other materials. For some years, in major practice areas, commercial publishers have compiled these various sources into what have traditionally been called "loose-leaf ser-vices," based on their publication format.

One advantage of a loose-leaf service is the accumulation of sources. The best loose-leafs also offer several other advantages: treatise-like material providing an overview of the law, a digest of the decisions set out within a logical framework, and updating publications. Increasingly these services are available online, some through Westlaw or LexisNexis, typically as a special subscription.

Selection of a loose-leaf service is best made by consulting a reference librarian or specialist in the area. To obtain the full benefit of a loose-leaf (in print or online), spend some time learning about its components and their connections. Often a sound place to start is in the overview or treatise com-ponent, to obtain a framework for your analysis and references to other components.

TEST YOUR UNDERSTANDING

Reflection Questions

1. When you operate in an area governed by an agency, you may be dealing with a wide range of sources and resources. Can you develop a set of steps or checklist that you could follow most of the time, to be sure your research is both thorough and cost-effective?

EXHIBIT 7.9   Guidance Document

NATIONAL LABOR RELATIONS BOARD

OFFICE OF THE GENERAL COUNSEL

WASHINGTON, D.C.   20570

REPORT OF THE GENERAL COUNSEL

On August 18, 2011, I issued a report presenting case developments arising in the context of today's social media. As I noted in that report, social media include various online technology tools that enable people to communicate easily via the internet to share information and resources. These tools can encompass text, audio, video, images, podcasts, and other multimedia communications. Cases concerning the protected and/or concerted nature of employees' social media postings and the lawfulness of employers' social media policies and rules continue to be presented to the Regional Offices and are then submitted to the Division of Advice in Washington for my consideration. In addition, these issues and their treatment by the NLRB continue to be a "hot topic" among practitioners, human resource professionals, the media, and the public. Accordingly, I am issuing this second report on fourteen recent cases that present emerging issues in the context of social media.

I hope that this report will continue to provide guidance as this area of the law develops.

/s/
Lafe E. Solomon
Acting General Counsel

2. Why should administrative agencies exist? One answer is that they enforce laws through such procedures as awarding licenses and inspecting operations of companies. But why should they have lawmaking authority? Why should a legislature leave the details of a legal rule up to an agency to determine?

Your Scenario

Assume that the dispute between your client, Elaine Wilson, who seeks to have a companion animal in her apartment to help her deal with her PTSD, and her landlord, who opposes this plan, is governed by the federal Fair Housing Act.

- Research whether an agency is involved in enforcing that statute and what its organic statute provides as to regulatory authority.
- Research whether a federal regulation governs your issue.
- Research whether the regulation has been applied in judicial cases.

RESEARCH IN RULES OF PROCEDURE

Contents

This chapter explores two issues: a lawyer's failure to sign a key document and contact between former coworkers now an opposite sides of a lawsuit.

Key Concepts and Tools in This Chapter

- Substantive versus procedural law
- Sources of procedural law
- Major rules of procedure
- Advisory committee notes
- Local rules
- Procedural law in judicial decisions
- Deskbooks
- Court websites

(continued)

- Procedural forms
- Procedure treatises
- Annotated rules
- Case law research
- Rules of professional responsibility
- ABA Model Rules
- Ethics opinions

The United States is widely described as a litigious culture.[1] Certainly litigation is a common occurrence. In fiscal year 2010,[2] over 360,000 cases were filed in the federal district courts alone. Civil cases numbered over 280,000. Major growth areas involved consumer credit, foreclosures, and bankruptcy as well as employment disputes with the types of issues discussed in this book. Roughly 80,000 criminal cases were filed; cases involving nearly 100,000 criminal defendants were concluded, about ninety percent through guilty pleas.

The conduct of these cases is regulated by various rules of procedure. Thus, when litigating a case, a lawyer attends not only to what is called the "substantive law" of the case (for example, whether discrimination has occurred and what the employer's defenses might be) but also to "procedural law," such as how promptly the defendant must file an answer to the plaintiff's complaint. Rules of procedure assure that cases proceed fairly and efficiently.

Rules of procedure are law, binding on the lawyers and through them on the litigants. Failure to follow applicable rules can have mild to dramatic consequences, depending on the situation. In serious situations, a client may lose a case[3] or a lawyer and the client may be fined.[4]

This chapter first provides an overview of the types of rules of procedure that operate in American court systems and the sources that are used to supplement the rules themselves. With this background set, the chapter then turns to the many resources for researching rules of procedure, with a focus on federal procedure. The chapter concludes with a discussion of rules of professional responsibility. These rules broadly cover lawyers' conduct, both while litigating cases and in other settings.

The chapter returns, for its illustration, to a case introduced in Chapters 3 and 4. The firm's client, Casey Nichols, was fired from his job at a grocery

1. See Jeff Yates, Belinda Creel Davis, & Henry R. Glick, *The Politics of Torts: Explaining Litigation Rates in the United States*, 1 St. Pol. & Pol'y Q 127 (2001).

2. See the report of the Administrative Office of the U.S. Courts, *Judicial Business of the United States Courts*, posted at the AOUSC website, www.uscourts.gov/Statistics.

3. For example, failure to respond to a complaint may lead to default judgment against the non-responding party under Federal Rule of Civil Procedure 55.

4. See Rule 11 of the Federal Rules of Civil Procedure, featured in this chapter.

store in Lawrence, Kansas. Not only was he fired; his manager told coworkers that he was fired for giving food to friends, a violation of the store's anti-pilferage policy. He now believes that word has spread of his situation around the town of Lawrence, probably by his manager; this is making it difficult for him to find a job in town. Negotiations with the employer proved utterly fruitless, and the decision was made to sue. Because the company's headquarters were in Missouri, not Kansas, and the suit sought damages in excess of $75,000,[5] the suit was venued in the U.S. District Court for the District of Kansas, through the use of diversity jurisdiction.

Not surprisingly, the grocery store chain filed an answer denying any liability, which arrived the exact date it was due. Surprisingly, the answer was not signed by the lawyer or the client. Hence one issue for this chapter: how serious was this mistake and what should be done about it?

Furthermore, Nichols reported to you that he shared some hobbies with someone he used to work with at the store, who was still working there as a manager in the bakery department. He wondered whether he could be in touch with this person for reasons unrelated to the litigation. Our first instinct was to forbid this; we decided to research it.

PROCEDURAL LAW

In every jurisdiction, procedural law, viewed broadly, is an amalgam of statutes, rules of procedure, and case law. For example, statutes govern such matters as jurisdiction and timing of claims (statutes of limitation). If litigation can be analogized to a game, rules of procedure regulate the moves one makes as a lawyer representing a party. Courts interpret and apply these statutes and rules. A few procedural law topics, such as the admissibility of certain types of evidence at trial, are governed by case law alone. This chapter focuses on procedural law that stems from rules of procedure.

Reflecting our federalist system, rules of procedure exist at both the federal and state levels. A federal court applies its rules; a state court applies its rules. This is so whether the substantive law of the claim being adjudicated is federal or state law.

Federal and state court systems each have various sets of rules of procedure. For example, in handling a civil case in federal court, one would apply federal rules of civil procedure, evidence, and appellate procedure that apply across all federal trial and appellate courts, respectively. Criminal cases and cases in specialized courts, such as family court, are governed by separate sets of rules.[6]

---

5. 28 U.S.C. §1332 (2006), amended by Pub. L. No. 112-63, 2012 U.S.C.C.A.N. (125 Stat.) 758 (2012).
6. Furthermore, nonjudicial forums, such as agency hearings and arbitration, have their own rules of procedure.

Rules of procedure are created by the legislature, court, or combination of the two. As to the federal rules, the U.S. Constitution is not clear whether Congress or the Supreme Court has the power to create procedural rules. As a practical matter, Congress has delegated this task to the Supreme Court through the Rules Enabling Act of 1934.[7] The Federal Rules of Civil Procedure were presented to Congress in 1937, became effective in 1938 (although Congress never formally adopted them), and have been amended from time to time since then.

In many states, the highest court or a special body drafts the rules, which may then be reviewed and adopted by the legislature. In others, the legislature enacts rules through its usual statutory process. Many state rules are modeled more or less closely after the federal rules.

A new or amended rule becomes effective on the date specified when the rule is adopted. A rule continues in effect until it is amended or eliminated.

In general, a set of procedural rules is organized more or less chronologically, charting the sequence of a case through the litigation process it governs. For example, the Federal Rules of Civil Procedure are organized as follows: introductory matters, commencement and framing of a lawsuit, discovery (the process through which lawyers exchange factual information), trial, judgment and remedies, and miscellaneous matters. Each rule resembles a statute, stating what is permissible or required; many have numbered and lettered subdivisions. Exhibit 8.1 is Federal Rule of Civil Procedure 11.

Many rules of procedure are accompanied by advisory committee notes or comments. However a set of rules is created, a committee of experts in litigation, such as judges and professors, often is involved in reviewing current rules and recommending and analyzing changes. The notes prepared by the committee generally discuss the previous rule and the purpose of the changes. These notes thus resemble legislative history materials and can be thought of as "quasi-authority."

Because of their similarity to statutes, working with a rule of procedure resembles working with a statute. Often, thorough research into a procedural issue involves not only one but several rules; just as sections of a statute interlock, so do the rules in a set of rules of procedure. A sound step after locating and reading a pertinent rule is to summarize it; a sound follow-up step is to study the advisory committee notes for additional insight and to incorporate any useful information into your summary. Example 8.1 is a summary of Rule 11 and historical notes bearing on our research topic.

---

7. 28 U.S.C. § 2072 (2006).

Rule 9   RULES OF CIVIL PROCEDURE

make it unnecessary to consider the admiralty claim and
have the same effect on the case and parties as disposition of
the admiralty claim. Or the admiralty and non-admiralty
claims may be interdependent. An illustration is provided by
Roco Carriers, Ltd. v. M/V Nurnberg Express, 899 F.2d 1292
(2d Cir.1990). Claims for losses of ocean shipments were
made against two defendants, one subject to admiralty jurisdiction and the other not. Summary judgment was granted
in favor of the admiralty defendant and against the nonadmiralty defendant. The nonadmiralty defendant's appeal was
accepted, with the explanation that the determination of its
liability was "integrally linked with the determination of non-
liability" of the admiralty defendant, and that "section
1292(a)(3) is not limited to admiralty claims; instead, it
refers to admiralty cases." 899 F.2d at 1297. The advantages of permitting appeal by the nonadmiralty defendant
would be particularly clear if the plaintiff had appealed the
summary judgment in favor of the admiralty defendant.

It must be emphasized that this amendment does not rest
on any particular assumptions as to the meaning of the
§ 1292(a)(3) provision that limits interlocutory appeal to orders that determine the rights and liabilities of the parties.
It simply reflects the conclusion that so long as the case
involves an admiralty claim and an order otherwise meets
statutory requirements, the opportunity to appeal should not
turn on the circumstance that the order does—or does not—
dispose of an admiralty claim. No attempt is made to invoke
the authority conferred by 28 U.S.C. § 1292(e) to provide by
rule for appeal of an interlocutory decision that is not
otherwise provided for by other subsections of § 1292.

GAP Report on Rule 9(h). No changes have been made
in the published proposal.

2006 Amendment

Rule 9(h) is amended to conform to the changed title of the
Supplemental Rules.

2007 Amendment

The language of Rule 9 has been amended as part of the
general restyling of the Civil Rules to make them more easily
understood and to make style and terminology consistent
throughout the rules. These changes are intended to be
stylistic only.

Rule 15 governs pleading amendments of its own force.
The former redundant statement that Rule 15 governs an
amendment that adds or withdraws a Rule 9(h) designation
as an admiralty or maritime claim is deleted. The elimination
of paragraph (2) means that "(3)" will be redesignated as
"(2)" in Style Rule 9(h).

Rule 10.   Form of Pleadings

(a) **Caption; Names of Parties.** Every pleading must
have a caption with the court's name, a title, a file
number, and a Rule 7(a) designation. The title of
the complaint must name all the parties; the title
of other pleadings, after naming the first party on
each side, may refer generally to other parties.

(b) **Paragraphs; Separate Statements.** A party must
state its claims or defenses in numbered para-

graphs, each limited as far as practicable to a
single set of circumstances. A later pleading may
refer by number to a paragraph in an earlier
pleading. If doing so would promote clarity, each
claim founded on a separate transaction or occurrence—and each defense other than a denial—
must be stated in a separate count or defense.

(c) **Adoption by Reference; Exhibits.** A statement in
a pleading may be adopted by reference elsewhere
in the same pleading or in any other pleading or
motion. A copy of a written instrument that is an
exhibit to a pleading is a part of the pleading for
all purposes.

(Amended April 30, 2007, effective December 1, 2007.)

1937 Adoption

The first sentence is derived in part from the opening
statement of former Equity Rule 25 (Bill of Complaint—
Contents). The remainder of the rule is an expansion in
conformity with usual state provisions. For numbered paragraphs and separate statements, see Conn.Gen.Stat., 1930,
§ 5513; Smith-Hurd Ill.Stats. ch. 110, § 157(2); N.Y.R.C.P.,
(1937) Rule 90. For incorporation by reference, see
N.Y.R.C.P., (1937) Rule 90. For written instruments as
exhibits, see Smith-Hurd Ill.Stats. ch. 110, § 160.

2007 Amendment

The language of Rule 10 has been amended as part of the
general restyling of the Civil Rules to make them more easily
understood and to make style and terminology consistent
throughout the rules. These changes are intended to be
stylistic only.

Rule 11.   Signing Pleadings, Motions, and Oth-
er Papers; Representations to the
Court; Sanctions

(a) **Signature.** Every pleading, written motion, and
other paper must be signed by at least one attorney of record in the attorney's name—or by a
party personally if the party is unrepresented.
The paper must state the signer's address, e-mail
address, and telephone number. Unless a rule or
statute specifically states otherwise, a pleading
need not be verified or accompanied by an affidavit. The court must strike an unsigned paper
unless the omission is promptly corrected after
being called to the attorney's or party's attention.

(b) **Representations to the Court.** By presenting to
the court a pleading, written motion, or other
paper—whether by signing, filing, submitting, or
later advocating it—an attorney or unrepresented
party certifies that to the best of the person's

EXHIBIT 8.1   *(continued)*

PLEADINGS AND MOTIONS   **Rule 11**

knowledge, information, and belief, formed after an inquiry reasonable under the circumstances:

(1) it is not being presented for any improper purpose, such as to harass, cause unnecessary delay, or needlessly increase the cost of litigation;

(2) the claims, defenses, and other legal contentions are warranted by existing law or by a nonfrivolous argument for extending, modifying, or reversing existing law or for establishing new law;

(3) the factual contentions have evidentiary support or, if specifically so identified, will likely have evidentiary support after a reasonable opportunity for further investigation or discovery; and

(4) the denials of factual contentions are warranted on the evidence or, if specifically so identified, are reasonably based on belief or a lack of information.

(c) Sanctions.

(1) *In General.* If, after notice and a reasonable opportunity to respond, the court determines that Rule 11(b) has been violated, the court may impose an appropriate sanction on any attorney, law firm, or party that violated the rule or is responsible for the violation. Absent exceptional circumstances, a law firm must be held jointly responsible for a violation committed by its partner, associate, or employee.

(2) *Motion for Sanctions.* A motion for sanctions must be made separately from any other motion and must describe the specific conduct that allegedly violates Rule 11(b). The motion must be served under Rule 5, but it must not be filed or be presented to the court if the challenged paper, claim, defense, contention, or denial is withdrawn or appropriately corrected within 21 days after service or within another time the court sets. If warranted, the court may award to the prevailing party the reasonable expenses, including attorney's fees, incurred for the motion.

(3) *On the Court's Initiative.* On its own, the court may order an attorney, law firm, or party to show cause why conduct specifically described in the order has not violated Rule 11(b).

(4) *Nature of a Sanction.* A sanction imposed under this rule must be limited to what suffices to deter repetition of the conduct or comparable conduct by others similarly situated. The sanction may include nonmonetary directives; an order to pay a penalty into court; or, if imposed on motion and warranted for effective deterrence, an order directing

payment to the movant of part or all of the reasonable attorney's fees and other expenses directly resulting from the violation.

(5) *Limitations on Monetary Sanctions.* The court must not impose a monetary sanction:

(A) against a represented party for violating Rule 11(b)(2); or

(B) on its own, unless it issued the show-cause order under Rule 11(c)(3) before voluntary dismissal or settlement of the claims made by or against the party that is, or whose attorneys are, to be sanctioned.

(6) *Requirements for an Order.* An order imposing a sanction must describe the sanctioned conduct and explain the basis for the sanction.

(d) Inapplicability to Discovery. This rule does not apply to disclosures and discovery requests, responses, objections, and motions under Rules 26 through 37.

(Amended April 28, 1983, effective August 1, 1983; March 2, 1987, effective August 1, 1987; April 22, 1993, effective December 1, 1993; April 30, 2007, effective December 1, 2007.)

1937 Adoption

This is substantially the content of [former] Equity Rules 24 (Signature of Counsel) and 21 (Scandal and Impertinence) consolidated and unified. Compare former Equity Rule 36 (Officers Before Whom Pleadings Verified). Compare to similar purposes, *English Rules Under the Judicature Act* (The Annual Practice, 1937) O. 19, r. 4, and *Great Australian Gold Mining Co. v. Martin*, L.R. 5 Ch.Div. 1, 10 (1877). Subscription of pleadings is required in many codes. 2 Minn.Stat. (Mason, 1927) § 9265; N.Y.R.C.P. (1937) Rule 91; 2 N.D.Comp.Laws Ann. (1913) § 7455.

This rule expressly continues any statute which requires a pleading to be verified or accompanied by an affidavit, such as: U.S.C., Title 28:

§ 381 [former] (Preliminary injunctions and temporary restraining orders)

§ 762 [now 1402] (Suit against the United States)

U.S.C., Title 28, § 829 [now 1927] (Costs; attorney liable for, when) is unaffected by this rule.

For complaints which must be verified under these rules, see Rules 23(b) (Secondary Action by Shareholders) and 65 (Injunctions).

For abolition of former rule in equity that the averments of an answer under oath must be overcome by the testimony of two witnesses or of one witness sustained by corroborating circumstances, see 12 P.S.Pa. § 1222; for the rule in equity itself, see *Greenfield v. Blumenthal*, C.C.A.3, 1934, 69 F.2d 294.

Complete Annotation Materials, see Title 28 U.S.C.A.

EXHIBIT **8.1**   *(continued)*

| PLEADINGS AND MOTIONS | **Rule 11** |

to do so has been made explicit in order to overcome the traditional reluctance of courts to intervene unless requested by one of the parties. The detection and punishment of a violation of the signing requirement, encouraged by the amended rule, is part of the court's responsibility for securing the system's effective operation.

If the duty imposed by the rule is violated, the court should have the discretion to impose sanctions on either the attorney, the party the signing attorney represents, or both, or on an unrepresented party who signed the pleading, and the new rule so provides. Although Rule 11 has been silent on the point, courts have claimed the power to impose sanctions on an attorney personally, either by imposing costs or employing the contempt technique. See 5 Wright & Miller, *Federal Practice and Procedure: Civil* § 1334 (1969); 2A Moore, *Federal Practice* ¶ 11.02, at 2104 n. 8. This power has been used infrequently. The amended rule should eliminate any doubt as to the propriety of assessing sanctions against the attorney.

Even though it is the attorney whose signature violates the rule, it may be appropriate under the circumstances of the case to impose a sanction on the client. See *Browning Debenture Holders' Committee v. DASA Corp.*, supra. This modification brings Rule 11 in line with practice under Rule 37, which allows sanctions for abuses during discovery to be imposed upon the party, the attorney, or both.

A party seeking sanctions should give notice to the court and the offending party promptly upon discovering a basis for doing so. The time when sanctions are to be imposed rests in the discretion of the trial judge. However, it is anticipated that in the case of pleadings the sanctions issue under Rule 11 normally will be determined at the end of the litigation, and in the case of motions at the time when the motion is decided or shortly thereafter. The procedure obviously must comport with due process requirements. The particular format to be followed should depend on the circumstances of the situation and the severity of the sanction under consideration. In many situations the judge's participation in the proceedings provides him with full knowledge of the relevant facts and little further inquiry will be necessary.

To assure that the efficiencies achieved through more effective operation of the pleading regimen will not be offset by the cost of satellite litigation over the imposition of sanctions, the court must to the extent possible limit the scope of sanction proceedings to the record. Thus, discovery should be conducted only by leave of the court, and then only in extraordinary circumstances.

Although the encompassing reference to "other papers" in new Rule 11 literally includes discovery papers, the certification requirement in that context is governed by proposed new Rule 26(g). Discovery motions, however, fall within the ambit of Rule 11.

1987 Amendment

The amendments are technical. No substantive change is intended.

1993 Amendments

Purpose of revision. This revision is intended to remedy problems that have arisen in the interpretation and application of the 1983 revision of the rule. For empirical examina-

tion of experience under the 1983 rule, see, *e.g.*, New York State Bar Committee on Federal Courts, *Sanctions and Attorneys' Fees* (1987); T. Willging, *The Rule 11 Sanctioning Process* (1989); American Judicature Society, *Report of the Third Circuit Task Force on Federal Rule of Civil Procedure 11* (S. Burbank ed., 1989); E. Wiggins, T. Willging, and D. Stienstra, *Report on Rule 11* (Federal Judicial Center 1991). For book-length analyses of the case law, see G. Joseph, *Sanctions: The Federal Law of Litigation Abuse* (1989); J. Solovy, *The Federal Law of Sanctions* (1991); G. Vairo, *Rule 11 Sanctions: Case Law Perspectives and Preventive Measures* (1991).

The rule retains the principle that attorneys and pro se litigants have an obligation to the court to refrain from conduct that frustrates the aims of Rule 1. The revision broadens the scope of this obligation, but places greater constraints on the imposition of sanctions and should reduce the number of motions for sanctions presented to the court. New subdivision (d) removes from the ambit of this rule all discovery requests, responses, objections, and motions subject to the provisions of Rule 26 through 37.

Subdivision (a). Retained in this subdivision are the provisions requiring signatures on pleadings, written motions, and other papers. Unsigned papers are to be received by the Clerk, but then are to be stricken if the omission of the signature is not corrected promptly after being called to the attention of the attorney or pro se litigant. Correction can be made by signing the paper on file or by submitting a duplicate that contains the signature. A court may require by local rule that papers contain additional identifying information regarding the parties or attorneys, such as telephone numbers to facilitate facsimile transmissions, though, as for omission of a signature, the paper should not be rejected for failure to provide such information.

The sentence in the former rule relating to the effect of answers under oath is no longer needed and has been eliminated. The provision in the former rule that signing a paper constitutes a certificate that it has been read by the signer also has been eliminated as unnecessary. The obligations imposed under subdivision (b) obviously require that a pleading, written motion, or other paper be read before it is filed or submitted to the court.

Subdivisions (b) and (c). These subdivisions restate the provisions requiring attorneys and pro se litigants to conduct a reasonable inquiry into the law and facts before signing pleadings, written motions, and other documents, and prescribing sanctions for violation of these obligations. The revision in part expands the responsibilities of litigants to the court, while providing greater constraints and flexibility in dealing with infractions of the rule. The rule continues to require litigants to "stop-and-think" before initially making legal or factual contentions. It also, however, emphasizes the duty of candor by subjecting litigants to potential sanctions for insisting upon a position after it is no longer tenable and by generally providing protection against sanctions if they withdraw or correct contentions after a potential violation is called to their attention.

The rule applies only to assertions contained in papers filed with or submitted to the court. It does not cover matters arising for the first time during oral presentations to the court, when counsel may make statements that would not have been made if there had been more time for study and reflection. However, a litigant's obligations with respect to

| EXAMPLE 8.1 | Summary of Rule of Procedure and History Notes |

Rule 11. Signing of Pleadings etc.

(a) "Every pleading . . . must be signed by at least one attorney of record in the attorney's name. The court must strike an unsigned paper unless the omission is promptly corrected after being called to the attorney's or party's attention."

Sections (b) and (c) cover pleadings that are presented for improper purposes, have claims or defenses not warranted by existing law or nonfrivolous arguments to extend the law, or contain allegations or denials of factual contentions lacking sufficient evidentiary support. Clients and lawyers may be sanctioned for these problems—but not for violating (a).

Notes re 1993 Amendments

Unsigned papers are to be received by the clerk but stricken if the omission is not corrected promptly after being called to the attention of the attorney. Correction occurs through signing the paper on file or submitting a signed duplicate. Notes refer to local rules that may require more information.

Many courts within a court system supplement the main rules of procedure with local rules governing matters of detail. Indeed, some judges have their own individual rules or guidelines. While these rules do not have the authoritativeness of the main rules, judges and other court personnel do not look kindly on lawyers who do not know and follow local rules.

Rules of procedure are applied by the courts every day as they handle the cases brought before them; just as the lawyers must follow the rules, so must the courts. For example, a court must follow the standard and procedures set out in Rule 11 before it sanctions a lawyer for frivolous litigation. Thus, many decisions written by a court include a procedural component in which the court at least identifies the applicable rule. Many decisions also quote and discuss the applicable rule, explain its application to the particular case, and provide sometimes significant judicial gloss on the rule's language. These decisions constitute precedent; the standard rules of court hierarchy fix which courts' decisions are mandatory and which are weightiest. For example, U.S. Supreme Court decisions bind all federal courts on issues under the various federal rules.

Finally, given the pervasiveness of litigation and importance of rules of procedure, procedural law is covered in many commentary sources. A good commentary source can assist you in putting together all of the pieces described in this section.

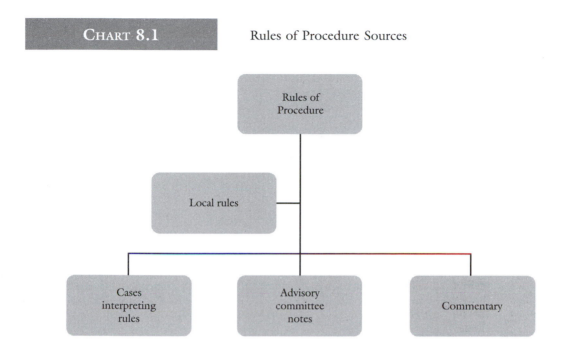

| CHART 8.1 | Rules of Procedure Sources |

OVERVIEW OF PROCEDURAL RESEARCH OPTIONS

It is critical to remember that thorough research into a procedural issue may involve not only rules and any pertinent advisory committee comments but also cases and commentary. The hierarchy of authority for these sources is as follows: the rules, cases (with jurisdiction and hierarchy setting their relative authoritativeness), advisory committee notes, and commentary. As noted previously, local rules supplement the main rules.

Resources for compiling these various sources abound, not surprisingly, with each resource offering varying amounts of information. The following discussion begins with resources that provide the rules and advisory committee notes and proceeds through resources that provide increasingly more information.

DESKBOOKS

Rules of procedure for a jurisdiction are published in their most compact form in deskbooks. A deskbook is an annual publication with rules currently in force; it may also contain advisory committee notes, history notes, and forms. The advantage of a deskbook is its compact size;[8] indeed, litigators generally keep their deskbooks at hand and take them to court. Finding a pertinent rule within a deskbook is aided by the classic means of access for well-organized sources: tables of contents and indexes.

In researching the issue of failure to sign an answer, we first looked up *signature* in the index to *Federal Civil Judicial Procedure and Rules*, a deskbook, which proved, surprisingly, not particularly helpful. Our next try, *pleading—signature*, led to Rule 11. We found Exhibit 8.1, which included the current rule and history notes from various versions.

COURT WEBSITES

American litigation is increasingly electronic; one helpful dimension of electronic litigation for researchers is the availability of procedural materials on court websites. Many, if not most, court websites provide not only the various main rules of procedure but also local rules for that court and forms to use for common procedures.

To learn more about the issue of the missing signature, we turned to the website of the U.S. District Court for the District of Kansas. There we found the Federal Rules of Civil Procedure. We also found pertinent local rules. One rule detailed the signature requirement for that court, which required additional information beyond Rule 11 and also covered electronic signatures. Even more interesting was the local rule implementing Rule 11, excerpted in Exhibit 8.2. That rule indicated that sanctions could be granted for violation of local rules—providing us an opportunity to seek sanctions for the failure to sign.[9]

We also found a variety of forms on the same website. Exhibit 8.3 is a form summons, the form used to give notice to a defendant that it was being sued.

COMMENTARY

Although the Restatements are not useful in researching procedural law, the other forms of commentary covered in Chapter 3—encyclopedias, treatises, periodicals, A.L.R. Annotations, and practice guides—are. Of these, the standard choice is a treatise. Strong treatises on procedural law include not only the discussion and references to other sources that are the hallmark of treatises but also the rules and supporting materials, such as the advisory committee comments.

---

8. Compactness is a relative concept. *Federal Civil Judicial Procedure and Rules* is 1,400 pages long.
9. The expansiveness of the local rule raised an interesting issue: if Rule 11 did not provide for sanctions for failure to sign, could a local rule do so?

EXHIBIT 8.2	Local Rule (U.S. District Court for the District of Kansas Website)

Local Rules

The following sections may contain rules and standing orders which are not yet reflected in the printed version.

View PDF version

I. Scope of Rules

II. Commencement of Actions; Process; Service & Filing of Pleadings, Motions and Orders

III. Pleadings and Motions

- **7.1 - MOTIONS IN CIVIL CASES**
- **7.2 - ORAL ARGUMENTS ON MOTIONS**
- **7.3 - MOTIONS TO RECONSIDER**
- **7.4 - FAILURE TO FILE AND SERVE MOTION PAPERS**
- **7.5 - APPLICATION OF THIS RULE**
- **7.6 - BRIEFS AND MEMORANDA**
- **9.1 - HABEAS CORPUS, MOTIONS TO VACATE AND CIVIL RIGHTS COMPLAINTS BY PRISONERS**
- **11.1 - SANCTIONS**

(a) Sanctions Under These Rules, Fed. R. Civ. P. 11, and Other Rules and Statutes.

(1) On Court's Own Initiative. The court, upon its own initiative, may issue an order to show cause why sanctions should not be imposed against a party and/or an attorney for violation of these rules, Fed. R. Civ. P. 11, 28 U.S.C. § 1927, or other provisions of the federal rules or statutes. The court will state the reasons for issuing the show cause order. Unless otherwise ordered, all parties may respond within 14 days after the filing of the order to show cause. The responses may include affidavits and documentary evidence as well as legal arguments.

(2) On a Party's Motion. A party may raise the issue of sanctions by a timely-filed motion. The responding party may respond in the same manner as specified above.

(3) Procedure. After the response time passes and without further proceedings, the court may rule on the issues of violation and the nature and extent of any sanction imposed. Discovery and evidentiary hearings on sanctions are permitted only by court order. The court will articulate the factual and legal bases for its rulings on sanctions.

(b) Imposition of Sanctions. If the court finds a violation of local rule or court order, the court may impose sanctions pursuant to Fed. R. Civ. P. 11 or other federal rules or statutes. In addition, the court may issue such orders as are just under the circumstances, including the following:

(1) an order that designated matters or facts are taken as established for purposes of the action;

(2) an order refusing to allow the failing party to support or oppose designated claims or defenses, or prohibiting it from offering specified witnesses or introducing designated matters in evidence;

(3) an order striking pleadings or parts thereof, or staying proceedings until the rule is complied with, or dismissing the action or any part thereof, or rendering a judgment by default against the failing party; and

(4) an order imposing costs, including attorney's fees, against the party, or its attorney, who has failed to comply with a local rule.

(c) Sanctions Within the Discretion of the Court. The court has discretion whether to impose sanctions for violation of a local rule or order. In considering sanctions, the court may consider whether a party's failure was substantially justified or whether other circumstances make sanctions inappropriate.

. . .

- **15.1 - MOTIONS TO AMEND AND FOR LEAVE TO FILE**
- **16.1 - PRETRIAL CONFERENCES, SCHEDULING, CASE MANAGEMENT**
- **16.2 - FINAL PRETRIAL CONFERENCE**
- **16.3 - ALTERNATIVE DISPUTE RESOLUTION**

IV. Parties

V. Depositions and Discovery

VI. Trials

VII. Judgment

VIII. Provisional and Final Remedies

COURTHOUSE INFORMATION
EDUCATION & OUTREACH
NATURALIZATION
NEWS
LOCAL RULES
MDL CASES
OUR JUDGES
CJA
CAMERAS IN COURTS

| EXHIBIT **8.3** | Form (U.S. District Court for the District of Kansas Website) |

AO 440 (Rev. 12/09) Summons in a Civil Action

UNITED STATES DISTRICT COURT
for the

_____)
         Plaintiff)
         v.)   Civil Action No.
)
_____)
        Defendant)

SUMMONS IN A CIVIL ACTION

TO: *(Defendant's name and address)*

A lawsuit has been filed against you.

Within 21 days after service of this summons on you (not counting the day you received it) — or 60 days if you are the United States or a United States agency, or an officer or employee of the United States described in Fed. R. Civ. P. 12 (a)(2) or (3) — you must serve on the plaintiff an answer to the attached complaint or a motion under Rule 12 of the Federal Rules of Civil Procedure. The answer or motion must be served on the plaintiff or plaintiff's attorney, whose name and address are:

If you fail to respond, judgment by default will be entered against you for the relief demanded in the complaint. You also must file your answer or motion with the court.

CLERK OF COURT

Date: _____   _____
                                     Signature of Clerk or Deputy Clerk

EXHIBIT **8.3**   *(continued)*

AO 440 (Rev. 12/09) Summons in a Civil Action (Page 2)

Civil Action No.

PROOF OF SERVICE
(This section should not be filed with the court unless required by Fed. R. Civ. P. 4 (l))

This summons for *(name of individual and title, if any)* _____

was received by me on *(date)* _____ .

☐ I personally served the summons on the individual at *(place)* _____

_____ on *(date)* _____ ; or

☐ I left the summons at the individual's residence or usual place of abode with *(name)* _____

_____ , a person of suitable age and discretion who resides there,

on *(date)* _____ , and mailed a copy to the individual's last known address; or

☐ I served the summons on *(name of individual)* _____ , who is

designated by law to accept service of process on behalf of *(name of organization)* _____

_____ on *(date)* _____ ; or

☐ I returned the summons unexecuted because _____ ; or

☐ Other *(specify):*

My fees are $ _____ for travel and $ _____ for services, for a total of $ 0.00   .

I declare under penalty of perjury that this information is true.

Date: _____

_____
Server's signature

_____
Printed name and title

_____
Server's address

Additional information regarding attempted service, etc:

On the federal side, many lawyers use either *Federal Practice and Procedure* by Charles Alan Wright, Arthur R. Miller, and others—hence its short name, Wright and Miller—or *Moore's Federal Practice*. Both are multivolume treatises covering civil, criminal, and appellate practice; Wright and Miller also covers evidence. These treatises, Wright and Miller more so perhaps than Moore's, are so well-regarded that they are highly citable, especially as to a routine point or a specific point as to which there is no mandatory case law. Westlaw carries Wright and Miller; LexisNexis carries Moore's.

Researching the issue of the missing signature, we turned to Wright and Miller. As explained in the excerpt in Exhibit 8.4, absent prejudice, a missing signature should be treated as a mere technical defect that can be corrected; the unsigned pleading may be stricken if appropriate.

ANNOTATED RULES

From a functional standpoint, rules of procedure operate much like statutes: they resemble codes, courts interpret and apply them, and commentators write about them. Thus, just as annotated codes are a major resource for statutory research, annotated rules can be very useful in procedural research. The advantages of annotated rules are the availability of the language of the rules, possibly also the advisory committee or history notes, synopses of cases presented within a logical framework, and references to various commentary sources. Research in annotated rules generally is most helpful after the pertinent rule has been identified and is done to find pertinent cases.

As discussed in detail in Chapter 5 as to statutory research, research in print can work well. Print annotated rules generally appear beside or within a jurisdiction's annotated statutes. Access tools include tables of contents and indexes. In print, a critical step is updating the main volume through supplementary publications, such as pocket parts.

Researching in online annotated rules databases also can work well. The advantages of researching online include additional search methods, such as key-word searches; seamless updating; and links to sources referred to in the annotation. One sound strategy for a key-word search is to include the number of the pertinent rule. As with statutes, KeyCite and Shepard's are available for rules of procedure; the rule is the cited source, and the citing sources include cases and commentary.

EXHIBIT 8.4	Treatise Discussion (Wright and Miller's *Federal Practice and Procedure*)

§ **1333**   SIGNING OF PLEADINGS   Ch. 4
Rule 11

pro se litigant's pleadings a more liberal construction than those drafted by an attorney. Moreover, the failure to sign a pleading shields an attorney from responsibility and accountability for his actions. Consequently, we have determined the failure of an attorney to acknowledge the giving of advice by signing his name constitutes a misrepresentation to this court by both the litigant and attorney. For these reasons, we have held "any ghostwriting of an otherwise *pro se* brief must be acknowledged by the signature of the attorney involved."[34]

Furthermore, the practice of "ghostwriting" has been "condemned as a deliberate evasion of the responsibilities imposed on counsel by" Rule 11 by another federal court because the attorney responsible for drafting the paper has not certified the document's legal and factual merit by including his or her signature.[35]

The 1993 amendment to Rule 11 requires that "[a]n unsigned paper shall be stricken unless omission of the signature is corrected promptly after being called to the attention of the attorney or party." Accordingly, the Advisory Committee Note to the 1993 amendments to the rule explains that "[u]nsigned papers are to be received by the Clerk, but then are to be stricken if the omission of the signature is not corrected promptly after being called to the attention of the attorney or the pro se litigant."[36] This language is virtually the same as it was under the 1983 amendment to Rule 11.[37] Thus, in the absence of prejudice, the district court can treat the defect as technical and should grant leave to correct a failure to

34. Tenth Circuit explained

Id. at 778 (Brorby, J.), quoting Duran v. Carris, C.A.10th, 2001, 238 F.3d 1268.

35. Deliberate evasion

Johnson v. Board of County Comm'rs for County of Fremont, D.C.Colo.1994, 868 F.Supp. 1226, 1231–1232 ("What we fear is that in some cases actual members of the bar represent petitioners, informally or otherwise, and prepare briefs for them which the assisting lawyers do not sign, and thus escape the obligation imposed on members of the bar, typified by F.R.Civ.P. 11, but which exists in all cases, criminal as well as civil, of representing to the court that there is good ground to support the assertions made. We cannot approve of such a practice. If a brief is prepared in any substantial part by a member of the

bar, it must be signed by him.") (Kane, J.).

See also

Wesley v. Don Stein Buick, Inc., D.C.Kan.1997, 987 F.Supp. 884.

36. Advisory Committee

Advisory Committee Note to the 1993 amendment to Rule 11, reprinted in 1993, 146 F.R.D. 577, 584, and in vol. 12A, App. C.

37. 1983 amendment

The 1983 amendment to Rule 11 stated that "[i]f a pleading, motion, or other paper is not signed, it shall be stricken unless it is signed promptly after the omission is called to the attention of the pleader or movant."

EXHIBIT 8.4   *(continued)*

Ch. 4   **SIGNATURE BY ATTORNEY OR PARTY**   **§ 1333**
                                                        Rule 11

sign;[38] if that is not done, an unsigned complaint may be dismissed or an unsigned paper stricken, as the district court deems appropriate. Although the rule requires that only the original of any paper submitted to the court must be signed,[39] as a matter of courtesy all copies should identify the person who signed the original document.

For a number of years, prior to the 1993 amendment of Rule 11, federal courts were divided on the question of who became sanctionable under Rule 11 when an attorney working for a law firm signed a pleading, motion, or other paper submitted to the district court. Some judges expressed an understanding that when a team of attorneys is conducting the litigation, the person who sign the paper may not necessarily be the one responsible for either the decision to file it or its preparation; for example, an associate or junior partner in a law firm may prepare, sign, and file a paper at the direction of a senior partner who made the relevant substantive decisions regarding the paper.[40] The rule's emphasis on the respon-

38. Defect technical

Becker v. Montgomery, 2001, 121 S.Ct. 1801, 532 U.S. 757, 149 L.Ed.2d 983.

Kovilic Constr. Co. v. Missbrenner, C.A.7th, 1997, 106 F.3d 768, 772, appeal after remand D.C.Ill.1997, 1997 WL 269630 (district court should not strike paper for failure to sign absent severe prejudice).

U.S. v. Kasuboski, C.A.7th, 1987, 834 F.2d 1345, **citing Wright & Miller.**

Operating Engineers Local 139 Health Benefit Fund v. Rawson Plumbing, Inc., D.C.Wis.2001, 130 F.Supp.2d 1022.

Stroud v. Senese, D.C.Ill.1993, 832 F.Supp. 1206.

Williams v. Frame, D.C.Pa.1992, 145 F.R.D. 65.

Duke v. Crowell, D.C.Tenn.1988, 120 F.R.D. 511.

See also

A legal malpractice complaint signed by the malpractice lawyer's wife was similar to one filed inadvertently without any signature, and therefore it was not necessary to strike the complaint as being in violation of Rule 11 when counsel's omission was a simple mistake, and a technically correct plead-

ing was filed shortly thereafter. Edwards v. Groner, D.C.Virgin Islands 1987, 116 F.R.D. 578.

Grant v. Morgan Guar. Trust Co. of New York, D.C.N.Y.1986, 638 F.Supp. 1528, 1531–1532 n. 6, **citing Wright & Miller** (irregularities treated as technical defects).

39. Original

Porto Transp., Inc. v. Consolidated Diesel Elec. Corp., D.C.N.Y.1956, 20 F.R.D. 1.

Pallant v. Sinatra, D.C.N.Y.1945, 7 F.R.D. 293.

Anderson v. Brady, D.C.Ky.1945, 5 F.R.D. 85.

40. Signing for another

Judge Schwarzer has remarked that "in such a situation, sanctions are more appropriately imposed on the principal rather than the agent carrying out his orders, and nothing in the rule bars its application in that manner." Schwarzer, Sanctions Under the New Rule 11—A Closer Look, 1985, 104 F.R.D. 181, 185.

521

Case Law

The resources just described generally suffice to identify pertinent cases. Various other approaches to cases research, as discussed in Chapter 4, can also be used. For example, procedural topics are covered in great detail by various West key numbers; thus digests are very useful. As another example, searching for cases in any online database can be fruitful. However, writing an effective search can be difficult because procedural terms are so common. One option is to include the number of the pertinent rule; another is to include an important substantive law or factual concept.[10] As with any cases research, citing a case through KeyCite or Shepard's is a critical step.

Cases involving issues of procedural law appear in reporters, commercial databases, and court websites. On the federal side, West publishes a reporter containing cases that are primarily of procedural significance, *Federal Rules Decisions*, which are covered in the *Federal Practice Digest*.

Researching the issue of the missing signature, we read the case of *Biocore Medical Technologies, Inc. v. Khosrowshahi*, a 1998 decision from the District of Kansas published in *Federal Rules Decisions*.[11] In that case, one litigant raised a series of concerns about the behavior of opposing counsel and sought to disqualify him. The lawyer whose conduct was at issue was from another state appearing by permission and with the assistance of local counsel. The out-of-state lawyer failed to obtain the signature of the Kansas lawyer on critical documents. As with the other sources described thus far in this chapter, the court ruled that, while the conduct violated the court's local rule regarding signatures, the defect was curable, was in fact nearly corrected, and had not prejudiced the other side.[12]

This decision confirmed the conclusion we were coming to already: the better course was not to make a federal case out of the failure to sign the answer. Litigation is adversarial enough when the focus is kept on the issues between the parties; conflict between the lawyers should be kept to a minimum. Thus the appropriate response was to contact opposing counsel to alert him of the mistake and suggest submission of a properly signed duplicate. This courtesy might be reciprocated when we needed it later in the litigation, and our reputation for being reasonable was important as well.

---

10. For some procedural issues, the facts and substantive law of the case matter little; the issue in this chapter is a good example. For other procedural issues, it is best to use cases involving similar facts and substantive law. A good example is a motion for summary judgment in an employment discrimination case.

11. 181 F.R.D. 660 (D. Kan. 1998).

12. However, continuing misconduct by the out-of-state lawyer led to his disqualification not long thereafter. *Biocore Med. Technologies, Inc. v. Khosrowshahi*, No. Civ. A. 98-2031-KHV, 1998 WL 919126 (D. Kans. Nov. 6, 1998).

Citation to Rules of Procedure and Related Sources

Rules of Procedure are cited as follows under both *Bluebook* rules B5.1.3, 3.4, and 12.9.3 and *ALWD* rule 17.1:
Fed. R. Civ. P. 11.

Advisory committee notes are cited as follows:

BLUEBOOK: Fed. R. Civ. P 11 advisory committee's note.
ALWD: Fed. R. Civ. P 11 advisory comm nn.

If more than one set of notes exist, adding a date would be helpful.

SUMMARY OF RESEARCH IN RULES OF PROCEDURE

The resources described previously provide various pieces of the procedural law pie; each also has, of course, certain advantages and disadvantages, as noted in Chart 8.2.

CHART 8.2	Optimal Options for Procedural Law Research

Resource	Information Provided	Advantages and Disadvantages
Deskbook	Rules, perhaps advisory committee or history notes, perhaps forms	Ease of use, but limited information
Court website	Varies; typically rules, including local rules, and forms	Range of rules and authoritative source, but limited information
Commentary	Discussion of rules and important cases, references, perhaps rules and notes	Legal framework with synthesis of sources, highly persuasive (in some cases) but not authoritative, leads to cases
Annotated Rules	Rules themselves, perhaps advisory committee or history notes, references to cases and commentary	References to many cases on specific points, less analytical and cohesive presentation than commentary
Case Law Resources	Interpretation of rules and application of rules to specific situations	Combine with rules to constitute procedural law

RULES OF PROFESSIONAL RESPONSIBILITY

Understanding professional responsibility rules. The well-being of our legal system—and by extension our government, society, and economy—depends in no small part on the conduct of lawyers. Lawyers not only represent clients; they also are "officer[s] of the legal system and . . . public citizen[s] with a special responsibility for the quality of justice," according to the preamble to the American Bar Association's Model Rules of Professional Conduct.

Rules of professional responsibility guide lawyers in carrying out these difficult roles ethically and professionally. They focus on the various relationships lawyers have, as shown in the titles of the main parts of the ABA Model Rules: client-lawyer relationship, counselor, advocate, transactions with persons other than clients, law firms and associations, public service, information about legal services, and maintaining the integrity of the profession.

Rules of professional responsibility typically are promulgated by a state's supreme court or bar association. Many state rules are based on the work of the ABA, which has created several sets of rules: the 1908 Canons of Professional Ethics, the 1969 Model Code of Professional Responsibility, and the 1983 Model Rules of Professional Conduct. The Model Rules are revised periodically, including a major revision in 2002, known as Ethics 2000.

In structure, professional responsibility rules based on the ABA Model Rules closely resemble the other rules discussed in this chapter. The rules are a set of interlocking rules. Each rule typically is followed by commentary, whether from the ABA or the state drafting committee or both, which operates as a form of "quasi-authority." See Exhibit 8.5, a Kansas rule pertinent to the second issue in this chapter.

Professional responsibility rules differ from rules of procedure in their enforcement mechanism. A typical model is that a disciplinary committee or board investigates a complaint of unprofessional conduct, holds a hearing, and issues a recommendation as to discipline; the state supreme court reviews these cases. In some areas, a local bar association may have an ethics committee serving some of these functions. Professional sanctions range from private or public censure to disbarment. Furthermore, violation of a rule may prompt a court to take protective measures if the violation occurs in the context of a case in litigation.[13]

Given the genesis and enforcement of rules of professional responsibility, an additional source exists in this area. Various ABA, state, and local bar associations as well as disciplinary committees consider issues arising under their rules upon the request of attorneys and issue advisory opinions as to how to proceed. These opinions are not authority, but they are more authoritative than commentary and thus fall in the category of "quasi-authority."

---

13. Furthermore, misconduct that entails incompetent representation may be the basis of a legal malpractice claim, and egregious misconduct may be the basis of a criminal prosecution.

Finally, as with rules of procedure, rules of professional responsibility are discussed at length in commentary. One notable source is the Restatement (Third) of the Law Governing Lawyers, promulgated in 2000, which is based not only on rules of professional responsibility but also on case law, including legal malpractice cases. As to some topics, the Restatement position diverges from the pre-2000 Model Rules.

Researching rules of professional responsibility. In many ways the approach to researching and working with professional responsibility rules parallels that discussed in this chapter for procedural rules. For example, many deskbooks contain the jurisdiction's professional responsibility rules, they are covered in annotated statutes, and case law research is integral.

To locate state or local ethics opinions, contact the appropriate organization or check its website. Opinions of the ABA Standing Committee on Ethics and Professional Responsibility are available through its website. Other strong options are the *ABA/BNA Lawyers' Manual on Professional Conduct* (a print source) and the LexisNexis and Westlaw legal ethics databases.

Researching the issue of Nichols' contact with his coworker, we turned to the Kansas Supreme Court website. We first found Rule 4.2 of the Kansas Rules of Professional Conduct, limiting a lawyer's ability to contact a person represented by another lawyer as to the subject of the representation. See Exhibit 8.5. We also learned that lawyers are not permitted to accomplish through others what they are not themselves permitted to do.[14]

However, comment 4 to the Kansas rule provided that communication regarding matters outside the representation was permitted, the parties could communicate directly with each other, and the lawyer could so advise the client. We also read ABA Formal Opinion 11-461, found on the ABA website, which permitted contact between parties, including discussion of the matter of the representation so long as the lawyer did not engage in overreaching. See Exhibit 8.6. Nonetheless, some boundaries existed. Through Westlaw we found a case in which a federal judge in Kansas issued a protective order against a lawyer's asking his client to seek affidavits from former coworkers.[15] All things considered, we determined that social contact was permissible—and the client should be encouraged to take care not to discuss the case.

---

14. Kan. Rule Prof'l Conduct 8.4.
15. *Holdren v. General Motors Corp.*, 13 F. Supp. 2d 1192 (D. Kan. 1998).

EXHIBIT 8.5	State Rule of Professional Responsibility with Comment

Kansas Courts

CONTACT INFORMATION

Clerk of the Appellate Courts
Kansas Judicial Center
301 SW 10th Avenue, Room 374
Topeka Kansas 66612-1507
Telephone: 785.296.3229
Fax: 785.296.1028
Email: appellateclerk@kscourts.org

Rules Adopted by the Supreme Court

Rules Relating to Discipline of Attorneys

Rule 226
Kansas Rules of Professional Conduct

4.2 Transactions with Persons other than Clients: Communication with Person Represented by Counsel

In representing a client, a lawyer shall not communicate about the subject of the representation with a person the lawyer knows to be represented by another lawyer in the matter, unless the lawyer has the consent of the other lawyer or is authorized to do so by law or a court order.

Comment

[1] This Rule contributes to the proper functioning of the legal system by protecting a person who has chosen to be represented by a lawyer in a matter against possible overreaching by other lawyers who are participating in the matter, interference by those lawyers with the client-lawyer relationship and the uncounselled disclosure of information relating to the representation.

[2] This Rule applies to communications with any person who is represented by counsel concerning the matter to which the communication relates.

[3] The Rule applies even though the represented person initiates or consents to the communication. A lawyer must immediately terminate communication with a person if, after commencing communication, the lawyer learns that the person is one with whom communication is not permitted by this Rule.

[4] This Rule does not prohibit communication with a party, or an employee or agent of a party, concerning matters outside the representation. For example, the existence of a controversy between a government agency and a private party, or between two organizations, does not prohibit a lawyer for either from communicating with nonlawyer representatives of the other regarding a separate matter. Nor does this Rule preclude communication with a represented person who is seeking advice from a lawyer who is not otherwise representing a client in the matter. A lawyer may not make a communication prohibited by this Rule through the acts of another. See Rule 8.4 (a). Parties to a matter may communicate directly with each other, and a lawyer is not prohibited from advising a client concerning a communication that the client is legally entitled to make. Also, a lawyer having independent justification for communicating with the other party is permitted to do so. Communications authorized by law include, for example, the right of a party to a controversy with a government agency to speak with government officials about the matter.

[5] Communications authorized by law may include communications by a lawyer on behalf of a client who is exercising a constitutional or other legal right to communicate with the government. Communications authorized by law may also include investigative activities of lawyers representing governmental entities, directly or through investigative agents, prior to the commencement of criminal or civil enforcement proceedings. When communicating with the accused in a criminal matter, a government lawyer must comply with this Rule in addition to honoring the constitutional rights of the accused. The fact that a communication does not violate a state or federal constitutional right is insufficient to establish that the communication is permissible under this Rule.

[6] A lawyer who is uncertain whether a communication with a represented person is permissible may seek a court order. A lawyer may also seek a court order in exceptional circumstances to authorize a communication that would otherwise be prohibited by this Rule, for example, where communication with a person represented by counsel is necessary to avoid reasonably certain injury.

[7] In the case of a represented organization, this Rule prohibits communications with a constituent of the organization who supervises, directs or regularly consults with the organization's lawyer concerning the matter or has authority to obligate the organization with respect to the matter or whose act or omission in connection with the

EXHIBIT 8.6   ABA Formal Ethics Opinion

AMERICAN BAR ASSOCIATION
STANDING COMMITTEE ON ETHICS AND PROFESSIONAL RESPONSIBILITY

Formal Opinion 11-461   **August 4, 2011**
Advising Clients Regarding Direct Contacts with Represented Persons

Parties to a legal matter have the right to communicate directly with each other. A lawyer may advise a client of that right and may assist the client regarding the substance of any proposed communication. The lawyer's assistance need not be prompted by a request from the client. Such assistance may not, however, result in overreaching by the lawyer.[1]

A lawyer may not communicate with a person the lawyer knows is represented by counsel, unless that person's counsel has consented to the communication or the communication is authorized by law or court order. ABA Model Rule 4.2 (sometimes called the "no contact" rule). Further, a lawyer may not use an intermediary, i.e., an agent or another, to communicate directly with a represented person in violation of the "no contact" rule.[2]

It sometimes is desirable for parties to a litigation or transactional matter to communicate directly with each other even though they are represented by counsel. Two examples may be where the parties wish to cement a settlement or break an impasse in settlement negotiations. In this opinion, the Committee explores the limits within which it is ethically proper under the Model Rules of Professional Conduct for a lawyer to assist a client regarding communications the client has a right to have with a person the lawyer knows is represented by counsel. Even though parties to a matter are represented by counsel, they have the right to communicate directly with each other.[3]   In addition, a client may require the lawyer's assistance and a lawyer may be reasonably expected to advise or assist the client regarding communications the client desires to have with a represented person. A client may ask the lawyer for advice on whether the client may lawfully communicate directly with a represented person without their lawyer's consent or their lawyer being present. The comments to Rules 4.2 and 8.4(a) state that such advice is proper.[4]   Even if the client has not asked for the advice, the lawyer may take the initiative and advise the client that it may be desirable at a particular time for the client to communicate directly with the other party.

For example, a lawyer represents a client in a marital dissolution. The client's husband also is represented by counsel. The parties and their lawyers have reached an impasse in their negotiations over various issues. The client may ask her lawyer if she may communicate directly with her husband to see if an agreement can be reached on some contested issues. Alternatively, the lawyer might independently

---

[1] This opinion is based on the ABA Model Rules of Professional Conduct as amended by the ABA House of Delegates through August 2011. The laws, court rules, regulations, rules of professional conduct, and opinions promulgated in individual jurisdictions are controlling.

[2] Rule 8.4(a). The Rule states: "[i]t is professional misconduct for a lawyer to violate or attempt to violate the Rules of Professional Conduct, knowingly assist or induce another to do so, or do so through the acts of another." ABA Comm. on Ethics and Professional Responsibility, Formal Op. 95-395 (1995) ("Since a lawyer is barred under Rule 4.2 from communicating with a represented party about the subject of the representation, she [under Rule 8.4(a)] may not circumvent the Rule by sending an investigator to do on her behalf that which she is herself forbidden to do."); ANNOTATED MODEL RULES OF PROFESSIONAL CONDUCT 408 (ABA 7th ed. 2011) ("A lawyer may not, however, "mastermind" a client's communication with a represented person.").

[3] *See* Holdren v. General Motors Corp., 13 F.Supp.2d 1192, 1195 (D. Kan. 1998) ("there is nothing in the disciplinary rules which restrict a client's right to act independently in initiating communications with the other side, or which requires that lawyers prevent or attempt to discourage such conduct." (citing New York City Bar Association Formal Opinion No.1991-2, at 5-6)); Dorsey v. Home Depot U.S.A., Inc., 271 F.Supp.2d 726, 730 (D.Md.2003) ("Nothing in the law prohibits litigants or potential litigants from speaking among and between themselves, as opposed to attorneys for such parties attempting direct communications with represented parties."); Northwest Bypass v. U.S. Army Corps of Engineers, 488 F.Supp.2d 22, 28-29 (D.N.H. 2007) (not improper for represented party to communicate directly with represented opponent).

[4] *See* Rule 4.2 cmt. 4 ("A lawyer may not make a communication prohibited by this Rule through the acts of another. *See also* Rule 8.4(a) cmt. 1 ("Lawyers are subject to discipline when they violate or attempt to violate the Rules of Professional Conduct, knowingly assist or induce another to do so or do so through the acts of another, as when they request or instruct an agent to do so on the lawyer's behalf. Paragraph (a), however, does not prohibit a lawyer from advising a client concerning action the client is legally entitled to take.").

TEST YOUR UNDERSTANDING

Reflection Questions

1. Review the language of the rest of Rule 11. What does its existence say about the conduct of lawyers? How can you avoid exceeding the boundaries it sets through your research practices?

2. Many rules governing the behavior of lawyers are fairly straightforward. Why should a lawyer ever be excused from failing to follow one of these rules, as seems to be the case in the signature rule?

Your Scenario

Assume that, according to your research and analysis of the substantive law governing the situation set out in Chapter 2, your client has a strong case for occupying her apartment with a companion animal given her PTSD. However, the landlord has refused to budge. So you are considering beginning a lawsuit in federal court in West Virginia's Southern District.

Research the rules of procedure to learn how to start a lawsuit in that court, under the Federal Rules of Civil Procedure and the local rules.

- What documents are required? What does each state, in general terms? To whom must you convey these documents?
- As to the complaint, how complete must it be to survive a motion to dismiss for failure to state a claim? Include case law in your research.

INTERNATIONAL LAW AND TRIBAL LAW

Contents

- Legal Research in Public International Law
  - A. Foreign Law
  - B. Public International Law
  - C. Private International Law
- Legal Research in Tribal Law
  - A. Federal Indian Law
  - B. Tribal Law

The law that governs activities in the United States is, in some situations, broader than that covered in the preceding chapters. In certain situations, international law governs. In others, the law of Indian tribes—separate sovereignties located in various areas around the United States—comes into play.

Legal Research in Public International Law
by Prof. Anthony S. Winer

The first thing to realize is that there is a distinction between foreign law, public international law, and private international law. This part focuses on researching in the second of these areas, public international law. Nonetheless, the chapter opens with a discussion of foreign law and closes with private international law.

A. FOREIGN LAW

The phrase "foreign law" refers to any domestic law or legal system other than that of the person using the phrase. So, to a legal researcher located in the U.S. who is practicing law in the U.S., the domestic law of France, China, or Peru (or any other non-U.S. country) would be foreign law. However, to a legal researcher in France, China, or Peru, the domestic law of the U.S. would be foreign law.

Often lawyers in the U.S. are confronted with a situation involving the domestic law of a country other than the U.S. When that happens, the U.S. lawyer is presented with an issue of foreign law, not of international law. In those circumstances, there are several websites and other authorities that provide a basic overview of the legal systems of various countries around the world. Among these are:

- The Yale Law School Country-by-Country Guide to Foreign Law Research,
- The Harvard Law School Library Research Guide Web Resources for Foreign Law,
- The World Law Guide,
- The World Legal Information Institute, and
- The Law Library of the U.S. Congress.

Lawyers in the U.S. can, if they wish, consult these websites and other similar authorities to get basic background regarding the law or legal systems in a foreign country with which their clients may be involved. However, utmost caution is warranted. Most lawyers practicing law in the U.S. are not educated, trained, or licensed regarding the domestic legal systems of other countries. Unless a lawyer is also educated, trained, and licensed under the domestic law of a foreign country, that lawyer should generally not give advice to U.S. clients regarding any foreign country's law, if that advice purports to be thorough, comprehensive, and of the type that the client can rely on.[1] If the client of a U.S. lawyer needs reliable advice on the domestic law of a foreign country, the usual approach is for the U.S. lawyer to obtain for the client competent co-counsel in that country. This, of course, usually involves added time and expense for the client and can only be undertaken with the client's informed consent.

B.   PUBLIC INTERNATIONAL LAW

The phrase "public international law" generally refers to the legal rules affecting the relations of different countries, in this context called "states," while acting vis-à-vis one another. So, legal rules involving the creation and enforcement of international treaties, the external use of armed force by states, the so-called "law of war," and other similar subjects are all aspects of public international law. Unlike foreign law, public international law does not necessarily concern the domestic law of any particular state. It is instead a legal system that generally operates largely externally to the domestic legal systems of states.

Unlike the situation with foreign law, there is no formal restriction against a U.S. lawyer, educated, trained, and licensed only under the law of a U.S. jurisdiction from providing advice on public international law.

---

1. *See, e.g.,* American Bar Association Model Rule of Professional Conduct 5.5 (stating, *inter alia*, that a lawyer "shall not practice law in a jurisdiction in violation of the regulation of the legal profession in that jurisdiction, or assist another in doing so"). The textual provisions of Rule 5.5 do not explicitly address the case of a U.S. lawyer in the U.S. practicing the law of a foreign state in violation of the law of that foreign state, but it is clear that such behavior can raise serious ethical issues.

The sources of public international law are listed in a United Nations (UN) document, the Statute of the International Court of Justice. The International Court of Justice (also called the "ICJ" or the "World Court") is the chief judicial body of the UN. It sits in The Hague, a city that is the seat of government of The Netherlands. The ICJ's Statute is the document through which the ICJ was established, along with the UN itself, in 1945. Article 38(1) of the ICJ Statute establishes five types of sources for public international law.[2] These are:

(1)   International treaties and conventions,
(2)   Customary international law,
(3)   General principles of law,
(4)   Judicial decisions in courts and tribunals, and
(5)   Scholastic works of prominent commentators on public international law.

The last two types of authority are stated to be a "subsidiary means" for determining rules of public international law. They are therefore not primary sources for rules of public international law, but rather secondary sources that serve as indirect indications. The extent to which there is a hierarchical relationship among the other three types of sources is itself a subject of interpretation and discussion.

1.   Treaties and Conventions

Treaties are international agreements among states, usually in written form, that the parties intend to be binding.[3] Many international agreements that states enter into have significance only for building mutual foreign relations and are not formal documents with binding effect. It is only when states enter into agreements that they intend to be internationally binding that a treaty is created.

Treaties can be viewed as falling into distinct categories. For example, bilateral treaties (treaties between only two states) can be distinguished from multilateral treaties (treaties among three or more states). Each state that has become party to a multilateral treaty is often called a "state party" to that treaty, while each party to a bilateral treaty is often called a "counter-party." A "convention" is usually a special kind of treaty, generally multilateral, that enunciates new rules of legal conduct for the parties to it. Conventions are thus sometimes called "law-making" treaties, as opposed to "treaty-

2. The language of Article 38(1) of the ICJ Statute varies somewhat from the five points stated here, but the presentation of the points here reflects a more conversational vocabulary and more pragmatic arrangement.

3. Vienna Convention on the Law of Treaties, May 23, 1969, 1155 U.N.T.S. 331 (effective Jan. 27, 1980) [hereinafter "VCLT"], at Art. 2(1)(a). The VCLT "constitutes the basic framework for any discussion of the nature and characteristics of treaties." Malcolm N. Shaw, *International Law* 903 (6th ed. 2008).

contracts," which would be treaties that only resolve certain more particular issues between their parties.[4]

The UN Charter requires that all treaties entered into by any UN members be registered with the UN secretary-general.[5] The secretary-general then publishes them in a hard-copy serial set called the *United Nations Treaty Series* (or "UNTS"). The UNTS also appears as an online electronic database, maintained by the UN, called the "United Nations Treaty Collection." The current URL for the UN Treaty Collection is: http://treaties.un.org/Home.aspx?lang=en. This online database allows for searching by title, party names, full-text search, and certain other parameters. The UN Treaty Collection also contains an online database for the now-discontinued League of Nations Treaty Series (or "LNTS"). The online LNTS is also searchable by a variety of parameters.

For access to treaties dating from before 1945, one often refers to treaty collections maintained by individual states. Over the generations, the United States has done a reasonably complete job of recording, cataloguing, and publishing the treaties to which it has become a party. The Treaty Affairs Office of the U.S. State Department's Legal Advisor has general authority in this regard. Retrieving a treaty to which the U.S. is a party, and which is not retrievable through the UNTS or UN Treaty Collection, involves two steps.

The first step is using an index. The indexing tool most commonly used is *Treaties in Force*, published annually by the Treaty Affairs Office. It is now available both in hard copy at most comprehensive law libraries and online at the Treaty Affairs page of the State Department website. One list covers all bilateral treaties to which the U.S. is a party as of the relevant year, arranged alphabetically by counter-party. The second covers all multilateral treaties to which the U.S. is a party that year, arranged alphabetically according to subject matter. Because *Treaties in Force* serves only as an index, its entries for each treaty merely give bibliographic data. These include the dates of signature and effectiveness, the names of other parties (for multilateral treaties), and the dates of any amendments. Also, most of the index entries (but not all) provide a citation to a treaty source publication or a serial number.

Second, several publications contain treaty texts. From 1778 to 1949, treaties were published chronologically in *Statutes at Large*. So when an entry in *Treaties in Force* lists a "Stat." citation, the text for that treaty can be found in *Statutes at Large*. From 1950 to 1984, treaties were published in a multi-volume, hard-copy series called *U.S. Treaties and Other International Agreements* (or "UST"). This is available in hard copy at most comprehensive law libraries and electronically through HeinOnline.

Entries in *Treaties in Force* also often refer to a serial number, called a "TIAS" number; the acronym refers to "Treaties and Other International Acts Series." The TIAS serial number, assigned to all U.S. treaties chronologically since 1945, can be used to find treaty texts not available through *Statutes at Large* or UST. Under the TIAS system, virtually all treaties to which the U.S. becomes a party, before appearing in a UST volume, are

---

4. *Starke's International Law*, 37–41 (I.A. Shearer, ed., 11th ed. 1994).
5. UN Charter Article 102(1).

initially published in the form of a slip pamphlet. There is one slip pamphlet per treaty, and each slip pamphlet is given a chronologically consecutive TIAS serial number. The slip pamphlets are available in hard-copy form at many law libraries and are also available electronically through HeinOnline. The TIAS releases are currently updated through 2006. (A small number of releases from 2007 are becoming available at press time.) Many more recent treaty texts can be retrieved electronically by TIAS number at the Treaty Affairs page of the State Department website.

These official resources have been complemented by unofficial compilers of U.S. treaties during various time periods. Of these perhaps the most frequently cited is the Bevans Series, which was compiled by Charles I. Bevans for U.S. treaties from 1776 to 1949. Another private treaty compilation (1987 through 2011) is by Igor Kavass, who has also maintained a separate Kavass finding index.

The issues of *Treaties in Force* from recent years and the UST series also are searchable databases in Westlaw. LexisNexis offers a database with a wide variety of treaties, including UST.

When a treaty cannot easily be located in an official source or a major unofficial source, it may have been published in periodical form by the American Society of International Law in either of its two flagship publications. These are *International Legal Materials* and the *American Journal of International Law*. These can be retrieved and searched in the same manner one would retrieve and search any other legal periodical. These two periodicals can also be researched electronically through Westlaw and LexisNexis.

Also, treaties can sometimes be located in other unofficial sources (such as additional academic periodicals or the websites of related professional organizations) or other official sources (such as the websites of sovereign states that serve as depositaries for multilateral treaties).

| **CHART 9.1** | Major Treaty Resources |

Organization	Resources
United Nations	*United Nations Treaty Series* United Nations Treaty Collection *League of Nations Treaty Series*
United States Government	*Treaties in Force* (index)* *Statutes at Large* *U.S. Treaties and Other International Agreements** Treaty Affairs page of State Department website
Unofficial Sources	Bevans and Kavass Series *International Legal Materials** *American Journal of International Law**

*Available through HeinOnline, LexisNexis, or Westlaw.

2.   Customary International Law

Rules of customary international law develop over time through the real-world practice of states. There is no written or published source or catalog of all these rules. Rather, they are determined to exist on a case-by-case basis by courts, arbitration tribunals, academic treatise authors, and other authorities.

For a pattern of state behavior to develop into a rule of customary international law, two things must be true. First, the behavior pattern must be engaged in by a sufficient number of states as to be considered a general practice, and it must be sufficiently uniform and of sufficient duration over time to be considered a consistent practice.[6] This is sometimes referred to as the "material" requirement. Second, the states engaging in this behavior pattern must do so out of a conviction that the behavior is required under international law. This is sometimes referred to as the "psychological" requirement and is frequently described by the Latin phrase "*opinio juris.*"[7]

Using formal research methods, one would accumulate evidence of state practice to establish compliance with the material requirement. This evidence could come from news reports, historical works, legal treatises, government press releases and policy statements, and other similar materials.[8] Similarly, one would retrieve evidence of official opinion regarding the psychological requirement. This evidence could come from diplomatic correspondence, official government manuals, executive decisions, military orders, and other similar materials.[9] These kinds of materials used in formal research can be difficult to obtain and use, however.

As a practical matter, for most non-specialists, research into customary international law can begin with academic articles in law journals, legal treatises, and other academic publications (especially those specializing in international subjects). These authorities frequently simply declare and discuss their views as to the existence of various rules of customary international law. Depending on the extent of influence of each authority and the degree of unanimity among them, these declarations and discussions can for many purposes be a substantial indication of the rules' existence.

Determinations derived from academic sources can (and usually should) be fortified by research in other sources. Prominent among these would be treaties and conventions. If a particular treaty or convention has a very large number of states as parties to it, and there is general compliance with its terms over an appreciable period, it arguably satisfies the requirements for a rule of customary international law. To the extent the treaty or convention has these characteristics, the customary international law rules it embodies will apply to all states, whether or not they are parties to the treaty or convention. Sometimes advocates even assert that draft treaties, or treaties not yet in

---

6. *E.g.,* Ian Brownlie, *Principles of Public International Law,* 7–8 (7th ed. 2008).
7. *E.g.,* Rebecca M.M. Wallace & Olga Martin-Ortega, *International Law,* 16–18 (6th ed. 2009).
8. *E.g.,* Brownlie, *supra* note 6, at 6.
9. *E.g., id.*

force, state rules of customary international law, if they believe that states generally and consistently comply with their terms out of a sense of legal obligation.

The decisions of courts and arbitration tribunals also frequently declare the existence of rules of customary international law and discuss their application. This is especially true of courts and arbitration tribunals charged with international duties. (Examples are the ICJ and the arbitration tribunals established by the Permanent Court of Arbitration.)[10]

Additionally, resolutions passed by the UN General Assembly and other international deliberative bodies can be helpful in identifying rules of customary international law. Indeed, it is not unusual for the resolutions themselves to purportedly declare rules of customary international law. Such declarations can be useful in building the case for a rule of customary international law, but they are usually not dispositive absent other evidence of general and consistent practice engaged in out of a sense of legal obligation.

CHART 9.2	Components of Customary International Law

The "Material" Component: State Practice—

- The observed practice of states should demonstrate *general* and *consistent* state behavior.
  General state behavior is engaged in by a sufficient quantity of states around the world.
  Consistent state behavior is engaged in by states that is sufficiently uniform and of sufficient duration over time.
- Among the sources from which one could discern state practice would be:
  - news reports,
  - historical works,
  - legal treatises,
  - domestic state legislation,
  - international and national judicial decisions,
  - government press releases,
  - government policy statements,
  - treaties and conventions, and
  - UN General Assembly resolutions addressing legal issues.

---

10. The Permanent Court of Arbitration was established through the Hague Peace Conventions of 1899.

The "Psychological" Component: *Opinio Juris—*

- States must engage in the general and consistent state behavior out of a conviction that the behavior is required under international law.
- Among the sources from which one could discern *opinio juris* would be:
  - diplomatic correspondence;
  - official government manuals;
  - opinions of legal advisors to governments and international organizations;
  - executive decisions;
  - manuals of military law;
  - military orders;
  - international and national judicial decisions;
  - treaties and conventions, in draft and completed form; and
  - UN General Assembly resolutions addressing legal issues.

3.   Decisions by Courts and Arbitration Panels

Decisions by courts and arbitration panels are a tool for building arguments about customary international law. Furthermore, Article 38(1) of the ICJ Statute also refers to "judicial decisions" directly as a "subsidiary" means for the determination of rules of law.

The ICJ, also called the "World Court," located at The Hague, is perhaps the most authoritative international court currently operating in the world. However, it hears and decides only cases between sovereign states.[11] No private persons, individual or corporate, can be parties to contested actions before it. In fact, not even international organizations can be parties before the ICJ. The ICJ is authorized, however, to give advisory opinions at the request of the UN General Assembly and certain other bodies.[12]

The decisions of the ICJ, both for contentious cases and for advisory opinions, are published in a print, annual, multi-volume set called the *International Court of Justice Reports of Judgments, Advisory Opinions and Orders* (or "*ICJ Reports*"). These decisions are available online at the ICJ website: http://www.icj-cij.org/; the International Court of Justice database from Westlaw; and the International Court of Justice Decisions, Combined database from LexisNexis.

11. ICJ Statute Art. 34(1).
12. *Id.* Arts. 65–68.

Decisions by international arbitration panels are also available in both print resources and online databases. The Permanent Court of Arbitration (PCA) has been for generations the administrator of some of the most influential international arbitration proceedings. Since the establishment of the UN, the UN has published the PCA's most significant arbitration decisions (even including those issued before 1945) in a multi-volume print set called the *Report of International Arbitration Awards* (or "RIAA"). The disputes addressed in these arbitrations all involve at least one state, although sometimes private persons (individuals or corporate) have also been parties. States have therefore chosen arbitration under PCA auspices when jurisdiction would not exist in the ICJ or when for other reasons the parties have chosen arbitration over the established framework of the ICJ. The RIAA is available at many law libraries and online in conjunction with the UN website at http://www.un.org/law/riaa/.

Westlaw maintains a database for international commercial arbitrations, its International Commercial Arbitration Cases database. While some decisions there are from arbitrations between or among states, others are arbitrations among or with private parties, either corporations or individuals or both. While these private international arbitrations might involve issues of public international law, their decisions would not normally have the same influence on later arbitrations between states as would decisions for arbitrations among states.

LexisNexis maintains various databases in the area of international arbitration, the most prominent being International Arbitration: Mealey's Litigation Report. Some of the LexisNexis databases feature secondary sources addressing arbitration decisions over the texts of the arbitration decisions themselves.

There are also several important regional and special-purpose courts and tribunals. Some of the most significant with websites including the decisions issued by the relevant courts and tribunals, are:

- International Criminal Court
  http://www.icc-cpi.int
- International Criminal Tribunal for the Former Yugoslavia
  www.icty.org
- International Criminal Tribunal for Rwanda
  www.unictr.org
- European Court of Human Rights
  www.echr.coe.int
- Inter-American Court on Human Rights
  http://www.oas.org/en/iachr/default.asp
- African Court of Justice and Human Rights
  http://www.au.int/en/organs/cj

Westlaw also maintains databases for documents of the ICTFY and ICTR, the Iran-U.S. Claims Tribunal, and panels of the World Trade Organization.

4.   UN Materials

Certain official documents issued by some bodies of the UN can also have a significant effect on the development of public international law. This is especially true of resolutions passed by the General Assembly (the "UNGA") and the Security Council (the "UNSC").

Many UNSC resolutions are binding in accordance with their terms. Article 25 of the UN Charter requires UN members to "accept and carry out the decisions" of the UNSC.

UNGA resolutions can be influential in the development of customary international law, although they are not in themselves customary international law or indeed any kind of binding international law. Indeed, they do not come within any of the classifications set out in Article 38(1) of the ICJ Statute. However, UNGA resolutions often make statements about rules of customary international law. These can be especially useful when the statements asserting a particular point appear in a large number of UNGA resolutions, these resolutions are frequent enough to be consistent, and the resolutions are carried by large enough majorities to indicate very broad consensus. Then the resolutions are good evidence that the point of law asserted has attained the required *opinio juris* to become a rule of customary international law.[13]

Similarly, some authorities have also used UNGA resolutions, if they are sufficiently unanimous and consistent over time, to fulfill the material requirement for a rule of customary international law, as well. That is, the resolutions can be used to show a general and consistent state practice. This is more controversial, because resolutions may reflect simply what states say, rather than be real reflections of their actions.

For many purposes, the easiest way to retrieve and work with UN resolutions is to use the UN website. The UNGA and the UNSC maintain separate catalogs of resolutions, dating back to the founding of the UN. The resolutions can be easily retrieved, by resolution number and by date, at the UNGA and UNSC pages of the UN website.

If you are researching a subject but do not know the resolution number or date of a resolution, you can use several search features at the UN website. First, the UN Bibliographic Information System Network (or "UNBISNet") uses a sophisticated advanced search protocol to access all the titles indexed in the official library of the UN in New York (called the Dag Hammarskjøld Library) and the official UN library in Geneva. It therefore includes all UNGA and UNSC resolutions. If you know the title of a resolution, it can be easily retrieved in the "title" field of the advanced search, and full-text searching is also available. However, at the present time UNBISNet goes only back to 1979, and the search protocol is relatively unyielding for even minor imprecisions.[14]

---

13. UNGA resolutions can also serve as a basis for later adoption in the form of conventions, as occurred with the International Covenant on Civil and Political Rights and the International Covenant on Economic, Social and Cultural Rights.

14. UNBISNet also allows searching for voting records for UN resolutions (back to 1946) and maintains an index to speeches made before the principal bodies of the UN, generally from 1983.

The second major UN tool is the UN Official Document System (or "ODS"). The scope of its covered database is more narrow than for UNBIS-Net: it does not extend to all titles indexed in the UN libraries, but rather all types of official UN documents. In addition to resolutions, verbatim records of meetings (called by their French name, "procès-verbaux"), letters to and from the UN principal bodies that are admitted into their records, reports delivered to or issued by the UN principal bodies and/or their subsidiary bodies, and other official matters are included. In general, ODS goes back only to 1993, but its database of UN resolutions goes back to the establishment of the UN in 1945.

Some of the other documents retrievable through UNBISNet and ODS (such as procès-verbaux, letters, and reports) can also be used to build cases for both the material and psychological requirements for the existence of a rule of customary international law.

There is also a third major UN bibliographic tool, called UN Info Quest (or "UNIQue"). It is mostly useful for advanced researchers who are using the UN's complex system of document numbering as a basis for their searching. Readers interested in this feature are urged to consult a specialized resource work specifically devoted to UN Documentation.

5. Commentary and General Principles

Commentary, particularly treatises and articles in law journals, can be used to build arguments regarding customary international law. In addition, Article 38(1) of the ICJ Statute directly refers to "the teachings of the most highly qualified publicists of the various nations" as a "subsidiary means for the determination of rules of law."

The discovery, retrieval, and use of treatises and articles in law journals to research issues of public international law is not much different from the methods used to research issues of U.S. domestic law. Most of the significant journals focused on public international law issues are included within appropriate Westlaw and LexisNexis databases. The leading treatises on public international law are available in print at most comprehensive law libraries. Among the leading treatises on public international law in the English language are:

- Anthony Aust, *Handbook of International Law* (2d ed. 2010);
- J.L. Brierly, *The Law of Nations* (6th ed. 1963);
- Ian Brownlie, *Principles of Public International Law* (7th ed. 2008);
- Antonio Cassese, *International Law* (2d ed. 2005);
- Malcolm N. Shaw, *International Law* (6th ed. 2008);
- *Starke's International Law* (I.A. Shearer, ed., 11th ed. 1994); and
- Rebecca M.M. Wallace & Olga Martin-Ortega, *International Law* (6th ed. 2009).

The third category of sources for public international law, listed above, is "general principles of law." There are varying interpretations of this phrase, and it has been reasonably interpreted as covering a variety of principles of various types. One category is principles "intrinsic to the idea of law and basic to all legal systems."[15] Examples are the idea that no one can transfer more rights than (s)he possesses and the canon that the later of two rules supersedes the earlier, if both address the same subject and both have the same source. Basic concepts of equity, proportionality, and fairness could also be cited in this connection.

The language of the ICJ Statute on this point is somewhat vague and general. The availability of this potential source of public international law can be viewed by some advocates as an opportunity to mold arguments based on considerations most conducive to their cause. For most purposes, it is best to base the arguments in court or tribunal decisions or in the works of commentators.

C. PRIVATE INTERNATIONAL LAW

Private international law is distinct from public international law. There are basically two different conceptions of private international law. The first traditional conception views private international law as identical to international conflict of laws.[16] The phrase "conflict of laws" refers to the body of rules used to determine which state's law applies to a litigated fact pattern that has plausible connections to more than one state. When two or more private parties are involved in a contested matter that involves more than one national jurisdiction, an international conflict of laws problem can arise.

Classically, each state develops and maintains its own conflict of laws rules. The institutions of the European Union have promulgated certain conflict of laws rules for contractual disputes adjudicated within the EU.[17] However, in general there are no universally applicable treaties or conventions setting forth conflict of laws rules. General treatises exist in the area, and the case law of a common-law state will in many instances contain that state's conflict of laws regime. A detailed discussion of conflict of laws rules is beyond the scope of this chapter.

Under the more modern and expansive interpretation, the phrase "private international law" applies to all treaties and other legal rules that pertain to the activities of private persons acting across national boundaries. For example, to a much greater extent now than before, treaties and conventions as instruments of public international law apply to and restrict the actions of private persons. When a treaty or convention does so, it can be thought of as also being an instrument of private international law. An

---

15. Oscar Schachter, *International Law in Theory and Practice*, 53 (1991).
16. James R. Fox, *Dictionary of International and Comparative Law*, 66 & 264 (3d ed. 2003).
17. Regulation (EC) No. 593/2008 of 17 June 2008, 2008 O.J. (L 177) 6.

example would be the Convention on Contracts for the International Sale of Goods, which directly applies to many private buyers and sellers of goods in international trade.

Similarly, when individual states issue laws that affect the international operations of their citizens or residents, those domestic laws can also be viewed as rules of private international law. An example would be the immensely influential U.S. Foreign Corrupt Practices Act, which applies to U.S. persons engaging in corrupt activities with officials of foreign states.

Furthermore, international organizations such as the Hague Conference on Private International Law have a role in creating international agreements directly affecting private persons acting internationally. Finally, some private organizations, such as the International Chamber of Commerce (the "ICC") and the International Law Institute (known by the acronym for its French title, the "IDI"), also promulgate or help develop rules that can be applied to private persons acting internationally.

The methods used when researching these instruments of private international law depend on the source involved. Treaties and conventions involving private international law are researched in much the same manner as any other treaty and convention, as discussed previously. Domestic statutes in any state setting forth rules of private international law are researched in whatever manner is normal for statutory research in that state. And materials issued by the Hague Conference, the ICC, and the IDI are researched as one would research the activities of any other modern association or organization, especially including their online databases.

Legal Research in Tribal Law
by Prof. Sarah Deer[18]

Another complex dimension of American legal research is how to research laws for the various tribes existing in the United States. Over 560 indigenous tribal nations are recognized by the United States federal government. These tribal nations have existed on the North American continent for thousands of years and therefore pre-date the United States government. Tribal governments retain limited forms of legal independence under the United States legal system; each tribal nation retains its own capacity as a self-governing entity.

Tribal nations have a wide range of qualities. In terms of population, the smallest tribe has less than fifty citizens. The largest tribes have over 200,000 citizens. There are dozens of distinct cultural groups, languages, and legal traditions represented among the many tribes. Some tribal governments still operate under ancient traditional governance structures. Other tribal governments have a contemporary structure identical to most state governments. Most tribal governments, however, are hybrid systems that include components from both tribal and Western (European) legal traditions. Each tribal nation has an independent government, and most operate a tribal court.

18. For more detail, consult Sarah Deer & J. B. Richland, *Introduction to Tribal Legal Studies* (AltaMira Press 2010).

Many Americans (including lawyers) are not familiar with tribal governments or tribal courts. This is likely because indigenous people make up a very small portion of the overall population. However, tribal courts have become more prominent in recent years and are growing in strength and visibility. For this reason, a comprehensive approach to legal research in the United States should include basic information on tribal law.

There are two major categories of Indian law: federal Indian Law (the law governing the relationship between tribal governments and the U.S. government) and tribal law (the internal laws of individual tribal governments).

A.   FEDERAL INDIAN LAW

Federal Indian law has an extraordinarily complicated set of statutes and case law that govern the extent of tribal legal authority. This brief introduction cannot cover all of the complex rules. An example of an issue of federal Indian law is this increasingly common situation: A tribal government is planning to form a contract with a privately owned business to develop a new business on tribal land. Because the title to the tribal land is legally held in trust by the federal government, the privately owned business needs to negotiate a contract that will be approved by the federal government.

Federal Indian law is reasonably accessible to the legal researcher but complex due to the many different agencies that may be involved with Indian issues. The United States Code has a specific title governing federal Indian law, Title 25, but Indian law issues arise in a variety of other contexts. There are also specific regulatory agencies that govern much of the administrative law pertaining to tribal governments. For example, the Department of Interior includes the Bureau of Indian Affairs, a sub-agency of which administers much of the relationship between the United States and tribal governments. All of these federal agencies have publically accessible websites including all of the applicable statutes and regulations.

The U.S. Supreme Court is the final arbiter on federal Indian law, and there are a number of crucial decisions that form the foundation for the relationship between the United States and tribal governments. Decisions dating back to the early 1800s still have significant relevance today. For this reason, legal research in Indian law usually requires historical research.

The most well-known legal treatise on Indian law is *Cohen's Handbook of Federal Indian Law*, which was most recently updated in 2005. It is published by LexisNexis and is available in a LexisNexis online database.

B.   TRIBAL LAW

An example of an issue arising in tribal law is the following: Two tribal citizens are seeking a divorce in tribal court. They are having a dispute about custody of their children. The tribal judge has determined that the custody matter should be referred to a respected tribal elder who has traditional spiritual authority in times of conflict.

Tribal courts are difficult to generalize about due to the number and variety of legal structures. However, there are some common philosophical differences between indigenous legal theory and Anglo-American legal theory. Tribal laws tend to be more community-based than individual-based. Tribal criminal law is usually based on reparation rather than on punishment. Tribal legal procedure is more likely to be collaborative rather than adversarial.

Another common difference is the appellate process. Most tribal governments have only one appellate court rather than two. In addition, some tribal courts rely on an inter-tribal court of appeals, which is a collaborative appellate court established by agreement by the tribal governments. Since tribal caseloads are typically much lower than those of state and federal courts, the appellate infrastructure is not as complicated.

A case that arises in tribal court will be governed first and foremost by the tribal government's own laws. Tribal courts may consider and consult laws from other tribes, the states, and federal government in deciding cases, but usually they are not bound by decisions other than those issued by the highest court of the tribal government. Tribal laws sometimes incorporate tribal customary law or oral tradition, which may or may not be codified in written form. This makes tribal legal research especially difficult. Some tribal law may be accessed only through ceremony, song, or prayer by the people of that community.

Researching tribal law requires more time and preparation than researching other areas of American law. The main reason is that there is no centralized comprehensive electronic database of tribal laws. Each tribe publishes laws, regulations, and cases differently. The oldest Indian law case reporter is the *Indian Law Reporter*, which contains tribal court opinions dating back to the 1970s. It is available in print in most academic law libraries. In 2009, West introduced *West's American Tribal Law Reporter* in paper and a tribal law database, both containing laws and cases from a few tribes.

Most tribal courts have a court clerk or a court judge who can usually provide an overview of where to find tribal law specific to that tribe. It may or may not be digital and searchable. Some tribal laws include indigenous (non-English) words.

INDEX